THE
EVIDENCE-BASED
PRACTICE

THE EVIDENCE-BASED PRACTICE

Methods, Models, and Tools for Mental Health Professionals

Edited by Chris E. Stout and Randy A. Hayes

WILEY

John Wiley & Sons, Inc.

Copyright © 2005 by John Wiley & Sons, Inc. All rights reserved.

Published by John Wiley & Sons, Inc., Hoboken, New Jersey.
Published simultaneously in Canada.

For general information on our other products and services please contact our Customer Care Department within the United States at (800) 762-2974, outside the United States at (317) 572-3993 or fax (317) 572-4002.

Wiley also publishes its books in a variety of electronic formats. Some content that appears in print may not be available in electronic books. For more information about Wiley products, visit our web site at www.wiley.com.

Library of Congress Cataloging-in-Publication Data:

The evidence-based practice : Methods, models, and tools for mental health professionals / edited by Chris E. Stout and Randy A. Hayes
    p.   cm.
  Includes bibliographical references.
  ISBN 0-471-46747-2 (cloth: alk. paper)
  1. Evidence-based medicine. I. Stout, Chris E. II. Hayes, Randy A.

  R723.7.E963   2004
  616—dc22
                                                2004047811

Printed in the United States of America.

10 9 8 7 6 5 4 3 2

To those who are able to navigate between the worlds of science, practice, and humanity, wanting to make a difference and willing to do so; and to the consumers who will ultimately benefit in an improved quality of life.

Contents

Foreword

It is with great pleasure and professional pride that I accepted Randy Hayes's invitation to write this foreword. The implementation and successful use of evidence-based treatments, described in the following chapters, will assist both care providers and consumers in achieving a more satisfying quality of life. For consumers, this is data evident. For providers, nothing succeeds like success, and the satisfaction generated by concrete evidence that your work has helped others is the professional's ultimate level of satisfaction. This is, after all, basic to the mission of all behavioral healthcare treatment providers.

The Joint Commission on the Accreditation of Healthcare Organizations has long been a proponent of evidence-based treatment within healthcare settings. As an acknowledgment and celebration of Joint Commission accredited organizations that achieve a high level of evidence collection and use, the Joint Commission on the Accreditation of Healthcare Organizations established the Ernst A. Codman Award. This award, initiated in 1997, is presented to organizations and individuals for the use of process and outcomes measures to improve organization performance and quality of care and services as a model for others.

Both the volume editor and the subjects addressed in this volume are linked to the Codman Award by experience and focus. The first Codman Award given in the behavioral health field recognized the value of data use in community-based settings. The Center for Behavioral Health in Bloomington, Indiana, received the first Codman Award in behavioral healthcare for their project entitled "Transporting Evidence-Based Treatments into Behavioral Health Care Settings." Attending the 1999 ceremony when the Center for Behavioral Health received the Codman Award was Randy Hayes, one of the co-editors of this volume. Randy took back to his organization, Sinnissippi Centers, his excitement regarding this concept. Within 1 year, Sinnissippi Centers had submitted one of their evidence-based programs for consideration, and in another 2 years, in 2002, Sinnissippi was the recipient of the Codman Award. The protocols and suggestions for implementing evidence-based treatments within a community-based setting are thus based on his experience in the real word of community agencies and practices.

Indeed, the experience of all of the winners of the Codman Award, as well as the applicants for the award is either in applying evidence-based treatments or collecting evidence on their own treatment protocols to determine their effectiveness. These agencies, as well as other treatment providers who are involved in similar endeavors, are the living proof that evidence-based treatment protocols and methodologies, such as those found within this book, can be applied within community settings. Their experience is that evidence-based practices can not only be applied within community settings, these practices can make significant improvements in the lives of the con-sumers who receive the evidence-based services.

I thus commend this work to you with the hope that it can inspire you and guide your practice, program, agency, leadership, and board in their approach to care and services and location of resources.

MARY CESARE-MURPHY, PhD
Executive Director, Behavioral Health
Joint Commission on the Accreditation
of Healthcare Organizations

Acknowledgments

No book is ever the result of one person, and this effort is certainly a fine example. I would first like to thank my co-author and co-editor, Randy Hayes. His work as well as his many e-mail consultations were critical to the production and quality of this volume (as well as helping me keep perspective in spite of the stresses and strains associated with a project such as this). Similarly, Tracey Belmont and Peggy Alexander have been critically helpful from the very start when I first approached John Wiley & Sons, Inc. about executing this book.

I very much feel like I have been, metaphorically speaking, "standing on the shoulders of giants" in regard to the caliber of the contributing authors and the quality of their work herein. I wish to personally thank the contributing authors for their scholarship, their work, and for their commitment to others and to the field.

And of course, behind the scenes there are an outstanding cadre of colleagues who have guided me in the realm of evidence-based practice issues, including Leigh Steiner, Daniel Luchins, Pat Hanrahan, Christopher Fichtner, Peter Nierman, Richard Barton, and Charlotte Kauffman.

Paramount to my ability to function, and ironically, the first to sacrifice time in order for me to work during vacation, evenings, weekends, and early morning hours that this book necessitated, are my family, Karen, Grayson, and Annika—without whom I would not be able to function. My thanks to you all.

CHRIS E. STOUT

Kildeer, Illinois

Authors' Bios

William A. Anthony, PhD, is the director of Boston University's Center for Psychiatric Rehabilitation, and a professor in Sargent College of Health and Rehabilitation Sciences at Boston University. For the past 35 years, Anthony has worked in various roles in the field of psychiatric rehabilitation, and has been honored for his performance as a researcher, an educator, and a clinician. He is currently co-editor of the *Psychiatric Rehabilitation Journal.* In 1988, Anthony received the Distinguished Services Award from NAMI. Anthony has appeared on ABC's *Nightline,* which featured a rehabilitation program developed and implemented by Boston University's Center for Psychiatric Rehabilitation. In 1992, Anthony received the Distinguished Service Award from the president of the United States.

Anthony has authored over 100 articles in professional journals, 14 textbooks, and several dozen book chapters—the majority of these publications on the topic of psychiatric rehabilitation.

Susan J. Boust, MD, is a psychiatrist on an ACT team in Omaha, Nebraska. She is also the director of Public and Community Psychiatry for the University of Nebraska Medical Center Department of Psychiatry. She has worked as the Mental Health Clinical Leader with the Nebraska Department of Health and Human Services. Boust has also consulted with the state of Florida in their statewide implementation of Assertive Community Treatment.

Timothy J. Bruce, PhD, is associate professor of clinical psychology in the Department of Psychiatry and Behavioral Medicine at the University of Illinois College of Medicine–Peoria, where he is also co-director of the Anxiety and Mood Disorders Clinic and director of Medical Student Education. A summa cum laude graduate of Indiana State University, he received his PhD in Clinical Psychology from the State University of New York at Albany and did his residency at Wilford Hall Medical Center, San Antonio, Texas. Bruce is a consultant to public and private mental health agencies on issues such as patient assessment and treatment, clinical training and supervision, and outcome management systems. He has been the principal or co-principle investigator on grants aimed at improving mental healthcare and service delivery systems. Bruce has authored several professional publications including professional journal articles, books, chapters, and professional educational materials in psychology and psychiatry. He has been cited frequently as an outstanding educator, having won more than a dozen awards for teaching excellence.

Judith A. Cook, PhD, is professor of psychiatry at the University of Illinois at Chicago (UIC), Department of Psychiatry. She received her PhD in sociology from the Ohio State University and completed a National Institute of Mental Health postdoctoral training program in clinical research at the University of Chicago. Currently she directs the Mental Health Services Research Program (MHSRP) which houses several federally funded centers, two of which focus on employment and vocational rehabilitation services research. The UIC Coordinating Center for the Employment Intervention Demonstration Program is a federally funded (by the Center for Mental Health Services-CMHS) multisite study of vocational rehabilitation service interventions for persons with major mental disorders in eight states around the country. The UIC National Research and Training Center on Psychiatric Disability is funded (by CMHS and the U.S. Department of Education) for 5 years to conduct a series of research and training projects addressing self-determination in the areas of psychiatric disability, employment, and rehabilitation. Her published research includes studies of vocational rehabilitation outcomes, employer attitudes toward workers with psychiatric disabilities, multivariate statistical approaches to studying employment among mental health consumers, the role of work in recovery from serious mental illness, policy issues in disability income support programs, and postsecondary training and educational services for persons with mental illness. Cook is an expert consultant on employment and income supports for the president's New Freedom Commission on Mental Health. She also consults with a variety of federal agencies.

Patrick W. Corrigan, PsyD, is professor of psychiatry at the University of Chicago where he directs the Center for Psychiatric Rehabilitation—a research and training program dedicated to the needs of people with serious mental illness and their families. Corrigan has been principal investigator of federally funded studies on rehabilitation, team leadership, and consumer operated services. Two years ago, Corrigan became principal investigator of the Chicago Consortium for Stigma Research (CCSR), the only NIMH-funded research center examining the stigma of mental illness. CCSR comprises more than two dozen basic behavioral and mental health services researchers from 9 Chicago area universities and currently has more than 20 active investigations in this area. Corrigan has published more than 150 papers and seven books including *Don't Call Me Nuts! Coping with the Stigma of Mental Illness,* co-authored with Bob Lundin.

Lisa Dixon, MD, is a professor of psychiatry at the University of Maryland School of Medicine. She serves as director of the Division of Services Research in the School's Department of Psychiatry. Dixon is also the associate director for research of the VA Mental Illness Research, Education, and Clinical Center (MIRECC) in VISN 5, the Capitol Health Care Network. Dixon is a graduate of Harvard College and the Cornell University Medical School. She completed her psychiatric residency at the Payne Whitney Clinic/New York Hospital, a research fellowship at the Maryland Psychiatric Research Center, and a master's degree at the Johns Hopkins School of Public Health. Dixon is an active researcher with grants from the NIMH, NIDA, and the VA as well as numerous foundations. Her research activities have focused on improving the health outcomes of persons with severe mental illnesses and their families. She has published over 80 refereed papers and numerous book chapters. She was previously director of education and residency training in the Department of Psychiatry as well as ethical issues in human research. She is currently a vice chair of the University of Maryland Institutional Review Board.

Marianne Farkas, ScD, is currently the director of training and international services at Boston University's Center for Psychiatric Rehabilitation, and a research associate professor in Sargent College of Health and Rehabilitation Sciences at Boston University. Farkas has authored and co-authored over 40 articles in professional journals, four textbooks, a dozen book chapters, and six multimedia training packages. Farkas's latest professional books were published in 2001 and 2002. For the past 25 years, Farkas has worked in various capacities in the field of psychiatric rehabilitation and has been recognized for her contributions to the field. Farkas is in charge of the World Health Organization Collaborating Center in Psychiatric Rehabilitation, providing training, consultation, and research expertise to the WHO network around the globe. She has developed training, consultation, and organizational change methodologies to support programs and systems in their efforts to adopt psychiatric rehabilitation and recovery innovations. She is currently on the editorial review board of journals ranging from *Psychiatric Services, la Riabilitazione Psichiatrica,* to the *Psychiatric Rehabilitation Journal.* Farkas has been elected for the past 16 years to the Board of the World Association of Psychosocial Rehabilitation, most recently chairing a committee on evidence base for PSR Programs. As an educator, Farkas received Boston University's Award of Merit in 1993. In 1998, Farkas received the John Beard Award from the International Association of Psychosocial Rehabilitation Services.

Randy A. Hayes, MS, is the director of quality assurance for Sinnissippi Centers, Inc., Dixon, Illinois, a position he has held for the past 12 years. With experience in both child welfare and behavioral health, Hayes has 30 years' experience in human services and holds multiple certifications in addition to being a licensed clinical professional counselor. He is a contractual lecturer for the Joint Commission Resources in addition to lecturing and consulting around the United States. He is co-author of *A Handbook of Quality Change and Implementation for Behavioral Health* and has both professional and faith-based publications. Sinnissippi Centers, received the 2002 Joint Commission for the Accreditation of Healthcare Organizations' Ernst A. Codman Award for Behavioral Healthcare and the 2003 American Psychiatric Association's Psychiatric Services Award for one of their evidence-based programs for MISA consumers.

Thomas C. Jewell, PhD, is an assistant professor of psychiatry (psychology) at the University of Rochester School of Medicine and Dentistry, and the director of the Family Institute for Education, Practice, and Research in Rochester, New York. He received his PhD from Bowling Green State University (Ohio), completed his internship training at the University of Rochester Medical Center, and completed a postdoctoral fellowship in the psychiatric rehabilitation of schizophrenia at the University of Rochester Medical Center and the Rochester Psychiatric Center. Jewell's research activities focus on staff training in evidence-based practices, family interventions, and caregiving in severe mental illness, and behavioral treatments of schizophrenia. Jewell is currently directing a project that established the Family Institute for Education, Practice, and Research to teach mental health professionals in New York State how to work effectively with families of people with severe mental illness. The Family Institute is a partnership between the New York State Office of Mental Health and the University of Rochester Medical Center's Department of Psychiatry, in collaboration with The Conference of Local Mental Hygiene Directors and the New York State Chapter of the National Alliance for the Mentally Ill. In addition, since 1994 Jewell has been conducting quantitative and qualitative research on the potential transfer of caregiving from aging parents to adult well siblings of people with severe mental illness. He has several publications in peer-reviewed journals and frequently presents his work at professional conferences throughout the United States.

Melody C. Kuhns, MS, has a master's degree in public administration and 20 years' experience developing services for persons with serious mental illness. She has worked both in a provider capacity for Tarrant County Mental Health and Mental Retardation in Ft. Worth, Texas, and as a program developer for the Texas Department of Mental Health. From 1994 to 1998, she served as the Texas state coordinator of Assertive Community Treatment. Recently, she worked with the Florida Department of Children and Families to coordinate a national cadre of PACT experts to help Florida with their statewide implementation of ACT.

John S. Lyons, PhD, is a professor of psychiatry and community medicine and the director of the Mental Health Services & Policy Program at Northwestern University's Feinberg School of Medicine. His research interests involve the use of assessment processes and findings to drive service system transformation. He has published nearly 200 peer-reviewed publications and four books.

Stanley G. McCracken, PhD, LCSW, is associate executive director at the University of Chicago Center for Psychiatric Rehabilitation and the Illinois MISA Institute. He holds joint appointments at the University of Chicago as associate professor of Clinical Psychiatry and as senior lecturer in the School of Social Service Administration. He has an MA and PhD in social work from the University of Chicago, School of Social Service Administration. He has conducted research at the Center for Psychiatric Rehabilitation and with the University of Chicago Human Behavioral Pharmacology Research Group. While with the latter group, McCracken conducted a series of research studies investigating the relationship between mood, mental illness, and drug taking behavior. He has published in the areas of psychiatric rehabilitation, chemical dependency, behavioral medicine, mental illness, and methods of staff training. He is a respected clinician with 25 years' experience working with individuals with mental illness, physical illness, and chemical dependence. He is a nationally known educator and teacher who has taught and supervised a variety of healthcare professionals. He has provided training, program development, and clinical consultation, throughout the United States to a number of inpatient and outpatient programs serving individuals with mental illness and substance abuse problems.

William R. McFarlane, MD, is professor of psychiatry at the University of Vermont, Department of Psychiatry, and director of research and former chairman, Department of Psychiatry of Maine Medical Center. Previously, he was director of the Biosocial Treatment Research Division of the New York State Psychiatric Institute and an associate professor in the Department of Psychiatry, College of Physicians and Surgeons, Columbia University. He was director of family therapy training for the residency training program and the director of the Fellowship in Public Psychiatry at Columbia. He has been working with families of the mentally ill, especially in multiple family groups, since his training at Albert Einstein College of Medicine in Social and Community Psychiatry, from 1970 to 1975. He edited *Family Therapy in Schizophrenia,* published in 1983. He published *Multifamily Groups in the Treatment of Severe Psychiatric Disorders* in 2003. He is a graduate of Earlham College and Columbia University, College of Physicians and Surgeons. His main interests are in developing and testing family and psychosocial treatments for major mental illnesses and their application in the public sector. He has published more than 40 articles and book chapters, is an associate editor of *Family Process* and *Families, Systems and Health* and has served on the board of directors of the American Orthopsychiatric Association, on the Council of the Association for Clinical Psychosocial Research, and as president of the Maine Psychiatric Association.

Catherine McNeilly, PsyD, is the director of the MISA Institute at the University of Chicago Center for Psychiatric Rehabilitation. McNeilly has served as the manager for Mentally Ill Substance Abuser (MISA) programs for the Division of Alcoholism and Substance Abuse (DASA) in Illinois and was manager for clinical services in the Illinois Department of Children and Family Services. She also worked as project administrator and research associate at two federally funded programs that studied perinatal addiction and recovery. In addition, she was the project director at a federally funded program aimed at evaluating attachment between drug using mothers and their preschool children. McNeilly received her degree in clinical psychology from the Adler School of Professional Psychology in Chicago. She has extensive experience as a trainer, both nationally and locally. She is a certified drug and alcohol counselor who has worked in the field for 15 years.

David J. Miklowitz, PhD, did his undergraduate work at Brandeis University, Waltham, Massachusetts, and his doctoral and postdoctoral work at University of California, Los Angeles. He was on the psychology faculty at the University of Colorado in Boulder from 1989 to 2003, and is now professor of psychology and director of clinical training at the University of North Carolina, Chapel Hill. His research focuses on family environmental factors and family psychoeducational treatments for adult-onset and childhood-onset bipolar disorder. Miklowitz has received the Joseph Gengerelli Dissertation Award from UCLA, the Young Investigator Award from the International Congress on Schizophrenia Research, the National Alliance for Research on Schizophrenia and Depression (NARSAD), a Research Faculty Award from the University of Colorado, and a Distinguished Investigator Award from NARSAD. He also has received funding for his research from the National Institute for Mental Health and the John D. and Catherine T. MacArthur Foundation. Miklowitz has published over 100 research articles and book chapters on bipolar disorder and schizophrenia. His articles have appeared in the *Archives of General Psychiatry,* the *British Journal of Psychiatry,* the *Journal of Nervous and Mental Disease, Biological Psychiatry,* the *Journal of Consulting and Clinical Psychology,* and the *Journal of Abnormal Psychology.* His book with Michael Goldstein, *Bipolar Disorder: A Family-Focused Treatment Approach,* won the 1998 Outstanding Research Publication Award from the American Association of Marital and Family Therapy. His latest book is *The Bipolar Disorder Survival Guide.*

Purva H. Rawal is a doctoral student in clinical psychology in the Mental Health Services and Policy Program at Northwestern University's Feinberg School of Medicine. Her research interests are children's mental health service delivery and outcomes management.

Lisa A. Razzano, PhD, is a social psychologist and associate professor of psychiatry in the Department of Psychiatry, University of Illinois at Chicago. She is the director of research for the UIC National Research and Training Center on Psychiatric Disability, and she also is principal investigator (or co-PI) for several federally funded programs at the department's Mental Health Services Research Program (MHSRP). Since 1995, she has served as project coordinator for the Employment Intervention Demonstration Program (EIDP). Razzano has more than 14 years of experience in mental health services and rehabilitation research, including projects in areas such as psychosocial rehabilitation, vocational services and employment outcomes, and the mental health aspects of HIV/AIDS, with particular expertise in evaluation and biostatistics. Razzano is the author of numerous peer-reviewed journal articles, book chapters, technical reports, and training materials regarding psychiatric rehabilitation research, and has presented outcomes and results from her own projects, as well as those of the MHSRP, at more than 100 professional conferences, federal project meetings, and consumer/advocacy organizations.

E. Sally Rogers, PhD, is director of research at the Center for Psychiatric Rehabilitation at Boston University. The Center focuses on the rehabilitation and recovery of persons with psychiatric disability. Rogers joined the Center in 1981 as a research associate. Rogers currently serves as co-principal investigator for a Research and Training Center grant which is funded to carry out nine research studies on the recovery of individuals with mental illness. She was principal investigator of a postdoctoral fellowship award from NIDRR for 10 years and principal investigator of a grant to study consumer-operated services funded by the Center for Mental Health Services. Rogers is also a research associate professor at Boston University, Sargent College of Health and Rehabilitation Sciences where she teaches master's and doctoral-level research courses and seminars. She is the recipient of the Loeb Research Award from the International Association of Psychosocial Rehabilitation Services. Rogers has written more than 50 peer-reviewed papers on various topics related to the vocational rehabilitation, vocational assessment, and the recovery of persons with severe psychiatric disability.

Sy Atezaz Saeed, MD, is professor and chairman, Department of the Psychiatry Medicine, Brody School of Medicine at East Caroline University. Until recently, he served as Professor and Chairman, Department of the Psychiatry and Behavioral Medicine at the University of Illinois College of Medicine at Peoria where he was also the Clinical Director for the Comprehensive Community Mental Health Service netWork of North Central Illinois, a state-operated *netWork* serving seriously and persistently mentally ill patients in 23 counties in north central Illinois. Dr. Saeed is board certified in Psychiatry, Psychiatric Administration and Management, and in Medical Psychotherapy. He also holds a MS degree in Counseling and Psychotherapy and a Diploma in Clinical Hypnotherapy. Dr. Saeed is the Editor of the American Association of Psychiatric Administrator's Journal, *Psychiatric Administrator*. Dr Saeed is currently involved in clinical work, teaching, research, and administration. He has published in the areas of evidence-based practices; anxiety and mood disorders; cross-cultural issues; psychiatric administration; and psychiatric treatment integration. His current scholarly and research interests area include: the *study of the impact* of implementing evidence-based practices in mental health setting; the *process* of implementing evidence-based treatments in psychiatry; psychiatric disorders in primary care settings; anxiety and mood disorders; and systems approach to psychiatric administration and management. He has been involved in funded research both as a principal investigator and co-investigator. He is the principal investigator and Project Director for the Illinois Medication Algorithm Project, focused on the study of the impact of implementing evidence-based treatment algorithms. He has lectured and presented nationwide.

William C. Sanderson, PhD, is professor of psychology at Hofstra University, Long Island, New York, where he directs the Anxiety and Depression Treatment Program. Sanderson received his PhD from the University of Albany, where he worked under the mentorship of Dr. David Barlow at the Center for Stress and Anxiety Disorders. He then completed a fellowship in Cognitive Therapy with Dr. Aaron T. Beck (the founder of Cognitive Therapy) at the Center for Cognitive Therapy, University of Pennsylvania. He has participated on numerous national committees, including the American Psychiatric Association's *DSM-IV* Anxiety Disorders Workgroup, and was recently the chair of the American Psychological Association Division of Clinical Psychology's Committee on Science and Practice (a Task Force aimed at identifying and promoting the practice of empirically supported psychological interventions). He has published six books and over 80 articles and chapters, primarily in the areas of anxiety, depression, personality disorders, and cognitive behavior therapy.

Chris E. Stout, PsyD, is a licensed clinical psychologist and a clinical professor at the University of Illinois College of Medicine's Department of Psychiatry. He holds a joint governmental appointment and serves as Illinois' first chief of psychological services for the Department of Human Services/Division of Mental Health. He also holds an academic appointment in the Northwestern University Feinberg Medical School, Department of Psychiatry and Behavioral Sciences' Mental Health Services and Policy Program, and is a visiting professor in the Department of Health Systems Management at Rush University. He was appointed by the Secretary of the U.S. Department of Commerce to the Board of Examiners for the Baldrige National Quality Award, he served on Mrs. Gore's *White House Conference on Mental Health,* and he served as an advisor to the White House on national education matters. He holds the distinction of being one of only 100 worldwide leaders appointed to the World Economic Forum's Global Leaders of Tomorrow 2000, and he was an invited faculty at the Annual Meeting in Davos, Switzerland. Stout is a fellow of the American Psychological Association, past-president of the Illinois Psychological Association, and a distinguished practitioner in the National Academies of Practice. Stout has published or presented over 300 papers and 29 books/manuals on various topics in psychology. His works have been translated into six languages. He has lectured across the nation and internationally in 10 countries, visited six continents and over 60 countries. He was noted as being "one of the most frequently cited psychologists in the scientific literature" in a study by Hartwick College. He is one of only four psychologists to have won the American Psychological Association's International Humanitarian Award.

Lynette Studer, MA, received her master's degree in social work from the University of Wisconsin-Madison and specialized in assertive community treatment. For the past 12 years, she has been working as a team leader with Dr. William Knoedler in Green County's Assertive Community Treatment program in Monroe, Wisconsin, the third oldest ACT team and the first rural team in the nation. Over the past 6 years, Studer has also been a PACT consultant in several states including Florida, Nebraska, Pennsylvania, and Alabama, focusing on issues of implementation specific to the team leader role, team based service delivery, rural ACT and consumer-centered treatment planning. Her team in Wisconsin is a national training model, hosting people who want to see a high fidelity model team.

James H. Zahniser, PhD, is assistant professor of psychology at Greenville College, Illinois. He has extensive experience in mental health services research and in the evaluation of psychiatric rehabilitation programs. He also has worked with psychiatric rehabilitation programs in articulating their program models, developing new psychosocial rehabilitation interventions, defining the appropriate outcomes of psychosocial rehabilitation services, and training consumers and nonconsumer providers in the delivery of psychosocial rehabilitation and recovery-oriented interventions. Zahniser served on the Federal Center for Mental Health Services panel, which identified competencies for working with adults diagnosed with serious mental illnesses in a managed care environment. He currently is working with the National Empowerment Center to evaluate the Personal Assistance in Community Existence (PACE) program, a consumer-driven model.

CHAPTER 1

Introduction to Evidence-Based Practices

Randy A. Hayes

Simply stated, evidence-based treatment is the use of treatment methodologies for which there is scientifically collected evidence that the treatment works. Much of this book discusses treatments for which there is an overwhelming set of evidence for their effectiveness. But before learning about these evidence-based treatments, before discovering the necessary prerequisites for establishing these treatments within a clinic, agency, or practice, we review the history of evidence-based treatment and discuss the reasons why evidence-based practice has come to the forefront at this time.

EARLY BEGINNINGS

Evidence-based treatment had its earliest contemporary beginnings in the collection of evidence regarding the causes of disease—epidemiology. But in a larger sense, evidence-based therapy began at the start of Western medical care with Hippocrates. The Hippocratic Oath has *beneficence* at its core—to help or at least do no harm. Perhaps the originator of this oath was considering overt acts of harm, indicating a point that would not be argued even to this day. The healthcare provider shall not knowingly provide a service whose purpose is ultimately harmful rather than helpful. On the one hand, this oath is exceptionally simple. Healthcare providers of any of the myriad of iterations of the past or current healthcare related professions did not, would not, do not provide services or treatments that they believe would ultimately be harmful to their patients, a few notable exceptions aside. However, as often is the case, simplicity can be deceptive and lead the professional down a twisted road: How does the healthcare professional know that the services they provide are ultimately helpful or hurtful?

For centuries, the decision as to the helpfulness or harmfulness of any treatment was dependent primarily on the practitioner's ethical intent, as well as his or her judgment of the effectiveness of the treatment. However, is ethical intent (that is, the clear intent toward beneficence) and individual observation as to effectiveness sufficient for the judgment of harm or helpfulness of treatment? Sufficient or not, for centuries, ethical intent and individual observation were the only tools available to the healthcare practitioner.

As medical instruction became organized and eventually institutionalized, beneficence in terms of treatment could be considered as following the practices learned as part of the medical education. However, much of the history of such medical education

1

preceded the development of modern scientific understandings and methodologies, including not only bacteriology and epidemiology (and thus the understanding of disease causation) but also the modern methods of collecting evidence in support of scientific theories. Thus, the practices taught in these early times, although beneficent in intent, may not have been beneficent in actual practice. Before the development of these scientific practices, there was no available methodology to determine the beneficence of actual practice. Patients simply got better or they got worse and died. The methodology, including the theoretical thought sets, necessary for the determination of practice beneficence (as compared to intent beneficence), did not exist.

It was not until scientific understanding, methods, and practices came together that *practice beneficence* had its beginnings. There is no better illustration of this point than the life and work of Florence Nightingale (1820–1910). Nightingale used the collection, analysis, and graphical display of healthcare data from the Crimean War to change the face of healthcare in the United Kingdom.

Nightingale used data (that is to say, evidence) to prove that conditions at the time in military hospitals were not beneficent, but in fact harmful to the lives of the soldiers being treated (Small, 1998). Inventing new forms of graphical representation of statistical analysis, Nightingale showed a statistically significant number of preventable deaths. Much of her data analysis showed the deleterious effects of uncleanliness in terms of healthcare survival. Many of the improvements she instituted based on this evidence had to do with improved cleanliness. Further, Nightingale used this evidence to successfully campaign for improved conditions in military hospitals and in general hospitals. It is interesting to note that illness from lack of cleanliness, now called nosocomial infections, is still cited, some 150 years following Nightingale's irrefutable proof of the potentially devastating effects of uncleanliness in healthcare, as a significant negative contributor to public health. See Martinez, Ruthazer, Hansjosten, Barefoot, and Snydman (2003) for one example of this continuing concern.

The collection of data regarding the cause, spread, and eventual containment of infectious disease developed slowly into the science of epidemiology during the nineteenth and twentieth centuries. Wade Hampton Front, MD, became the first American professor of epidemiology in 1921 at the Johns Hopkins School of Hygiene and Public Health (Stolley & Lasky, 1995). Joseph Goldberger moved the science solely from the realm of infectious diseases into the study of noninfectious diseases with his concentration on the effects of diet on public health (Stolley & Lasky, 1995) during the same time period. The investigation of the causes of lung cancer was included in the data collection efforts of the epidemiologists also during the early and mid-twentieth century leading eventually to the link with cigarette smoking. Epidemiology as a science held the collection and analysis of disease-related data in terms of the causes and containment of disease as its standard. However, it did not include treatment effectiveness, as such, as a focus.

The collection of medical and health-related data in terms of treatment effectiveness came to the fore, albeit briefly, with the systems of Ernst A. Codman, MD, during the turn of the past century as the science of epidemiology was developing. A graduate of Harvard Medical School in 1895, Codman had a keen interest in all of the aspects of the effectiveness of medical treatment (Brauer, 2001). Codman, an avid collector of data of all kinds, believed that the outcomes of surgery should be openly documented, monitored, and reported. Developing an elaborate system of recording the results of his own surgeries using a card system, he encouraged other physicians to do the same. Calling his system the "End Results System" (Brauer, 2001). Codman was strongly influenced by engineering concepts and was a friend of efficiency expert Frank Gilbreth. In 1911, Codman opened his own 20-bed hospital in Boston to fully apply his system of tracking the outcomes of the care he provided. Continuing the use of the index card system, each patient was categorized in terms of presenting symptoms, diagnoses (initial and discharge), complications while in the hospital, and status one year following hospitalization. Further, Codman developed a system for identifying medical errors and adverse outcomes, which he not only published, but gave to patients before their treatment (Brauer, 2001). Codman encouraged other physicians and hospitals to follow the same course.

Codman's "End Results System" processes were way ahead of his time. Perhaps because of Codman's fierce advocacy of his system, he angered many of his fellow physicians and eventually left the local medical society. His hospital closed due to lack of referrals from his colleagues. Codman then practiced medicine in Nova Scotia and in the army. Eventually returning to Boston and reuniting with Massachusetts General Hospital, he studied the Registry of Bone Sarcoma—a registry that he had initiated. Codman recognized that his "End Result" concepts would not come to fruition in his lifetime. He died in 1940 (Brauer, 2001) although the ideas did not die with him.

Some 32 years following the death of Codman, the cause of evidence-based treatment was taken up by an epidemiologist in the United Kingdom. In 1972, the Nuffield Provincial Hospitals Trust (NPHT) published the landmark work of A. L. Cochrane, MD. The NPHT had invited Cochrane, a well-known and highly respected epidemiologist, to evaluate the United Kingdom's National Health Service. Titling his work *Effectiveness and Efficiency: Random Reflections on Health Services,* Cochrane called for the use of evidence-based treatment practices.

Cochrane's evaluation of healthcare services, by his own admission, was crude due to the lack of properly collected evidence. Nevertheless, Cochrane used the techniques available to an epidemiologist, for example, demographics and mortality rates, and so on. He analyzed healthcare services/treatments as compared to healthcare costs and found a huge gap—increased national funding for healthcare services had not led to increased positive outcomes for patients (Cochrane, 1972/1999).

Based on these findings, Cochrane made a series of recommendations regarding the improvement of outcomes by improving treatment. These recommendations focused on the use of applied medical research in the form of random controlled trials to determine those treatments that produced improved health. It is interesting and informative to note that Cochrane discusses both in his introduction and through his evaluation the differences between pure research and applied research. He further devotes one entire chapter to the use of evidence, and another on exploring and defining the meaning of both effectiveness and efficiency as they relate to healthcare services.

The need for these discussions, begun three decades ago, continues to this day both in the field of medical services and behavioral healthcare services. In doing training for the Joint Commission Resources, both on implementing evidence-based practices in behavioral healthcare and in the use of data in this field, the problems noted by Cochrane

30 years ago, as well as Codman 80 years ago, continue to be evident in healthcare and behavioral healthcare. Few clinicians, either in medicine or behavioral healthcare, have had sufficient and meaningful training in research design or data analysis to negate the need for elementary discussion and training so that the healthcare professional who is not a professional researcher, can appreciate, understand, and properly apply the findings of research to their practice or agency. This book, in part, exists to help overcome this continuing need.

Cochrane discussed a third metric—equity—that may be coming more into play this first decade of the new millennium. *Equity* means effective and efficient healthcare services for all who need them. Cochrane was discussing the disparity of services that were available through the National Health Service in the United Kingdom. This had been a concern discussed a century earlier by Nightingale (Small, 1998). During Nightingale's time, public hospitals were solely for the poor and indigent. People with means were seen and treated in their homes. By Cochrane's time, although not as evident as during Nightingale's time, a disparity of treatment continued, not only between social classes, noted Cochrane, but also between geographic areas.

Although far beyond the scope of this book to discuss in length, equity of services for all people in all places may be becoming an area of concern within the United States. With the severe state budgetary crises following the tragedy of September 11, 2001, many publicly supported behavioral healthcare agencies have seen significant reductions in funding. These reductions have forced agencies to limit both the numbers of and types of consumers who receive healthcare and behavioral healthcare services.

These budgetary restrictions have also limited the staff devoted to evidence collection and analysis in service of evidence-based practice development. At a recent workshop conducted by the author on data analysis, one participant disclosed that his agency was forced to eliminate its research and analysis staff in order to provide basic behavioral health services.

Because of budgetary restrictions and limitations, the use of proven treatments, that is, evidence-based treatments, is absolutely critical, and yet agencies and practices who were in the forefront of the field in terms of having staff to do this needed work, are having to reduce or eliminate staff who are capable of doing this needed work. At some point, directors and boards of agencies will need to ask the same or similar questions Codman and Cochrane were asking many years ago. Can agencies or practices save money by providing treatment that may not be producing any effect? Is it efficient to provide treatment that has not been proven to be effective? Is it efficient in tight budgetary times to either not hire, or to reduce the professional staff who are able to provide the research necessary to "prove" what treatments actually produce statistically significant results? We hope to help you answer these questions, or minimally, understand better the importance of these questions.

Some 40 years following the death of Codman, and within a decade of Cochrane's work, McMaster University in Hamilton, Ontario Canada, took up the cause by producing a series of articles that helped the healthcare professional begin to address these questions.

The Department of Epidemiology and Biostatistics published a series of five articles in the *Canadian Medical Association Journal* in 1981 [(124) 5–9] from March through May entitled "How to read clinical journals." The series of articles had following subtitles: I. Why to read them and how to start reading them critically; II. To learn about a diagnostic test; III. To learn the clinical course and prognosis of a disease; IV. To determine etiology or causation; and V. To distinguish useful from useless or even harmful therapy (1981a, 1981b, 1981c, 1981d, 1981e). This series is credited (Baker & Kleijnen cited in Rowland & Goss, 2000) as being the actual starting point of the type of evidence-based therapy that this book addresses.

From McMaster University, the advance of evidence-based treatment was pursued vigorously in the United Kingdom as part of a redesign of the National Health Service in 1991 (Baker & Kleijnen as cited in Rowland & Goss, 2000). Not only has the British National Health Service adopted evidence-based practices for medical care, the institution has adopted, as of 2001, a set of evidence-based practices for behavioral health (Department of Health, 2001). These guidelines list the evidence for various treatment methodologies for the following diagnoses: depressive disorders, panic disorder and/or agoraphobia, social phobia, generalized anxiety disorder, posttraumatic stress disorder, obsessive compulsive disorder, eating disorder, somatic complaints, personality disorders, and deliberate self-harm. Also reviewed are "other factors" that impact behavioral health therapy. These practices are available not only for clinicians working within the Department of Health but an abbreviated version is available for potential consumers of the services.

Within the United Kingdom are a number of centers that promote evidence-based treatment research, including the Cochrane Collaboration, a Web site instituted for "preparing, maintaining and promoting the accessibility of systematic reviews of the effects of health care interventions" (http://www.cochrane.de). This collaboration reviews research, based on a set of principles, and makes the reviews available to subscribers. It also conducts workshops and training on this topic. A similar British institution is the Centre for Evidence Based Medicine.

DATA COLLECTION AND APPLICATION: THE RECENT PRESENT

Although data or evidence-collection methodologies have been in use for a variety of scientific endeavors for decades, the application of scientific methodology to prove the effectiveness of various medical treatments has been a long time coming. Further, even as effectiveness evidence has been collected, it has not been used in the healthcare field.

For example, the University of Sheffield evidence-based Web site references a study done in 1963 (Forsyth, 1963) of medical practitioners' use of prescription medicine. The two-week study indicated that only 9.3% of prescriptions written during the period were specific for the condition for which they were intended. Another investigation in 1973 (Wennberg & Gittelsohn, 1973) documented "serious and inexplicable regional variations in health care providers' clinical practices." Thirteen years later, the situation had not changed. The Lohr study (1986) documented the inappropriate overuse or underuse of healthcare services. A study by Brook (1989) called into question the effectiveness of many medical interventions. Six years later, the Rosen study (Rosen, Proctor, Morrow-Howell, & Staudt, 1995) indicated that fewer than 1% of the practice decisions of social work were justified by empirical findings. In the October 12, 1998, issue of *Time* magazine, Dr. Robert Califf, director of the Duke University Clinical Research Institute estimated that less than 15% of U.S. healthcare is evidence-based.

As recently as 2002, the *CNS News: Neurology and Psychiatry* journal indicated that the American Psychiatric Association's bipolar disorder best-practice guidelines were not being followed. Reporting on a 1999 APA Practice Research Network Study of Psychiatric Patients and Treatments, 20% of these patients did not receive treatment with a mood stabilizer and 40% did not receive any sort of psychotherapy, both of which are recommended in the APA's best-practice guidelines ("Bipolar Treatment Guidelines," 2002).

This article mirrors the findings of "Mental Health: Report of the Surgeon General" (USDHHS, 1999). This extensive report summarized the current state of mental health treatment models, pointing out that there were numerous psychiatric and/or psychological treatments that were of proven value for even the most severe cases of mental illness. The findings also emphasized, however, that these state-of-the-art treatments refined through years of research were not being transferred into actual practice in community settings. Calling this lack of transfer "a gap" that exists between research and application, the report concludes, in part, indicating the reasons this application gap exists. Foremost among the reasons listed for the practice gap is the practitioners' lack of knowledge of research results. Other reasons cited are the lag time between reporting of research results and translation into practice and the cost of introducing innovations into the various healthcare systems.

Adding to the so-called transfer gap is the response of behavioral healthcare clinicians themselves to the collection and use of data, as well as the use of evidence-based guidelines within their practices. Azocar, Brian, Goldman, and McCarter (2003) studied the use of evidence-based guidelines within managed behavioral healthcare organizations using random control trial methodology. Participants in the study ($N = 443$) either received guidelines for the treatment of major depression from a general mailing (independently practicing clinicians); received the guidelines from a targeted mailing (client/patient receiving treatment from an independently practicing clinician); or received no guideline (i.e., neither clinician nor client/patient received the guideline). The study showed no effects of the guideline dissemination, either through clinician or client/patient self-report or through analysis of claim data, and so on. We suggest that dissemination strategies other than mailings should be examined to improve the standard of care.

A later study published in the same year may shed some light on this possible reluctance to use evidence-based practice guidelines. Garland, Kruse, and Aaron (2003) studied the attitudes regarding the use of standard outcome measures in practice. Fifty behavioral healthcare practitioners were interviewed individually or in focus groups as to their attitudes regarding the use of outcome measurements. The findings of this study are quite telling: Although all practitioners interviewed received some type of scored assessment profiles on their patients/clients at the initiation of assessment treatment, the vast majority reported that they did not use the measures as part of their treatment planning or monitoring. Further, the clinicians reported that outcome measures were not believed to be clinically useful.

The reader might conclude that clinician/practitioner attitudes regarding receptive uses of evidence-based treatment guidelines as well as the measurement sets that play a significant part of these guidelines, could play a significant role in whether such guidelines would be used. Evidence-based guideline usage may not be swayed by the preponderance of evidence as to the effectiveness of the guideline as much as by the individual clinicians attitude toward the use and usefulness of evidence and guidelines in general. This is one area in terms of the adoption of evidence-based practices that could benefit from significant research.

The so-called transfer gap helps explain the purposes and outline of this book. Six evidence-based practices (sometimes known as the *Tool Kit*) follow this introductory chapter. These are all practices that have been extensively researched using controlled scientific methodology. These are all practices that have shown outstanding outcomes when applied within the research settings. These practices have all shown exceptional outcomes when applied in a variety of practice and agency settings.

In terms of clinician acceptance, this volume also presents first the various general considerations regarding the state and use of evidence-based treatments within both private practices and behavioral healthcare agencies. A second series of chapters by this author outlines some of the very practical considerations that need to be considered before and during the attempts at implementation of evidence-based practices.

The need for the latter is highlighted by Frances Cotter, MA, MPH (personal communication, September 24, 2003) team leader—Science to Service Program, Center for Substance Abuse Treatment-Division of Services Improvement, the federal sponsor of the Tool Kit development. Cotter has pointed out the need for an examination of the processes within an agency in which evidence-based practices are being installed. "Too often, the substance abuse field has neglected looking into the black box in which we want to place evidence-based practices. If we want to increase the success of these practices, we need to understand what is occurring within the organization and how the organization can support and sustain the evidence-based practices."

Thus, the last chapters provide an initial look into the "black box" with suggestions for understanding and overcoming possible resistance to evidence-based treatment implementation. CSAT and the Robert Wood Johnson Foundation are in the process of researching both barriers to best practice implementation as well as promising practices for treatment engagement and retention within the substance abuse field. This author's agency, Sinnissippi Centers, Dixon, Illinois, is part of that research effort. Further, and more to the point of this volume, we present suggestions based on the experiences at this agency in designing and implementing data collection for the development of evidence-based practices regarding treatment of the mentally ill substance abusing client/patient/consumer. These are practices that have been awarded the Joint Commission on the Accreditation of Healthcare 2002 Ernst A. Codman Behavioral Healthcare Award (Hayes, Andrews, Baron-Jeffrey, Conley, Gridley, et al., 2003) and the 2003 American Psychiatric Association's Bronze Psychiatric Services Award.

The call for the use of evidence-based practices both in healthcare in general, and in behavioral healthcare specifically, has been long in development. From the ancient practitioner's intuitive collection of the "evidence" of what worked and what did not work through trial and error to the current use of scientific methodologies to discover what treatment methodologies work and which do not work has been a long and sometimes arduous journey. It has been a journey replete with heroines and heroes, working against the practices and thought patterns of their day to begin the current movement toward evidence-based practices. It is a journey that continues to have heroes and heroines, both in researching the treatment methodologies, and in attempting to implement those proven treatment methods within their own practices and agencies. And it is a journey that we welcome you to join, as we, in our own practices, attempt to live out the oath promulgated so long ago: To help, or at least to do no harm.

REFERENCES

Azocar, F., Brian, C., Goldman, B., & McCarter, L. (2003, January/February). The impact of evidence-based guideline dissemination for the assessment and treatment of major depression in a managed behavioral health care organization. *Journal of Behavioral Health Services and Research, 20*(1), 109–118.

Bipolar treatment guidelines not widely followed. (2002, February). *CNS News: Neurology and Psychiatry, 4*(2).

Brauer, C. (2001). *Champions of quality in health care: A history of the Joint Commission on Accreditation of Healthcare Organizations.* Lyme, CT: Greenwich.

Brook, R. H. (1989). Practice guidelines and practicing medicine: Are they compatible? *Journal of the American Medical Association, 262,* 3027–3030.

Cochrane, A. L. (1999). *Effectiveness and efficiency: Random reflections on health services.* London: Royal Society Medical Press Limited. (Original work published 1972)

Department of Clinical Epidemiology and Biostatistics, McMaster University Health Sciences Centre. (1981a). How to read clinical journals I. Why to read them and how to start reading them critically. *Canadian Medical Association Journal, 124*(5), 555–558.

Department of Clinical Epidemiology and Biostatistics, McMaster University Health Sciences Centre. (1981b). How to read clinical II. To learn about a diagnostic test. *Canadian Medical Association Journal, 124*(6), 703–710.

Department of Clinical Epidemiology and Biostatistics, McMaster University Health Sciences Centre. (1981c). How to read clinical III. To learn the clinical course and prognosis of a disease. *Canadian Medical Association Journal, 124*(7), 869–872.

Department of Clinical Epidemiology and Biostatistics, McMaster University Health Sciences Centre. (1981d). How to read clinical IV. To determine etiology or causation. *Canadian Medical Association Journal, 124*(8), 985–990.

Department of Clinical Epidemiology and Biostatistics, McMaster University Health Sciences Centre. (1981e). How to read clinical V. To distinguish useful from useless or even harmful therapy. *Canadian Medical Association Journal, 124*(8), 1156–1162.

Department of Health. (2001). *Treatment choice in psychological therapies and counselling: Evidence-based clinical practice guideline.* London: Crown Copyright, Department of Health. Available free of change from DH web site: http://www.doh.gov.uk/mentalhealth/treatmentguideline.

Forsyth, G. (1963). An enquiry into the drug bill. *Med Care, 1,* 10–16. Available from http://www.shef.ac.uk/~scharr/ir/percent.html#prehistory.

Garland, A., Kruse, M., & Aaron, G. (2003). Clinicians and outcome measurement: What's the use? *Journal of Behavioral Health Services and Research, 20*(4), 393–405.

Hayes, R., Andrews, N., Baron-Jeffrey, M., Conley, C., Gridley, K., Norman, R., et al. (2003). Service enhancement to a dual-diagnosis population: Mental illness/substance abuse. *Quality Management in Health Care, 12*(3), 133–150.

Lohr, K. N., Brook, R. H., Kamberg, C. J., Goldberg, G. A., Leibowitz, A., Keesey, J., et al. (1986). Use of medical care in the Rand Health Insurance Experiment. Diagnosis and service-specific analysis in a randomized controlled trial. *Medical Care, 24,* S1–S87.

Martínez, J., Ruthazer, R., Hansjosten, K., Barefoot, L., Snydman, D. R., et al. (2003). Role of environmental contamination as a risk factor for acquisition of Vancomycin-Resistant Enterococci in patients treated in a medical intensive care unit. *Archives of Internal Medicine, 163,* 16.

Rosen, A., Proctor, E. E., Morrow-Howell, N., & Staudt, M. (1995). Rationales for practice decisions: Variations in knowledge use by decision task and social work service. *Research on Social Work Practice, 5,* 501–523.

Rowland, N., & Goss, S. (Eds.). (2000). *Evidence-based counselling and psychological therapies: Research and applications.* London: Routledge.

Small, H. (1998). *Florence Nightingale: Avenging angel.* New York: St. Martin's Press.

Stolley, P. D., & Lasky, T. (1995). *Investigating disease patterns: The science of epidemiology.* New York: Scientific American Library.

U.S. Department of Health and Human Service. (1999). *Mental health: A Report of the Surgeon General.* Rockville, MD: Author.

Wennberg, J. E., & Gittelsohn, A. (1973). Small-area variation in health care delivery. *Science, 182,* 1102–1108.

CHAPTER 2

Evidence-Based Practices in Supported Employment

Lisa A. Razzano and Judith A. Cook

Research from diverse fields in the behavioral sciences has provided abundant evidence supporting the importance of employment to people with psychiatric disabilities (Cook & Pickett, 1995; Gatens-Robinson & Rubins, 1995). People with mental illness not only are interested in working, but numerous studies demonstrate their successful participation in the labor market in a multitude of competitive employment settings (Bond, Becker, et al., 2001; Cook & Razzano, 2000; Crowther, Marshall, Bond, & Huxley, 2001; Rogers, Anthony, Toole, & Brown, 1991). Overall, work is an important goal for many mental health consumers, and gainful employment opportunities afford consumers the chance to promote their own economic independence, as well as enhance other factors related to their overall well-being (Lehman et al., 2002). A substantial amount of research also has identified the benefits of working for mental health consumers, including alleviation of poverty (Polak & Warner, 1996), higher levels of functioning (Anthony, Rogers, Cohen, & Davies, 1995; Bond, Resnick, et al., 2001; Lehman, 1995), and improvements in quality of life (Arns & Linney, 1995), self-esteem (Mueser et al., 1997), and greater satisfaction with both vocational services and finances (Mueser et al., 1997). Work among people with psychiatric disabilities has positive social benefits, such as less reliance on public disability entitlements (Kouzis & Eaton, 2000; Polak & Warner, 1996) and the overall costs of care (Baron, 2000; Drake, McHugo, Becker, Anthony, & Clark, 1996).

Contemporary developments in both the social and scientific arenas have provided greater opportunities for people with psychiatric disabilities to enter and remain in the labor force (Cook & Burke, 2002). Past, as well as new federal initiatives, such as the Americans with Disabilities Act (ADA, 1990) and the passage of the Ticket to Work and Work Incentives Improvement Act, Public Law Number 106-170 (1999), which supports people with disabilities in the workplace and removes the financial and health coverage disincentives for employment, point to the value our society is now placing on employment of its citizens with disabilities (Cook & Razzano, 2000). Along with these developments, the advocacy movement among mental health consumers, including community activism and training in self-advocacy and legal protections, has promoted the employment goal for a wider and wider range of clientele (Cook & Wright, 1995). Furthermore, advancements in psychiatric services, such as formulation and use of new psychopharmacologic agents, also have provided consumers with more treatment options and hope

10

for recovery than ever before (Lehman, 1999; Meyer, Bond, Tunis, & McCoy, 2002). Despite these many developments, however, the vast majority of people with psychiatric disabilities in the United States remain outside of the labor force. By some estimates, 75% to 85% of people with severe mental illnesses are unemployed in the United States (Anthony & Blanch, 1987; Lehman, 1995).

In addition to the basic goal of reducing unemployment among mental health consumers, supported employment programs seek to improve other aspects of recovery. In particular, employment has been viewed as a means to foster improvement in other rehabilitation outcomes, including mental health symptoms, level of functioning, substance use, and self-esteem (Bond, Resnick, et al., 2001; Lehman, 1999; Mueser et al., 1997). Yet despite targeted efforts to develop and implement evidence-based best practice programs designed to assist all mental health consumers find work, the overwhelming majority of consumers still remain outside of the competitive labor force (Jacobs, Wissusik, Collier, Stackman, & Burkeman, 1992; Mueser et al., 1997). Although some studies suggest that concerns regarding the deleterious effects of work on other clinical factors and quality of life indicators continue to loom (Blankertz & Robinson, 1996; Lehman, 1988; Marrone & Golowka, 1999; Schied & Anderson, 1995), other investigations report that there is no empirical evidence that participation in supported employment programs adversely affects clinical or other indicators, such as number of psychiatric hospitalizations (Bond, Resnick, et al., 2001; Drake, 1998), severity of psychiatric symptoms (McFarlane et al., 2000; Mueser et al., 1997), or quality of life (Fabian, 1992).

RESEARCH-BASED PRINCIPLES OF VOCATIONAL REHABILITATION AND SUPPORTED EMPLOYMENT

The existing literature on people with psychiatric disabilities provides support for a series of research-based principles related to vocational rehabilitation services. Although several of these principles have been demonstrated in the multidisability vocational rehabilitation field, others have emerged from specific efforts designed to address the unique employment needs of people with psychiatric disabilities. To provide an overall understanding of the evidence-based best practices in vocational rehabilitation among psychiatric populations, these principles are reviewed and relevant supporting research is discussed. However, as others have provided comprehensive reviews of this research (e.g., Bond, Drake, Mueser, & Becker, 1997; Lehman, 1995), this section presents an overview of the critical issues related to these studies and their findings, as well as their role in supported employment services within the larger context of vocational rehabilitation.

Supported employment is, as defined in the 1998 Amendments to the Rehabilitation Act, Title IV of the Workforce Investment Act, "competitive work in integrated work settings [that is] consistent with strengths, resources, priorities, concerns, abilities, capabilities, interests, and informed choices of individuals." The Act goes on to note that, in particular, supported employment services should be provided to those individuals with "the most significant disabilities for whom competitive employment has not traditionally occurred," and "for whom competitive employment has been interrupted or intermittent as a result of a significant disability" (Rehabilitation Act Amendments, 1998). Based on this definition, several overarching principles of supported employment have emerged.

As stated in the Act, the first principle indicates that clients should be provided with *competitive or supported employment* services rather than programs leading to sheltered or unpaid work. In supported employment settings, clients are rehabilitated by being placed and trained in community-based jobs in integrated settings where they earn minimum wage or above. In a series of studies, Wehman and others (Kregel, Wehman, & Banks, 1989; Wehman & Moon, 1988) demonstrated that employment outcomes were significantly better for individuals with severe disabilities, including those with mental illness and other behavioral health concerns, when clients received rehabilitation services in community job placements at minimum wage or above in socially integrated settings. In a comparison of two different day programs that provided sheltered work to former psychiatric patients, Drake et al. (1994) also demonstrated that conversion of one program into a continuous supported employment approach yielded superior competitive employment outcomes than the intact sheltered work model.

One goal of supported employment programs, competitive work, also appears to offer several additional rehabilitative advantages over sheltered or enclave jobs, as well as volunteer or unpaid work. In particular, work skills training occurring within integrated settings alongside nondisabled coworkers offers clients positive role modeling opportunities (Cook & Razzano, 1992). Competitive employment at minimum wage or above also has been shown in several surveys to be preferred among people with psychiatric disabilities (Polak & Warner, 1996; Rogers, Walsh, Masotta, Danley, & Smith, 1991) and offers obvious economic advantages to clients. Finally, the place-then-train approach provides on-the-job training, allowing workers to learn skills in the same environments in which they will later use them, helping to prevent "transfer of training" difficulties that can occur when skills are applied in different settings (Cook & Hoffschmidt, 1993).

The next principle supports the use of *situational assessment* to evaluate vocational skills and potential. This involves longitudinal observation of jobs by trained evaluators who rate job behaviors and attitudes within actual or simulated work environments (Cook et al., 1991). Included in typical rating scales are aspects such as clients' work quality (e.g., error rate) and quantity (e.g., percent of industrial production rate), their ability to perform specific work tasks (e.g., alphabetizing), their work attitudes (e.g., work motivation), and their interpersonal relations with supervisor(s) and other coworkers. Situational assessment recognizes that work behaviors and attitudes comprise a complex constellation of factors that should be assessed systematically within real work settings (Massel et al., 1990). For example, situational assessment appropriately takes into account that accurate assessments of people with mental illnesses may be complicated by numerous behavioral health issues, including the symptoms of mental health disorders themselves, side-effects from use of psychoactive medications, and other forms of co-occurring cognitive impairments (Cook & Pickett, 1995). In addition, other studies have demonstrated that situation-specific assessment is preferred over traditional psychiatric assessments (Anthony & Jansen, 1984) or traditional vocational assessments designed for people with physical disabilities or mental retardation (Cook & Razzano, 1994), since many people with psychiatric disorders perform differently in different types of work environments (Schultheis & Bond, 1993). For example, in one study by Anthony et al. (1995), ratings from situational assessments of work behaviors for 275 clients receiving psychosocial rehabilitation significantly predicted employment status, even when controlling for symptoms, diagnosis, race, living arrangement, and lifetime number of hospitalizations. Several correlational studies also have revealed zero-order level relationships among situational assessment scores and later employment status (Black, 1986). In a study of youth (late teens and early 20s) with severe mental illness, Cook (1991) found that a 23-item situational assessment significantly predicted likelihood of employment, as well as hourly wage, at 6 months and 1 year after the beginning of clients' first jobs. Likewise, Bond and Friedmeyer (1987) found that a 22-item checklist predicted total number of weeks worked, as well as total earnings, among 77 adults receiving psychosocial rehabilitation services within the community. Other situational assessment studies (Rogers, Sciarappa, & Anthony, 1991; Schultheis & Bond, 1993) also have demonstrated good reliability, discriminative validity, and content validity.

The third principle involves *rapid placement* into paid community employment rather than undergoing lengthy periods of prevocational training. By placing clients swiftly into community-based jobs, this principle acknowledges the importance of avoiding the demoralization that can accompany lengthy periods of job training and evaluation (Schultheis & Bond, 1993). Similarly, Bond and Dincin (1986) showed when clients were randomly assigned to an "accelerated" job placement model, they were significantly more likely to be employed at 9-month follow-up and to be working full-time at 15-month follow-up compared with those in a comparison group who underwent several months in unpaid, segregated work adjustment training. In another randomized study, Bond, Dietzen, McGrew, and Miller (1995) found that superior outcomes (higher employment rate, higher job satisfaction) were achieved among supported employment clients who were placed in jobs immediately compared with those receiving prevocational services prior to their first jobs. In a discriminant function analysis of 602 severely mentally ill clients following vocational rehabilitation, those who had worked in sheltered workshops on their first paid placement were significantly less likely to achieve later competitive employment, even controlling for demographic factors (e.g., ethnicity, gender, education), functional impairment, illness severity, length of time receiving services, and the nature of employment services received (Cook & Razzano, 1995).

A fourth principle focuses on the availability of *ongoing vocational supports* that are appropriate to individuals' needs and situations. Continuous availability of vocational supports following job placement is one hallmark of supported employment services (Wehman, 1988). Given the relapsing and remitting nature of severe mental illness, this principle suggests that vocational supports should not be completely removed from clients upon their attainment of a job, creating a challenge for providers to avoid over- or underserving successfully employed clients (Cook & Razzano, 1992). In another study including 550 outpatients receiving vocational rehabilitation, Cook and Rosenberg (1994) used logistic regression analysis in a model predicting employment status at

6-month follow-up after program exit. This analysis revealed that ongoing support was a significant factor, even when controlling for client demographic features (e.g., age, education, ethnicity), prior work history, degree of functional impairment, hospitalization history, length of time in treatment, and types of job supports received. In another study of a model program at the same agency, Cook and Razzano demonstrated that the addition of ongoing, as-needed employment support services resulted in an agency-wide increase in employment rates from 50% to over 80% throughout the 36-month program period.

Tailoring job development and support to *clients' individual preferences* is yet another principle which, to some extent, grew out of a reaction against "one-size-fits-all" approaches in some vocational rehabilitation service delivery models in which clients have little to say over the nature of the jobs they are offered and/or the level of intrusiveness of the job supports they receive (Danley, Sciarappa, & MacDonald-Wilson, 1992; Mowbray et al., 1994). Contrary to this line of thinking, more contemporary research supports that clients have better employment-related outcomes when their services are designed and delivered to coincide with their job preferences. For example, in one study by Becker, Drake, Farabaugh, and Bond (1996) examining 143 clients with severe mental illness, findings suggested that the clients who worked in their preferred fields reported job tenure twice as long as those not employed in their preferred area, as well as significantly greater levels of job satisfaction.

A final principle involves the explicit acknowledgment of and planning for the ways in which changes in clients' work status may alter their disability income and associated healthcare coverage. This principle identifies the necessity to addresses potential *economic disincentives* to achieve certain levels of paid employment, inherent in the structure of disability entitlements (Noble, 1998). One study of vocational rehabilitation involving job-seeking skills training reported that Supplemental Security Income (SSI) recipients were significantly less likely to become employed or enter job training than nonrecipients of SSI; however, this was linked by the authors to the recipient group's poorer work histories and greater illness severity and chronicity (Jacobs et al., 1992). A multivariate study of 1,634 male Vietnam-era veterans found differences in likelihood and nature of employment according to the *monthly amount* the men were receiving (Rosenheck, Frisman, & Sindelar, 1995). Veterans who received Department of Veteran's Affairs disability compensation payments of less than $500 a month were no less likely to work or earn less money than those who received no disability income (and presumably had no disincentive). However, even controlling for illness status, functional impairment, and traditional labor force predictors such as ethnicity and education, veterans whose compensation was greater than $500 per month were significantly less likely to work and earned significantly less than all groups of eligibles. Interestingly, veterans with psychiatric disabilities were no less likely to be employed than their disabled counterparts with *physical and other nonpsychiatric* disabilities (Rosenheck et al., 1995). While research in this area has yet to persuasively answer many questions about the relationship between disability payments and employment activity, it *has* highlighted the importance of benefits counseling and financial planning to both service providers and recipients (Donegan & Palmer-Erbs, 1998).

METHODS OF ASSESSMENT FOR OUTCOMES/EFFICACY

As noted by Cook (1995), the need to provide evidence regarding the efficacy and effectiveness of services for mental health consumers has grown within the field. Efficacy involves the examination and testing of service models under more methodologically controlled conditions by providers with relevant training and expertise. Effectiveness, however, generally has characterized research involving more rigorous designs and methods to examine services that have been delivered in real-world settings, by existing providers and staff at community-based service organizations. With the growing emphasis on evidence-based practices, service systems of all types, including vocational rehabilitation and supported employment, strategies to implement evidence-based services are critical now more than ever (Cook, Toprac, & Shore, in press). However, to date, ongoing research continues to investigate and document the best methods with which to implement supported employment services (Bond, Becker, et al., 2001; Rogers, McDonald-Wilson, Danley, Martin, & Anthony, 1997). In addition, while barriers to implementation of supported employment exist at a number of levels, including governmental, programmatic, clinical, and among consumers and their families (Bond, Becker, et al., 2001; Shafer, Pardee, & Stewart, 1999), newer projects have focused on strategies with which to expand the implementation of supported employment services at all levels (Drake et al., 1998; McCarthy, Thompson, & Olsen, 1998). Furthermore, new methods to address or supplement the implementation of evidence-based practices, such as the structured consensus process, have been successfully adopted (Baker, 2001; Cook, Toprac, & Shore, in press; Crimson et al., 1999).

Supported Employment Outcomes

There are numerous indicators used within the field to characterize employment outcomes (Cook & Razzano, 2000). Published accounts have included measures of work skills (Lysaker & Bell, 1995), sheltered work, defined as paid, piece-rate work activity in nonintegrated settings (Bond, Resnick, et al., 2001), and more recently, competitive work outcomes (Lehman et al., 2002). Currently, there is a growing emphasis within the field, particularly within supported employment, on assisting mental health consumers to achieve competitive work outcomes, characterized by regular/open market jobs (i.e., not set aside for people with disabilities), located within integrated community settings, and paying at minimum wage or above (Bond, Becker, et al., 2001; Cook & Razzano, 2000; Drake et al., 1999; Lehman et al., 2002).

Within the field, supported employment has emerged as an area with evidence for both its efficacy and effectiveness. Several accounts, including those with randomized intervention methodologies, have demonstrated the ways in which supported employment promotes improvements in the vocational and nonvocational outcomes compared to other types of employment models, including standard community care services (Chandler, Meisel, The-wei, McGowen, & Madisom, 1997); prevocational training service models (Drake et al., 1996; McFarlane et al., 2000); and most recently, traditional psychosocial interventions, including transitional and placement employment services (Lehman et al., 2002; Mueser et al., in press). Overall, evidence from quasi-experimental studies, as well as randomized clinical trials, indicates that supported employment is not only evidence-based, but also has been shown to be more successful than other types of vocational rehabilitation interventions (Bond, Becker, et al., 2001).

PROVIDER COMPETENCY AND TRAINING IN VOCATIONAL REHABILITATION

Service providers working within the field of vocational rehabilitation and supported employment engage in a variety of activities, including job development and placement, job coaching, and on-the-job support. Based on previous studies (Danley & Mellen, 1987; Farrell, 1991), Baron (2000) describes three overarching categories for vocational competencies that support best practices psychosocial rehabilitation services: encouragement, assistance, and ongoing support. These provider competencies have been formulated with and reflect the current state of the science for evidence-based best practices in rehabilitative employment services.

Encouragement Competencies

There are seven encouragement-related competencies. These initial steps focus on strategies with which providers can forge alliances with mental health consumers to identify and begin to build upon their values and interests in working:

1. *Engagement:* Engaging mental health consumers in the overall rehabilitation process (Blankertz, 1994; Cohen, 1989).

2. *Encouragement:* Encouraging each mental health consumer to establish employment as a central goal in his or her rehabilitation and recovery experience (Blankertz, 1994; Blankertz & Cnaan, 1993).

3. *Empowerment:* Assisting mental health consumers to establish the employment goals, nature, and pace of their rehabilitation/recovery process (Blankertz, 1994; Harp, 1992).

4. *Education:* Providing information to mental health consumers regarding the nature of and available options within employment programs (Blankertz, 1994; Rogers, Danley, & Anthony, 1992).

5. *Assessment:* Providing initial and ongoing assessment of mental health consumers' strengths and weaknesses related to employment (Anthony & Jansen, 1984; Shepherd, 1990).

6. *Financial Counseling:* Working with mental health consumers to understand the impact of working on their financial status and resources (Hill, Wehman, Kregel, Banks, & Metzler, 1987).

7. *Program Planning:* Coordinating services within complex and multi-dimensional vocational rehabilitation plans (Isbister & Donaldson, 1987; Test, 1992).

Assistance Competencies

Eight competencies have been identified that relate to assistance over the course of the rehabilitation process. They focus on activities that support the ongoing growth of consumers' vocational rehabilitation experiences:

1. *Teaching:* Teaching mental health consumers the skills that are required technically and interpersonally within the workplace (Mueser & Liberman, 1988; Rogers et al., 1992).

2. *Monitoring:* Observing mental health consumers' attainment of and ability to use technical and interpersonal skills while on the job (Furlong, Jonikas, & Cook, 1994).

3. *Job Development:* Working to develop viable employment opportunities for mental health consumers within integrated community settings (Goodall, 1987; Young, Rosati, & Vandergroot, 1986).

4. *Job Finding:* Working with mental health consumers to assist in their ability to find appropriate jobs independently (Azrin & Phillip, 1979).

5. *Coordination of Services:* Working to coordinate services through ongoing and consistent communication with other services providers, including employers (Frey & Godfrey, 1991; Test, 1992).

6. *Reasonable Accommodations:* Supporting mental health consumers, employers, and other stakeholders to request, develop, and implement appropriate and effective reasonable accommodations within the workplace to support continued job tenure (Combs & Omvig, 1986; Mancuso, 1990).

7. *Transportation:* Helping mental health consumers to identify and utilize consistent sources of transportation to and from the workplace (Danley, Ridley, & Cohen, 1982).

8. *Stabilization:* Providing initial and ongoing support to mental health consumers as they become accustomed to employment settings (Jacobsen, 1993).

Ongoing Supports

Providing ongoing vocational supports is characterized by five provider competencies. These areas not only focus on supports for initial jobs but also build on strategies to assist consumers to develop and sustain employment over time and remain active in the labor market:

1. *Managing Crises:* Given the chronic nature of psychiatric disabilities, providers should work with consumers and employers in advance to develop intervention plans that allow consumers to maintain employment.

2. *Social Networks:* Assisting mental health consumers to develop social skills and relationships with peers and coworkers that support continued employment (Henderson & Argyle, 1985; Nisbet & Hagner, 1988).

3. *Career Mobility:* Working with mental health consumers to regularly examine and address changes on the job (Baumgart, 1987; Toms-Barker, 1994).

4. *Job Loss:* Assisting mental health consumers to respond appropriately to job ending and loss to avoid discouragement and disengagement with employment activities (McLoughlin, Garner, & Callahan, 1987).

5. *Vocational Independence:* Supporting mental health consumers in their efforts to develop the types of individual supports they need to sustain independence within the workplace (McDonald-Wilson, Mancuso, Danley, & Anthony, 1989; McLoughlin et al., 1987).

With the demanding nature of contemporary labor markets, developing and maintaining competency in all of these areas is a challenge for vocational providers. Now more than ever, mental health consumers are able to facilitate their own recovery within the community. Employment is a focal aspect of that recovery. Thus, it is essential that practitioners from many diverse behavioral and social science disciplines address their ability to actively support consumers in attaining their goals for meaningful employment experiences.

ASSESSING FIDELITY AND OTHER SUPPORTED EMPLOYMENT SERVICE TOOLS

With the growing body of evidence regarding the success of supported employment programs, it has become increasingly important for mental health consumers (and service providers) to have resources and tools with which they can characterize the vocational services available, as well as identify consumers' employment goals. There are some assessment tools available to measure program fidelity within specific models, including supported employment, such as the Individual Placement and Support Fidelity Scale (Bond, Becker, Drake, & Vogler, 1997), as well as other service interventions, for example, the Dartmouth Assertive Community Treatment Scale (Bond, Drake, Mueser, & Latimer, 2001; Teague, Bond, & Drake, 1998). Yet due to the model-specific nature of these types of assessments, their ability to characterize programs and the inclusion of the "active ingredients" of supported employment overall is limited. However, one such tool, "Seeking Supported Employment: What You Need to Know," recently was developed (Cook & Petersen, 2003). In creating this tool, several issues were fundamental: consumer choice, policy relevance, and state-of-the-science implications. With regard to consumer choice, it was necessary to incorporate mental health consumers' views on work and employment. This is a central theme in the tool since achieving higher levels of economic well-being is accorded primary importance by consumers. In addition, the relevance of work and employment from a policy perspective was considered, per the heavy emphasis on employment in the *Final Report* of President George W. Bush's New Freedom Mental Health Commission (2003). Finally, the Seeking Supported Employment tool incorporates recommendations from the current state of the science. For example, the instrument incorporates factors that build on other core principles recently published by the Center for Mental Health Services (CMHS), Substance Abuse and Mental Health Services Administration, the federal funding agency of the Employment Intervention Demonstration Program (EIDP). CMHS has completed and released a supported employment service provider toolkit to the field.

Seeking Supported Employment educates mental health consumers about different "roads to employment," affording consumers the opportunity to choose the best-fitting employment options for them. Using an integrated scoring system, the self-guided and user-friendly instrument allows mental health consumers more control in choosing the best-fitting program and includes open-ended sections to allow for self-expression and self-exploration of mental health consumers' employment goals. All of the program evaluation questions included in Seeking Supported Employment are based on research-based principles of supported employment derived from the EIDP. The first five questions represent principles having the strongest research evidence, so program features have extra "weight." Furthermore, the integrated scoring system identifies program's overall level of adherence to these evidence-based practices (see Figure 2.1).

SUPPORTED EMPLOYMENT SUCCESS STORIES AND A CASE EXAMPLE

The following success stories and case example in supported employment are drawn from a series compiled in the Employment Intervention Demonstration Program (EIDP; Cook, Carey, Razzano, Burke & Blyler, 2002). These brief accounts describe some of the supported employment experiences of people with psychiatric disabilities, and highlight how supported employment program models responded to participants' needs in attaining their employment goals. A common thread in all of these cases is that attention was paid to the specific individual needs and preferences among these mental health consumers, and that ongoing support both in and out of the workplace, an important feature of supported employment programs, was provided. In reviewing the case example and the success stories, bear in mind that the individuals described are those who have typically been considered "unemployable" by most traditional vocational rehabilitation standards (Cook & Razzano, 2000; Simmons, Selleck, Steele, & Sepetauc, 1993). In particular, all of these clients are people living with serious and persistent mental illnesses. They also represent great diversity, not only in geographic region, but in primary *DSM-IV* diagnosis (i.e., schizophrenia spectrum and mood disorders), age (i.e., 31 to 53 years), level of formal education (i.e., grade school through graduate school), and race/ethnicity (i.e., African American, American Indian, Hispanic/Latino, and White). Their experiences and jobs reflect their individuality, and also are diverse in nature, hours, and salary/earnings. Furthermore, as a result of their participation in supported employment programs, none are engaged in sheltered work or being paid at less than minimum wage (Burke, Cook, & Razzano, 2002).

Supported Employment Success Stories

One type of supported employment program that is a "promising practice" is the Individual Placement and Support (IPS) model. IPS includes several of the active ingredients of many supported employment programs, including rapid placement, continued follow-along support, and finding employment opportunities that are consistent with mental health consumers' preferences, skills, and abilities.

One EIDP study participant from the Connecticut (CT) site had approximately an eighth grade education, had never held a paying job, and had been hospitalized for

Check off each answer ☒

Question	Green Zone	Red Zone
How many of your clients work in competitive jobs that are open to anyone who applies? At least 80% or less than 80%?	At least 80% ☐	Less than 80% ☐
How many of your clients work in settings where none of the coworkers is disabled? At least 80% or less than 80%?	At least 80% ☐	Less than 80% ☐
Can people who are working continue to receive support from program staff for as long as they want?	Yes ☐	No ☐
Does your program place clients in jobs that are permanent?	Yes ☐	No ☐
How many of your clients earn minimum wage or above? At least 80% or less than 80%?	At least 80% ☐	Less than 80% ☐
Add 1 point for each answer in the Green Zone and 0 for each answer in the Red Zone.		
Score for first 5 questions only =		
How many of your clients earn $10 an hour or more? At least 10% or less than 10%?	At least 10% ☐	Less than 10% ☐
How many of your clients get a job in a field they want? At least 50% or less than 50%?	At least 50% ☐	Less than 50% ☐
Does your program work with anyone interested in working, regardless of her/his abilities?	Yes ☐	No ☐
Does your program have in-person vocational support after 5 P.M.?	Yes ☐	No ☐

Check off each answer ☒

Question	Green Zone	Red Zone
Does your program terminate clients from services even though the clients still want to continue receiving services?	No ☐	Yes ☐
What is the average amount of time people take to get a job in your agency? 6 months or less or more than 6 months	6 months or less ☐	More than 6 months ☐
Do staff at your agency provide benefits counseling for people on SSI/SSDI?	Yes ☐	No ☐
Will your agency accept clients who want to work AND keep their SSI and SSDI benefits at the same time?	Yes ☐	No ☐
Does your program offer peer support services from people who have had mental health problems?	Yes ☐	No ☐
Does your program allow family or friends to be involved in the process of finding and keeping a job?	Yes ☐	No ☐
How many of your clients also are clients of our state Vocational Rehabilitation agency? At least 50% or less than 50%?	At least 50% ☐	Less than 50% ☐
Does your program help clients keep their jobs if they go in the hospital or need to take some time off for mental health reasons?	Yes ☐	No ☐
Will your staff talk frequently with my case manager or psychiatrist if I ask them to?	Yes ☐	No ☐
How many of your clients have a psychiatric disability? At least 25% or less than 25%?	At least 25% ☐	Less than 25% ☐
TOTAL SCORE for all 19 questions =		

Figure 2.1 Key Questions for Identifying Supported Employment Services

psychiatric symptoms six times in the 4 years prior to joining the EIDP. She also was a single parent of three children, and coping with other family members who have difficulties with alcohol. The IPS program helped her to get a job as a greeter at a child care center that was part of a larger chain. Shortly thereafter, another location in the chain hired her into a position closer to her home and promoted her to teacher's assistant, a position that also brought a salary increase. The IPS team helped with the job development, and continued to work with this participant providing vocational and individual counseling, case management, and clinical care services. She continued to work in this job for over a year and a half, leaving the position only because she elected to move away from the area. In addition, throughout the course of her job and IPS program support, she experienced no psychiatric hospitalizations.

The Maryland EIDP site also studied the IPS model as part of a comprehensive community-based services program. This participant had no previous competitive work history, and was open to suggestions regarding types of employment goals when he entered into the program. However, his psychiatric symptoms, including delusional thinking and paranoia, made it difficult for him to engage successfully with IPS. After about 7 months of program involvement, he approached his therapist with a renewed interest in work. The participant, his therapist, and vocational staff then met to develop an action plan. Initially, the consumer asked that the job search be restricted to only certain days and hours during the week because he was concerned that working would conflict with his usual activities. Once it was determined that IPS staff would help him to rearrange his daily routine, he started applying for part-time positions regardless of the hours or days. During this time, it also became apparent to IPS staff that this participant was an avid sports fan. Vocational staff accompanied him to a job fair at Camden Yards (the home of the Baltimore Orioles) prior to the start of baseball season. During this visit, he was hired on the spot as a member of the janitorial crew, and continues to work for the ballpark over the baseball season. He also has been able to rearrange his daily activities without assistance, and IPS staff have not observed symptoms of paranoia or delusional thinking since he began working.

At the Texas EIDP site, the intervention program consisted of combined "rapid entry" supported employment services with social network enhancement. These services are designed to help mental health consumers move from support networks characterized primarily by professional support to more balanced networks that are larger, more diverse, and more reciprocal, that is, include more peers. The participant profiled here had been employed intermittently for 10 years prior to joining the EIDP. After 3 months in the combined supported employment program, she was hired as manager of an apartment complex, consisting of approximately 40 affordable housing units for lower-income mental health consumers. Her duties included those traditionally associated with apartment management, but also included providing peer counseling. Clinical and vocational service staff were concerned, however, that she was working so hard that she might be vulnerable for a reoccurrence of psychiatric symptoms. However, with support from project staff and her social network peers, she developed appropriate strategies to manage the stressors of her job, such as turning her pager off at night and over the weekends when she was not on call. She maintained this job for over 2 years, and as of the conclusion of the EIDP study follow-up period, she was still employed at this salaried position and receiving full benefits. Yet, despite her success, she requested that program staff not close her case, believing that the ongoing support of the program helps her maintain her job, including helping her to develop a balance between her work and personal life. In addition, she continues to refer consumers to the supported employment program, and volunteers to speak to groups of job seekers about her experiences. After hearing her speak, another consumer who had been negative, frustrated, and withdrew from employment-related activities experienced a change of heart, saying, "if she [can do this], then maybe there is hope for me, too."

────────────── A Supported Employment Case Example ──────────────

Mr. Smith is a 34-year-old African American male mental health consumer receiving services from an outpatient mental health center affiliated with the University of Maryland, Baltimore. He had untreated depression and substance abuse as a youth, culminating in a suicide attempt at age 18. Mr. Smith reported that his substance abuse problems began in late adolescence, and that the abuse became quite heavy for several years, peaking with approximately a fifth of alcohol consumed daily and regular crack cocaine use. He sought treatment at the University's clinic in 1991, after being discharged from a psychiatric hospitalization that lasted 3.5 months and was attributed to a series of co-occurring factors, including another suicide attempt, active crack cocaine use, and alcohol dependence. At the time of hospitalization, he was diagnosed with Major Depressive Disorder on Axis I and Borderline Personality Disorder on Axis II. Mr. Smith was hospitalized a second time for psychiatric reasons in 1992. He reported being clean and sober for more than three years at the time he entered the vocational services program.

Mr. Smith is a high school graduate, and he completed some technical training in preparation for work as a nurse's aide. He was employed as a nurse's aide for five years before the reoccurrence of symptoms of depression, as well as continued use of alcohol and drugs, resulted in his inability to maintain employment. Except for a brief 5-month period, Mr. Smith remained unemployed from 1992 to 1996.

In 1996, Mr. Smith joined a supported employment program that was part of the EIDP. At this time, he continued to struggle with symptoms of depression, but was no longer drinking alcohol or using any recreational drugs. He reported being unemployed, living on Social Security Disability Income (SSDI) support, and participating in a psychosocial day treatment program at the University. He was, however, eager to make use of supported employment services in order to help him achieve his goal of going back to work. Mr. Smith actively participated in an Individual Placement and Support (IPS) program, and he soon applied for and accepted a job as a janitor at the Social Security Administration (SSA) in Baltimore, where he continued to work for over two years (and was still employed at the conclusion of the EIDP study follow-up period). Included among the vocational services Mr. Smith received from the IPS program were several key ingredients of supported employment services overall: rapid job placement, intensive on-the-job support, as well as the 24-hour-a-day availability of service provision, and the integration of a number of treatment teams, all of which were key to his success in obtaining and maintaining this job. Subsequently, Mr. Smith was married and reported feeling better about himself and his life situation. Most recently, Mr. Smith made the decision to work full-time and stop receiving financial support from SSDI. Since doing so, he continued to work independently at the same job, and reported significant ongoing job satisfaction and improvements in his overall quality of life.

As illustrated in these case examples, the experiences of mental consumers' desire and commitment to find and maintain meaningful employment are inspiring. Equally inspiring are the efforts of supported employment service delivery staff who often "go that extra mile" and "think outside the box" when designing individually tailored vocational services and providing unobtrusive job supports. The final analyses of EIDP data are well underway; study results indicate the success of the supported employment programs tested, as well as provide new support for the growing evidence-based literature in this area. However, in addition to the empirical proof that supported employment is a promising practice, it is essential to remember that there are important human stories behind the numbers, and to celebrate the achievements of mental health consumers who pursue and accomplish their vocational goals and those who help them to do so.

FUTURE DIRECTIONS

Clearly, research on supported employment has accumulated a strong body of evidence-based best practices for people with psychiatric disabilities. With the "key ingredients" outlined in this chapter, including rapid placement, ongoing supports, competitive work in integrated settings, more mental health consumers are able to accomplish their employment and vocational goals than ever before. As demonstrated by this literature, there are numerous benefits for mental health consumers engaged in competitive employment over time. However, many continue to confront barriers to employment, including depressed labor markets, financial disincentives, and loss of health benefits. Thus, many challenges remain for mental health consumers and service providers working to achieve and sustain employment. Consumers, family members, providers, and stakeholders at a variety of levels must work together in order to continue to move the field of supported employment forward. This can be accomplished with a renewed focus on providing best practices services with a demonstrated ability to lead to work, as well as those which focus on remediating deficits in other areas of consumers' lives, including cognitive impairments, educational achievement, social skills and competence, and financial education and planning. Despite the lingering stigma regarding the "unemployability" of mental health consumers, supported employment provides substantial evidence to the contrary, demonstrating that competitive employment not only affects positive changes in vocational goals among consumers, but also positively affects outcomes in other, nonemployment-related areas. Based on the evidence to date, supported employment can and does improve vocational outcomes in a myriad of settings for a variety of individuals living with psychiatric disabilities.

REFERENCES

Americans with Disabilities Act. (1990). Public Law 101-336, 42, U.S.C., 12101-12132.

Anthony, W. A., & Blanch, A. (1987). Supported employment for persons who are psychiatrically disabled: An historical and conceptual perspective. *Psychosocial Rehabilitation Journal, 11*(2), 5–23.

Anthony, W. A., & Jansen, M. A. (1984). Predicting the vocational capacity of the chronically mentally ill. *American Psychologist, 39*(5), 537–544.

Anthony, W. A., Rogers, E. S., Cohen, M., & Davies, R. R. (1995). Relationships between psychiatric symptomatology, work skills, and future vocational performance. *Psychiatric Services, 46*(4), 353–358.

Arns, P., & Linney, J. A. (1995). Relating functional skills of severely mentally ill clients to subjective and societal benefits. *Psychiatric Services, 46*(3), 260–265.

Azrin, N. H., & Phillip, R. A. (1979). The job club method for the job handicapped: A comparative outcome study. *Rehabilitation Counseling Bulletin, 23,* 144–155.

Baker, J. G. (2001). Engaging community mental health stakeholders in pharmacy cost management. *Psychiatric Services, 52*(5), 650–653.

Baron, R. C. (2000). Vocational rehabilitation. In R. Hughes & D. Weinstein (Eds.), *Best practices in psychosocial rehabilitation* (pp. 245–263). Columbia, MD: International Association of Psychosocial Rehabilitation Services.

Baumgart, D. (1987). Career focus: A curriculum manual for students with moderate or severe handicaps. *Secondary Transition and Employment Project: STEP.* Moscow: Idaho University, Department of Special Education.

Becker, D., Drake, R., Farabaugh, A., & Bond, G. R. (1996). Job preferences of clients with severe psychiatric disorders participating in supported employment programs. *Psychiatric Services, 47*(11), 1223–1226.

Black, B. J. (Ed.). (1986). *Work as therapy for the mentally ill.* New York: Altro Institute for Rehabilitation Studies.

Blankertz, L. (1994). *The employment specialist manual.* Philadelphia: Matrix Research Institute.

Blankertz, L., & Cnaan, R. (1993). Serving the dually-diagnosed homeless: Program development and interventions. *Journal of Mental Health Administration, 20*(2), 100–112.

Blankertz, L., & Robinson, S. (1996). Adding a vocational focus to mental health rehabilitation. *Psychiatric Services, 47,* 1216–1222.

Bond, G. R., Becker, D. R., Drake, R. E., Rapp, C. A., Meisler, N., Lehman, A. F., et al. (2001). Implementing supported employment as an evidence-based practice. *Psychiatric Services, 52*(3), 313–322.

Bond, G. R., Becker, D. R., Drake, R. E., & Vogler, K. M. (1997). A fidelity scale for the Individual Placement and Support model of supported employment. *Rehabilitation Counseling Journal, 40,* 265–284.

Bond, G. R., Dietzen, L., McGrew, J., & Miller, L. (1995). Accelerating entry into supported employment for persons with severe psychiatric disabilities. *Rehabilitation Psychology, 40,* 75–94.

Bond, G. R., & Dincin, J. (1986). Accelerating entry into transitional employment in a psychiatric rehabilitation agency. *Rehabilitation Psychology, 32,* 143–155.

Bond, G. R., Drake, R. E., Mueser, K. T., & Becker, D. R. (1997). An update on supported employment for people with severe mental illness. *Psychiatric Services, 48*(3):335–346.

Bond, G. R., Drake, R. E., Mueser, K. T., & Latimer, E. (2001). Assertive community treatment for people with severe mental illness: Critical ingredients and impact on patients. *Disability Management and Health Outcomes, 9,* 141–159.

Bond, G. R., & Friedmeyer, M. H. (1987). Predictive validity of situational assessment as a psychiatric rehabilitation center. *Psychosocial Rehabilitation Journal, 11,* 61–77.

Bond, G. R., Resnick, S. G., Drake, R. E., Xie, H., McHugo, G. J., & Bebout, R. R. (2001). Does competitive employment improve non-vocational outcomes for people with severe mental illness? *Journal of Consulting and Clinical Psychology, 69*(3), 489–501.

Burke, J. K., Cook, J. A., & Razzano, L. A. (2002). *Courage and commitment: Success stories from the Employment Intervention Demonstration Program.* Unpublished manuscript, University of Illinois at Chicago.

Chandler, D., Meisel, J., The-wei, H., McGowen, M., & Madison, K. (1997). A capitated model for a cross-section of severely mentally ill clients: Employment outcomes. *Community Mental Health Journal, 33*(6), 501–516.

Cohen, M. B. (1989, November). Social work practice with homeless mentally ill people: Engaging the client. *Social Work,* 505–508.

Combs, I. H., & Omvig, C. P. (1986). Accommodation of disabled people into employment: Perceptions of employers. *Journal of Rehabilitation, 52*(2), 42–45.

Cook, J. A. (1991). *Vocational rehabilitation for youth with severe mental illness: Predictive validity of situational assessment for later employment.* Paper presented at the annual meeting of the American Public Health Association, Atlanta, GA.

Cook, J. A. (1995). Research on psychosocial rehabilitation services for persons with psychiatric disabilities. *Psychotherapy and Rehabilitation Research Bulletin, 4,* 5–11.

Cook, J. A., Bond, G. R., Hoffschmidt, S., Jonas, E., Razzano, L. A., & Weakland, R. (1991). *Assessing vocational performance among persons with severe mental illness.* Chicago: Thresholds National Research and Training Center on Rehabilitation and Mental Illness.

Cook, J. A., & Burke, J. (2002). Public policy and employment of people with disabilities: Exploring new paradigms. *Behavioral Science and the Law, 20*(6), 541–557.

Cook, J. A., Carey, M. A., Razzano, L. A., Burke, J. K., & Blyler, C. (2002). The Pioneer: The Employment Intervention Demonstration Program—A multisite study of vocational rehabilitation interventions. In J. M. Herrell & R. B. Straw (Eds.), *New directions in evaluation: Conducting multiple site evaluations in real-world settings* (pp. 31–44). San Francisco: Jossey-Bass/American Evaluation Association.

Cook, J. A., & Hoffschmidt, S. (1993). Comprehensive models of psychosocial rehabilitation. In R. W. Flexor & P. Solomon (Eds.), *Psychiatric rehabilitation in practice* (pp. 81–97). Boston: Andover Medical.

Cook, J. A., & Petersen, C. A. (2003). *Seeking supported employment: What you need to know.* Chicago, IL: UIC National Research and Training Center on Psychiatric Disability.

Cook, J. A., & Pickett, S. A. (1995). Recent trends in vocational rehabilitation for people with psychiatric disability. *American Rehabilitation, 20*(4), 2–12.

Cook, J. A., & Razzano, L. A. (1992). Natural vocational supports for persons with severe mental illness: Thresholds supported competitive employment program. In L. Stein (Ed.),

New directions in mental health services: Innovations in mental health services (pp. 23–42). San Francisco: Jossey-Bass.

Cook, J. A., & Razzano, L. A. (1994). Predictive validity of the McCarron-Dial testing battery for employment outcomes among psychiatric rehabilitation clientele. *Vocational Evaluation and Work Adjustment Bulletin, 27*(2), 39–47.

Cook, J. A., & Razzano, L. A. (1995). Discriminant function analysis of competitive employment outcomes in a transitional employment program for persons with severe mental illness. *Journal of Vocational Rehabilitation, 5,* 127–139.

Cook, J. A., & Razzano, L. A. (2000). Vocational rehabilitation for persons with schizophrenia: Recent research and implications for practice. *Schizophrenia Bulletin, 26*(1), 87–103.

Cook, J. A., & Rosenberg, H. (1994). Predicting community employment among persons with psychiatric disability: A logistic regression analysis. *Journal of Rehabilitation Administration, 18*(1), 6–22.

Cook, J. A., Toprac, M., & Shore, S. (in press). Combining evidence-based practice with stakeholder consensus to enhance psychosocial rehabilitation services in the Texas benefit design initiative. *Psychiatric Rehabilitation Journal.*

Cook, J. A., & Wright, E. R. (1995). Medical sociology and the study of severe mental illness: Reflections on past accomplishments and directions for future research. *Journal of Health and Social Behavior, 36,* 95–114.

Crimson, M., Trivedi, M., Pigott, T., Rush, A. J., Hirschfeld, R. M., Kahn, D. A., et al. (1999). The Texas Medication Algorithm Project: Report of the Texas consensus conference panel on medication treatment of major depressive disorder. *Journal of Clinical Psychiatry, 60,* 142–156.

Crowther, R. E., Marshall, M., Bond, G. R., & Huxley, P. (2001). Helping people with severe mental illness to obtain work: Systematic review. *British Medical Journal, 322,* 204–208.

Danley, K. S., & Mellen, V. (1987). Training and personnel issues for supported employment programs which serve persons who are severely mentally ill. *Psychosocial Rehabilitation Journal, 11*(2), 87–102.

Danley, K. S., Ridley, D. E., & Cohen, M. R. (1982). *Review of skills teaching guides.* Boston: Boston University, Center for Psychiatric Rehabilitation.

Danley, K. S., Sciarappa, K., & MacDonald-Wilson, K. (1992). Choose-get-keep: A psychiatric rehabilitation approach to supported employment. In R. Liberman (Ed.), *New directions in mental health services: In effective psychiatric rehabilitation* (pp. 87–97). San Francisco: Jossey-Bass.

Donegan, K. R., & Palmer-Erbs, V. K. (1998). Promoting the importance of work for persons with psychiatric disabilities: The role of the psychiatric nurse. *Journal of Psychosocial Nursing, 36*(4), 13–14.

Drake, R. E. (1998). A brief history of the Individual Placement and Support Model. *Psychiatric Rehabilitation Journal, 22*(1), 3–7.

Drake, R. E., Becker, D. R., Biesans, J., Torrey, W., McHugo, G. J., & Wyzik, P. (1994). Rehabilitative day treatment vs. supported employment: I. Vocational outcomes. *Community Mental Health Journal, 30,* 519–532.

Drake, R. E., Fox, T. S., Leather, P. K., Becker, D. R., Musumeci, J. S., Ingram, W. F., & McHugo, G. J. (1998). Regional variation in competitive employment for persons with severe mental illness. *Administration and Policy in Mental Health, 25,* 493–504.

Drake, R. E., McHugo, G. J., Bebout, R. R., Becker, D. R., Harris, M., Bond, G. R., et al. (1999). A randomized controlled trial of supported employment for inner city patients with mental illness. *Archives of General Psychiatry, 56,* 627–633.

Drake, R. E., McHugo, G. J., Becker, D. R., Anthony, W. A., & Clark, R. E. (1996). The New Hampshire study of supported employment for people with severe mental illness. *Journal of Consulting and Clinical Psychology, 64*(2), 391–399.

Fabian, E. (1992). Longitudinal outcomes in supported employment: A survival analysis. *Rehabilitation Psychology, 37,* 23–35.

Farrell, D. (1991). Case management issues in a supported competitive employment setting for young adults with mental illness. In J. A. Cook (Ed.), *Issues in supported employment for youth with mental illness: Theory, research and practice* (pp. 22–40). Chicago: Thresholds National Research and Training Center on Rehabilitation and Mental Illness.

Frey, J. L., & Godfrey, M. (1991). A comprehensive clinical vocational assessment: The PACT approach. *Applied Rehabilitation Counseling, 22,* 25–28.

Furlong, M., Jonikas, J. A., & Cook, J. A. (1994). *Job coaching and on-going job support for persons with psychiatric disabilities.* Chicago, IL: Thresholds National Research and Training Center on Rehabilitation and Mental Illness.

Gatens-Robinson, E., & Rubins, S. E. (1995). Societal values and ethical commitments that influence rehabilitation service delivery behavior. In S. E. Rubin & R. T. Roessler (Eds.), *Foundations of the vocational rehabilitation process* (pp. 157–174). Austin, TX: ProEd.

Goodall, P. (1987). Benefits to employers who hire workers with disabilities. *Virginia Commonwealth University Rehabilitation Research and Training Center Newsletter, 3*(1), 1–2.

Harp, H. T. (1992). *Empowerment of mental health consumers in vocational rehabilitation* (Resource papers, Consensus Validation Conference). Washington, DC: National Institute on Disability and Rehabilitation Research.

Henderson, M., & Argyle, M. (1985). Social support by four categories of work colleague: Relationships between activities, stress, and satisfaction. *Journal of Occupational Behavior, 6,* 229–239.

Hill, M. L., Wehman, P. H., Kregel, J., Banks, P. D., & Metzler, H. M. (1987). Employment outcomes for people with moderate and severe disabilities: An eight-year longitudinal analysis of supported competitive employment. *Journal of the Association for Persons with Severe Handicaps, 12*(3), 182–189.

Isbister, F., & Donaldson, G. (1987). Supported employment for individuals who are mentally ill: Program developments. *Psychosocial Rehabilitation Journal, 9*(2), 87–96.

Jacobs, H. E., Wissusik, D., Collier, R., Stackman, D., & Burkeman, D. (1992). Correlations between psychiatric disabilities and vocational outcome. *Hospital and Community Psychiatry, 43,* 365–369.

Jacobsen, S. G. (1993). *Use of workplace supports to promote growth opportunities with mental illness: Baltimore Supported Employment Project.* Baltimore: Kennedy Krieger Community Resources.

Kouzis, A. C., & Eaton, W. W. (2000). Psychopathology and the initiation of disability payments. *Psychiatric Services, 51,* 908–913.

Kregel, J., Wehman, P., & Banks, P. D. (1989). The effects of consumer characteristics and type of employment model on individual outcomes in supported employment. *Journal of Applied Behavior Analysis, 22*(4), 407–415.

Lehman, A. F. (1988). A quality of life interview for the chronically mentally ill. *Evaluation and Program Planning, 11,* 51–62.

Lehman, A. F. (1995). Vocational rehabilitation in schizophrenia. *Schizophrenia Bulletin, 21*(4), 645–656.

Lehman, A. F. (1999). Developing an outcomes-based approach for the treatment of schizophrenia. *Journal of Clinical Psychiatry, 60*(Suppl. 19), 30–35.

Lehman, A. F., Goldberg, R., Dixon, L. B., McNary, S., Postrado, L., Hackman, A., et al. (2002). Improving employment outcomes for persons with severe mental illness. *Archives of General Psychiatry, 59,* 165–172.

Lysaker, P., & Bell, M. (1995). Work performance over time for persons with schizophrenia. *Psychosocial Rehabilitation Journal, 18,* 141–145.

Mancuso, L. L. (1990). Reasonable accommodations for workers with psychiatric disabilities. *Psychosocial Rehabilitation Journal, 14*(2), 3–19.

Marrone, J., & Golowka, E. (1999). If work makes people with mental illness sick, what do unemployment, poverty, and social isolation cause? *Psychiatric Rehabilitation Journal, 23*(2), 187–193.

Massel, H., Liberman, R., Mintz, J., Jacobs, H., Rush, T., Gianni, C., et al. (1990). Evaluating the capacity to work in the mentally ill. *Psychiatry, 53,* 31–43.

McCarthy, D., Thompson, D., & Olsen, S. (1998). Planning a statewide project to convert day treatment to supported employment. *Psychiatric Rehabilitation Journal, 22*(1), 30–33.

McDonald-Wilson, K. L., Mancuso, L. L., Danley, K. S., & Anthony, W. A. (1989). Supported employment for people with psychiatric disability. *Journal of Applied Rehabilitation Counseling, 20*(3), 50–57.

McFarlane, W. R., Dushay, R. A., Deakins, S. M., Stastny, P., Lukens, E. P., Toral, J., et al. (2000). Employment outcomes in family-aided assertive community treatment. *American Journal of Orthopsychiatry, 70*(2), 203–214.

McLoughlin, K., Garner, B., & Callahan, M. (1987). *Getting employed and staying employed.* Baltimore: Paul H. Brookes.

Meyer, P. S., Bond, G. R., Tunis, S. L., & McCoy, M. L. (2002). Comparison between the effects of atypical and traditional antipsychotics on work status for clients in a psychiatric rehabilitation program. *Journal of Clinical Psychiatry, 63,* 108–116.

Mowbray, C. T., Rusilowski-Clover, G., Arnold, J., Allen, C., Harris, A., McCrohan, H., et al. (1994). Project WINS: Integrating vocational services on mental health case management teams. *Community Mental Health Journal, 30*(4), 347–362.

Mueser, K. T., Becker, D. R., Torrey, W. C., Xie, H., Bond, G. R., Drake, R. T., et al. (1997). Work and non-vocational domains of functioning in persons with severe mental illness: A longitudinal analysis. *Journal of Nervous and Mental Diseases, 185*(7), 419–426.

Mueser, K. T., Clark, R. E., Haines, M., Drake, R. E., McHugo, G. J., Bond, G. R., et al. (in press). The Hartford Study of supported employment for persons with severe mental illness. *Journal of Consulting and Clinical Psychology.*

Mueser, K. T., & Liberman, R. P. (1988). Skills training in vocational rehabilitation. In J. A. Ciardiello & M. D. Bell (Eds.), *Vocational rehabilitation of persons with prolonged mental illness* (pp. 81–103). Baltimore: Johns Hopkins University Press.

New Freedom Mental Health Commission. (2003). *Achieving the promise: Transforming mental health care in America, Final Report* (Publication No. SMA-03-3832). Rockville, MD: Department of Health and Human Services.

Nisbet, J., & Hagner, D. (1988). Natural supports in the workplace: A re-examination of supported employment. *Journal of the Association for Persons with Severe Handicaps, 3*(4), 3–11.

Noble, J. H. (1998). Policy reform dilemmas in promoting employment of persons with severe mental illness. *Psychiatric Services, 49*(6), 775–781.

Polak, P., & Warner, R. (1996). The economic life of seriously mentally ill people in the community. *Psychiatric Services, 47*(2), 270–274.

Rehabilitation Act Amendments. Title IV of the Workforce Investment Act of 1998, Pub. L. No. 105–220, 112 Stat. 936. (1998).

Rogers, E. S., Anthony, W. A., Toole, J., & Brown, M. A. (1991). Vocational outcomes following psychosocial rehabilitation: A longitudinal study of three programs. *Journal of Vocational Rehabilitation, 1*(3), 21–29.

Rogers, E. S., Danley, K. S., & Anthony, W. A. (1992). *Survey of client preferences for vocational and educational services.* Boston: Boston University, Center for Psychiatric Rehabilitation.

Rogers, E. S., McDonald-Wilson, K., Danley, K. S., Martin, R., & Anthony, W. A. (1997). A process analysis of supported employment services for persons with serious psychiatric disability: Implications for program design. *Journal of Vocational Rehabilitation, 8,* 233–242.

Rogers, E. S., Sciarappa, K., & Anthony, W. A. (1991). Development and evaluation of situational assessment instruments and procedures for persons with psychiatric disability. *Vocational Evaluation and Work Adjustment Bulletin, 24*(2), 61–67.

Rogers, E. S., Walsh, D., Masotta, L., Danley, K., & Smith, K. (1991). *Massachusetts survey of client preferences for community support services* [Final report]. Boston: Boston University, Center for Psychiatric Rehabilitation.

Rosenheck, R., Frisman, L., & Sindelar, J. (1995). Disability compensation and work among veterans with psychiatric and nonpsychiatric impairments. *Psychiatric Services, 46*(4), 359–365.

Schied, T. L., & Anderson, C. (1995). Living with chronic mental illness: Understanding the role of work. *Community Mental Health Journal, 31,* 163–176.

Schultheis, A. M., & Bond, G. R. (1993). Situational assessment ratings of work behaviors: Changes across time and between settings. *Psychosocial Rehabilitation Journal, 17*(2), 107–119.

Shafer, M. S., Pardee, R., & Stewart, M. (1999). An assessment of training needs of rehabilitation and community mental health workers in a six-state region. *Psychiatric Rehabilitation Journal, 23*(2), 161–169.

Shepherd, G. (1990). A criterion-oriented approach to skills training. *Psychosocial Rehabilitation Journal, 13*(3), 11–13.

Simmons, T. J., Selleck, V., Steele, R. B., & Sepetauc, F. (1993). Supports and rehabilitation for employment. In R. W. Flexor & P. Solomon (Eds.), *Psychiatric rehabilitation in practice* (pp. 119–153). Boston: Andover Medical.

Teague, G. B., Bond, G. R., & Drake, R. E. (1998). Program fidelity in assertive community treatment: Development and use of a measure. *American Journal of Orthopsychiatry, 68,* 216–232.

Test, M. A. (1992). Training in community. In R. P. Liberman (Ed.), *Handbook of psychosocial rehabilitation living* (pp. 153–170). New York: MacMillan & Co.

Toms-Barker, L. (1994). *Cultivating a career development orientation in employment programs.* Santa Fe, NM: International Association of Psychosocial Rehabilitation Services.

Wehman, P. (1988). Supported employment: Toward a zero exclusion of persons with severe disabilities. In P. Wehman & M. Moon (Eds.), *Vocational rehabilitation and supported employment* (pp. 3–14). Baltimore: Paul H. Brookes.

Wehman, P., & Moon, M. (1988). *Vocational rehabilitation and supported employment.* Baltimore: Paul H. Brookes.

Young, J., Rosati, R., & Vandergroot, D. (1986). Initiating a marketing strategy by assessing employer needs for rehabilitation services. *Journal of Rehabilitation, 52*(2), 37–41.

CHAPTER 3

Assertive Community Treatment

Susan J. Boust, Melody C. Kuhns, and Lynette Studer

Assertive Community Treatment (ACT) is a proven model of community care intended for a small percentage of people with serious and persistent mental illness who have demonstrated difficulties with stable community living. The model provides individualized treatment, rehabilitation, and support services by a multidisciplinary team in an intense and continuous manner in a community setting. The model has been widely disseminated and is also known by such names as Program of Assertive Community Treatment (PACT), continuous treatment teams, intensive psychiatric community care within the Department of Veteran's Affairs (VA), and has been referred to as a "hospital without walls."

The model is intended for people with the most serious and persistent mental illness. Those generally identified as most appropriate to receive ACT services are the 10% to 20% of people disabled by serious and persistent mental illness who have the most severe symptoms and functional impairments or who have frequent or prolonged hospitalization.

Extensive research demonstrating positive outcomes has resulted in ACT being recommended as an essential mental health service. This recommendation has been made by the schizophrenia PORT studies (Lehman, 1998a, 1998b, 1999; Lehman & Steinwachs, 1998a, 1998b), by the Surgeon General in the 1999 report on mental health (U.S. Department of Health and Human Services, 1999), and the *President's New Freedom Commission Report* (2003). The National Alliance for the Mentally Ill (NAMI), a family and consumer advocacy organization, has established a policy of support for ACT and initiated a movement to make ACT available to everyone who needs it (Burns, 1998).

ACT has been included as one of the six practices identified by the Evidence-Based Practices Project (Drake, Goldman, et al., 2001; Drake, Torrey, & McHugo, 2003; Drake et al., 2000; Mueser, Torrey, Lynde, Singer, & Drake, 2003). This project is sponsored by the Robert Wood Johnson Foundation, the Center for Mental Health Services, NAMI, and several state and local agencies. The goal of this project is to develop tool kits and standardized guidelines and training materials to assist in the implementation of identified evidence-based practices (Mueser et al., 2003).

This chapter reviews the history and development of the model and identifies the issues that must be addressed for its successful implementation.

HISTORY AND DEVELOPMENT OF THE ACT MODEL

In the 1970s, a pioneering group of researchers in Madison, Wisconsin, developed a model of care that was distinctly different from case management (Test, 1992). Initially the innovative program was called Training in Community Living and later was renamed the Program for Assertive Community Treatment (PACT; Allness & Knoedler, 1998). At the time, these researchers were concerned about "revolving door hospitalization" seen in their patients (Dixon, 2000). Rather than changing the care provided inside the hospital, they moved their clinical work outside the hospital to the community and developed a model intended to provide care to a group of patients who heretofore had been unsuccessful at stable community living.

This model retained many of the processes that had been used in the hospital setting, and additionally clearly documented the processes and the outcomes achieved by this new model of care. This model has been replicated, disseminated, modified, and researched for over 3 decades. The literature demonstrating its successful outcomes is definitively positive (Bond, Drake, Mueser, & Latimer, 2001; Dixon, 2000; Drake & Burns, 1995; Marshall & Lockwood, 2004; Mueser, Bond, Drake, & Resnick, 1998).

Distinguishing ACT from Case Management Models

ACT is frequently confused with case management; however, the two services have only superficial similarities (Marshall, Gray, Lockwood, & Green, 2004; Essock & Kontos, 1995). ACT is a model of community-based care, which combines psychiatric rehabilitation, clinical treatment, and case management provided by a multidisciplinary team. Scott and Dixon (1995) differentiate case management models from ACT: "ACT directly and intensively provides all or nearly all of the treatment, rehabilitation, and support services needed by individuals with schizophrenia; case management models offer a limited array of direct services delivered with less intensity than ACT programs." Research outcomes for case management are not as positive as they are for ACT (Bedell, Cohen, & Sullivan, 2000). Case management, as a model for community care for people with serious mental illness, falls far short of ACT's success (Holloway & Carson, 2001; Marshall & Lockwood, 2004; Marshall et al., 2004).

Case management is a general term used to describe the coordination, integration, and allocation of care within limited resources (Thornicroft, 1991). A variety of models including brokered, clinical, strengths, and intensive case management have been described, however, none of these definitions of case management has been standardized, and there is no current broad body of evidence that supports the inclusion of case management in a continuum of services (Table 3.1).

Intensive case management (ICM), with staff-to-client ratios approaching those of ACT has frequently been compared to ACT. Schaedle, McGrew, Bond, and Epstein (2002) outlined expert ratings of the critical elements between ACT and ICM. Results indicated that the experts see ICM as having the same treatment goals as ACT; however, ICM does not have a team structure, and ICM models are not clearly defined. ACT is viewed as a medical model with the psychiatrist and nurse having important roles on the team. ACT provides most treatment and rehabilitation services, while ICM frequently coordinates and connects consumers with services.

Table 3.1   Description of Models of Case Management

Model	Description
Brokerage	Provides coordination of services in a fragmented system. No direct care provided.
Strengths	Emphasizes working with strengths rather than problems or deficits.
Clinical	Professional staff directly provides some services such as therapy or skill training. Also coordinates care with other services.
Intensive	Poorly defined except for emphasis on small caseloads.
Rehabilitation	Focuses on direct assistance with skill building.

Case management based on any of these models is much more widely available than ACT, and is generally thought to be an essential service in community care, however; a systematic review has shown that this consensus is questionable (Marshall & Lockwood, 2004). Unlike ACT or other well-documented evidence-based practices, case management has not outlined a model of care and demonstrated its ability to replicate findings of positive outcomes by dissemination and testing of a model.

The Cochrane meta analysis of case management (Marshall et al., 2004) indicates that more people are ensured to remain in contact with psychiatric services with case management (one extra person remains in contact for every 15 people who receive case management), but case management also increases hospital admission rates. The currently available evidence suggests that case management also increases duration of hospitalization. It has not been demonstrated that case management produces clinically significant improvement in mental state, social functioning, or quality of life. Marshall et al. (2004) question whether case management should be offered at all by community psychiatric services.

Principles of ACT

The Training in Community Living (TCL) model employs a multidisciplinary self-contained team, structured communication tools, and 24-hours a day, 365-days-a-year coverage. Staff continues to be the fixed point of responsibility for assuring that all needs are met. Treatment, rehabilitation, and support services are distinctly individualized rather than being a group model.

The model is different from other services available to people with serious mental illness. Services are delivered in the community, and services are delivered by a team of professionals who provide most or all of the treatment, rehabilitation, and support needed by the person. Care is individualized, focusing on the needs of a single person rather than trying to meet the needs of a group of people. Responses to interventions are monitored and treatment adjusted on a frequent basis. Services are available 24 hours a day, 7 days a week for as long as needed—frequently for years. Services are delivered out of the office or in vivo. Examples of services are listed in Table 3.2.

The professionals work as a team rather than as individual case managers. Because of extensive cross-training, all team members know all people who receive services from the team. The staffing ratio is low (1:10), and staffing must include a psychiatrist, nurses, and the other professionals necessary to meet the needs of the person—

Table 3.2   Elements of the Training in Community Living Model

Service Organization	Treatment, Rehabilitation, and Support Services Provided

Team approach:
  –The team is accountable for assuring that all needs are met. The team is the fixed point of responsibility.
  –Team provides most needed services.
  –Continuity and dependability of care and caregivers.
	Direct assistance with psychiatric symptoms:
	  –Medication prescription and monitoring
	  –24-hour crisis availability
	  –Assistance with arranging brief hospitalization when needed
	  –1:1 clinical relationship with more than one team member

Assertive outreach for people who are failing appointments or having a relapse.	Assistance in developing an optimally supportive environment:
In vivo treatments: People are seen in their home and community.	–Assistance with basic needs when necessary, i.e., housing, finances –Supportive social environment –Family psychoeducation and counseling
Individualized treatment based on assessment of the individual needs and desires.	Direct assistance with role functioning (work, social relations, activities of daily living):
Services for as long as necessary. Ongoing treatment rehabilitations and support.	–In vivo skill teaching –In vivo support –Environmental modifications

Adapted from Table 7.1 in "Training in Community Living" by M. A. Test, (pp. 153–170). In Liberman, R. P., ed. *Handbook of Psychiatric Rehabilitation.* New York: Macmillan Press, 1992.

such as substance abuse providers and vocational rehabilitation specialists. Team size must be large enough to meet the needs of all people receiving care from the team and to assure availability for 24-hour/7-days-a-week coverage without burning out the team.

The team uses specific communication tools and strategies to assure coordination of care and rapid response to the needs of the person.

There have been many variations and modifications of the model; however, the basic principles are clear (Allness & Knoedler, 1998; Bond, 1991; Mueser et al., 1998). They include the following:

- Treatment rehabilitation and support services are provided directly by a multidisciplinary team of professionals.
- Team members share responsibilities for the provision of services to all consumers under team care.
- Each consumer's care is directed by an individualized treatment plan.
- Staff-to-consumer ratio is low (approximately 1:10).
- Treatment rehabilitation and support services are comprehensive and flexible.
- Treatment is in vivo—carried out in the places where the consumer lives and works, rather than in hospitals or clinics.

- Services are targeted to people with serious and persistent mental illness (SPMI) who have high needs and may be high users of service.
- There is no arbitrary length of time for receiving services.
- Treatment and support services are individualized and adjusted based on need and consumer input.
- Services are available 24 hours a day, 365 days a year.
- The team is assertive in engaging people in treatment.

Examples of services provided by ACT teams—adapted from Phillips et al. (2001):

- Symptom identification and assistance in coping with symptoms
- Rehabilitation for problems with daily living skills
- Assistance with developing and maintaining relationships
- Crisis management
- Coordination with family service agencies
- Employment and volunteer work support and assistance
- Assistance with entitlements
- Health education and assistance with acute medical care
- Medication support and education
- Housing assistance
- Assistance with financial management skills
- Counseling and psychotherapy as necessary

In the original Wisconsin Training in Community Living model, the consumers were individuals with severe mental illness who had severe psychiatric symptoms and difficulties in problem solving, stress management, and had been considered "un-dischargeable" (Dixon, 2000). These individuals lived in the community and saw team members several times a week—even several times a day. The philosophy of the team was to provide whatever assistance was needed to help these people to continue to live in the community. Services included a variety of assessment, treatment, rehabilitation, and support services, including assistance in developing the skills necessary for community living, as well as solving concrete problems of living in the community.

Initial research indicated success at helping people with serious mental illness live in the community. Indeed, the program received the American Psychiatric Society's Gold Award in 1974 (Mendota Mental Health Institute, 1974).

Research Findings and Outcomes in Support of ACT

The Assertive Community Treatment model has been the subject of more than 25 randomized, controlled trials (Burns & Santos, 1995; Dixon, 2000; Essock, Drake, & Burns, 1998; Herinckx, Kinney, Clarke, & Paulson, 1997; Marshall & Lockwood, 2004;

Mueser et al., 1998; Olfson, 1990; Ziguras & Stuart, 2000). Research has shown that this type of program is effective in reducing hospitalization, is no more expensive than traditional care, and is more satisfactory to consumers and their families than standard care (Phillips et al., 2001).

One group of researchers (Bond et al. 2001) summarized the outcomes from 25 randomized clinical trials and found that ACT substantially decreased hospitalization, improved housing stability and had a moderate improvement on symptoms and quality of life. There was no improvement on other outcomes studied, as illustrated in Table 3.3.

Researchers (Bond, McGrew, & Fekete, 1995) looked at retention in mental health services after 1 year and found that 83% of people receiving ACT services were still in treatment compared to 51% of people in control services. They summarized ACT as having a clear positive impact on hospital use, housing stability, and retention in treatment with less clear positive impact on symptoms and quality of life and little evidence of positive impact on employment, substance use, incarceration, and social adjustment.

In the review of ACT costs, Latimer (1999) examined 34 ACT studies and looked at the economic impact of the teams. The most reliable effect was a reduction in costs for hospitalization. The study estimates that ACT can reduce hospitalizations by 58% to 78% over 1 year. He further estimated that costs for ACT would be offset if the people admitted to the program where hospitalized at least 50 days a year. For cost savings to be realized, ACT must target the right people (Essock, Frisman, & Kontos, 1998).

Disseminations and Variations

At this point, it is important to emphasize that medical advancement occurs when a successful program is shown to be effective in one setting and replicable in another with similar success. The term *fidelity* is used to describe adherence to the principles (the organization and structure) of the original model. The research indicates that some of the best outcomes are from the original Wisconsin program. Programs that had the highest

Table 3.3   Significant Outcomes in 25 Randomized Controlled Trials of ACT

Substantial improvement
Hospital use
Housing stability

Moderate improvement
Quality of life
Symptoms

No improvement
Social adjustment
Jails/arrests
Substance use
Med compliance
Vocational outcomes
Client satisfaction
Family satisfaction

fidelity (more closely adhered to the principle elements) with the original Wisconsin model had the best outcomes.

Test (1992) outlined the early (1970s) dissemination of the model to Michigan, Australia, Chicago, Illinois, and Indiana. Each of these programs adopted many of the key elements of the original team, but also made some modifications. All early modifications maintained a team approach, identified the team as the fixed point of responsibility for services, and provided assertive outreach and in vivo services. Significant differences included the amount of services provided by the team as opposed to being provided by other rehabilitation services.

During the 1980s, the model was disseminated in Michigan, Rhode Island, Delaware, Maryland, and Missouri. In the 1990s, the program as adopted in seven more states: Indiana, Illinois, New Jersey, New Mexico, North Carolina, South Dakota, and Texas (Meisler, 1997). ACT is available in at least 33 U.S. states (Deci, Santos, Hiott, Schoenwald, & Dias, 1995), and in Canada, England, Sweden, and Australia (Bond et al., 2001; Burns, Fioritti, Holloway, Malm, & Rossler, 2001; Holloway & Carson, 2001).

There have been many adaptations based on local needs, including rural areas (Santos et al., 1993), teams with special focus on problem substance abuse (Drake, Essock, et al., 2001; Drake, McHugo, et al., 1998; Drake, Mercer-McFadden, Mueser, McHugo, & Bond, 1998; Teague, Drake, & Ackerson, 1995), and special services to enhance employment (Becker, Meisler, Stormer, & Brondino, 1999; Drake, McHugo, Becker, Anthony, & Clark, 1996). Another special target group has been homeless people with mental illness (Calsyn, Morse, Klinkenberg, Trusty, & Allen, 1998; Dixon, Krauss, Kernan, Lehman, & DeForge, 1995; Lehman, Dixon, Kernan, DeForge, & Postrado, 1997). Some teams include peer support (Dixon, Hackman, & Lehman, 1997; Dixon et al., 1995) or family member providers as key elements of the team (McFarlane, 1997; McFarlane, Dushay, Stastny, Deakins, & Link, 1996). It has been demonstrated that specific program elements—such as focus on substance abuse treatment or vocational placement and rehabilitation—impact the outcomes in those areas.

Outcome Effects of Adaptations

Movement away from the principles used by the Wisconsin team may decrease costs for the services, but also may decrease outcomes. Programs with high fidelity to the model as measured by critical elements have demonstrated better outcomes including fewer days in the hospital, less cost, and high satisfaction from the people receiving the services than programs with lower fidelity (Latimer, 1999; McGrew, Bond, Dietzen, & Salyers, 1994; McHugo, Drake, Teague, & Xie, 1999).

Current research does not clarify which elements of the model (in other words, which structure works best for which patient population) are essential to obtain the outcomes demonstrated by previous teams. It does appear evident that the cost outcomes are best when the service is made available to people who have been high users of services, particularly if they used over 50 days of hospitalization a year because of the high cost of such care.

Research supports the practice of the entire ACT model, not the selective adoption of any of its particular elements, to achieve the best outcomes. Extensive work has been done to identify the critical elements of the ACT model. Current evidence indicates that the more closely a team replicates the original Wisconsin model for Training in Community Living (and has fidelity to that model), the better the outcomes. Because of the high cost of the service and the desire for program planners to maximize resources, it would be beneficial to know which components are critical and which could be modified based on local needs and the characteristics of patients to be served.

GUIDELINES AND ISSUES RELATED TO FIDELITY

Overview of Model Fidelity

It is clear that there are benefits to using evidence-based practices. For a practice to be called evidence-based, there must be a clear description of what was done, how it was done, to whom and by whom. With this clear description, other programs can attempt to replicate the findings and prove that the model can work in other locations.

Clarity of the model is important. Early researchers (Brekke, 1988; Brekke & Test, 1987) outlined a process to study community support programs and applied this process to the original ACT model, TCL. They documented the operationalization of the TCL program to assist mental health planners in implementing the program in other locations.

The adaptations and modifications to the model were extensive; however, the principal elements described here in the previous sections were present in most adaptations. Although the general principles were well documented, a clear description of the model with enough specificity to categorize programs, as being high in fidelity or low in fidelity, was not available.

By 1994, a group of researchers (McGrew & Bond, 1995; McGrew et al., 1994) interviewed the experts to further clarify the critical elements of the model. Examples of the elements that were identified as critical (7—very important) by more than 50% of the experts include these:

Team Structure

- One team member as coordinator
- Team approach
- Shared case load for treatment planning
- Psychiatrist, social worker, and registered nurse on team
- All team members attend all meetings

Structure

- In vivo treatment
- Low client : staff ratio
- Petty cash fund
- Responsibility for client

Discharge, Retention, and Engagement

- Assertive, persistent engagement
- No close policy

Hospitalization and Coordination of Services
- Team members work to prevent hospitalization
- Team continues to work with hospitalized client
- ACT team consulted prior to hospitalization

Treatment Goals and Foci
- Team works with family
- Assistance with living skills
- Build on strengths

Service Elements
- Intake assessments at admission
- Clients involved in treatment planning
- Clients consulted prior to major decisions

Client Characteristics
- Severe and persistent mental illness

Program Capacity
- Limited team caseload size
- New clients admitted at a controlled rate

This work was a great resource in examining the relationship between program characteristics and outcomes associated with ACT programs (McGrew & Bond, 1997; McGrew, Bond, Dietzen, McKasson, & Miller, 1995).

Several organizations attempted to further clarify the model. One such attempt was the States Helping States meeting in 1996 in Fort Worth, Texas, that brought together national experts, researchers, policymakers, and advocates to review the work of these practitioners. The meeting helped clarify the current state of assertive community treatment in the United States and confirmed the need to build consensus regarding national standards and to define practices necessary for model fidelity.

A number of events were happening at the same time on a national level to encourage evidence-based practice in mental health. In 1998, for example, the national ACT standards were published by SAMHSA. At that time, NAMI had begun strategic planning and commitment to ACT dissemination in all states by 2002. NAMI commissioned the writing of the PACT manual and mobilized their local advocates to push for inclusion of ACT services in all state plans.

In addition, accreditation agencies and individual states adopting the model established standards, although these vary from national standards. The Rhode Island Department of Mental Health, Retardation and Hospitals was one exception as it committed to replicating the Madison model by developing standards for its Mobile Treatment Teams and a process of certifying programs in the state for Medicaid reimbursement.

It was estimated that at the time national standards were developed there were 400 teams in the United States that called themselves ACT, but only 75 achieved adequate fidelity to the model to achieve the anticipated outcomes (Kanapaux, 2000). Clearly, there was a need for a tool to assess fidelity to the model.

Development of the Dartmouth Assertive Community Treatment Scale

A group of researchers (Teague, Bond, & Drake, 1998) developed a criterion-based assessment tool by a combination of expert consensus, review of the literature, and previous research on critical elements. The Dartmouth Assertive Community Treatment Scale (DACTS) organized the critical elements into three categories and identified scoring criteria. The categories are human resources: structure and composition (11 elements); organizational boundaries (7 elements); and nature of services (10 elements). Each element has a potential score from 1 (low) to 5 (high; see Table 3.4).

The DACTS is currently our best tool for measuring fidelity to the model. This tool assists program managers, funders, and the program itself in measuring how well a team follows the principles of the model. Again, high fidelity to the model predicts better outcomes. The critical ingredients that were most predictive were nurse on team, shared caseloads, daily team meetings, team leaders see clients, and total number of contacts.

There is still no clearly accepted cutoff guideline to assess fidelity to the model. This continuing issue needs to be defined through further research.

McHugo et al. (1999) looked at teams providing care for dually diagnosed patients in New Hampshire. Using a modified fidelity scale, they identified five teams as high fidelity and three teams as low fidelity to the ACT model. People in the high-fidelity programs had significantly fewer days of alcohol and drug use than people in the low-fidelity programs. They concluded that the fidelity of the program affected the outcomes (see Table 3.5).

Table 3.4   Examples of High and Low Anchors for the Dartmouth Assertive Community Treatment Scale (DACTS)

Category	Element	Low Rating/Anchor	High Rating/Anchor
Human resources: structure/ composition	Team approach	<10% of clients see more than one staff a week.	> 90% of clients have contact with more than one staff a week.
	Psychiatrist on staff	Program for 100 clients has < 0.10 FTE psychiatrist.	At least one FTE psychiatrist for a program with 100 clients.
Organizational boundaries	Responsibility for crisis services	Program has no responsibility after hours.	Program provides 24-hour coverage.
	Time unlimited services	> 90% of clients expected to be discharged within one year.	All clients served on time unlimited basis.
Nature of services	In vivo services	Staff spends < 20% of time in community.	80% of total service time in community.
	Intensity of service	Average < 15 minutes/week per client.	Average 2 hours/week per client or more.

Table 3.5   Relationship between Outcomes and Fidelity

Mean outcomes	Programs	
	High Fidelity	Low Fidelity
Number of days alcohol use	35	79
Hospital admissions	2.87	4.96
Treatment dropouts	15	30

Conclusion: Better implementation of programs leads to better outcomes for both staff and clients.

The DACTS can assist in the assessment of a program's fidelity to the ACT model, differentiating between programs that are of high or low fidelity. This instrument, while important in evaluating structure and some organizational features, falls short in evaluating staff attitudes, outcomes, and does not emphasize the depth of assessment and treatment planning as the national standards do.

Even so, the DACTS is one of the best resources for new teams to use now (the DACTS instrument over the years has moved closer to the national standards, but has some minor variations in staffing and emphasis on substance abuse). (Additional resources of choice in the area of team development are the Allness & Knoedler manual, 1998, and the book by Stein & Santos, 1998, *Assertive Community Treatment of Persons with Severe Mental Illness.*)

More recently, a study by the Lewin group (2000), funded by SAMHSA, indicated that the most important elements are team approach, in vivo services, assertive engagement, a small caseload, and explicit admission criteria. The study was done only on programs with high fidelity to the mode, so limited variability may make it difficult to identify which elements are critical in programs that adhere less closely to the model.

IMPLEMENTATION ISSUES

Administrators and team leaders may underestimate the amount of change and learning necessary for successful implementation of ACT. In starting an ACT team, the principles to support any change apply. Execution requires strong leaders who understand the new service and have the ability to help staff embrace change; adequate resources including financial resources; clear administrative rules and regulations that support the new practice; staff who are willing to learn new methods of practice; and a process to monitor and provide feedback on the practice.

Steps necessary for ACT implementation have been outlined and include educating and building consensus among key stakeholders, identifying funding, identifying leaders, and developing a plan that includes training and monitoring for fidelity (Drake et al., 2000).

The immense research supporting ACT—as well as the unequaled support for the service by NAMI, the Surgeon General, and the President's New Freedom Commission—makes it easy to gain stakeholder support. Of course, there will be competing services and concern that many consumers require a hospital or residential level of care rather than ACT. It is essential that these concerns be heard and addressed in the process of building consensus. There is indication that ACT should be available to 10% to 20% of people with the most disabling, serious, and persistent mental illness. Each state is easily able to calculate the number of people who would benefit from the service and at a cost that would not exceed what is currently being spent.

Several issues may derail support for the model. Despite the structural and philosophical aspects of ACT that support recovery, there are some authors who do not think the model goes far enough to support recovery (Anthony, Rogers, & Farkas, 2003). There are other people who are opposed to the model based on the belief that it is coercive. Obviously, the model could be used to provide coercive treatment—forcing people to accept services, taking unwanted medications, or being assertively outreached. The team approach can even be perceived as one against many. Coercion is an issue primarily in poorly implemented, low-fidelity programs. ACT is intended to be collaborative, individualized, and supportive of consumers' goals, and has demonstrated consumer satisfaction (Gerber & Prince, 1999).

In addition, the model may be perceived as expensive, especially when compared to case management services. Yet, case management costs generally do not include the cost for medication checks, substance abuse treatment, and rehabilitation services, so care must be taken in making this comparison. Current evidence is clear that the outcomes, including financial outcomes, are better when ACT is targeted to people with high services use, especially hospital use, and when the model is fully implemented. ACT is a model that may be especially useful when shifting services from institutional care to community care.

Funding for new ACT teams frequently comes from a combination of state money and federal money in the form of Medicaid. Funding may range from payment for each service provided to a client to a per diem for each consumer receiving care from the team. Medicaid has established guidelines for funding ACT, and this may actually increase the resources to the state for providing services (Clark et al., 1998; Dixon et al., 1997).

ACT is a complex model with a vast literature supporting it, with many variations on the model. Implementation is enhanced by identifying someone in the organization who is responsible for the implementation and who becomes familiar with the model. It is recommended that this leader read the *PACT Manual* (Allness & Knoedler, 1998) and *ACT for Persons with Severe Mental Illness* (Stein & Santos, 1998). These manuals outline the extensive literature and provide assistance in getting started. It is a good idea to refer to these books when answering questions, not only to provide consistent answers, but also to encourage interested people to turn to these excellent resources themselves. In addition, onsite visits to several established programs are an excellent investment and should precede the development of local policies.

The Internet contains a wealth of information about the model. A search for Assertive Community Treatment will bring hundreds of sites to your attention—some less than credible. Some recommended sites are those hosted by:

NAMI (http://www.nami.org)

Assertive Community Treatment Association (ACTA) (http://www.actassociation .org)

ACT Center of Indiana (http://psych.iupui.edu/ACTCenter/ACTHome.htm)

Implementing   Evidence-Based   Practice   Project   for   ACT   (http://www
.mentalhealthpractices.org/act.html)

ACT teams require a paradigm shift from both organizations and the staff members
of the team. During the initial development of the team, a team leader is hired who will
be a resource to support the change process necessary for the full implementation of
the model and to maintain communication with the parent organization. Other programs in the organization will need to be educated about the fixed point of responsibility, understand the team concept, and learn how to collaborate with the team. In
addition, it is a misconception that ACT can be a panacea for all the organization's
problems, and it is essential that clear admission criteria be maintained.

Teams are at risk of being isolated from the rest of the organization, which decreases the support they will feel from their colleagues and peers. In addition, teams
need the benefits of a larger organization for training, credentialing, and accreditation.
The organizational leader can help establish the right balance for team autonomy and
inclusion in the general program.

Finally, the organization must support the implementation and ongoing delivery of
services that have high fidelity to the model. This will require intense initial training,
ongoing training, and a method to measure fidelity and feed the results back to the
team. It is essential to have ACT consultants available to assist the team in learning the
model and in continuing the practices that will support better outcomes. Ongoing measurement of outcomes is strongly encouraged as one method to monitor team function.

When a new team is developing, it is best to require faithful replication of the model
before allowing teams to deviate. Teams frequently want to make changes to the model
before understanding the entire concept. Because they don't know what they don't
know, this practice should be discouraged. The data are clear that the higher the fidelity to the original model, the better the outcomes will be. Many experts also agree
that it takes over 2 years for a new team to fully implement the model.

Although there is no specific research on best practices to implementing ACT, implementation strategies have been outlined by Phillips et al. (2001) in preparation for
tool kits that are being developed with funding from the Robert Wood Johnson Foundation and SAMHSA. There is already a great deal of experience with initiating ACT
teams, and there are numerous experts who have assisted with the implementation of
many teams, as well as national resources to provide assistance.

These implementation strategies are outlined as they relate to four key stakeholders:
mental health administrators, program directors, team members, and consumers.

Mental Health Administrators

As organizations or states attempt to develop ACT programs, they also have to balance
the cost of the services against the needs of other programs and against the anticipated
benefits of ACT. Special concerns about cost have resulted in modifications of the
structures of the program such as going above the recommended 1:10 staffing ratio,
decreasing the number of staff, the professional nature of the staff, changing eligibility
for admission, decreasing the requirements for the team to attend a daily team meeting,
and in general moving to a less intense, team-based service.

It is important that the people responsible for the organization and oversight of the behavioral health system understand the principles of the model, the anticipated outcomes, and have a broad understanding of the issues that will be faced by the program directors and team staff. The support of system administrators is essential for the successful implementation of ACT, whether it is as a single demonstration project or in a statewide effort. They provide the vision and mission, set the goals, and ensure adequate support to the organizations and front-line workers. Issues that confront administrators include funding, ensuring adherence to the model, and planning the implementation of multiple programs.

Program Directors

Success of ACT within an agency is facilitated when program directors have a clear understanding of the principles of the model and an appreciation of the difference between ACT and other services within the agency (Table 3.6). If the program director is committed to the principles of the model, the director is better able to provide the support the staff will need to follow the model and hold them accountable for fidelity to the model. Program directors must educate themselves on the model by attending training, visiting successful programs, and establishing a relationship with an expert mentor.

They must provide leadership in the development of separate and specific policies that support the model dealing with such issues as increased training needs, transportation of clients, staff safety in the community, communication among the ACT

Table 3.6   Key Things Program Administrators and Directors Can Do to Make ACT a Success

Understand and communicate the vision of ACT to the organization and its stakeholders. Be clear on the outcomes you want the team to achieve.

Ensure adequate resources for team success, especially sufficient resources for staff salaries and training.

Know the PACT manual for start-up.

Hire a competent team leader. This will be your most important decision. The team leader must be a skilled clinician as well as a good administrator who is willing to embrace the move from traditional mental healthcare to a new philosophy. Understand the team leader's role prior to the hire.

Learn about team functioning by shadowing a team member; attend team meetings.

Work with the team leader to develop a monitoring/feedback system to ensure the team is developing in a positive direction.

Understand the complexities and challenges faced by the team and its leader. Remove barriers to implementation (e.g., support necessary changes in policies procedures and assist with inter- and intra-agency issue resolution).

Establish clear admission criteria and monitor admissions to avoid "dumping."

Establish procedures and support for service funds and petty cash. This ensures responsiveness to individual needs and accountability.

Establish mechanisms for collecting and analyzing system and person-specific level outcomes.

Develop an advisory/steering committee to assist with maintaining focus, resources, and positive outcomes. Attend meetings.

team and other providers within the agency, medication management, delivery and monitoring, and management of client funds.

The ability to fund appropriate salaries is important. If the agency has provided primarily psychosocial services in the past, there may be learning issues for the agency leadership in managing credentialed professionals. It is also important to have competitive salaries to avoid frequent staff turnover.

Outlining the appropriate autonomy of the team is another important area. The team must have the flexibility to adjust staff hours, services, and policies to meet the changing needs of consumers; however, it is not good for the ACT program to be so independent that they essentially separate from the parent agency.

Hiring the right team leader and psychiatrist are two of the most important tasks. The team leader must be able to work with a diverse group of professionals and provide clinical leadership and supervision to the team as they care for people with serious illness and functional impairments. It is essential that the team leader and psychiatrist agree to work as a team to meet the needs of those who receive services.

Team Members

Teamwork is an essential component of ACT just as it is in hospital, residential, and day rehabilitation care. Knowledge of team development and function is imperative to the development of successful ACT teams.

These beliefs about teamwork underlie ACT services:

- Teamwork and group decision making translate into improved client care.
- Strong leadership leads to better teamwork and service delivery.
- Team members can hold each other accountable for keeping services focused on the consumer's needs and preferences.
- Communication among the team and utilizing organizational tools are essential to good teamwork.

Although there are excellent reasons to use a team of people to provide services, there are some potential pitfalls in using a team, such as these:

- Increased time necessary to reach decisions and for communication between team members.
- Change in productivity as the team moves through the stages of team development.
- Potential to send inconsistent messages to the consumer.
- Worse accountability in the absence of good leadership.
- Requires a focus on good organization.

Even with the potential pitfalls, ACT services depend on teamwork. A good team leader will recognize these issues and remedy the problems quickly and with fairness. There are several "tools" that support the teamwork of ACT; most importantly are the initial and on-going assessments, individualized treatment plans, staff schedules, and daily communication via team meetings.

ACT assessment is done at reoccurring stages in an interdisciplinary manner with all staff working with the consumer to completely review the consumer's prior experiences and care. This comprehensive look at the person's life starts to build trust that the team cares about what the consumer thinks and feels, and that the team members understand what the consumer has experienced. The assessment lays the foundation for identification of problems that are present or tend to recur in the person's life and may require treatment.

Identification of problems is important, but it is equally important to identify a consumer's strengths, preferences and goals. It's the person's life; positive outcomes should be their goals in the treatment plan. It is the art of making sure that the team is working toward the goals identified by the consumer, yet still having measurable goals and adequately addressing problems that makes ACT treatment planning a challenge.

To avoid being overwhelmed by daily crises, it is important to follow the established ACT process as outlined in available manuals (Allness & Knoedler, 1998; Stein & Santos, 1998). The goals, interventions, and assigned staff identified in the treatment plan for a single consumer are transcribed to their client card. Each day during team meeting, scheduled interventions outlined on each client's card are transcribed to that day's plan for staff activities. It is the daily plan for services (The Board) that allows a team to coordinate the schedules of 8 to 100 consumers and 10 to 12 staff with minimizing chaos. This organizational tool of the client weekly card in essence is how the consumer's treatment plan is operationalized. It is how the plan stays relevant, real, and focuses the teamwork on the treatment, rehabilitation, and support services necessary for that specific client.

This may seem like a lot of process, but this process is key to the implementation of a new team. Each consumer can depend on the structure of the team keeping scheduled appointments and learn skills to keep their own appointments. Team members hold each other accountable to follow through with interventions outlined in the treatment plan. Crisis decisions can be shared by the team members, and the team leader can help the team move away from a crisis mode into a treatment and rehabilitation mode. If the team is in chaos because of disorganization, the consumer will sense this and lose trust in the team.

Much of the work of developing a new ACT team centers on learning the processes that support good teamwork. Although this could be done by allowing a new team to develop their own processes, this would be time consuming and would not take advantage of the vast experience about what tools will support the principles of ACT. In fact, experienced ACT trainers report that when new teams deviate from the proven ACT processes, they remain in crisis mode rather than being able to move into planned treatment and rehabilitation and overall implementation is significantly delayed.

Members of a newly formed team will be asked to work in an entirely new manner. It is essential they learn to work as a member of a team in order to coordinate care with other team members and make collaborative decisions both with other team members, including the psychiatrist, and with the people receiving services. Team members must learn new skills, cross-train each other, and learn to work interdependently. Various skills must be valued, taught, nurtured and cross-trained. Equitable workload distribution among team members is essential and is the responsibility of the team leader. Scheduling and maintenance of routines is also essential and difficult in the face of critical client needs and inevitable crises. The ACT team may have a peer support person, and this may be the first such position in the agency. Team leaders and members as well as the peer support person will need to demonstrate respect and support for each other.

Training and retraining needs are high during the first 2 years of a new ACT team's implementation. Team members will need training on skills, attitudes, and behaviors. ACT consultants can assist with this, as well as provide intensive training at the start of the work with the use of videos, manuals, workbooks, tool kits and on-site teaching and mentoring. It will be tempting for staff to revert to old patterns and habits and most will in the absence of logic to do otherwise. A process must be in place to avoid this. Continuous onsite and telephone mentoring is essential. It is the job of the administrators and team leader to assure that this happens.

Obviously, one of the most crucial team members in creating and sustaining an ACT team is the team leader. The team leader will be required to implement the changes in practice that are essential for the function of the team. He or she will also be responsible for maintaining good working relationships between the team and the larger agency and must possess the ability to take the ACT concept and vision and implement those constructs into practical daily services and activities the treatment team delivers. This requires a tremendous amount of skill and where many new team leaders struggle. Further, there are several roles the ACT team leader should understand and embrace to maximize the likelihood of success (see Table 3.7).

Consumers

Consumers of ACT services have generally felt satisfied by the service; however, there is some concern in the consumer advocacy community that ACT services may be coercive. This point of view must be respected. Training of teams in the philosophy of recovery, and careful monitoring to assure that people receiving services are respected and in charge of establishing the goals for treatment must be included in ACT teams. It is also vital to remember that consumer satisfaction is highest when receiving services for a high fidelity ACT program.

Implementation of evidence-based practices can be time-consuming and expensive, but to the extent possible, such practices should be the foundation of care provided. In fact, the process necessary to implement a well-defined, proven program is well worth the effort as long as the program actually follows the model intended.

FUTURE DIRECTIONS

Although the research evidence regarding the efficacy of the ACT intervention is substantial, outcomes have varied. This variability in outcomes will require further research on the critical program elements that produce desired outcomes. Future research should clarify changes in outcomes in reaction to such structural changes as staffing ratio, admission criteria, inclusion of specific credentialed providers, and deviation from use of specific communication tools and processes. In addition, controlled research on the best practices for implementing new programs should be a focus of future research.

Table 3.7 Key Things Team Leaders Can Do to Successfully Implement PACT

Become an expert on the PACT model of care and know the PACT manual for start-up. Educate yourself with the ACT literature as well as information on teamwork, group dynamics, and change management. This will prove essential when you are asked to hire team members.

Examine your present philosophical orientation to treatment. Embrace the ideas of providing treatment in a new way and set a positive attitude for the team in changing how mental health services are provided. The team leader must accept and promote ACT attitudes, values, and ideals.

Lead by clinical example. The team leader acts as a primary clinician for clients and has more clinical work and less of an administrative role within the agency structure. This allows the team leader to stay involved, know resources, have an idea of how long things take other team members and keeps the team leader current. Model expected attitudes, work practices, and behavior.

Be a leader. The team leader is the clinical focal point through which all communication goes through. Role model teamwork by consulting the psychiatrist for decisions. Act as the gate-keeper of clinical information and for continuity of care.

Continue to assure that through daily transactions of the program implementation that the ACT model is being followed. Maintain high standards and expectations for all staff and model these behaviors. Learn to hold staff accountable. Must be able to articulate and educate staff on the principles of the model and keep them focused.

Become an expert in psychiatric assessment and treatment planning. Lead all treatment planning meetings with the psychiatrist and model this so other team members can learn.

Provide clinical supervision to all team members on an on-going basis. This will not only assist in the reviewing of client care and the development of individual staff clinical skills, but also assure that client contacts are driven by the treatment plan. This is essential to the building of teamwork and in managing different styles and attitudes of team members.

Understand how to organize all the work across the team, including implementation of the ACT organizational tools. Create policies and procedures that are specific to ACT and not modeled from other parts of the agency. A team leader may need administrative assistance with this.

Have a strong relationship with your administrators of your agency. Assist them in understanding the variables that contributes to bringing up an ACT program and the length of time this will take. Express input regarding key factors such as screening procedures, admissions rates into ACT and know the funding of your ACT program so you can provide relevant input into the ACT budget.

Create a macro plan for the program including objectives you, the team and your agency would like to see attained. Collect the data, analyze it and provide it back to the team.

Identify an ACT expert consultant and initiate an on-going collaboration of mentoring. Create a training plan for a minimum of two years to assist in the implementation of ACT.

The efforts of the Evidence-Based Practice Project now under way are intended to improve the ability of states to succeed at large-scale implementation of evidence-based practices, including ACT. Implementation resource kits will contain education and training materials for state administrators, providers, and consumers and family members. These tool kits and the information from the Project will provide future guidance for implementation of ACT teams.

In addition, ACT is a model that supports the delivery of other evidence-based practices. In the future, research should focus on outcomes as ACT teams incorporate specific practices that focus on supported employment, integrated treatments of people with dual disorders, family psycho education, illnesses management, and medication guidelines.

Other ACT research should address the following questions:

- What should the admission criteria be?
- What is the value of time-limited ACT and clarification of outcomes when planned discharge/transfer to a lesser level of community care takes place?
- What modifications of the model are appropriate for rural programs?
- What modifications could improve outcomes in areas that have only modest or no improvement with the current model, such as quality of life, symptoms, and functional status?
- Can ACT be modified to produce desired outcomes for special populations such as people with personality disorders, mental retardation, or dementia?
- What are the best methods of funding services to encourage program fidelity and obtain desired outcomes?
- What accreditation standards will encourage high-quality ACT services?

———————————————— Case Example ————————————————

One illustrative example related to ACT implementation involves this scenario: the habit of individual work with little or no psychiatric assessment (case management) versus teamwork reliant on psychiatric information (ACT) and also the desire to continue to broker services outside of ACT (brokerage management) versus seeing team responsibility to get the client's needs met (ACT). The following is an example of this.

John N. was a 33-year-old single male residing in a residential-type home. He had an Axis I diagnosis of schizophrenia, paranoid type and alcohol dependence. While he had no official diagnosis on Axis II, he was known among professionals at the agency to be "challenging" and somewhat "noncompliant" with treatment. He was admitted to the newly formed ACT team.

The ACT team kept going to the residential program and seeing John in soiled clothing and smelling of urine. The primary ACT member consulted with the residential staff who reported that John was resistant to showering despite their repeated attempts. They were clearly becoming quite frustrated with John. They believed hygiene was in his control and his refusal seemed purposeful. He had lost many previous residential placements prior to this one for similar reasons and was now in jeopardy of also losing his sheltered workshop job secondary to complaints of poor hygiene and his seemingly "poor attitude" toward this issue. The ACT team did little to assess the situation independently because they trusted the residential program's assessment. It was clear that the new team members were used to being case managers who relied heavily on other programs to provide care to John and while they did well to try to manage the situation, they did little to evaluate and make preventive changes.

When it was pointed out to the team that the proper ACT response would be for them to assess and respond to the problem directly, they did this with trepidation citing they "knew" John so well, but here is what was discovered. The primary team member began ongoing, consistent, individualized psychiatric interviews to better understand the symptoms John was dealing with. John, after a few months, disclosed that he believed that the water coming out of the showerhead was poisonous and that his life was endangered when he showered. This explained some previous history when he would become combative when other residential providers would "force" a shower.

The response of the primary team member was to consult immediately with the psychiatrist who decided to increase John's antipsychotic medication. The fear of showering was explained to John as a symptom of his illness, and although he disagreed with the logic, he agreed to an increase in his medications. With the increase in medications, John became more willing to discuss the issues related to his compromised hygiene and agreed to try to bathe at least once a week (an every-other-day shower was the rule at the residential facility). The primary team member needed to meet with the providers at the residential facility to ask for this accommodation of rules.

Through weekly symptom discussions with a consistent team member, John was able to work through some of his paranoia regarding the shower and attempted to meet this goal of weekly showers. (Note the goal was set so it was attainable and John was not expected to bathe daily or every other day—a compromise that is essential to client-centered treatment planning.)

Also during this time, the ACT RN coordinated and accompanied John to a medical appointment where it was discovered he had a bladder infection. She assisted John with the appointment because in the past he had poor follow-through because of his anxiety and paranoia of medical providers. He was given an antibiotic that cleared up his infection.

Through the ongoing supportive therapy that was occurring, John voiced his desire to move out of the residential facility citing several valid reasons. The team agreed to this reluctantly. They again evaluated the level of support John would need and decided that initially they would see him 2 times per day/14 times per week and that he would need a high level of structure. There were many skeptics on the team, but what the team discovered was that John improved by moving out of the residential facility, and his paranoia decreased because there were fewer conflicts. John displayed a better sense of worth.

Finally, John had the goal of getting a "real" job integrated in the community. The team initially assessed that John was not ready, but he himself proceeded to go out and find work on his own. Instead of leaving John without support, the team proactively provided supportive counseling prior to his work shift and transportation to the worksite (thus increasing his contacts to 18 times per week). John maintained his job for 8 months. During that time, his drinking buddies, who would come around and offer John beer in exchange for a place to crash, were told by John that they could not come over because he needed to get to sleep in order to get up to work in the morning. The team helped John explain this to his friends and helped him "take the heat" when his social supports put pressure on him. John explained to his ACT team members that, while he still dealt daily with his symptoms and liked hanging out with his friends, he now felt as if he had purposeful reasons to stay out of the hospital, take his medications, maintain his job and apartment, and bathe once a week.

While there were some "glitches" to John's treatment during that period of time, this is a typical scenario with ACT services. This example shows that teamwork, individualized psychiatric assessment and treatment, and coordinated interventions are the foundation of true ACT work. Without this, John likely would be moving from placement to placement and be seen as a "terror" to the system, thus taxing the system financially as well. This is what has been seen by ACT consultants over and over as new teams try to implement ACT with their institutionalized knowledge of the case management brokerage model. Case managers for the most part are not the direct care providers and, if so, do it on a limited basis and typically are not trained in psychiatric interviewing to get at the root of the issue.

REFERENCES

Allness, D., & Knoedler, W. (1998). *The PACT model of community-based treatment for persons with severe and persistent mental illness: A manual for PACT start-up.* Arlington, VA: National Alliance for the Mentally Ill.

Anthony, W. A., Rogers, E. S., & Farkas, M. D. (2003). Research on evidence-based practices: Future directions in an era of recovery. *Community Mental Health Journal, 39*(2), 101–114.

Becker, R. E., Meisler, N., Stormer, G., & Brondino, M. J. (1999). Employment outcomes for clients with severe mental illness in a PACT model replication. *Program for Assertive Community Treatment Psychiatry Service, 50*(1), 104–106.

Bedell, J. R., Cohen, N. L., & Sullivan, A. (2000). Case management: The current best practices and the next generation of innovation. *Community Mental Health Journal, 36*(2), 179–194.

Bond, G. R. (1991). Variations in an assertive outreach model. *New Directions for Mental Health Services, 52,* 65–80.

Bond, G. R., Drake, R. E., Mueser, K. T., & Latimer, E. (2001). Assertive community treatment for people with severe mental illness: Critical ingredients and impact on patients. *Disease Management and Health Outcomes, 9,* 141–159.

Bond, G. R., McGrew, J. H., & Fekete, D. M. (1995). Assertive outreach for frequent users of psychiatric hospitals: A meta-analysis. *Journal of Mental Health Administration, 22*(1), 4–16.

Brekke, J. S. (1988). What do we really know about community support programs? Strategies for better monitoring. *Hospital and Community Psychiatry, 39*(9), 946–952.

Brekke, J. S., & Test, M. (1987). An empirical analysis of services delivered in a model community support program. *Psychosocial Rehabilitation Journal, 10*(4), 51–61.

Burns, B. J. (1998). Links between research findings and the future of assertive community treatment: A commentary. *American Journal of Orthopsychiatry, 68*(2), 261–264.

Burns, B. J., & Santos, A. B. (1995). Assertive community treatment: An update of randomized trials. *Psychiatric Services, 46*(7), 669–675.

Burns, T., Fioritti, A., Holloway, F., Malm, U., & Rossler, W. (2001). Case management and assertive community treatment in Europe. *Psychiatric Services, 52*(5), 631–636.

Calsyn, R. J., Morse, G. A., Klinkenberg, W. D., Trusty, M. L., & Allen, G. (1998). The impact of assertive community treatment on the social relationships of people who are homeless and mentally ill. *Community Mental Health Journal, 34*(6), 579–593.

Clark, R. E., Teague, G. B., Ricketts, S. K., Bush, P. W., Xie, H., McGuire, T. G., et al. (1998). Cost-effectiveness of assertive community treatment versus standard case management for persons with co-occurring severe mental illness and substance use disorders. *Health Services Research, 33*(5, Pt. 1), 1285–1308.

Deci, P. A., Santos, A. B., Hiott, D. W., Schoenwald, S., & Dias, J. K. (1995). Dissemination of assertive community treatment programs. *Psychiatric Services, 46*(7), 676–678.

Dixon, L. B. (2000). Assertive community treatment: Twenty-five years of gold. *Psychiatric Services, 51*(6), 759–765.

Dixon, L. B., Hackman, A., & Lehman, A. (1997). Consumers as staff in assertive community treatment programs. *Administration and Policy in Mental Health, 25*(2), 199–208.

Dixon, L. B., Krauss, N., Kernan, E., Lehman, A. F., & DeForge, B. R. (1995). Modifying the PACT model to serve homeless persons with severe mental illness. *Psychiatric Services, 46*(7), 684–688.

Drake, R. E., & Burns, B. J. (1995). Special section on assertive community treatment: An introduction. *Psychiatric Services, 46*(7), 667–668.

Drake, R. E., Essock, S. M., Shaner, A., Carey, K. B., Minkoff, K., Kola, L., et al. (2001). Implementing dual diagnosis services for clients with severe mental illness. *Psychiatric Services, 52*(4), 469–476.

Drake, R. E., Goldman, H. H., Leff, H. S., Lehman, A. F., Dixon, L. B., Mueser, K. T., et al. (2001). Implementing evidence-based practices in routine mental health service settings. *Psychiatric Services, 52*(2), 179–182.

Drake, R. E., McHugo, G. J., Becker, D. R., Anthony, W. A., & Clark, R. E. (1996). The New Hampshire study of supported employment for people with severe mental illness. *Journal of Consulting and Clinical Psychology, 64*(2), 391–399.

Drake, R. E., McHugo, G. J., Clark, R. E., Teague, G. B., Xie, H., Miles, K., et al. (1998). Assertive community treatment for patients with co-occurring severe mental illness and substance use disorder: A clinical trial. *American Journal of Orthopsychiatry, 68*(2), 201–215.

Drake, R. E., Mercer-McFadden, C., Mueser, K. T., McHugo, G. J., & Bond, G. R. (1998). Review of integrated mental health and substance abuse treatment for patients with dual disorders. *Schizophrenia Bulletin, 24*(4), 589–608.

Drake, R. E., Mueser, K. T., Torrey, W. C., Miller, A. L., Lehman, A. F., Bond, G. R., et al. (2000). Evidence-based treatment of schizophrenia. *Current Psychiatry Reports, 2*(5), 393–397.

Drake, R. E., Torrey, W. C., & McHugo, G. J. (2003). Strategies for implementing evidence-based practices in routine mental health settings. *Evidence-Based Mental Health Notebook, 6*(1), 6–7.

Essock, S. M., Drake, R. E., & Burns, B. J. (1998). A research network to evaluate assertive community treatment: Introduction. *American Journal of Orthopsychiatry, 68*(2), 176–178.

Essock, S. M., Frisman, L. K., & Kontos, N. J. (1998). Cost-effectiveness of assertive community treatment teams. *American Journal of Orthopsychiatry, 68*(2), 179–190.

Essock, S. M., & Kontos, N. (1995). Implementing assertive community treatment teams. *Psychiatric Services, 46*(7), 679–683.

Gerber, G. J., & Prince, P. N. (1999). Measuring client satisfaction with assertive community treatment. *Psychiatric Services, 50*(4), 546–550.

Herinckx, H. A., Kinney, R. F., Clarke, G. N., & Paulson, R. I. (1997). Assertive community treatment versus usual care in engaging and retaining clients with severe mental illness. *Psychiatric Services, 48*(10), 1297–1306.

Holloway, F., & Carson, J. (1998). Intensive case management for the severely mentally ill: Controlled trial. *British Journal of Psychiatry, 172*(1), 19–22.

Holloway, F., & Carson, J. (2001). Case management: An update. *International Journal of Social Psychiatry, 47*(3), 21–31.

Kanapaux, W. (2000). A question of standards. *Behavioral Healthcare Tomorrow, 9*(1), 14–16, 45.

Latimer, E. A. (1999). Economic impacts of assertive community treatment: A review of the literature. *Canadian Journal of Psychiatry, 44*(5), 443–454.

Lehman, A. F. (1998a). Public health policy, community services, and outcomes for patients with schizophrenia. *Psychiatric Clinics of North America, 21*(1), 221–231.

Lehman, A. F. (1998b). The role of mental health service research in promoting effective treatment for adults with schizophrenia. *Journal of Mental Health Policy and Economics, 1*(4), 199–204.

Lehman, A. F. (1999). Improving treatment for persons with schizophrenia. *Psychiatric Quarterly, 70*(4), 259–272.

Lehman, A. F., Dixon, L. B., Kernan, E., DeForge, B. R., & Postrado, L. T. (1997). A randomized trial of assertive community treatment for homeless persons with severe mental illness. *Archives of General Psychiatry, 54*(11), 1038–1043.

Lehman, A. F., & Steinwachs, D. M. (1998a). Patterns of usual care for schizophrenia: Initial results from the Schizophrenia Patient Outcomes Research Team (PORT) Client Survey. *Schizophrenia Bulletin, 24*(1), 11–20.

Lehman, A. F., & Steinwachs, D. M. (1998b). Translating research into practice: The Schizophrenia Patient Outcomes Research Team (PORT) treatment recommendations. *Schizophrenia Bulletin, 24*(1), 1–10.

Marshall, M., Gray, A., Lockwood, A., & Green, R. (2004). Case management for people with severe mental disorders. *Cochrane Database System Review* (2) CD000050.

Marshall, M., & Lockwood, A. (2004). Assertive community treatment for people with severe mental disorders. *Cochrane Database System Review* (2) CD001089.

McFarlane, W. R. (1997). Fact: Integrating family psychoeducation and assertive community treatment. *Administration and Policy in Mental Health, 25*(2), 191–198.

McFarlane, W. R., Dushay, R. A., Stastny, P., Deakins, S. M., & Link, B. (1996). A comparison of two levels of family-aided assertive community treatment. *Psychiatric Services, 47*(7), 744–750.

McGrew, J. H., & Bond, G. R. (1995). Critical ingredients of assertive community treatment: Judgments of the experts. *Journal of Mental Health Administration, 22*(2), 113–125.

McGrew, J. H., & Bond, G. R. (1997). The association between program characteristics and service delivery in assertive community treatment. *Administration and Policy in Mental Health, 25*(2), 175–189.

McGrew, J. H., Bond, G. R., Dietzen, L., McKasson, M., & Miller, L. D. (1995). A multisite study of client outcomes in assertive community treatment. *Psychiatric Services, 46*(7), 696–701.

McGrew, J. H., Bond, G. R., Dietzen, L., & Salyers, M. (1994). Measuring the fidelity of implementation of a mental health program model. *Journal of Consulting and Clinical Psychology, 62*(4), 670–678.

McHugo, G. J., Drake, R. E., Teague, G. B., & Xie, H. (1999). Fidelity to assertive community treatment and client outcomes in the New Hampshire dual disorders study. *Psychiatric Services, 50*(6), 818–824.

Meisler, N. (1997). Assertive community treatment initiatives: Results from a survey of selected state mental health authorities. *Community Support Network News, 11*(4), 3–5.

Mendota Mental Health Institute. (1974). The 1974 APA achievement award winners. Gold award: A community treatment program (Madison, Wisconsin). *Hospital and Community Psychiatry, 25*(10), 669–672.

Mueser, K. T., Bond, G. R., Drake, R. E., & Resnick, S. G. (1998). Models of community care for severe mental illness: A review of research on case management. *Schizophrenia Bulletin, 24*(1), 37–74.

Mueser, K. T., Torrey, W. C., Lynde, D., Singer, P., & Drake, R. E. (2003). Implementing evidence-based practices for people with severe mental illness. *Behavior Modification, 27*(3), 387–411.

New freedom commission on mental health, achieving the promise: Transforming mental health care in America. (2003). Available from http://www.mentalhealthcommission.gov.

Olfson, M. (1990). Assertive community treatment: An evaluation of the experimental evidence (discussion 649–651). *Hospital and Community Psychiatry, 41*(6), 634–641.

Phillips, S. D., Burns, B. J., Edgar, E. R., Mueser, K. T., Linkins, K. W., Rosenheck, R. A., et al. (2001). Moving assertive community treatment into standard practice. *Psychiatric Services, 52*(6), 771–779.

Santos, A. B., Deci, P. A., Lachance, K. R., Dias, J. K., Sloop, T. B., Hiers, T. G., et al. (1993). Providing assertive community treatment for severely mentally ill patients in a rural area. *Hospital and Community Psychiatry, 44*(1), 34–39.

Schaedle, R. W., McGrew, J. H., Bond, G. R., & Epstein, I. (2002). A comparison of experts' perspectives on assertive community treatment and intensive case management. *Psychiatric Services, 53*(2), 207–210.

Scott, J. E., & Dixon, L. B. (1995). Assertive community treatment and case management for schizophrenia. *Schizophrenia Bulletin, 21*(4), 657–668.

Stein, L. I., & Santos, A. (1998). *Assertive community treatment of persons with severe mental illness.* New York: Norton.

Teague, G. B., Bond, G. R., & Drake, R. E. (1998). Program fidelity in assertive community treatment: Development and use of a measure. *American Journal of Orthopsychiatry, 68*, 216–232.

Teague, G. B., Drake, R. E., & Ackerson, T. H. (1995). Evaluating use of continuous treatment teams for persons with mental illness and substance abuse. *Psychiatric Services, 46*(7), 689–695.

Test, M. A. (1992). Training in community living. In R. P. Liberman (Ed.), *Handbook of psychiatric rehabilitation (pp. 153–170).* New York: McMillan.

Thornicroft, G. (1991). The concept of case management for long-term mental illness. *International Review of Psychiatry, 3,* 125–132.

U.S. Department of Health and Human Services. (1999). *Mental health: A Report of the Surgeon General.* Rockville, MD: Author. Available from http://www.surgeongeneral.gov /library/mentalhealth/home.html.

Ziguras, S. J., & Stuart, G. W. (2000). A meta-analysis of the effectiveness of mental health case management over 20 years. *Psychiatric Services, 51*(11), 1410–1421.

CHAPTER 4

Evidence-Based Family Services for Adults with Severe Mental Illness

Thomas C. Jewell, William R. McFarlane, Lisa Dixon, and David J. Miklowitz

Family members and other persons involved in the lives and care of adults who have serious mental illnesses often provide emotional support, case management, financial assistance, advocacy, and housing to their mentally ill loved ones. These family members often have limited access to the resources and information they need (Adamec, 1996; Marsh, 1992; Marsh & Johnson, 1997), which results in considerable burdens for those serving in this capacity (Cochrane, Goering, & Rogers, 1997; Leff, 1994; McFarlane, Lukens, et al., 1995; Schene, van Wijngaarden, & Koeter, 1998). Evidence-based practice guidelines for using psychoeducational approaches to address the needs of family members have been developed. These guidelines are supported by over a decade of research that has consistently shown that clients' outcomes improve when the needs of family members are met.

In general, evidence-based practices are clinical practices for which scientific evidence of improvement in consumer outcomes has been consistent (Drake et al., 2001). The scientific evidence of the highest standard is the randomized clinical trial. Often, several clinical trials are pooled by using a technique such as meta-analysis to identify evidence-based practices. Quasi-experimental studies, and to a lesser extent open clinical trials, can also be used. However, the research evidence for an evidence-based practice must be consistent and sufficiently specific for the quality and outcome of the intervention to be assessed. This chapter describes *family psychoeducation,* the basis for its identification as an evidence-based practice, barriers to its implementation, strategies for overcoming these barriers, and future directions in the field.

HISTORICAL BACKGROUND

Family psychoeducation originated in the late 1970s. Among the sources were family members themselves and their rapidly growing advocacy organizations, such as the National Alliance for the Mentally Ill (NAMI). NAMI developed in 1979 from a lack of professional responsiveness to the needs and issues of families who have a relative with mental illness (Backer & Richardson, 1989; Hatfield, 1987). Family members and their advocacy organizations were acutely aware that living with an illness such as schizophrenia is difficult and confusing for clients and families alike.

It became increasingly clear that a well-functioning family has to possess the available knowledge about the illness itself and coping skills specific to a particular disorder, skills that are often nascent and even counterintuitive in families. For instance, it may be natural for well-meaning family members to want to adamantly argue with an ill loved one on a daily basis that his or her delusions are not true, even though such direct and frequent confrontations may result in increased stress and symptom exacerbation. Given that perspective, the most adaptive family was seen to be the one that has access to information, with the implication that the treatment system is a crucial source of that information. As to coping skills, many families develop methods of dealing with positive (psychotic) and negative (functional and cognitive deficits, such as flattened affect, loss of energy, and apathy) symptoms, functional disabilities, and the desperation of their ill relatives through painful trial and error. Successes, however, are rare. Many families need access to each other to learn of other families' successes and failures and to establish a repertoire of coping strategies that are closely tailored to the disorder. Further, family members and significant others involved in the lives and care of adults with serious mental illnesses often provide emotional and instrumental support, case management functions, financial assistance, advocacy, and housing to their relative with mental illness. Doing so can be rewarding but poses considerable burdens (Adamec, 1996; Cochrane et al., 1997; Leff, 1994; McFarlane, Lukens, et al., 1995). Family members often find that access to needed resources and information is lacking (Adamec, 1996; Marsh, 1992; Marsh & Johnson, 1997).

Even with this new perspective, it took many years to revive interest and effort in the treatment of families coping with severe mental illness. Investigators began to recognize the crucial role families played in outcomes after an acute episode of schizophrenia had occurred and endeavored to engage families collaboratively. Therapists shared illness information, suggested behaviors to promote recuperation, and taught coping strategies to reduce their sense of burden (Anderson, Hogarty, & Reiss, 1980; Falloon, Boyd, & McGill, 1984; Goldstein, Rodnick, Evans, May, & Steinberg, 1978; Leff, Kuipers, Berkowitz, Eberlein-Vries, & Sturgeon, 1982). The group of interventions that emerged became known as family psychoeducation.

The psychoeducational approach recognizes that schizophrenia and other severe mental illnesses, such as bipolar disorder, are biological disorders that are only partially remediable by medication and that family members' behavior can significantly impact the relative's recovery. Thus, the psychoeducational approach shifted away from attempting to get families to change their "disturbed" communication patterns toward educating and persuading families on how to behave toward the ill member to facilitate recovery. This education included methods to compensate for deficits and sensitivities specific to the various psychotic disorders. For example, family members might interfere with recuperation if in their natural enthusiasm to promote progress they created unreasonable demands and expectations. The same family members could have a dramatically positive effect on recovery by gradually increasing expectations and supporting an incremental return of functioning.

Several models have evolved to address the needs of families of persons with mental illness: individual consultation and family psychoeducation conducted by a mental health professional (Anderson, Reiss, & Hogarty, 1986; Falloon et al., 1984), various forms of more traditional family therapy (Marsh, 2001), and a range of professionally led short-term family education programs (Amenson, 1998; Mannion, 2000), sometimes referred to as therapeutic education. Also available are family-led information and support classes or groups, such as those provided by NAMI (Burland, 1998; Pickett-Schenk, Cook, & Laris, 2000). Family psychoeducation has a deep enough research and dissemination base to be considered an evidenced-based practice. However, the term psychoeducation can be misleading: family psychoeducation includes many therapeutic elements, often uses a consultative framework, and shares characteristics with other types of family interventions.

DESCRIPTION OF FAMILY PSYCHOEDUCATION

Originally developed by Anderson et al. (1980), family psychoeducation for schizophrenia is a specific, empirically based model that includes an intensive engagement effort with family and client and extended education about the disease and guidelines for recovery based on research and best clinical practice. It pursues a careful, gradual treatment process to promote a strong stable symptomatic recovery and relapse prevention. It includes a careful social and vocational rehabilitation effort and problem solving based on the needs of both family and client. It emphasizes partnering and joining with family members (Anderson, 1983), incorporating family members' and clients' desires and ambitions as the core of the treatment plan, and empathic acceptance of the family's suffering, burdens, and frustrations in caretaking.

This approach was heavily influenced by Hogarty and Ulrich's (1977) finding that psychotic relapse is a major impediment to longer term clinical and functional improvement, but that after roughly a year of remission, most people with schizophrenia make significant functional gains, are more resistant to stress, and can tolerate increasing mental and physical demands. This translated into working closely with the family, making coordinated efforts to take the next steps toward improved community participation, and using clinical condition as the guide to what a client might be able to handle. A hallmark is that a considerable period of time is allowed for recovery from the last episode of psychosis—as much as a year, as is done for heart attacks. The assumption is that psychosis is traumatic for the brain, the person having the episode, and the immediate social support system, and requires recuperation to allow functional recovery.

Finally, the approach uses clinical approaches in training families to assist in creating an optimal psychosocial environment for recovery from schizophrenia, especially one that is somewhat quieter, less intense, less complex, and moves a bit slower than the world in general. This is perhaps the point on which there is the greatest contrast with family therapy: Here the family is assumed to be functional until proven otherwise (for example, by resisting or failing to use the treatment). Its members need to adopt a special interactional style and create a low-stimulation social environment to adapt to, and compensate for, the specific sensory and cognitive characteristics of a given disorder.

PSYCHOEDUCATIONAL MULTIFAMILY GROUPS

The psychoeducational multiple family group (PMFG) brings together aspects of family psychoeducation, family behavioral management, and multiple-family approaches

(McFarlane, Dixon, Lukens, & Lucksted, 2003). As such, it is a second-generation treatment model that incorporates the advantages of each of its sources, diminishes their negative features, and leads to a number of synergistic effects that appear to enhance efficacy. Building on the psychoeducational family approach and the family behavioral management approach, the model attempts to reflect contemporary understanding of schizophrenia and other severe mental illnesses from biological, psychological, and social perspectives.

Multiple family group work arose nearly 3 decades ago in attempts by Laqueur, LaBurt, and Morong (1964), and Detre, Sayer, Norton, and Lewis (1961) to develop psychosocial treatments for hospitalized consumers. The emphasis was more pragmatic than theoretical. Indeed, the first reported successful experience with the modality emerged serendipitously from a need to solve ward management problems. In the process, Laqueur et al. noted improved ward social functioning in patients who insisted on attending a group organized for visiting relatives. Detre and his colleagues started a multiple family group to encourage cooperation between resident psychiatrists and social workers on an acute inpatient service. They found a high level of interest in the group among patients and family members alike, as well as improvements in social functioning among patients and in family communication and morale.

Many practitioners have observed that specific characteristics of the multiple family group have remarkable effects on a number of social and clinical management problems commonly encountered in schizophrenia and other severe mental illnesses. Further, the PMFG approach is based on research showing that families attempting to cope with mental illness experience stressors that exasperate and discourage them. These responses often take the form of high expressed emotion, in which relatives are highly critical and/or overinvolved, a factor empirically shown to predict relapse (Hooley, Rosen, & Richters, 1995). Multifamily groups address social isolation, stigmatization, and increased financial and psychological burden directly. They achieve these by increasing the size and richness of the social support network, connecting the family to other families like themselves, providing a forum for mutual aid, providing an opportunity to hear the experiences of others who have had similar experiences and have found workable solutions, and building hope through mutual example and experience.

The general character of the PMFG approach can be summarized as consisting of three components that roughly correspond to the phases of the group. In the first phase, the content of the model follows that developed by Anderson (1983), with its emphasis on joining with each family in a single-family format, conducting a multifamily educational workshop, focusing on preventing relapse and fostering social and vocational rehabilitation. The second phase involves moving beyond stability to gradual increases in consumers' community functioning, a process that uses PMFG-based problem solving. This usually occurs during the second year of the PMFG. The third phase consists of deliberate efforts to mold the group into a social network that can persist for an extended period and satisfy family and consumer needs for social contact, support, and ongoing clinical monitoring. This format is also an efficient context in which to continue psychopharmacologic treatment and routine case management. Expansion of the families' social networks occurs through problem solving, direct emotional support, and out-of-group socializing, all involving members of different families in the group. McFarlane's recent book (2002) provides a more comprehensive description that may serve as a how-to manual for implementing PMFGs in the treatment of severe mental illnesses.

RESEARCH REVIEW

You may ask why clinicians should consider investing the time and energy to implement PMFGs. There is a range of possible answers to this question. One simple answer relates to the identification of family psychoeducation as an evidence-based practice: "Because we now know that family psychoeducation helps the people we care about—adults with severe mental illness." Studies spanning over 2 decades indicate the positive effects of PMFGs on the lives of people with schizophrenia. There is also a rapidly growing and promising database that suggests similar beneficial effects of family involvement on the course of bipolar disorder.

Schizophrenia

A large number of studies have shown markedly higher reductions in relapse and rehospitalization rates among adults with schizophrenia whose families received psychoeducation than among those who received standard individual services (Dixon & Lehman, 1995; Falloon, Held, Coverdale, Roncone, & Laidlaw, 1999; Lam, Kuipers, & Leff, 1993; Penn & Mueser, 1996), with differences ranging from 20% to 50% over 2 years. For programs of more than 3 months' duration, the reductions in relapse rates were at the higher end of this range. In addition, the well-being of family members improved (Falloon & Pederson, 1985), clients' participation in vocational rehabilitation increased (McFarlane, Dushay, Stastny, Deakins, & Link, 1996), and the costs of care decreased (Cardin, McGill, & Falloon, 1985; Falloon et al., 1999; McFarlane, Lukens, et al., 1995; Tarrier, Lowson, & Barrowclough, 1991).

Goldstein and Miklowitz (1995) concluded that family psychoeducation for people afflicted with schizophrenia was highly effective when compared to standard care or medication alone. Going beyond basic efficacy, they described a number of studies in progress or very recently published that addressed the question as to whether there were technical variants that were more or less effective and/or specific subpopulations of clients with schizophrenia for which a given approach was superior. They went on to note that in the United States, where the bulk of the research had been done, there was little application in routine clinical practice. In the United Kingdom, by contrast, there was at least one national and one major large urban initiative to implement the approach. Finally, they noted that the approach had been tested in other disorders, beginning with bipolar disorder.

At least nine literature reviews have been published in the past decade, all finding a large and significant effect for the family psychoeducational model of intervention (Baucom, Shoham, Mueser, Daiuto, & Stickle, 1998; Dixon, Adams, & Lucksted, 2000; Dixon & Lehman, 1995; Dixon, McFarlane, et al., 2001; Falloon et al., 1999; Goldstein & Miklowitz, 1995; Lam, 1991; McFarlane & Lukens, 1998; McFarlane et al., 2003; Penn & Mueser, 1996; Pitschel-Walz, Leucht, Bauml, Kissling, & Engel, 2001). Since 1978, with the publication of Goldstein's study showing dramatic short-term effects of educational and coping skills training intervention (Goldstein et al., 1978), there has been a steady stream of rigorous validations of the positive effects of psychoeducational approaches on relapse in schizophrenic disorders. Overall, the relapse rate for clients provided family psychoeducation has hovered around 15% per year, compared to a consistent 30% to 40% for individual therapy and medication or medication alone (Baucom et al., 1998). Table 4.1 presents the major studies and relapse outcomes for schizophrenia, divided by the format of the treatment model tested.

Medication was provided to patients in all treatment conditions. In fact, family psychoeducational approaches encourage regular adherence to medications.

As a result of the compelling evidence, the Schizophrenia Patient Outcomes Research Team (PORT) project included family psychoeducation in its set of treatment recommendations. The PORT recommended that all families in contact with a relative with mental illness be offered a family psychosocial intervention spanning at least 9 months and including education about mental illness, family support, crisis intervention, and problem-solving skills training (Lehman et al., 1998). Other best practice standards (APA, 1997; Frances & Kahn, 1996) have also recommended that families receive education and support programs. In addition, an expert panel that included clinicians from various disciplines, families, clients, and researchers emphasized the importance of engaging families in the treatment and rehabilitation process (Coursey, Curtis, & Marsh, 2000a, 2000b).

Other Psychiatric Disorders

Most of the preceding studies evaluated family psychoeducation for schizophrenia or schizoaffective disorder only. However, several controlled studies support the effects of family interventions for other psychiatric disorders, such as dual diagnosis of schizophrenia and substance abuse (Barrowclough et al., 2001; McFarlane, Lukens, et al., 1995), bipolar disorder (Clarkin, Carpenter, Hull, Wilner, & Glick,

Table 4.1 Relapse in Major Outcome Trials of Family Psychoeducation

			Relapsed during Study			
	n	Duration of Treatment (Months)	SF	SF + MF (%)	MF (%)	Standard Treatment (%)
Falloon (1984)	36	24	17			83
Leff (1985)	19	24		14		78
Tarrier (1989)	44	9	33			59
Leff (1990)	23	24	33		36	
Hogarty (1991)	67	24	32			67
Xiong (1994)	63	18		44		64
Zhang (1994)	83	18		15		54
Randolph (1994)	41	12	10			40
McFarlane (1995)	34	48	83		50	
McFarlane (1995)	172	24	44		25	
Schooler (1997)	313	12/24		29	35	
N and means	895	19.7	29.0	25.5	28.0	63

SF = Single family format.
MF = Multifamily format.
Source: From McFarlane et al. (2003). p. 230. Reprinted by permission from author.

1998; Miklowitz & Goldstein, 1997; Miklowitz et al., 2000; Moltz, 1993; Parikh et al., 1997; Simoneau, Miklowitz, Richards, Saleem, & George, 1999; Tompson, Rea, Goldstein, Miklowitz, & Weisman, 2000), major depression (Emanuels-Zuurveen, 1997; Emanuels-Zuurveen & Emmelkamp, 1996; Leff et al., 2000), mood disorders in children (Fristad, Gavazzi, & Soldano, 1998), obsessive-compulsive disorder (Van Noppen, 1999), anorexia (Geist, Heinmaa, Stephens, Davis, & Katzman, 2000), and borderline personality disorder (Gunderson, Berkowitz, & Ruizsancho, 1997), including single- and multifamily approaches. Gonzalez and Steinglass have extended this work to deal with the secondary effects of chronic medical illness (Gonzalez, Steinglass, & Reiss, 1989; Steinglass, 1998).

Bipolar Disorder

The best-studied and developed versions of family psychoeducation beyond those for schizophrenia have focused on bipolar disorder. Given the relatively recent developments in family psychoeducation for this disorder, it is worthwhile to extensively review the existing literature for the reader. The first family psychoeducational approach for bipolar disorder was proposed by Clarkin et al. (1990; Glick et al., 1990) at the Cornell University Medical Center. Their model involved nine sessions of inpatient family intervention for a mixed group of psychotic, unipolar affective, and bipolar affective patients. The model focused on enhancing posthospital adjustment and maximizing drug adherence. Inpatients ($N = 186$) randomized to inpatient family intervention had better symptomatic and global functioning 6 to 18 months after hospital discharge than clients who were assigned to standard care alone. A post hoc analysis by Clarkin et al. (1990) revealed benefits in their small sample of bipolar clients ($n = 21$), although only among the female subjects.

More recently, Clarkin et al. (1998) examined married, recently ill clients with bipolar disorder ($N = 33$) who were randomly assigned to a 25-session psychoeducational couple therapy plus mood stabilizers or mood stabilizers only. The couple's intervention involved an educational focus on bipolar disorder, methods to enhance spousal communication, and drug compliance. There were no differential effects of the marital intervention over 11 months on either recurrence or symptoms. However, clients in the couple intervention had higher functional outcomes and higher medication compliance scores than the comparison clients.

More consistent results have been reported in studies of family-focused therapy (FFT; Miklowitz & Goldstein, 1997). This psychoeducational model is administered in 21 sessions (weekly, biweekly, then monthly) over 9 months once the client has begun to recover from an acute manic or depressive episode. In the first segment, psychoeducation (usually seven or more sessions), clients and their caregiving relatives (typically parents or spouses) learn about the nature, symptoms, course, and treatment of bipolar disorder; the notion that episodes come about as an interaction among genetic, biological, and stress factors; the importance of continued adherence to medications to delay recurrences; and the role of stress management in reducing the likelihood of future episodes. Families are taken through a "relapse drill" (Marlatt, 1985) in which they learn to identify incipient signs of relapse and develop a plan for how they will act as a family should those signs appear (for example, who will call the physician, arranging a hospitalization; how to communicate with the symptomatic family member; how to keep the environment low in stress).

The intermediate and later phases of FFT focus on enhancing the emotional atmosphere of the family through skill training. These techniques are directed at reducing levels of negative expressed emotion. In communication enhancement training (7 to 10 sessions), clients and relatives learn through role playing and behavioral rehearsal to listen actively, deliver positive feedback and constructive criticisms, and to diplomatically ask for changes in other family members' behaviors. Between-session homework assignments help these skills to generalize to other settings. In the late phases of FFT, the focus shifts to problem solving. Specific illness, family, or work-related problems are defined, and the family is taught a series of steps to brainstorm solutions, evaluate the pros and cons of each solution, choose one or a set of solutions, and develop an implementation plan. Once the family or couple has learned the problem-solving method, families are encouraged to practice these techniques on their own.

In the first of two randomized trials of FFT (Miklowitz, George, Richards, Simoneau, & Suddath, 2003) conducted at the University of Colorado, Boulder, 101 bipolar I clients who began in a manic, mixed, or depressive phase were assigned to 9 months of FFT and standard medication maintenance or a comparison condition known as crisis management (CM) and medication maintenance. Crisis management was delivered over 9 months and consisted of two sessions of family education, crisis intervention sessions as needed, and face-to-face research follow-ups. Clients were included only if they had family members active in their care. Over a 2-year follow-up, clients in FFT had a 35% reduction in relapse likelihood, longer survival intervals without relapsing (73.5 weeks versus 53.2 weeks), and a greater likelihood of completing the study without relapsing or dropping out (52% versus 17%). They also showed greater stabilization of depressive symptoms and, to a lesser extent, manic symptoms.

Family-focused therapy led to modifications over the first year in positive affect and positive communication skills, as expressed within family interactions. Improvements in the degree with which clients were able to engage with their family members during directed interaction exercises (conducted before and after treatment) predicted clinical improvement, particularly of depression symptoms (Simoneau et al., 1999). FFT was also associated with better medication adherence than CM over the course of the 2-year study. Adherence predicted improvements in mania symptoms, but not depression symptoms. Thus, FFT may operate through two avenues: improving family relationships, which may help alleviate depression symptoms, and improvements in drug compliance, which mediates improvement in mania symptoms. These findings need to be replicated in larger samples that examine more systematically the timing of changes in adherence, family communication, and mood symptoms.

The Colorado study compared FFT to a treatment-as-usual comparison condition. A randomized study at the University of California, Los Angeles, examined FFT against a comparably paced individual therapy (Rea et al., 2003). These investigators randomly assigned 53 hospitalized, bipolar I manic clients to FFT and medications or a comparison individual therapy called individually focused client management (IFPT), also with medications. IFPT had many of the same elements as FFT—support, psychoeducation, encouragement of drug adherence, and managing symptoms and life stressors—but did not involve family members. IFPT consisted of half-hour individual sessions delivered on the same time schedule as FFT (21 sessions over 9 months).

Clients in FFT had fewer relapses and fewer hospitalizations over the 2-year study than clients in IFPT. FFT assisted participants in avoiding rehospitalizations through teaching them to recognize relapses early and obtain medical treatment. When clients in FFT did relapse, they were less likely (55%) to be hospitalized than clients in IFPT who relapsed (88%). However, the effects of FFT were not seen until the 1-year posttreatment interval, during which rehospitalizations were observed in 12% of the FFT group and 60% of the IFPT group. No differences in hospitalization or relapse rates were seen during the first year of treatment. Clients and relatives may not have begun to absorb the relapse prevention, communication skills, or problem-solving skills until the treatments had been largely completed. Alternatively, education of family members increases the likelihood that relapses will be caught early and treated during intervals in which patients are not engaged in active psychosocial treatment.

Thus, in bipolar disorder, the combination of family psychoeducation and drug treatment appears to improve symptom functioning, enhance family functioning, and help clients and caregivers to avoid hospitalization through early intervention. The positive effects of FFT and other family approaches on drug compliance deserve further investigation. Involving family members in the psychoeducational process increases the likelihood that clients learn skills to manage their bipolar disorder.

Nonreplication Studies

Reviewing studies in which there has been no effect found for family psychoeducation is simpler than reviewing studies in which a positive effect has been demonstrated: three studies to date, of nearly 30 (Kottgen, Sonnichsen, Mollenhauer, & Jurth, 1984; Linszen et al., 1996; Telles et al., 1995). In the Kottgen study, the ongoing sessions were oriented toward exploring psychodynamic and dysfunctional aspects of families, now generally considered as contraindicated for families of clients with schizophrenia (Lehman et al., 1998). In the Telles study, conducted in a Spanish-speaking immigrant sample, there was a reversed effect for behavioral family management among those from a less acculturated subgroup and no effect for those from the more acculturated subgroup. Other recent studies in Spain have demonstrated the same robust effects as the prior studies in English-speaking countries, suggesting that it was the sample's immigrant status that may have negated the effects of family intervention, not a difference between languages or cultures. It is also possible that the family treatment in the Telles study was not fully adapted to the stressors, beliefs, or cultural norms of less acculturated families. In the Linszen study, the control group received individual therapy, which was well designed and achieved low relapse rates comparable to those in the family intervention sample (15% to 16% in both conditions). In other words, family psychoeducation was added to an already intense and comprehensive treatment program and overall relapse rates were low for both conditions. This study utilized family intervention only during an inpatient admission and not during outpatient treatment. Finally, a study of personal therapy by Hogarty and his colleagues produced mixed results (Hogarty, Greenwald, et al., 1997; Hogarty, Kornblith, et al., 1997). In clients living with family, personal therapy had lower relapse rates than family or supportive therapy, but personal adjustment was better in family psychoeducation. In clients living independent of their families, personal therapy was associated with more psychotic relapses than supportive therapy.

Thus, the nonconfirming studies tend to validate the effectiveness of the studies in which an effect was found by suggesting that the core elements make a difference, that some clients and families may require cultural and/or contextually specific adaptations of the approach, that longer term participation by families is required to achieve outcomes, and that other methods may also achieve comparable short-term effects. Consistent efficacy of family psychoeducation when evaluated against comparison treatments has been demonstrated only in those studies in which intervention was provided on an ongoing basis, lasting at least 6 months, and incorporated problem-solving, coping skills training, expanded social support, and communication skills training. It has become clear that education alone has at least short-term salutary effects for family members (Dixon, Stewart, et al., 2001), but other studies have found that there is no lasting effect on client clinical or functional outcomes (Abramowitz & Coursey, 1989). Further, given the long-term course of illness of schizophrenia, it has appeared to many observers that even the shorter term positive effects for family members of the education-only models erode under the influence of the persisting deficits, symptoms, and burdens. Thus, the critical elements include those that involve changes in behavior and ongoing training in diagnosis-specific and coping skills training. Increasingly, as the focus of intervention has shifted to functional aspects, especially employment, the client has been included in these skills training and behavioral interventions. In the multifamily group approaches, there is another element added—ongoing social support and social network expansion for family members and the client.

Effects of Family Psychoeducation on Functioning

Many studies reported in the past few years have demonstrated significant effects on other areas of functioning. These studies and findings address a frequent criticism of the clinical trials: that relapse is only one dimension of outcome and course of illness. Many consumers and their family members are more concerned about the functional aspects of the illness, especially housing, employment, social relationships, dating and marriage, and general morale than about remission, a more abstract goal. More recently, several investigators have shifted focus to targeting these more human aspects of illness and life. Other effects have consequently been shown for:

- Improved family member well-being (Cuijpers, 1999; Falloon & Pederson, 1985; McFarlane et al., 1996; Shi, Zhao, Xu, & Sen, 2000)

- Increased client participation in vocational rehabilitation (Falloon et al., 1985)

- Substantially increased employment rates (McFarlane, Lukens, et al., 1995; McFarlane et al., 1996, 2000)

- Decreased psychiatric symptoms, including deficit syndrome (Dyck et al., 2000; Falloon et al., 1985; McFarlane, Lukens, et al., 1995; Zhao et al., 2000)

- Improved social functioning (Montero et al., 2001)
- Reduced costs of care (Cardin et al., 1985; McFarlane, Lukens, et al., 1995; Rund et al., 1994; Tarrier et al., 1991)

THE FAMILY-TO-FAMILY EDUCATION PROGRAM

In the historical absence of family psychoeducation or other professionally led family education or support programs, voluntary peer-led family education programs have developed, epitomized by NAMI's Family-to-Family Education Program (FFEP; Burland, 1998; Solomon, 2000; Solomon, Draine, & Mannion, 1996; Solomon, Draine, Mannion, & Meisel, 1996). FFEP is currently available in over 40 states, many of which have waiting lists. FFEP and other mutual-assistance family programs are organized and led by trained volunteers from families of persons who have mental illness.

These community programs are offered regardless of the mentally ill person's treatment status. They tend to be brief—for example, 12 weeks for FFEP—and mix families of persons with various diagnoses, although they focus on persons with schizophrenia or bipolar disorder. On the basis of a trauma-and-recovery model of a family's experience in coping with mental illness, FFEP merges education with specific support mechanisms to help families through the various stages of comprehending and coping with a family member's mental illness (Burland, 1998). The FFEP focuses first on outcomes of family members and their well-being, although benefits to the client are also considered to be important (Solomon, 1996).

Uncontrolled research on FFEP and its predecessor, Journey of Hope, suggests that the program increases the participants' knowledge about the causes and treatment of mental illness, their understanding of the mental health system, and their well-being (Pickett-Schenk et al., 2000). In a prospective, naturalistic study, FFEP participants reported that they had significantly less displeasure and concern about members of their family who had mental illness and significantly more empowerment at the family, community, and service-system levels after they had completed the program (Dixon, Stewart, et al., 2001). Benefits observed at the end of the program were sustained 6 months after the intervention (Dixon, Stewart, et al., 2001). This uncontrolled study of the effectiveness of FFEP was recently followed by a controlled evaluation that used a waiting-list control design (Dixon et al., 2004). This follow-up evaluation of FFEP revealed findings similar to the 2001 study by Dixon and her colleagues. Within the constraints of the follow-up study's nonrandomized design, this replication provides the strongest evidence available that FFEP has important salutary effects on the family experience of serious mental illness (Dixon et al., 2004).

Although FFEP currently lacks rigorous scientific evidence of efficacy such as a randomized controlled trial (RCT) in improving clinical or functional outcomes of persons who have mental illness, it shows considerable promise for improving the well-being of family members. In recent research and practice, attempts have been made to optimize the clinical opportunities provided by family psychoeducation and peer-based programs such as FFEP by developing partnerships between the two strategies. For example, family psychoeducation programs have used FFEP teachers as leaders, and participation in FFEP has facilitated eventual participation in family psychoeducation.

FAMILY PSYCHOEDUCATION PRACTICE GUIDELINES

A variety of family psychoeducation programs have been developed by mental health-care professionals over the past 2 decades. These programs have been offered as part of an overall clinical treatment plan for individuals who have mental illness. The interventions with the most research support last 9 months to 5 years, are usually diagnosis specific, and focus primarily on consumer outcomes, with the well-being of family members a secondary outcome. Family psychoeducation models differ in their format—for example, multiple-family, single-family, or mixed sessions—the duration of treatment, consumer participation, location—for example, clinic based, home, family practice, or other community settings—and the degree of emphasis on didactic, cognitive-behavioral, and systemic techniques.

Delivery of the *appropriate components* of family psychoeducation to clients and families appears important in determining the outcomes of families and clients. Several studies (Greenberg, Greenley, & Kim, 1995) have demonstrated that programs fail to reduce relapse rates if they present information without also providing family members with skills training, ongoing guidance concerning illness management, and emotional support. Additionally, a meta-analysis of 16 studies found that family interventions of fewer than 10 sessions had no important effects on relatives' burden (Cuijpers, 1999). The behaviors and disruptions of schizophrenia, in particular, may require more than education to ameliorate family burden and enhance client outcomes.

Overall, the consensus of previous reviews is that various family psychoeducational approaches, if they include the key elements and continue for a minimum duration, are equally effective. While not a rigorous criterion, there is nevertheless a remarkable consistency of effects on relapse rates, with minimum reductions of about 50% of the control groups' rates. The differences simply increase with time, so that at 24 months the family-based conditions are well below 50% of the rates in the control groups, approaching 75% in some studies. Baucom and colleagues found that in 11 of the most rigorously designed and conducted studies, with an average study duration of 19.7 months, the overall average for family intervention was about 27%; for the control groups, it was 64%, a reduction of about 58% of the standard or routine treatment rate (Baucom et al., 1998). These differences in outcome are some of the most substantial and consistent empirical effects achieved by any treatment in the mental health domain.

A strong consensus about the critical elements of family intervention emerged in 1999 under the encouragement of the leaders of the World Schizophrenia Fellowship (WSF; 1998). The resulting consensus as to goals, principles, and methods, that is, elements of family intervention that are critical to achieving the empirically validated outcomes reported, is summarized:

Goals for Working with Families

- To achieve the best possible outcome for the individual with mental illness through treatment and management that involves collaboration among professionals, families, and clients

- To alleviate suffering among the members of the family by supporting them in their efforts to foster their loved one's recovery

Principles for Working with Families

The models of treatment supported with demonstrated effectiveness required clinicians working with families to:

- Coordinate all elements of treatment and rehabilitation to ensure that everyone is working toward the same goals in a collaborative, supportive relationship.
- Pay attention to the social as well as the clinical needs of the client.
- Provide optimum medication management.
- Listen to families and treat them as equal partners in treatment planning and delivery.
- Explore family members' expectations of the treatment program and for the client.
- Assess the family's strengths and limitations in their ability to support the client.
- Help resolve family conflict through sensitive response to emotional distress.
- Address feelings of loss.
- Provide relevant information for client and family at appropriate times.
- Provide an explicit crisis plan and professional response.
- Help improve communication among family members.
- Provide training for the family in structured problem-solving techniques.
- Encourage the family to expand their social support networks, for example, participation in multifamily groups and/or family support organizations such as the National Alliance for the Mentally Ill.
- Be flexible in meeting the needs of the family.
- Provide the family with easy access to a professional should work with the family cease.

TRAINING AND DISSEMINATION ISSUES

An ongoing challenge in the mental health field is determining the most effective way to implement evidence-based practices in routine treatment settings. In spite of the body of research that shows the effectiveness of evidence-based treatments, many are not regularly available to people with severe mental illness (Lehman & Steinwachs, 1998), and traditional training opportunities for clinicians have been shown to be insufficient to promote their widespread use (Backer, Liberman, & Kuehnel, 1986; Corrigan, Steiner, McCracken, Blaser, & Barr, 2001).

Barriers to Implementing Family Psychoeducation

You may wonder why family psychoeducation is rarely offered in routine clinical practice despite the extensive documentation of its basic benefits. In general, low levels of any contact between programs/staff and family members in public and community-based settings may preclude the more substantial educational or support interventions. In addition, the availability of any intervention is limited by the availability of people to provide it and the training necessary to equip them. Such staffing requires willing clinicians, resources, time, and financial reimbursement that have not been forthcoming for family psychoeducation. These imply the existence of larger attitudinal, knowledge, practical, and systemic implementation obstacles.

Clients, Family Members

Implementation of family psychoeducation may be hindered by realities in the lives of potential participants. Practical issues such as transportation, time commitment, and competing demands for time and energy are common (Solomon, 1996). If family members perceive that "training" through family psychoeducation includes expectations that they will take on yet more caregiving responsibilities, they may stay away (WSF, 1998). Sessions must be scheduled when facilitators are available, but doing so may not mesh with potential participants' needs. Family members report significant caregiving burdens, such as providing transportation for their ill loved one, that pose barriers to attendance even though attendance may lighten these burdens (Gallagher & Mechanic, 1996; Mueser, Webb, Pfeiffer, Gladis, & Levinson, 1996).

Family members may not want to be identified with psychiatric facilities. Due to stigma, they may feel uncomfortable revealing to others the psychiatric illness in their families and airing their family problems in a public setting. Family members may also have had negative experiences in the past and be hesitant to open themselves to that possibility again. Most have not had access to information documenting the value of family programs and thus may not appreciate their potential (WSF, 1998). Indeed, hopelessness can be a barrier. Clients may experience some of the same hesitations about participating in family psychoeducation as their family members. In addition, they may worry about losing the confidential relationship with their treatment teams or losing autonomy.

Clinicians, Program Administrators

It may be that the lack of family psychoeducation availability reflects mental health providers' lack of knowledge about its utility and importance (Dixon & Lehman, 1995; Greenberg et al., 1995; Solomon, 1996). Providers may not know about the effectiveness of family psychoeducation and may not appreciate the impact of mental illness on families (WSF, 1998). They may focus on medication over psychosocial interventions and deem family involvement as superfluous to an individual's treatment and recovery. Additionally, some may still follow theories that blame family dynamics for causing schizophrenia. Bergmark (1994) noted the persistence of psychodynamic theories as a potential barrier since many families perceive them as blaming. Despite attempts by expressed emotion researchers to avoid any implication of blame, the findings about expressed emotion that were the original basis for family psychoeducation are often perceived similarly.

Important though they are, individuals' knowledge and underlying assumptions are only part of the picture. Wright, Takei, Rifkin, and Murray (1995) found that job and organizational factors were much more predictive of the frequency of mental health professionals' involvement with families than were professionals' attitudes. Clinician work schedule and professional discipline were the strongest predictors, but other organizational factors have posed barriers as well. Dissemination of McFarlane's multiple family psychoeducation group model has been hindered by a paucity of programmatic leadership supporting implementation, conflicts between the model's philosophy and typical agency practices, insufficient resources supporting practice change, and inadequate attention to human dynamics on a systems level (Dixon, McFarlane, Hornby, & McNary, 1999; McFarlane et al., 1993). For example, reasonable concerns about confidentiality issues may be seen as roadblocks to family involvement rather than as opportunities to create useful innovations that respect everyone's right to privacy (Boise, Heagery, & Eskenazi, 1996).

Mental health professionals have also expressed concern about the cost and length of structured family psychoeducation programs (Dixon, Lyles, et al., 1999), although medication and case management services for clients usually have to be continued for much longer periods. Caseloads are universally very high, and staff time is stretched thin. Therefore, devoting substantial staff resources to training, organizing, leading, and sustaining family psychoeducation is seen as a luxury by most administrators and clinicians (WSF, 1998). In such an atmosphere, horizons tend to be short, and immediate organizational crises or short-term goals tend to overshadow the long-term investment and payoffs of family psychoeducation, such as reduced crises, hospitalizations, and total treatment costs.

Mental Health Authorities, Government

At the level of healthcare systems, pressures to focus on outcomes, cost effectiveness, and customer satisfaction would seem in principle to favor widespread adoption of family information/support interventions. However, other tenets of the current healthcare environment—such as emphasis on short-term cost savings, technical (as contrasted with human process-oriented) remedies, and individual pathology—encourage little attention to such services. Many of the impediments mentioned as client- and program-level issues have their parallels in larger administrative systems: inadequate resources, ingrained assumptions about how care should be structured, and lack of awareness of evidence.

Strategies for Overcoming Barriers to Implementing Family Psychoeducation

Research on technology transfer has identified four fundamental conditions that must be met for individual or system change to occur:

1. Dissemination of knowledge.
2. Evaluation of programmatic impact.
3. Availability of resources.
4. Efforts to address the human dynamics of resisting change (Backer, 1991).

Implementation strategies must include clear, widespread communication of the models and of their benefits to all stakeholders. This must be done through channels accessible and acceptable to the various stakeholders—including families, clients, providers, administrators, and policymakers. It must be accompanied by advocacy, training, and supervision/consultation initiatives to raise awareness and support at all organizational levels (McFarlane, 1994). Implementation strategies should also include training and consultation methods that provide choices for trainees, while maintaining faithfulness to the practice guidelines of the intervention. Clinicians, agency administrators, and recipients should all have input as to how the dissemination effort takes place in any given agency.

Clients, Family Members

At the level of individual family members and clients, effective family psychoeducation models include strategies for overcoming barriers to participation such as the family's sense of often overwhelming grief and stigma. For example, offering sessions at home, helping family members understand that the intervention is designed to improve the lives of everyone in the family (not just the client), being flexible about scheduling family meetings, and providing education during the engagement process can destigmatize mental illness and engender hope (Mueser & Glynn, 1999; Tarrier, 1991).

Recent efforts to disseminate family psychoeducation in New York State, Los Angeles, Maine, and Illinois have illustrated the importance of including representatives of the recipients—clients and their families and practitioners—of these services in their planning, adaptation, and eventual implementation. New York has been involved in two dissemination efforts: one in the 1980s to 1990s and one that is currently underway. In the earlier New York example, the dissemination was initiated and sponsored by the state's AMI (now NAMI New York) chapter (McFarlane et al., 1993). Presently in New York, a large-scale dissemination effort involves a partnership between the state mental health authority and an academic institution, in collaboration with the state's NAMI chapter and an association composed of mental health directors at the local level. In comparing dramatic differences in the outcome of dissemination in Maine and Illinois, one key difference is the strong, formal support from NAMI Maine for the effort there, versus occasional resistance by local chapters and the absence of involvement of the state NAMI in Illinois (McFarlane, McNary, Dixon, Hornby, & Cimett, 2001). Experience and now some empirical data illustrate the need to include clients and families in efforts to disseminate.

Clinicians, Program Administrators

Unfortunately, awareness and evidence, while necessary, are often not sufficient for adoption of new programs among mental health professionals. While interventions must maintain high fidelity to their model to obtain client and family outcomes, they also have to be responsive to local organizational and community cultures. Engagement and implementation strategies, as well as the interventions themselves, must be tailored for local and cultural characteristics, workload and other stresses facing clinicians and agencies, particular diagnoses, relationships, duration of disorder and disability, and/or whether the ill person is in medical treatment (Guarnaccia & Parra, 1996; Jordan, Lewellen, & Vandiver, 1995). Perhaps even more critical to adoption is matching administrative support and expectations for evidence-based practice with a rationale and explication of advantages that are meaningful to clinicians. Advantages can include avoidance of crises, more efficient case management, gratitude from families and clients, and more interesting, invigorating work lives for the clinicians. Knowledge about the reduced relapse and hospitalization rates associated with family psychoeducation carries almost no weight in convincing most working clinicians to change attitudes toward families and adopt a new clinical practice (McFarlane et al., 2001).

Successful implementations have required ongoing supervision, operational consultation, and general support to achieve high levels of adoption. Consensus-building among agency staff and directors, including a wide range of concerned parties in a top-down *and* bottom-up planning process, is critical but must be tailored to address local operational barriers and contrary beliefs. For instance, Amenson and Liberman's (2001) dissemination of a family psychoeducation program in Los Angeles County succeeded due to the persistent advocacy of the local NAMI group, the support of top management, the 9-month duration of training, the high quality and commitment of trainees, and the skill of the trainer.

Mental Health Authorities, Government

Although it is tempting to assume that state mental health authorities could mandate adoption of family psychoeducation centrally, experience suggests that a more complex approach is required. During the 1980s and early 1990s, New York partially succeeded in dissemination by partnering with the NAMI affiliate and an academic center; unfortunately, the mental health authority there terminated their large dissemination program before achieving a widespread impact. New York has recently reinvigorated its family psychoeducation dissemination efforts via a partnership with an academic medical center and by collaborating with the state NAMI chapter and the state association of local mental health directors. New York's recent efforts are part of an overall campaign to partner with multiple stakeholder groups to disseminate and implement a wide array of evidence-based practices throughout the state (Carpinello, Rosenberg, Stone, Schwager, & Felton, 2002). Maine's recent success was initiated by the trade association of mental health centers/services, with support but little involvement by the state authority, which has recently begun exploring a formal partnership to continue and deepen this largely successful effort. A simultaneous effort in Illinois, initiated by the state authority but distinctly lacking consensus by center directors or the state NAMI chapter, has had much less success. One exception is New Jersey, which succeeded in dissemination by setting expectations and requirements for family psychoeducation at the central level.

New Jersey aside, the most likely strategy based on experience to date is one in which provider organizations take the initiative while being supported in implementation by consumer and family organizations, the state mental health authority, and the key insurance payers as a consensus-driven partnership. Appropriate reimbursement for the service will follow from this collaboration. Experience also suggests that this process requires several years of consistent effort and ongoing monitoring to succeed.

There must also be accountability and tracking of delivery of services to families. While many states encourage the delivery of services to families, few monitor or make funding contingent on such services being delivered (Dixon, Goldman, Hirad, Adams, & Lucksted, 1999). One systems level option is for mental health centers to create the role of adult family intervention coordinator, who serves as the point person for such intervention, running interference, supervising clinicians, and monitoring fidelity (Mueser & Fox, 2000).

Few, if any, of the treatments described in this chapter have been examined within community mental health facilities, using the clinicians that work in them, focusing on the populations they serve, and limited by the financial constraints under which they work. To make the transition into regular use in community settings, family psychoeducation may benefit from being further distilled down to its most effective (and cost-effective) ingredients. If a clinician only has six to eight sessions in which to treat a person with schizophrenia or bipolar disorder in conjunction with his or her family, how should the clinician proceed? Using the example of bipolar disorder, it may be possible for the clinician to capitalize on the use of detachable modules or freestanding self-care exercises in FFT. A clinician may choose to conduct only the psychoeducational module of FFT (seven sessions), or he or she may decide to spend three to four sessions with a couple teaching the communication enhancement exercises (e.g., active listening). Clients or relatives, especially if already knowledgeable, may be able to rapidly draw up relapse prevention plans. Buttressing these brief treatments with monthly maintenance sessions may keep treatments economical while increasing the longevity of their effects. Indeed, one maintenance study for recurrent depression showed that monthly sessions of interpersonal therapy—even in the absence of medication—lengthened the time between episodes among clients who had been previously stabilized on the combination of imipramine hydrochloride and interpersonal therapy (Frank et al., 1990). Accomplishing these objectives depends on the availability of brief, efficient therapist training materials specific to each treatment modality. Clinical manuals supplemented by training videotapes can go far in influencing clinicians' routine practice. Weekend continuing education seminars may serve a similar purpose.

FIDELITY ASSESSMENT

Fidelity refers to the degree of implementation of the critical ingredients of an evidence-based practice. If clinicians from agency A and agency B all say that they are implementing PMFGs at their respective sites, how do you know what is actually taking place? Does this family service at each site reflect the family psychoeducation evidence-based practice guidelines? It may be that clinicians at site A are accurately implementing PMFGs with a high degree of fidelity, while clinicians at site B are implementing very few, if any, of the key ingredients. In part to help address this issue, a new family psychoeducation fidelity assessment tool has recently been developed by several leaders in the field in partnership with the Substance Abuse and Mental Health Services Administration and The Robert Wood Johnson Foundation (Family Psychoeducation Implementation Resource Kit, 2003). The Family Psychoeducation Fidelity Scale is a 12-item scale that was developed to measure the extent to which *programs,* as opposed to individual clinicians, are implementing family psychoeducation according to a set of practice guidelines similar to those described earlier. The items on the scale are each rated on a five-point rating scale ranging from 1 to 5 (1 = "Not implemented," 5 = "Fully implemented"). For research purposes, it is recommended that the scale be administered in person by an independent assessor to help ensure objectivity and facilitate the validity of the findings. However, for practical use by agencies, there is some flexibility in the fidelity assessment methods. The authors recommend that agencies choose a review process that will foster objectivity in ratings, such as involving a staff member who is not centrally involved in providing family psychoeducation at the agency (Family Psychoeducation Implementation Resource Kit, 2003).

In the New York State dissemination and implementation project currently underway, consultants are teaching and supervising staff from more than 25 agencies to implement PMFGs (McFarlane, 2002) in the treatment of adults with severe mental illness (Office of Mental Health Quarterly, 2002). Assessment of fidelity is planned as a routine investigation of the status of each agency's implementation efforts. Further, the team in New York is planning to use the fidelity assessment process as an opportunity to teach providers how assessing fidelity can be integrated with each agency's own continuous quality improvement strategies. The consulting team in New York is also finding it helpful to use newly developed, brief Family Psychoeducation Competency Checklists (McFarlane, personal communication, 2002) for teaching and supervision purposes. There are three separate one- to two-page checklists, one for each phase of the PMFG: Joining, Family Education Workshop, and Ongoing Problem-Solving Meetings. These brief checklists can serve as helpful notes for clinicians who are learning to implement family psychoeducation as part of their routine practices.

NEW DIRECTIONS AND FUTURE RESEARCH

Family psychoeducation has a solid research base and a consensus among leaders in the field as to its marked efficacy, essential components, and techniques. It should continue to be recommended for application in routine practice. However, there are many important gaps in the knowledge needed to make comprehensive evidence-based practice recommendations and to implement them with a wide variety of families in a wide variety of settings.

Consumers' outcomes and experiences need to be better understood and described, both quantitatively and qualitatively. Most clients have been increasingly enthusiastic about family psychoeducation, but would often not view it as useful or even tolerable at the outset. In addition, in routine clinical practice, treatment teams need to link the benefits sought by primary participants to the benefits that occur for them. This most often occurs around employment, less around relapse. Although not typically emphasized in respective research reports, the client's perspectives, feelings, hopes, and pains are central to family psychoeducation. It is important to include clients' descriptions in the treatment manuals as the basis for developing further research on client/consumer experiences and outcomes.

The minimal ingredients of a successful family intervention are still uncertain, although the World Schizophrenia Fellowship and others have delineated the core components, highlighted by the Treatment Strategies in Schizophrenia study by Schooler et al. (1997). The investigators found no significant difference in relapse rates between families receiving the more intensive program that consisted of a simplified version of behavioral family management plus a multiple family group and those receiving a less intensive psychoeducational (supportive) multifamily group program. However, both conditions provided support and education to families far beyond that found in usual services, including most of the key elements of the psychoeducational multifamily groups approach described previously (Schooler et al., 1997). To increase the cost effectiveness of the model and to decrease the burden on families, we need more studies that are designed to identify the least intensive dose of family psychoeducation that is necessary to achieve specific outcomes.

We need to develop more sophisticated measurement tools to evaluate what is beneficial for whom and at what cost. Commonly used benchmarks such as relapse are often associated with unmeasured intervening variables. Future evaluations need to consider the differing needs of diverse family members and routinely measure family well-being and health. Further, research is needed to refine the interventions so they better address different types of families, in different situations, and at different points in the course of illness. For example, there is some evidence that individualized consultation may have more benefit than group psychoeducation for families who already have ample natural supports or are part of a support group (Solomon, 1996; Solomon, Draine, Mannion, & Meisel, 1997).

Since the development of family psychoeducation, other psychosocial programs have also developed a substantial evidentiary base, including supported employment and assertive community treatment (ACT; Bond et al., 2001). For instance, ACT in combination with family psychoeducation (FACT) led to better noncompetitive employment outcomes than ACT alone (McFarlane et al., 1996); and the combination of ACT, family psychoeducation, and supported employment led to better competitive employment outcomes than conventional vocational rehabilitation (McFarlane et al., 2000). We have yet to fully explore the combination or comparison of family psychoeducation with these new psychosocial models.

Although family psychoeducation has been tested in a wide range of national and global settings, there remains a need to assess modifications in content and outcome among particular American subcultures as well as internationally. As noted previously, in the United States, the one study involving Latino family members reached mixed conclusions, while several studies in Spain have found the expected robust results (Canive et al., 1995; Telles et al., 1995). However, studies completed in China and underway with Vietnamese refugees in Australia have found effects comparable to those conducted with Anglo populations (Xiang, Ran, & Li, 1994; Xiong et al., 1994; Zhang, Wang, Li, & Phillips, 1994). The single-family format may be more effective in low-expressed emotion African American families than multifamily groups (McFarlane, 2002).

Additional research is needed to answer the question of what happens after a family has completed a family psychoeducation program. Families of clients with long-term problems and disability may need ongoing support and problem-solving skills to deal with the vicissitudes of illnesses. Lefley (2001) has described ad hoc psychoeducation in informal settings such as an ongoing medical center family support group. McFarlane's multifamily group structure is usually open-ended for families in need. As described earlier in this chapter, the Family-to-Family program of the National Alliance for the Mentally Ill in the United States is limited to 12 sessions of formal education, but offers continuity in the NAMI support and educational group structure (Burland, 1998).

CONCLUSIONS

The efficacy and effectiveness of family psychoeducation as an evidence-based practice have been established. Its use in routine clinical practice is alarmingly limited. This is particularly unfortunate, because nearly all practitioners of the approach report marked increases in their sense of professional satisfaction, gratification and enjoyment of their work, and gratitude and appreciation from families and clients. Recent research has begun to develop dissemination interventions targeted at programmatic and organizational levels with some success. Ongoing research must continue to develop practical and low-cost strategies to introduce and sustain family psychoeducation in typical practice settings. More research is also needed on identifying the barriers to implementing family psychoeducation in various clinical settings (i.e., the impact of clinicians' attitudes, geographic factors, funding, disconnection of clients from family members, stigma), as well as the extent to which modifications in these factors mediate the outcomes of educational interventions. Dissemination could also be facilitated by further exploration of integration of family psychoeducation with psychosocial interventions such as assertive community treatment, supported work and social skills training, and other evidence-based cognitive behavioral strategies to improve client treatment outcomes.

Perhaps the most immediate implication for clinicians is that family psychoeducational approaches are not difficult to learn or competently apply in practice if training and some supervision are available. Further, in-office practice with a person with schizophrenia or bipolar disorder, using the key elements of family psychoeducation, is likely to achieve nearly the same results as a more formalized implementation in an organized practice setting. The technical aspects could be less important to outcome than simply having the right attitude and an empathic approach to both client and family. Families themselves are usually appreciative of the support of professionals. Anecdotal feedback tells us that it is the basics of family psychoeducation—support, guidance, sharing the burden, information—that families most value. The more technical aspects seem to be effective in achieving outcomes, but may not be noticed as much by the recipients. In short, it is far more effective for clinicians to incorporate the practice guidelines in whatever way seems feasible in their ongoing work than to not include the family in treatment at all. Investing the time and effort to start family psychoeducation programs and build rapport and trust in relationships among consumers, family members, and providers may pay off in ways that exceed everyone's expectations.

REFERENCES

Abramowitz, I. A., & Coursey, R. D. (1989). Impact of an educational support group on family participants who take care of their schizophrenic relatives. *Journal of Consulting and Clinical Psychology, 57,* 232–236.

Adamec, C. (1996). *How to live with a mentally ill person.* New York: Wiley.

Amenson, C. S. (1998). *Schizophrenia: A family education curriculum.* Pasadena, CA: Pacific Clinics Institute.

Amenson, C. S., & Liberman, R. P. (2001). Dissemination of educational classes for families of adults with schizophrenia. *Psychiatric Services, 52*(5), 589–592.

American Psychiatric Association. (1997). *Practice guidelines for the treatment of schizophrenia.* Washington, DC: Author.

Anderson, C. M. (1983). A psychoeducational program for families of patients with schizophrenia. In W. R. McFarlane (Ed.), *Family therapy in schizophrenia* (pp. 99–116). New York: Guilford Press.

Anderson, C. M., Hogarty, G., & Reiss, D. (1980). Family treatment of adult schizophrenic patients: A psychoeducational approach. *Schizophrenia Bulletin, 6,* 490–505.

Anderson, C. M., Reiss, D., & Hogarty, G. (1986). *Schizophrenia and the family: A practitioner's guide to psychoeducation and management.* New York: Guilford Press.

Backer, T. E. (1991). *Drug abuse technology transfer.* Rockville, MD: National Institute on Drug Abuse.

Backer, T. E., Liberman, R., & Kuehnel, T. (1986). Dissemination and adoption of innovative psychosocial interventions. *Journal of Consulting and Clinical Psychology, 54*(1), 111–118.

Backer, T. E., & Richardson, D. (1989). Building bridges: Psychologists and families of the mentally ill. *American Psychologist, 44,* 546–550.

Barrowclough, C., Haddock, G., Tarrier, N., Lewis, S. W., Moring, J., O'Brien, R., et al. (2001). Randomized controlled trial of motivational interviewing, cognitive behavior therapy, and family intervention for patients with comorbid schizophrenia and substance use disorders. *American Journal of Psychiatry, 158*(10), 1706–1713.

Baucom, D. H., Shoham, V., Mueser, K. T., Daiuto, A. D., & Stickle, T. R. (1998). Empirically supported couples and family interventions for marital distress and adult mental health problems. *Journal of Consulting and Clinical Psychology, 66,* 53–88.

Bergmark, T. (1994). Models of family support in Sweden: From mistreatment to understanding. *New Directions for Mental Health Services, 62,* 71–77.

Boise, L., Heagery, B., & Eskenazi, L. (1996). Facing chronic illness: The family support model and its benefits. *Patient Education and Counseling, 27,* 75–84.

Bond, G. R., Becker, D., Drake, R. E., Rapp, C., Meisler, N., Lehman, A., et al. (2001). Implementing supported employment as an evidenced-based practice. *Psychiatric Services, 52*(3), 313–322.

Burland, J. (1998). Family-to-Family: A trauma-and-recovery model of family education. *New Directions for Mental Health Services, 77,* 33–44.

Canive, J. M., Sanz Fuentenebro, J., Vazquez, C., Qualls, C., Fuentenebro, F., & Tuason, V. B. (1995). Family environment predictors of outcome in schizophrenic patients in Spain: A nine-month follow-up study. *Acta Psychiatrica Scandinavica, 92,* 371–377.

Cardin, V. A., McGill, C. W., & Falloon, I. (1985). An economic analysis: Costs, benefits, and effectiveness. In I. R. H. Falloon (Ed.), *Family management of schizophrenia: A study of clinical, social, family, and economic benefits* (pp. 115–123). Baltimore: Johns Hopkins University Press.

Carpinello, S. E., Rosenberg, L., Stone, J., Schwager, M., & Felton, C. J. (2002). New York State's campaign to implement evidence-based practices for people with serious mental disorders. *Psychiatric Services, 53,* 153–155.

Clarkin, J. F., Carpenter, D., Hull, D., Wilner, P., & Glick, I. (1998). Effects of psychoeducational intervention for married patients with bipolar disorder and their spouses. *Psychiatric Services, 49,* 531–533.

Clarkin, J. F., Glick, I. D., Haas, G. L., Spencer, J. H., Lewis, A. B., Peyser, J., et al. (1990). A randomized clinical trial of inpatient family intervention: V. Results for affective disorders. *Journal of Affective Disorders, 18,* 17–28.

Cochrane, J., Goering, P., & Rogers, J. (1997). The mental health of informal caregivers in Ontario: An epidemiological survey. *American Journal of Public Health, 87*(12), 2002–2008.

Corrigan, P., Steiner, L., McCracken, S., Blaser, B., & Barr, M. (2001). Strategies for disseminating evidence-based practices to staff who treat people with severe mental illness. *Psychiatric Services, 52*(12), 1598–1606.

Coursey, R., Curtis, L., & Marsh, D. (2000a). Competencies for direct service staff members who work with adults with severe mental illness in outpatient public mental health managed care systems. *Psychiatric Rehabilitation Journal, 23*(4), 370–377.

Coursey, R., Curtis, L., & Marsh, D. (2000b). Competencies for direct service staff members who work with adults with severe mental illness: Specific knowledge, attitudes, skills and bibliography. *Psychiatric Rehabilitation Journal, 23*(4), 378–392.

Cuijpers, P. (1999). The effects of family interventions on relatives' burden: A meta-analysis. *Journal of Mental Health, 8,* 275–285.

Detre, T., Sayer, J., Norton, A., & Lewis, H. (1961). An experimental approach to the treatment of the acutely ill psychiatric patient in the general hospital. *Connecticut Medicine, 25,* 613–619.

Dixon, L. B., Adams, C., & Lucksted, A. (2000). Update on family psychoeducation for schizophrenia. *Schizophrenia Bulletin, 26*(1), 5–20.

Dixon, L. B., Goldman, H., Hirad, A., Adams, C., & Lucksted, A. (1999). State policy and funding of services to families of adults with serious and persistent mental illness. *Psychiatric Services, 50*(4), 551–553.

Dixon, L. B., & Lehman, A. F. (1995). Family interventions for schizophrenia. *Schizophrenia Bulletin, 21*(4), 631–644.

Dixon, L. B., Lucksted, A., Stewart, B., Burland, J., Brown, C., Postrado, L., et al. (2004). Outcomes of the Peer-Taught 12-Week Family-to-Family Education Program for severe mental illness. *Acta Psychiatrica Scandinavica, 109,* 207–215.

Dixon, L. B., Lyles, A., Scott, J., Lehman, A., Postrado, L., Goldman, H., et al. (1999). Services to families of adults with schizophrenia: From treatment recommendations to dissemination. *Psychiatric Services, 50*(2), 233–238.

Dixon, L. B., McFarlane, W. R., Hornby, H., & McNary, S. (1999). Dissemination of family psychoeducation: The importance of consensus building. *Schizophrenia Research, 36,* 339.

Dixon, L. B., McFarlane, W. R., Lefley, H., Lucksted, A., Cohen, M., Falloon, I., et al. (2001). Evidence-based practices for services to families of people with psychiatric disabilities. *Psychiatric Services, 52*(7), 903–910.

Dixon, L. B., Stewart, B., Burland, J., Delahanty, J., Lucksted, A., & Hoffman, M. (2001). Pilot study of the effectiveness of the Family-to-Family Education Program. *Psychiatric Services, 52*(7), 965–967.

Drake, R. E., Goldman, H. H., Leff, H. S., Lehman, A. F., Dixon, L. B., Mueser, K. T., et al. (2001). Implementing evidence-based practices in routine mental health service settings. *Psychiatric Services, 52,* 179–182.

Dyck, D. G., Short, R. A., Hendryx, M. S., Norell, D., Myers, M., Patterson, T., et al. (2000). Management of negative symptoms among patients with schizophrenia attending multiple-family groups. *Psychiatric Services, 51*(4), 513–519.

Emanuels-Zuurveen, L. (1997). Spouse-aided therapy with depressed patients. *Behavior Modification, 21*(1), 62–77.

Emanuels-Zuurveen, L., & Emmelkamp, P. (1996). Individual behavioural-cognitive therapy v. marital therapy for depression in maritally distressed couples. *British Journal of Psychiatry, 169*(2), 181–188.

Falloon, I., Boyd, J., & McGill, C. (1984). *Family care of schizophrenia.* New York: Guilford Press.

Falloon, I., Boyd, J., McGill, C., Williamson, M., Razani, J., Moss, H., et al. (1985). Family management in the prevention of morbidity of schizophrenia. *Archives of General Psychiatry, 42,* 887–896.

Falloon, I., Held, T., Coverdale, J., Roncone, R., & Laidlaw, T. (1999). Psychosocial interventions for schizophrenia: A review of long-term benefits of international studies. *Psychiatric Rehabilitation Skills, 3,* 268–290.

Falloon, I., & Pederson, J. (1985). Family management in the prevention of morbidity of schizophrenia: The adjustment of the family unit. *British Journal of Psychiatry, 147,* 156–163.

Frances, A. D. J., & Kahn, D. A. (1996). Expert consensus guideline series: Treatment of Schizophrenia. *Journal of Clinical Psychiatry, 57*(50, Suppl. 12B), 5–58.

Frank, E., Kupfer, D. J., Perel, J. M., Cornes, C., Jarrett, D. B., Mallinger, A. G., et al. (1990). Three-year outcomes for maintenance therapies in recurrent depression. *Archives of General Psychiatry, 47,* 1093–1099.

Fristad, M. A., Gavazzi, S. M., & Soldano, K. W. (1998). Multi-family psychoeducation groups for childhood mood disorders: A program description and preliminary efficacy data. *Contemporary Family Therapy, 20*(3), 385–402.

Gallagher, S., & Mechanic, D. (1996). Living with the mentally ill: Effects on the health and functioning of other household members. *Social Science and Medicine, 42*(12), 1691–1701.

Geist, R., Heinmaa, M., Stephens, D., Davis, R., & Katzman, D. K. (2000). Comparison of family therapy and family group psychoeducation in adolescents with anorexia nervosa. *Canadian Journal of Psychiatry, 45*(2), 173–178.

Glick, I., Spencer, J., Clarkin, J., Haas, G., Lewis, A., Peyser, J., et al. (1990). A randomized trial of inpatient family intervention: IV. Follow-up results for subjects with schizophrenia. *Schizophrenia Research, 3,* 187–200.

Goldstein, M. J., & Miklowitz, D. J. (1995). The effectiveness of psychoeducational family therapy in the treatment of schizophrenic disorders. In W. M. Pinsof & L. C. Wynne (Eds.), *Family therapy effectiveness: Current research and theory* (pp. 361–376). Washington, DC: American Association for Marriage and Family Therapy.

Goldstein, M. J., Rodnick, E., Evans, J., May, P., & Steinberg, M. (1978). Drug and family therapy in the aftercare treatment of acute schizophrenia. *Archives of General Psychiatry, 35,* 1169–1177.

Gonzalez, S., Steinglass, P., & Reiss, D. (1989). Putting the illness in its place: Discussion groups for families with chronic medical illnesses. *Family Process, 28*(1), 69–87.

Greenberg, J., Greenley, J., & Kim, H. (1995). The provision of mental health services to families of persons with serious mental illness. *Research in Community and Mental Health, 8,* 181–204.

Guarnaccia, P., & Parra, P. (1996). Ethnicity, social status, and families experiences of caring for a mentally ill family members. *Community Mental Health Journal, 32,* 243–260.

Gunderson, J., Berkowitz, C., & Ruizsancho, A. (1997). Families of borderline patients: A psychoeducational approach. *Bulletin of the Menninger Clinic, 61*(4), 446–457.

Hatfield, A. B. (1987). The National Alliance for the Mentally Ill: The meaning of a movement. *International Journal of Mental Health, 15,* 79–93.

Hogarty, G. E., Anderson, C. M., Reiss, D. J., Kornblith, S. J., Greenwald, D. P., Ulrich, R. F., et al. (1991). Family psychoeducation, social skills training, and maintenance chemotherapy in the aftercare treatment of schizophrenia: II. Two-year effects of a controlled study on relapse and adjustment. *Archives of General Psychiatry, 48*(4), 340–347.

Hogarty, G. E., Greenwald, D., Ulrich, R. F., Kornblith, S. J., DiBarry, A. L., Cooley, S., et al. (1997). Three-year trials of personal therapy among schizophrenic patients living with or independent of family: II. Effects on adjustment of patients. *American Journal of Psychiatry, 154*(11), 1514–1524.

Hogarty, G. E., Kornblith, S. J., Greenwald, D., DiBarry, A. L., Cooley, S., Ulrich, R. F., et al. (1997). Three-year trials of personal therapy among schizophrenic patients living with or independent of family: I. Description of study and effects on relapse rates. *American Journal of Psychiatry, 154*(11), 1504–1513.

Hogarty, G. E., & Ulrich, R. (1977). Temporal effects of drug and placebo in delaying relapse in schizophrenic outpatients. *Archives of General Psychiatry, 34,* 297–301.

Hooley, J. M., Rosen, L. R., & Richters, J. E. (1995). Expressed emotion: Toward clarification of a critical construct. In G. A. Miller (Ed.), *The behavioral high-risk paradigm in psychopathology* (pp. 88–120). New York: Springer Verlag.

Jordan, C., Lewellen, A., & Vandiver, V. (1995). Psychoeducation for minority families: A social-work perspective. *International Journal of Mental Health, 23*(4), 27–43.

Kottgen, C., Sonnichsen, I., Mollenhauer, K., & Jurth, R. (1984). Group therapy with families of schizophrenic patients: Results of the Hamburg Camberwell Family Interview Study III. *International Journal of Family Psychiatry, 5,* 83–94.

Lam, D. H. (1991). Psychosocial family intervention in schizophrenia: A review of empirical studies. *Psychological Medicine, 21*(2), 423–441.

Lam, D. H., Kuipers, L., & Leff, J. P. (1993). Family work with patients suffering from schizophrenia: The impact of training on psychiatric nurses' attitude and knowledge. *Journal of Advanced Nursing, 18,* 233–237.

Laqueur, H. P., LaBurt, H. A., & Morong, E. (1964). Multiple family therapy: Further developments. *International Journal of Social Psychiatry, 10,* 69–80.

Leff, J. (1994). Working with the families of schizophrenic patients. *British Journal of Psychiatry, 23*(Suppl.), 71–76.

Leff, J., Kuipers, L., Berkowitz, R., Eberlein-Vries, R., & Sturgeon, D. (1982). A controlled trial of social intervention in the families of schizophrenic patients. *British Journal of Psychiatry, 141,* 121–134.

Leff, J., Kuipers, L., Berkowitz, R., & Sturgeon, D. (1985). A controlled trial of social intervention in the families of schizophrenic patients: Two year follow-up. *British Journal of Psychiatry, 146,* 594–600.

Leff, J., Vearnals, S., Brewin, C., Wolff, G., Alexander, B., Asen, E., et al. (2000). The London Depression Intervention Trial: Randomised controlled trial of antidepressants v. couple therapy in the treatment and maintenance of people with depression living with a partner: Clinical outcome and costs. *British Journal of Psychiatry, 177*(2), 95–100.

Lefley, H. (2001). Impact of mental illness on families and carers. In G. Thornicroft & G. Szmukler (Eds.), *Textbook of community psychiatry.* London: Oxford University Press.

Lehman, A. F., & Steinwachs, D. M. (1998). Patterns of usual care for schizophrenia: Initial results from the schizophrenia patient outcomes research team (PORT) client survey. *Schizophrenia Bulletin, 24*(1), 11–32.

Lehman, A. F., Steinwachs, D. M., Buchanan, R., Carpenter, W. T., Dixon, L. B., Fahey, M., et al. (1998). Translating research into practice: The Schizophrenia Patient Outcomes Research Team (PORT) treatment recommendations. *Schizophrenia Bulletin, 24*(1), 1–10.

Linszen, D., Dingemans, P., Van der Does, J. W., Nugter, A., Scholte, P., Lenior, R., et al. (1996). Treatment, expressed emotion and relapse in recent onset schizophrenic disorders. *Psychological Medicine, 26,* 333–342.

Mannion, E. (2000). *Training manual for the implementation of family education in the adult mental health system of Berks County, PA.* Philadelphia: University of Pennsylvania Center for Mental Health Policy and Services Research.

Marlatt, G. A. (1985). *Relapse prevention.* New York: Guilford Press.

Marsh, D. (1992). *Families and mental illness: New directions in professional practice.* New York: Praeger.

Marsh, D. (2001). *A family-focused approach to serious mental illness: Empirically supported interventions.* Sarasota, FL: Professional Resource Press.

Marsh, D., & Johnson, D. (1997). The family experience of mental illness: Implications for intervention. *Professional Psychology: Research and Practice, 28*(7), 229–237.

McFarlane, W. R. (1994). Multiple-family groups and psychoeducation in the treatment of schizophrenia. *New Directions for Mental Health Services, 62,* 13–22.

McFarlane, W. R. (2002). *Multifamily groups in the treatment of severe psychiatric disorders.* New York: Guilford Press.

McFarlane, W. R., Dixon, L. B., Lukens, E. P., & Lucksted, A. (2003). Family psychoeducation and schizophrenia: A review of the literature. *Journal of Marital and Family Therapy, 29,* 223–245.

McFarlane, W. R., Dunne, E., Lukens, E. P., Newmark, M., McLaughlin Toran, J., Deakins, S. M., et al. (1993). From research to clinical practice: Dissemination of New York State's family psychoeducation project. *Hospital and Community Psychiatry, 44*(3), 265–270.

McFarlane, W. R., Dushay, R. A., Deakins, S. M., Stastny, P., Lukens, E. P., Toran, J., et al. (2000). Employment outcomes in Family-Aided Assertive Community Treatment. *American Journal of Orthopsychiatry, 70*(2), 203–214.

McFarlane, W. R., Dushay, R. A., Stastny, P., Deakins, S. M., & Link, B. (1996). A comparison of two levels of family-aided assertive community treatment. *Psychiatric Services, 47*(7), 744–750.

McFarlane, W. R., Link, B., Dushay, R., Marchal, J., & Crilly, J. (1995). Psychoeducational multiple family groups: Four-year relapse outcome in schizophrenia. *Family Process, 34*(2), 127–144.

McFarlane, W. R., & Lukens, E. P. (1998). Insight, families, and education: An exploration of the role of attribution in clinical outcome. In X. F. Amador & A. S. David (Eds.), *Insight and psychosis* (pp. 317–331). New York: Oxford University Press.

McFarlane, W. R., Lukens, E. P., Link, B., Dushay, R., Deakins, S. A., Newmark, M., et al. (1995). Multiple-family groups and psychoeducation in the treatment of schizophrenia. *Archives of General Psychiatry, 52*(8), 679–687.

McFarlane, W. R., McNary, S., Dixon, L. B., Hornby, H., & Cimett, E. (2001). Predictors of dissemination of family psychoeducation in community mental health centers in Maine and IL. *Psychiatric Services, 52*(7), 935–942.

Miklowitz, D. J., George, E. L., Richards, J. A., Simoneau, T. L., & Suddath, R. L. (2003). A randomized study of family-focused psychoeducation and pharmacotherapy in the outpatient management of bipolar disorder. *Archives of General Psychiatry, 60,* 904–912.

Miklowitz, D. J., & Goldstein, M. J. (1997). *Bipolar disorder: A family-focused treatment approach.* New York: Guilford Press.

Miklowitz, D. J., Simoneau, T. L., George, E. L., Richards, J. A., Kalbag, A., Sachs-Ericsson, N., et al. (2000). Family-focused treatment of bipolar disorder: 1-year effects of a psychoeducational program in conjunction with pharmacotherapy. *Biological Psychiatry, 48,* 582–592.

Moltz, D. (1993). Bipolar disorder and the family: An integrative model. *Family Process, 32,* 409–423.

Montero, I., Asencio, A., Hernandez, I., Masanet, M. S. J., Lacruz, M., Bellver, F., et al. (2001). Two strategies for family intervention in schizophrenia: A randomized trial in a Mediterranean environment. *Schizophrenia Bulletin, 27*(4), 661–670.

Mueser, K., & Fox, L. (2000). Family-friendly services: A modest proposal. *Psychiatric Services, 51,* 1452.

Mueser, K., & Glynn, S. (1999). *Behavioral family therapy for psychiatric disorders.* Oakland: New Harbinger.

Mueser, K., Webb, C., Pfeiffer, M., Gladis, M., & Levinson, D. (1996). Family burden of schizophrenia and bipolar disorder: Perceptions of relatives and professionals. *Psychiatric Services, 47*(5), 507–511.

Office of Mental Health Quarterly. (2002, December). OMH and URMC announce new Family Institute for Education, Practice and Research. *OMH Quarterly, 8*(3), 12.

Parikh, S., Kusumakar, V., Haslam, D., Matte, R., Sharma, V., & Yatham, L. (1997). Psychosocial interventions as an adjunct to pharmacotherapy in bipolar disorder. *Canadian Journal of Psychiatry, 42,* 74S–78S.

Penn, D. L., & Mueser, K. T. (1996). Research update on the psychosocial treatment of schizophrenia. *American Journal of Psychiatry, 153,* 607–617.

Pickett-Schenk, S., Cook, J., & Laris, A. (2000). Journey of Hope program outcomes. *Community Mental Health Journal, 36,* 413–424.

Pitschel-Walz, G., Leucht, S., Bauml, J., Kissling, W., & Engel, R. R. (2001). The effect of family interventions in relapse and rehospitalization in schizophrenia: A meta-analysis. *Schizophrenia Bulletin, 27*(1), 73–92.

Randolph, E. T., Eth, S., Glynn, S. M., Paz, G. G., Leong, G. B., Shaner, A. L., et al. (1994). Behavioural family management in schizophrenia outcome of a clinic-based intervention. *British Journal of Psychiatry, 164*(4), 501–506.

Rea, M. M., Tompson, M., Miklowitz, D. J., Goldstein, M. J., Hwang, S., & Mintz, J. (2003). Family focused treatment vs. individual treatment for bipolar disorder: Results of a randomized clinical trial. *Journal of Consulting and Clinical Psychology, 71,* 482–492.

Rund, B. R., Moe, L., Sollien, T., Fjell, A., Borchgrevink, T., Hallert, M., et al. (1994). The Psychosis Project: Outcome and cost-effectiveness of a psychoeducational treatment programme for schizophrenic adolescents. *Acta Paediatrica Scandinavica, 89*(3), 211–218.

Schene, A. H., van Wijngaarden, B., & Koeter, M. W. J. (1998). Family caregiving in schizophrenia: Domains and distress. *Schizophrenia Bulletin, 24,* 609–618.

Schooler, N. R., Keith, S. J., Severe, J. B., Matthews, S. M., Bellack, A. S., Glick, I. D., et al. (1997). Relapse and rehospitalization during maintenance treatment of schizophrenia: The effects of dose reduction and family treatment. *Archives of General Psychiatry, 54*(5), 453–463.

Shi, Y., Zhao, B., Xu, D., & Sen, J. (2000). A comparative study of life quality in schizophrenic patients after family intervention. *Chinese Mental Health Journal, 14*(2), 135–137.

Simoneau, T. L., Miklowitz, D. J., Richards, J. A., Saleem, R., & George, L. (1999). Bipolar disorder and family communication: The effects of a psychoeducational treatment program. *Journal of Abnormal Psychology, 108,* 588–597.

Solomon, P. (1996). Moving from psychoeducation to family education for families of adults with serious mental illness. *Psychiatric Services, 47,* 1364–1370.

Solomon, P. (2000). Interventions for families of individuals with schizophrenia: Maximizing outcomes for their relatives. *Disease Management and Health Outcomes, 8*(4), 211–221.

Solomon, P., Draine, J., & Mannion, E. (1996). The impact of individualized consultation and group workshop family education interventions in ill relative outcomes. *Journal of Nervous and Mental Diseases, 184*(4), 252–255.

Solomon, P., Draine, J., Mannion, E., & Meisel, M. (1996). Impact of brief family psychoeducation on self-efficacy. *Schizophrenia Bulletin, 22*(1), 41–50.

Solomon, P., Draine, J., Mannion, E., & Meisel, M. (1997). Effectiveness of two models of brief family education: Retention of gains by family members with serious mental illness. *American Journal of Orthopsychiatry, 67*(2), 177–186.

Steinglass, P. (1998). Multiple family discussion groups for patients with chronic medical illness. *Families, Systems and Health, 16,* 55–70.

Substance Abuse and Mental Health Services Administration. (2002). *Family Psychoeducation Implementation Resource Kit,* Evaluation Edition, Draft Version. Washington, DC: Author.

Tarrier, N. (1991). Some aspects of family interventions in schizophrenia. I: Adherence to intervention programmes. *British Journal of Psychiatry, 159,* 475–480.

Tarrier, N., Barrowclough, C., Vaughn, C., Bamrah, J., Porceddu, K., Watts, S., et al. (1989). The community management of schizophrenia: A two-year follow-up of a behavioral intervention with families. *British Journal of Psychiatry, 154,* 625–628.

Tarrier, N., Lowson, K., & Barrowclough, C. (1991). Some aspects of family interventions in schizophrenia: II. Financial considerations. *British Journal of Psychiatry, 159,* 481–484.

Telles, C., Karno, M., Mintz, J., Paz, G., Arias, M., Tucker, D., et al. (1995). Immigrant families coping with schizophrenia: Behavioral family intervention v. case management with a low-income Spanish-speaking population. *British Journal of Psychiatry, 167,* 473–479.

Tompson, M. C., Rea, M. M., Goldstein, M. J., Miklowitz, D. J., & Weisman, A. G. (2000). Difficulty in implementing a family intervention for bipolar disorder: The predictive role of patient and family attributes. *Family Process, 39*(1), 105–120.

Van Noppen, B. (1999). Multi-family behavioral treatment (MFBT) for OCD. *Crisis Intervention and Time-Limited Treatment, 5,* 3–24.

World Schizophrenia Fellowship. (1998). *Families as partners in care: A document developed to launch a strategy for the implementation of programs of family education, training, and support.* Toronto, Ontario, Canada: Author.

Wright, P., Takei, N., Rifkin, L., & Murray, R. M. (1995). Maternal influenza, obstetric complications, and schizophrenia. *American Journal of Psychiatry, 152*(12), 1714–1720.

Xiang, M., Ran, M., & Li, S. (1994). A controlled evaluation of psychoeducational family intervention in a rural Chinese community. *British Journal of Psychiatry, 165*(4), 544–548.

Xiong, W., Phillips, M. R., Hu, X., Wang, R., Dai, Q., Kleinman, J., et al. (1994). Family-based intervention for schizophrenic patients in China: A randomised controlled trial. *British Journal of Psychiatry, 165*(2), 239–247.

Zhang, M., Wang, M., Li, J., & Phillips, M. R. (1994, August). Randomised-control trial of family intervention for 78 first-episode male schizophrenic patients: An 18-month study in Suzhou, Jiangsu. *British Journal of Psychiatry, 24*(Suppl.), 96–102.

Zhao, B., Shen, J., Shi, Y., Xu, D., Wang, Z., & Ji, J. (2000). Family intervention of chronic schizophrenics in community: A follow-up study. *Chinese Mental Health Journal, 14*(4), 283–285.

CHAPTER 5

Evidence-Based Psychopharmacotherapy: Medication Guidelines and Algorithms

Sy Atezaz Saeed

Empirically informed clinical practice guidelines have been around for over 4 decades. Since their initial introduction in the management of emergency medical conditions in the1960s, there has been a steady growth in the number, diversity, and popularity of these guidelines. However, they are relatively new to the area of mental health. The growth in the number of these guidelines for psychiatry has paralleled the substantial growth in the number of medication alternatives available for the treatment of people with mental illness.

At the most basic level, evidence-based practice is the integration of best research with clinical expertise, patient values, and available resources (Institute of Medicine, 2001). More specific definitions have also included a focus on lifelong, self-directed learning in which caring for patients creates the need for clinically important information, a bottom-up approach that integrates the best external evidence with individual clinical expertise and patient choice (Etminan, Wright, & Carleton, 1998; Wolf, 2000).

Clinical practice guidelines are designed to help decision making about appropriate healthcare for specific indications. They are commonly defined as "systematically developed statements to assist practitioner and patient decisions about appropriate health care for specific clinical circumstances" (Committee to Advise the Public Health Service on Clinical Practice Guidelines, Institute of Medicine, 1990). The Institute of Medicine task force has also described characteristics of a "good" guideline (Institute of Medicine, 1990). The best guidelines tend to have the following characteristics:

1. They are developed from a systematic examination and appraisal of evidence from well-conducted studies.

2. Great care is taken to maximize their validity.

3. They have reliability and reproducibility.

4. They are supported by an expert consensus.

5. They have multidisciplinary input.

6. They are supported by appropriate clinical expertise.

7. They allow for patients' participation in treatment selection process.

8. The recommendations they make are specific and unambiguous.

9. They are flexible.

10. They have clarity and good documentation.

11. They are regularly reviewed for revisions/updates as the new evidence evolves.

RATIONALE FOR USE OF EVIDENCE-BASED PSYCHOPHARMACOTHERAPY

It is obvious that clinicians need valid information about diagnosis, treatment, prognosis, and prevention as they work with patients. They need this information on a daily basis. The knowledge base that informs clinical decision has been growing with a very rapid pace making it a difficult challenge for the busy clinician to keep up with this growing and high volume of research findings. Practice guidelines facilitate dissemination of research findings that are of direct clinical relevance. Compared to the guidelines, the sources of information traditionally relied on by clinicians are typically inadequate. For example, textbooks may be outdated, experts may be wrong, didactic continuing medical education is known to be ineffective, and medical journals may be too overwhelming in their volume and too difficult to put them to practical clinical use.

Evidence-based guidelines not only help busy clinicians stay current, they also have an immediate goal of impacting practice behavior to promote the use of therapeutic interventions known to be effective. Use of practice guidelines can also serve as valuable educational tools (Berg, Atkins, & Tierney, 1997). Implementation of guidelines can also enhance treatment outcomes and facilitate cost management (Audet, Greenfield, & Field, 1999).

At the systems level, treatment guidelines can facilitate a systematic approach to medication management of chronic illnesses across treatment venues and prescribers (Mellman et al., 2001). They are also likely to reduce inappropriate variation in clinical practice.

Another system level issue has to do with the higher costs associated with newer psychotropic medications. This has been a growing concern for major stakeholders including mental health administrators, policymakers, consumers, and the public. Use of guidelines may reduce costs by eliminating ineffective practices. It is also likely that evidence-based treatment may result in better and more efficient outcomes that may in turn result in lower costs to the society. It is also likely that guidelines produce greater value per healthcare dollar. All this being said, how the implementation of evidence-based guidelines and algorithms impact treatment costs and what the payoff is to the society in terms of impact of the illness are the questions that are currently unanswered.

Polypharmacy is another system level issue that relates to cost. With a growing list of newer medications with fewer side effects, there has been an increasing level of comfort on the part of providers to prescribe medication combinations. This increase in potential medication combinations underscores the significance of defining and implementing evidence-based psychopharmacologic practice that is likely to minimize undesirable treatment variation, while at the same time raising treatment outcome goals by providing treatment combinations that are supported by empirical evidence.

It has also been argued that using treatment algorithms can help patients achieve remission in treatment of major depressive disorder (Trivedi, 2003). Many patients treated with antidepressants fail to reach full remission. Patients who experience incomplete remission from antidepressant treatment are candidates for a sequential treatment approach involving treatment options such as switching, augmentation, or combination of antidepressants. The goal of treatment in any algorithm should always be sustained remission—complete recovery—and not just the alleviation of symptoms or adequate response.

DIFFERENTIATING EVIDENCE-BASED PRACTICE OF PSYCHOPHARMACOTHERAPY FROM TRADITIONAL PRACTICE

Pharmacotherapy has always used research evidence to inform key decisions. The fundamental difference between evidence-based practice of psychopharmacotherapy and traditional practice is not so much whether evidence itself is used in relation to a particular question, rather evidence-based psychopharmacotherapy:

1. Gives healthcare decisions a structured process to help professionals and patients alike choose the best available healthcare interventions for the outcomes they are seeking.
2. Incorporates patients' preferences.
3. Consistently uses structured measures to assess outcome.

Discussions of evidence-based practices in mental health settings typically emphasize underutilization of effective practices. Pharmacologic treatment does not appear to be generally underused in the usual treatment of people with mental illness. The difference for guidelines and algorithms is mostly on their emphasis on using medication treatments that are evidence based and, whenever possible, on using them in sequences supported by research (Mellman et al., 2001).

AN OVERVIEW OF CLINICAL DECISION-MAKING PARAMETERS

There are a variety of clinical decision-making parameters that relate to the practice of psychopharmacotherapy. The main purpose of these parameters has been to facilitate appropriate healthcare decision making by synthesizing the treatment literature into a usable form. The following sections describe these parameters.

Evidence-Based Clinical Practice Guidelines

Evidence-based clinical practice guidelines are based on comprehensive literature reviews. Such reviews evaluate various aspects of treatment options, including areas such as the efficacy, spectrum of action, safety, and tolerability. When developed by professional organizations, these practice guidelines also require organizational approval. The typical process for developing such guidelines includes:

1. Working group(s) comprised of content experts
2. Comprehensive literature reviews
3. Secondary expert review
4. Revision
5. Organizational approval

Practice guidelines addressing psychopharmacotherapy for various mental disorders are now available. Several organizations have developed such guidelines for various disorders. For example, the American Psychiatric Association has developed practice guidelines for patients with major depressive disorder (American Psychiatric Association [APA], 2000), bipolar disorder (APA, 1994), and panic disorder (APA, 1998). Both American and Canadian Psychiatric Associations have developed guidelines for treatment of patients with schizophrenia (APA, 1997; Canadian Psychiatric Association, 1998). The International Society for Traumatic Stress Studies has developed practice guidelines for the treatment of posttraumatic stress disorder (Foa, Keane, & Friedman, 2000). The American Academy of Child and Adolescent Psychiatry has developed comprehensive practice guidelines for the treatment of disorders presenting in children and adolescents (The American Academy of Child and Adolescent Psychiatry, 1994). Tables 5.1 and 5.2 identify some of these guidelines along with the year of publication and the developer for child, adolescent, and adult populations.

Practice guidelines have proliferated in mental health and addiction services with more than 40 organizations having developed guidelines in the field (Stuart, Rush, & Morris, 2002). The National Guideline Clearinghouse (NGC), available at http://www

Table 5.1   A Selective List of Practice Guidelines: Adults

Practice Guideline	Sponsor	Year
Practice guideline for the treatment of patients with HIV/AIDS.	American Psychiatric Association	2000
Practice parameter for the use of stimulant medications in the treatment of children, adolescents, and adults.	American Academy of Child and Adolescent Psychiatry	2001
VHA/DOD clinical practice guideline for the management of substance use disorders.	Veterans Health Administration/ Department of Veterans Affairs/ Department of Defense	2001
Practice guideline for the treatment of patients with panic disorder.	American Psychiatric Association	1998
Treatment for stimulant use disorders.	Substance Abuse and Mental Health Services Administration (U.S.)	1999
Major depression, panic disorder and generalized anxiety disorder in adults in primary care.	Institute for Clinical Systems Improvement	1996 (revised 2002)
Practice guideline for the treatment of patients with borderline personality disorder.	American Psychiatric Association	2001
Practice guideline for the treatment of patients with major depressive disorder.	American Psychiatric Association	1993 (revised 2000)

Table 5.1   *Continued*

Practice Guideline	Sponsor	Year
Practice guideline for the treatment of patients with bipolar disorder (revision).	American Psychiatric Association	1994 (revised 2002)
Diagnosis and treatment of attention deficit/hyperactivity disorder.	National Institutes of Health (NIH) Consensus Development Panel on Diagnosis and Treatment of Attention Deficit/Hyperactivity Disorder (ADHD)	1998
The role of phenytoin in the management of alcohol withdrawal syndrome.	American Society of Addiction Medicine	1994 (revised 1998)
Practice guideline for the treatment of patients with delirium.	American Psychiatric Association	1999
Substance abuse treatment for persons with HIV/AIDS.	Substance Abuse and Mental Health Services Administration (U.S.)	2000
VHA/DOD clinical practice guideline for the management of major depressive disorder in adults.	Veterans Health Administration/ Department of Veterans Affairs	1997 (updated 2000)
Guidelines for Alzheimer's disease management.	Alzheimer's Association of Los Angeles, Riverside and San Bernardino Counties/California Workgroup on Guidelines for Alzheimer's Disease Management	1999 (revised 2002)
Substance use disorder treatment for people with physical and cognitive disabilities.	Substance Abuse and Mental Health Services Administration	(U.S.) 1998
Major depression in adults for mental health care providers.	Institute for Clinical Systems Improvement	1996 (revised 2002)
Pharmacological management of alcohol withdrawal: a meta-analysis and evidence-based practice guideline.	American Society of Addiction Medicine	1997
Naltrexone and alcoholism treatment.	Substance Abuse and Mental Health Services Administration (U.S.)	1998
Brief interventions and brief therapies for substance abuse.	Substance Abuse and Mental Health Services Administration (U.S.)	1999
Substance abuse among older adults.	Substance Abuse and Mental Health Services Administration (U.S.)	1998
Practice guideline for psychiatric evaluation of adults.	American Psychiatric Association	1995 (revised 2000)
Postnatal depression and puerperal psychosis. A national clinical guideline.	Scottish Intercollegiate Guidelines Network	2002
Evidence-based protocol. Elderly suicide: secondary prevention.	University of Iowa Gerontological Nursing Interventions Research Center, Research Dissemination Core	2002
Guidelines for smoking cessation.	New Zealand Guidelines Group	1999 (revised 2002)

Note: Brief summaries, major recommendations, bibliographic sources, and full-text availability information for these guidelines can be obtained at the National Guideline Clearinghouse. Retrieved May 24, 2004, from www.guideline.gov.

.guideline.gov, provides an accessible mechanism for obtaining objective, detailed information on clinical practice guidelines. This clearinghouse is a comprehensive database of evidence-based clinical practice guidelines and related documents produced by the Agency for Healthcare Research and Quality (AHRQ) in partnership with the American Medical Association (AMA) and the American Association of Health Plans (AAHP). The guidelines available at the NGC web site are not limited to pharmacological treatment. Neither are they limited to the field of mental health. The key components of NGC include:

1. Structured abstracts (summaries) about the guideline and its development
2. A utility for comparing attributes of two or more guidelines in a side-by-side comparison
3. Syntheses of guidelines covering similar topics, highlighting areas of similarity and difference
4. Links to full-text guidelines, where available, and/or ordering information for print copies
5. An electronic forum, NGC-L, for exchanging information on clinical practice guidelines, their development, implementation, and use
6. Annotated bibliographies on guideline development methodology, implementation, and use

Expert Consensus Guidelines

Expert Consensus Guidelines do not directly rely on empirical data or evaluation of the level or strength of evidence from the review of literature. Instead the recommendations contained in these guidelines are based on the results of surveying a relatively broad range of experts. Ideally, all of the recommendations within a treatment guideline would be supported by valid research literature comprised of replicated studies that are generalizable to the most important questions that arise in clinical practice. Since this is currently not achievable, the Expert Consensus Guidelines are meant to bridge the gap that currently lies between research and clinical practice. The stated rationale for this approach is that research literature does not always adequately address critical points for treatment decisions (Frances, Kahn, Carpenter, Frances, & Docherty, 1998). Generalizing from research to clinical practices is difficult because clinical trials emphasize acute treatment of precisely defined and homogeneous samples typically free from comorbid conditions. Research has also typically not addressed questions such as what to do when the first or second line treatments fail. Expert consensus is helpful in providing guidance in such areas.

Expert consensus guidelines for the treatment of several psychiatric disorders have been published and are also available on the Internet (www.psychguides.com). The documents present not only the guidelines synthesized from the survey results, but they also contain the statistical results of questionnaire-based surveys addressing the appropriateness of interventions for different stages of treatment. The available Expert Consensus Guidelines for psychiatric disorders, as listed on their web site (http://www .psychguides.com/index.htm Accessed July 11, 2003), are listed in Table 5.3.

Table 5.2   A Selective List of Practice Guidelines: Children and Adolescents

Practice Guideline	Sponsor	Year
Practice parameter for the use of stimulant medications in the treatment of children, adolescents, and adults.	American Academy of Child and Adolescent Psychiatry	2001
Practice parameters for the assessment and treatment of children, adolescents, and adults with mental retardation and comorbid mental disorders.	American Academy of Child and Adolescent Psychiatry	1999
The pediatrician's role in the diagnosis and management of autistic spectrum disorder in children.	American Academy of Pediatrics	2001
Practice parameters for the assessment and treatment of children and adolescents with depressive disorders.	American Academy of Child and Adolescent Psychiatry	1998
Practice parameters for the assessment and treatment of children, adolescents, and adults with autism and other pervasive developmental disorders.	American Academy of Child and Adolescent Psychiatry	1999
Treatment of adolescents with substance use disorders.	Substance Abuse and Mental Health Services Administration (U.S.)	1993 (updated 1999)
Diagnosis and treatment of attention deficit hyperactivity disorder.	National Institutes of Health (NIH) Consensus Development Panel on Diagnosis and Treatment of Attention Deficit/Hyperactivity Disorder (ADHD)	1998
Clinical practice guideline: treatment of the school-aged child with attention deficit/hyperactivity disorder.	American Academy of Pediatrics	2001
Practice parameters for the assessment and treatment of children and adolescents with posttraumatic stress disorder.	American Academy of Child and Adolescent Psychiatry	1998
Clinical practice guideline: diagnosis and evaluation of the child with attention deficit/hyperactivity disorder.	American Academy of Pediatrics	2000
Guidelines for primary care providers. Detection and management of young people at risk of suicide.	Royal New Zealand College of General Practitioners	1999
Practice parameter for the assessment and treatment of children and adolescents with suicidal behavior.	American Academy of Child and Adolescent Psychiatry	2000
Practice parameter for the prevention and management of aggressive behavior in child and adolescent psychiatric institutions with special reference to seclusion and restraint.	American Academy of Child and Adolescent Psychiatry	2001

Note: Brief summaries, major recommendations, bibliographic sources, and full-text availability information for these guidelines can be obtained at the National Guideline Clearing house. Retrieved May 24, 2004, from www.guideline.gov.

Table 5.3   Expert Consensus Guidelines

Practice Guideline	Reference
Pharmacotherapy of depressive disorders in older patients	Alexopoulos, G. S., Katz, I. R., Reynolds, C. F., Carpenter, D., & Docherty, J. P. (2001). *The expert consensus guideline series: Pharmacotherapy of depressive disorders in older patients* [A Postgraduate Medicine Special Report]. New York: McGraw-Hill.
Treatment of behavioral emergencies	Allen, M. H., Currier, G. W., Hughes, D. H., Reyes-Harde, M., & Docherty, J. P. (2001). *The expert consensus guideline series: Treatment of behavioral emergencies* [A Postgraduate Medicine Special Report]. New York: McGraw-Hill.
Treatment of depression in women	Altshuler, L. L., Cohen, L. S., Moline, M. L., Kahn, D. A., Carpenter, D., & Docherty, J. P. (2001). *The expert consensus guideline series: Treatment of depression in women* [A Postgraduate Medicine Special Report]. New York: McGraw-Hill.
Attention deficit/hyperactivity disorder	Conners, C. K., March, J. S., Frances, A., Wells, K. C., & Ross, R. (2001). The Expert Consensus Guideline Series: Treatment of attention deficit/hyperactivity disorder. *Journal of Attention Disorders, 4*(Suppl. 1).
Psychiatric and behavioral problems in mental retardation	Rush, A. J., & Frances, A. (2000). The expert consensus guideline series: Treatment of psychiatric and behavioral problems in mental retardation. *American Journal on Mental Retardation, 105,* 159–228.
Bipolar disorder	Sachs, G. S., Printz, D. J., Kahn, D. A., Carpenter, D., & Docherty, J. P. (2000). *The expert consensus guideline series: Medication treatment of bipolar disorder* [A Postgraduate Medicine Special Report]. New York: McGraw-Hill.
Posttraumatic stress disorder	Foa, E. B., Davidson, J. R. T., & Frances, A. (Eds.). (1999). The expert consensus guideline series: Treatment of posttraumatic stress disorder. *Journal of Clinical Psychiatry, 60*(Suppl. 16, 1–79).
Schizophrenia	McEvoy, J. P., Scheifler, P. L., & Frances, A. (Eds.). (1999). The expert consensus guideline series: Treatment of schizophrenia 1999. *Journal of Clinical Psychiatry, 60*(Suppl. 11, 1–83).
Agitation in older persons with dementia	Alexopoulos, G. S., Silver, J. M., Kahn, D. A., Frances, A., & Carpenter, D. (Eds.). (1998). *The expert consensus guideline series: Agitation in older persons with dementia* [A Postgraduate Medicine Special Report]. New York: McGraw-Hill.
Obsessive-compulsive disorder	March, J. S., Frances, A., Kahn, D. A., & Carpenter, D. (Eds.). (1997). The expert consensus guideline series: Treatment of obsessive-compulsive disorder. *Journal of Clinical Psychiatry, 58*(Suppl. 4, 1–63).

The Internet site for these guidelines reminds us of several limitations of these guidelines (http://www.psychguides.com/methodology.html. Accessed July 11, 2003):

1. Since these guidelines are based on a synthesis of the opinions of a large group of experts, from question to question some of the individual experts would differ with the consensus view.

2. As the history of medicine teaches us, the expert opinion at any given time can be very wrong.

3. The guidelines are financially sponsored by the pharmaceutical industry, which could possibly introduce biases.

4. These guidelines are comprehensive but not exhaustive; because of the nature of the method, some interesting topics are omitted from the expert panel query.

Treatment Algorithms

An algorithm is a procedure used to solve a problem. Development of evidence-based treatment guidelines has provided the foundation for developing more specific treatment algorithms that provide a step-by-step approach to clinical decisions.

As the practice in psychopharmacology rapidly evolves into much more complex science, it is becoming very difficult for clinicians to keep up with developments. It is particularly difficult to keep these advances in the knowledge base in mind during actual clinical decision making. Treatment algorithms are a helpful aid to clinicians. Although medication algorithms are not new to the field of medicine, for example, they have commonly been used in the treatment of cancer, asthma, arthritis, diabetes, and other chronic general medical disorders, they are relatively new to psychiatry. This is because diverse medication choices and the tools by which to measure outcomes (and therefore to consistently apply the algorithms in routine practice) have both become available only recently. Medication algorithms recommend more specific treatment sequences and are often accompanied by tactical recommendations (at what dose, over what period of time, at what therapeutic blood levels) for particular strategies (e.g., specific medications). Hence, treatment algorithms represent a level of specificity that goes beyond typical guidelines. For example, medication algorithms establish a sequence for use of medications in a particular illness, as well as dose ranges, criteria for response, and duration for each medication trial. Conceptually, algorithms are a way of operationalizing guidelines.

Treatment algorithms outline a suggested course of action in a patient with a particular disorder, under various clinical conditions that might influence best-course treatment decisions. In this regard, algorithms depict clinical choices to treat a specific disorder. Algorithms are an attractive approach to impact quality of care since they can be disseminated rapidly and widely. They are important tools that help clinicians make informed choices about how best to treat patients and to achieve better outcomes more quickly. They represent an effort to codify a consensus of the most effective and safe sequence by which to alter, augment, or introduce new agents in treating a disorder that is unresponsive to an initial course of treatment. The sequence of treatment recommended in an algorithm allows critical discussion of each decision point especially as it relates to the choice of switching versus augmenting in the presence of partial or nonresponse to initial treatment.

The Texas Medication Algorithm Project (TMAP) and the Texas Implementation of Medication Algorithms (TIMA) represents perhaps the most comprehensive and extensive development and implementation of medication algorithms for the treatment of schizophrenia, bipolar disorder, and major depression. TMAP, started in 1996, was designed to develop, implement, and evaluate not just a set of medication algorithms, but an algorithm-driven treatment philosophy for major psychiatric disorders in adults. The explicit goals also included improvement in the quality of care and an attempt to decrease some of the variation in psychiatric medication practice. As a treatment philosophy for the medication management portion of care, TMAP consisted of:

1. Evidence-based, consensually agreed upon medication treatment algorithms;
2. Clinical and technical support necessary to allow the clinician to implement the algorithms; and
3. Patient and family education programs that allow the patient to be an active partner in care.

Initiated by the Texas Department of Mental Health and Mental Retardation in collaboration with a consortium of Texas academic medical centers, TMAP has been a public and academic collaborative effort (Gilbert et al., 1998; Rush et al., 1999). The processes that led to the development of the TMAP algorithms included literature review, expert panels, consensus conferences, and input from consumers and advocacy groups. Processes were also put in place to seek ongoing input from consumers and providers to assist with the process of updates and revisions.

The general guiding principles in organizing treatment options into stage sequences has been:

- Most efficacious/safest treatments first
- Simplest interventions first
- Subsequent interventions that tend toward increased complexity and risk
- Multiple options for physicians when appropriate
- Patients' preference

Studies to evaluate the clinical and economic impact of implementing these algorithms are ongoing, largely in the Texas public mental health system. The TIMA is the implementation of TMAP at the real life, clinician-focused level. Detailed manuals for all three disorders that are the current focus of TIMA are available on the Internet at www.mhmr.state.tx.us/centraloffice/medicaldirector/tima. These manuals include flow charts and specific recommendations for various stages of treatment including elaborate stepwise strategies for nonresponse, partial response, or medication intolerance. The manuals also include information on dosing, side-effect profiles, and the tools used for assessment and monitoring.

Consistent with a disease management model, one of the strongest aspects of TMAP is a well-structured and elaborate patient and family education component. The component provides patients and families with the needed background to participate in treatment planning and implementation as full "partners" with clinicians. Such partnership is likely to increases the probability that appropriate and accurate treatment decisions will be made and that a treatment regimen will be followed.

More recently, Texas has developed a children's medication algorithm project (CMAP). CMAP currently addresses the use of medication for childhood and adolescent depression and attention-deficit hyperactivity disorder. (Hughes et al., 1999; Pliszka et al., 2000). Although developed initially for the public sector, the stated goals of these algorithms are to increase the uniformity of treatment and improve the clinical outcomes of children and adolescents in a variety of treatment settings.

There are several methods of creating treatment algorithms based on evidence. The Harvard Psychopharmacology Algorithm Project has approached treatment algorithms in a model based on the process of psychopharmacology consultation (Osser & Zarate, 1999). The algorithms are constructed from a series of questions and answers that evolve as a provider consults with an expert. This information is gathered through a series of "what if" scenarios. The algorithm thus constructed flows very much like the series of questions that a psychopharmacology consultant would ask about a patient. Each of these questions requires examination of pertinent evidence from the literature. In answering these questions, the "virtual consultant" also provides the pertinent evidence, indicates the strength of the evidence, and points out when the evidence is contradictory or inadequate. The recommendations made are discussed and referenced along with the clinical confidence ratings that indicate the strength of scientific support for them. Additionally, the merits and problems associated with alternatives to the first-line choices are reviewed. The algorithms and the disease management system in which they are embedded are available at the project's web site (http://www.mhc.com/Algorithms Accessed August 11, 2003).

Aside from these two approaches to developing medication algorithms, there are several other algorithms of varying quality available for use by the clinician prescriber. Table 5.4 lists some of the currently available treatment algorithms in the area of psychopharmacotherapy.

PRACTICING EVIDENCE-BASED PSYCHOPHARMACOTHERAPY

There are certain practices that are needed for pharmacologic treatment to conform to evidence-based principles (Mellman et al., 2001). Figure 5.1 on page 99 is a flow chart of the following practices in the general order of how they occur during a patient encounter:

1. A thorough evaluation leading to an accurate diagnosis.
2. Defining target symptoms and their severity (pretreatment baseline).
3. Choosing a medication and dosage range for the diagnostic condition and target symptoms. The research evidence supports the choice of the drug and the dose range.

Table 5.4   A Selective List of Psychopharmacology Algorithms

Algorithm	Reference
Depression	Crismon, M. L., Trivedi, M. H., Pigott, T. A., Rush, A. J., Hirschfeld, R. M. A., Kahn, D. A., et al. (1999). The Texas Medication Algorithm Project: Report of the Texas Consensus Conference Panel on medication treatment of major depressive disorder. *Journal of Clinical Psychiatry, 60,* 142–156. Available, with latest update, from http://www.mhmr.state.tx.us /centraloffice/medicaldirector/TIMA.html Retrieved September 2, 2003.
	DeBattista, C., Solvaason, B., Nelson, C., & Schatzberg, A. F. (1999). Major depression and its subtypes. In J. Fawcett, D. J. Stein, & K. O. Jobson (Eds.), *Textbook of Treatment Algorithms in Psychopharmacology* (pp. 38–57). New York: Wiley.
	Department of Veterans Affairs. (2000). *The pharmacologic management of major depression in the primary-care setting.* Veterans Health Administration Publication No. 00-0016. Retrieved September 2, 2003, from www.vapbm.org /PBM/treatment.htm.
	Mulsant, B. H., Alexopoulos, G. S., Reynolds, C. F., III, Katz, I. R., Abrams, R., Oslin, D., et al. (2001). Pharmacological treatment of depression in older primary care patients: The PROSPECT algorithm. *International Journal of Geriatric Psychiatry, 16,* 585–592.
	Osser, D. N., & Patterson, R. D. (1998). Algorithms for the pharmacotherapy of depression, part one (unipolar, dysthymia), part two (psychotic, treatment-refractory, comorbid). *Directions in Psychiatry, 18,* 303–333. Available, with latest updates, from www.mhc.com/Algorithms. Retrieved September 2, 2003.
	Schatzburg, A. F., DeBattista, C., Zarate, C., & Ketter, T. (2002). *The Stanford Algorithm Project: Treatment of psychotic major depression 2002.* Available from http://stagehand.stanford.edu/pmd/. Retrieved September 2, 2003.
Bipolar disorder	Dantzler, A., & Osser, D. N. (1999). Algorithms for the pharmacotherapy of acute depression in patients with bipolar disorder. *Psychiatric Annals, 29,* 270–284. Available, with latest updates, from www.mhc.com/Algorithms. Retrieved September 2, 2003.
	Post, R. M., Denicoff, K. D., Frye, M. A., & Leverich, G. S. (1997). Algorithms for bipolar mania. In A. J. Rush (Ed.), *Mood disorders: Systematic medication management* (pp. 114–145). Basel, Switzerland: Karger.
	Suppes, T., Dennehy, E. B., Swann, A. C., Bowden, C. L., Calabrese, J. R., Hirschfeld, R. M., et al. (2002). Report of the Texas Consensus Conference Panel on medication treatment of bipolar disorder 2000. *Journal of Clinical Psychiatry, 63,* 288–299. Available, with latest updates, from http://www .mhmr.state.tx.us/centraloffice/medicaldirector/TIMA.html. Retrieved September 2, 2003.
Schizophrenia	Buscema, C. A., Abbasi, Q. A., Barry, D. J., & Lauve, T. H. (2000). An algorithm for the treatment of schizophrenia in the correctional setting: The forensic algorithm project. *Journal of Clinical Psychiatry, 61*(10), 767–783.
	Miller, A. L., Chiles, J. A., Chiles, J. K., Crismon, M. L., Shon, S. P., & Rush, A. J. (1999). The Texas Medication Algorithm Project (TMAP) schizophrenia algorithms. *Journal of Clinical Psychiatry, 60,* 649–657. Available, with latest updates, from http://www.mhmr.state.tx.us/centraloffice/medicaldirector /TIMA.html. Retrieved September 2, 2003.
	Osser, D. N., & Sigadel, R. (2001). Short-term inpatient pharmacotherapy of schizophrenia. *Harvard Review of Psychiatry, 9,* 89–104. Available, with latest updates, from www.mhc.com/Algorithms. Retrieved September 2, 2003.

Table 5.4   *Continued*

Algorithm	Reference
Schizophrenia *(continued)*	Osser, D. N., & Zarate, C. A. (1999). Consultant for the pharmacotherapy of schizophrenia. *Psychiatric Annals, 29,* 252–267. Available, with latest updates, from www.mhc.com/Algorithms. Retrieved September 2, 2003.
Panic disorder	Coplan, J. D., & Gorman, J. M. (1999). Panic disorder. In J. Fawcett, D. J. Stein, & K. O. Jobson (Eds.), *Textbook of Treatment Algorithms in Psychopharmacology* (pp. 88–98). New York: Wiley.
	Rosenbaum, J. F., Pollack, M. H., & Friedman, S. J. (1998). The pharmacotherapy of panic disorder. In J. F. Rosenbaum & M. H. Pollack (Eds.), *Panic disorder and its treatment* (pp. 153–180). New York: Marcel Dekker.
Social anxiety disorder	Marshall, R. D., & Schneier, F. R. (1996). An algorithm for the pharmacotherapy of social phobia. *Psychiatric Annals, 26*(4), 210–216.
	Stein, D. J., Kasper, S., Matsunaga, H., Osser, D. N., Stein, M. B., van Ameringen, M., et al. (2001). Pharmacotherapy of social anxiety disorder: An algorithm for primary care. *Primary Care Psychiatry, 7*(3), 107–110.
	Sutherland, S. M., & Davidson, J. R. T. (1999). Social phobia. In J. Fawcett, D. J. Stein, & K. O. Jobson (Eds.), *Textbook of treatment algorithms in psychopharmacology* (pp. 107–118). New York: Wiley.
Obsessive-compulsive disorder	Greist, J. H., & Jefferson, J. W. (1998). Pharmacotherapy for obsessive-compulsive disorder. *British Journal of Psychiatry, 173*(Suppl. 35), 64–70.
Posttraumatic stress disorder	Alarcon, R. D., Glover, S., Boyer, W., & Balon, R. (2000). Proposing an algorithm for the pharmacological treatment of posttraumatic stress disorder. *Annals of Clinical Psychiatry, 12*(4), 239–246.
Anxiety disorders in patients with chemical abuse and dependence	Osser, D. N., Renner, J. A., & Bayog, R. (1999). Algorithms for the pharmacotherapy of anxiety disorders in patients with chemical abuse and dependence. *Psychiatric Annals, 29*(5), 285–301. Available, with latest updates, from www.mhc.com/Algorithms. Retrieved September 2, 2003.
Body dysmorphic disorder	Phillips, K. A. (2000). Pharmacotherapy of body dysmorphic disorder: A review of empirical evidence and a proposed treatment algorithm. *Psychiatric Clinics of North America Annals of Drug Therapy, 7,* 59–82.
Personality disorders	Soloff, P. H. (1998). Algorithms for pharmacological treatment of personality dimensions: Symptom-specific treatment for cognitive-perceptual, affective, and impulsive-behavioral dysregulation. *Bulletin of the Menninger Clinic, 62*(2), 195–214.
	Soloff, P. H. (2000). Psychopharmacology of borderline personality disorder. *Psychiatric Clinics of North America, 23*(1), 169–192.
ADHD in adults	Bhandary, A. N., Fernandez, F., Gregory, R. J., et al. (1997). Pharmacotherapy in adults with ADHD. *Psychiatric Annals, 27*(8), 545–555.
Developmental disabilities and behavioral disorders	Mikkelsen, E. J., & McKenna, L. (1999). Psychopharmacologic algorithms for adults with developmental disabilities and difficult-to-diagnose behavioral disorders. *Psychiatric Annals, 29*(5), 302–314.
Child and adolescent psychopharmacology	Birmaher, B., Brent, D., & Heydl, P. (1999). Childhood-onset depressive disorders. In J. Fawcett, D. J. Stein, & K. O. Jobson (Eds.), *Textbook of Treatment Algorithms in Psychopharmacology* (pp. 135–163). New York: Wiley.
	Hughes, C. W., Emslie, G. J., Crismon, M. L., Wagner, K. D., Birmaher, B., Geller, B., et al. (1999). The Texas Children's Medication Algorithm Project: Report of the Texas Consensus Conference Panel on medication treatment of

(continued)

Table 5.4   *Continued*

Algorithm	Reference
Child and adolescent psychopharmacology *(continued)*	childhood major depressive disorder. *Journal of the American Academy of Child and Adolescent Psychiatry, 38,* 1442–1454. Available, with latest updates, from http://www.mhmr.state.tx.us/centraloffice/medicaldirector /cmap.html. Retrieved September 2, 2003.
	Pliszka, S. R., Greenhill, L. L., Crismon, M. L., Sedillo, A., Carlson, C., Conners, C. K., et al. (2000). The Texas Children's Medication Algorithm Project: Report of the Texas Consensus Conference Panel on medication treatment of childhood attention deficit/hyperactivity disorder, Part I. Part II: Tactics. *Journal of American Academy of Child and Adolescent Psychiatry, 39*(7), 908–927. Latest update available from http://www.mhmr.state.tx.us /centraloffice/medicaldirector/cmap.html. Retrieved September 2, 2003.

4. Defining appropriate thresholds for adequate versus inadequate response.

5. Monitoring for changes in symptoms and adequacy of response, preferably with use of reliable and valid rating instruments to make these determinations more precise.

6. Monitoring for the occurrence and tolerability of side effects, preferably with use of reliable and valid rating instruments to make these determinations more precise.

7. Determining appropriate thresholds for adequate versus inadequate response.

8. In cases where medications are not tolerated well or when there is no response after an adequate trial, considering strategies recommended by the evidence-based guidelines specific for the condition/symptoms. Such strategies include raising the dosage, switching to another efficacious medication, or using an augmentation strategy.

9. Using the same approach (1 to 8) for the comorbid conditions.

10. Evaluating patient's response to co-administered medication treatments when using augmentation and/or combination strategies. An attempt should always be made to discontinue medications that have not helped to enhance the clinical response.

BARRIERS TO IMPLEMENTATION

Although treatment guidelines offer a tremendous promise, implementation has not been easy to achieve (Davis & Taylor-Vaisey, 1997). Several guidelines' characteristics are likely to impact their implementation. Milner and Valenstein (2002) have compared these characteristics for guidelines for schizophrenia. They examined three nationally prominent practice guidelines and one set of algorithms for schizophrenia. Such comparisons not only assist the decision-making process for practitioners and healthcare organizations that are considering the implementation of guidelines but are also likely to inform the development of future guidelines.

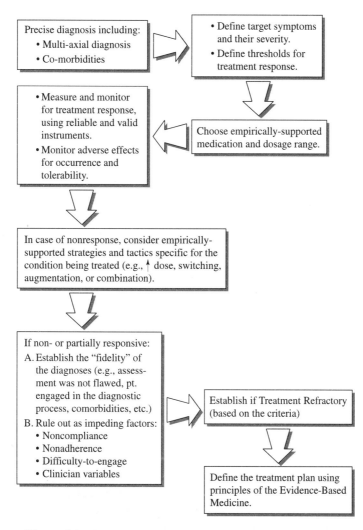

Figure 5.1 Practicing evidence-based psychopharmacotherapy.

Aside from the characteristics of a guideline itself, there are also several potential barriers that can impact implementation of evidence-based guidelines and algorithms.

Rapidly Growing Evidence Base

The rapidly growing evidence base requires a significant commitment of resources, both time and money, to develop and update meta-analyses and other organized databases to inform the process of guideline and algorithm development.

Integrating Evidence into Practice

Physicians do not always have easy access to timely, relevant evidence-based information, at least not on a consistent basis. When they do have such information, there are other challenges to integrating such information into their routine practice, for example, time constraints, demands of their work environments including the complexity of large healthcare organizations, access to medications, and so on (Guyatt, 1992).

Documenting Treatment History

Guidelines and algorithms require specific information regarding patients and their treatment histories. Often such information is not readily available. Staging patients require a treatment history that again is often incomplete or simply unavailable. Documenting an adequate trial of a certain medication is particularly difficult. Also, patients with severe mental illness often are unable to provide a thorough and accurate history of their illness and its treatment, due to symptoms that limit their ability to report their past treatment response adequately. Collateral informants may be very helpful in such cases, but they are not always available.

Partial Response as a Barrier to More Aggressive Treatment

Partial response to treatment, at times, can be a barrier to seeking more aggressive treatment. Often patients considered stable by the treatment team continue to have symptoms that are quite disabling. Despite these disabling symptoms, there is hesitancy on the part of physicians and other treatment staff to changing medications especially when the patient has a history of violence or if there was a worsening after previous medication changes. Sometime patients and family members are also resistant to medication change for the same reasons. Treatment providers may choose not to take the risk of clinical deterioration that is involved with any medication change. This leads to maintenance of the status quo at the cost of continued residual symptoms and disability.

Impacting Physicians Practice Behavior

Studies of impact of practice guidelines suggest that publication and distribution of guidelines is not enough to change clinical practice (Cabana et al., 1999; Kosecoff et al., 1987; Lomas, 1991; Lomas et al., 1989). Sustained change requires a restructuring of the flow of the daily work so that routine procedures make it natural for the clinician to give care in the new way. Hence, the treatment guidelines and algorithms must be contextualized to the actual process of care. For successful implementation of evidence-based guidelines and algorithms, both providers and consumers must see them as an approach to treatment that is likely to increase the possibility of a successful outcome. Intention to change is necessary but not sufficient. For the change in practice behavior to occur, intention to change must be combined with the necessary skill, and the environmental constraints must be removed (Fishbein, 1995). Additional efforts that may also be necessary before a change in practice behavior occurs include the following (Davis, Thomson, Oxman, & Haynes, 1995; Greco & Eisenberg, 1993):

- Using administrative rules and regulations
- Changing financial incentives and penalties
- Providing clinicians with ongoing supervision and feedback on practices
- Increasing consumer demand for services

Consumer and Family Members' Concerns

Considering them to be a cookbook approach, consumers and family members may fear that guidelines and algorithms limit consideration of their individuality or may take the choice away from them or their providers. Although this concern may be understandable, it is generally agreed that evidence-based practice within appropriate guidelines allows for consideration of the individualized treatment planning while reducing troublesome variation. The model of evidence-based practice suggested by Hayes, Devereaux, and Guyatt (2002) addresses physicians and patients choices in evidence-based practice as follows:

- Clinical decision must include consideration of:
  —Diagnosis and treatment options available
  —Research evidence concerning the efficacy, effectiveness, and efficiency of the options
  —Patient's preference, given the likely consequences associated with each option
- Clinical expertise is needed to bring these considerations together and recommend the treatment that the patient is agreeable to accepting.

Guideline materials developed for consumers and their families can help them understand the rationale for current medication treatments and serve as tools for initiating discussion of alternative considerations (Mellman et al., 2001).

A powerful argument for the use of algorithms, at least for depression, is made by Trivedi (2002), stating that the goal of the algorithm is the attainment of full and sustainable remission of symptoms. With such a goal, it is hoped that algorithm-driven pharmacotherapy of depression will increase the quality of care, leading to improved patient outcomes, reducing unnecessary practice variation, and increasing the overall cost-effectiveness of treatment intervention. Consumers, family members, and advocates may find this to be reassuring.

Misconceptions

There are many misperceptions about evidence-based practice across the professions, including that the approach ignores clinical experience and instinct, as well as standard aspects of clinical care (Guyatt, 1992). There also is concern that evidence-based practice will slow innovation and is too reliant on quantitative research methods.

Costs and Other System-Level Issues

There are significant costs and technical challenges associated with development of clinical decision-support systems that provide foundational basis to evidence-based practice. This is further complicated by the invisibility of nursings' contributions and consumer choices, which largely are not captured in computerized records and clinical and administrative databases.

For the implementation to be successful, there must be a commitment at the systemic level to providing necessary resources for guideline implementation. This may include areas such as ensuring that physicians' have access to the recommended medications (formulary), that adequate time is provided for required assessments (both frequency and duration of appointments), a record system that supports an evidence-based practice, an infrastructure that facilitates implementation, and so on.

There has been little discussion in the literature concerning how costs should be defined and measured in the context of algorithm-based practices. Kashner, Rush, and Altshuler (1999) have described the strategy to measure costs for TMAP in a multisite study investigating outcomes and costs of medication algorithms for bipolar disorder, schizophrenia, and depression.

Tools for Outcome Management

In research settings, standardized instruments are used for making a diagnosis and for determining treatment response. Clinical decisions regarding changes in treatment after an initial intervention are also based on assessments using such instruments to determine the adequacy of response at critical decision points. Such instruments are not typically used in the day-to-day clinical practice of psychiatry. While the option to use such instruments in everyday clinical practice is available, it adds demands on the time of clinical staff whose time may already be consumed by other routine responsibilities related to clinical practice. Many of these instruments can be quite time consuming and complicated. One solution is to use brief, pared-down, and clinician-friendly versions of these instruments. Although there is a gradual emergence of many such instruments designed and normed for clinical practice, more research is needed to establish the validity of many such pared-down versions. Even when brief and clinician-friendly, they still add time to daily work and that needs to be addressed. For assessment and tracking tools to be more widely accepted outside of research settings, they should not substantially increase, and ideally would decrease, the burden of documentation (Mellman et al., 2001).

Legal Issues

Evidence-based practice can be used selectively to define medical necessity and appropriateness in court or other venues. This has the potential to undermine support for evidence-based practice among clinicians and managers.

No Evidence

When environments start focusing on evidence-based practice, there are challenges in also preparing physicians to make decisions when there is little evidence to guide them, for example, combinations of medications, child psychopharmacotherapy, and so on.

DOES USE OF EVIDENCE-BASED GUIDELINES AND ALGORITHMS THREATEN THE PHYSICIAN'S AUTONOMY?

One of the reasons why there has been an increasing number of medication algorithms in recent years may be because algorithms respond to one of the major challenges of our times: how to keep abreast with an ever-increasing knowledge base. The speed with which the knowledge base for psychopharmacologic therapy has grown has been tremendous. Psychopharmacotherapy has become more complex and increasingly sophisticated. Clearly the value of information systems that can support clinical decision making is becoming more and more obvious. Evidence-based guidelines and algorithms are likely to make clinical decision making thoughtful and informed by empirical evidence. It does impose a new structure, a code of conduct, on decision makers. This may make the clinician's task more laborious. It also requires that certain kinds of interventions be justified. This all having been said, use of guidelines and algorithms is likely to enhance, rather than diminish, physicians' responsibility and autonomy, because it provides a much more reasoned basis for decision making. Practice guidelines and algorithms based on research evidence help physicians make complex decisions. Medication algorithms go one step further by providing clinicians a convenient, comprehensive elaboration of next-step alternatives. Development of consumer-oriented materials in programs such as TMAP facilitates clinician-consumer dialogue and shared decision making (Toprac et al., 2000).

Evidence-based practice enhances the overall care delivery system by providing treatments that are proven to be effective, by using systematic outcome management components, and then feeding this information back to the system to enhance training in the areas consistently shown to be areas where outcomes appear to be lagging behind the defined thresholds. Figure 5.2 illustrates the vicious cycle relationship between clinical care, outcome management, and training.

Evidence-based practice increases, rather than diminishes, professional responsibility and authority, because it provides a much more secure basis for decision making. It is probably most accurate to say that evidence-based practice enhances physicians' capacity for clinical autonomy, particularly within organizations and societies that require publicly accountable and more open decisions. Like anything else, evidence-based practice can be abused. For this reason, it is crucial that health professionals have the requisite skills to use evidence-based practice responsibly and to withstand its misapplication for purposes other than best practice.

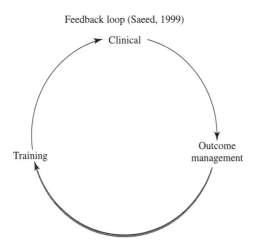

Figure 5.2   Designing effective and efficient systems of care delivery.

REFERENCES

Alarcon, R. D., Glover, S., Boyer, W., & Balon, R. (2000). Proposing an algorithm for the pharmacological treatment of posttraumatic stress disorder. *Annals of Clinical Psychiatry, 12*(4), 239–246.

American Academy of Child and Adolescent Psychiatry. (1994). Practice parameters for the assessment and treatment of children and adolescents with schizophrenia. *Journal of the American Academy of Child and Adolescent Psychiatry, 33*(Suppl. 5), 616–635.

Alexopoulos, G. S., Katz, I. R., Reynolds, C. F., Carpenter, D., & Docherty, J. P. (2001). *The expert consensus guideline series: Pharmacotherapy of depressive disorders in older patients.* [A postgraduate medicine special report]. New York: McGraw-Hill.

Alexopoulos, G. S., Silver, J. M., Kahn, D. A., Frances, A., & Carpenter, D. (Eds.). (1998). *The expert consensus guideline series: Agitation in older persons with dementia.* [A postgraduate medicine special report]. New York: McGraw-Hill.

Allen, M. H., Currier, G. W., Hughes, D. H., Reyes-Harde, M., & Docherty, J. P. (2001). *The expert consensus guideline series: Treatment of behavioral emergencies* [A postgraduate medicine special report]. New York: McGraw-Hill.

Altshuler, L. L., Cohen, L. S., Moline, M. L., Kahn, D. A., Carpenter, D., & Docherty, J. P. (2001). *The expert consensus guideline series: Treatment of depression in women* [A postgraduate medicine special report]. New York: McGraw-Hill.

American Psychiatric Association. (1994, December). Practice guideline for the treatment of patients with bipolar disorder. *American Journal of Psychiatry, 151*(Suppl.), 1–36.

American Psychiatric Association. (1998). Practice guideline for the treatment of patients with panic disorder. *American Journal of Psychiatry, 155,* 1–34.

American Psychiatric Association. (2000). Practice guideline for the treatment of patients with major depressive disorder. *American Journal of Psychiatry, 157,* 1–45.

American Psychiatric Association Practice. (1997, April). Guideline for the treatment of patients with schizophrenia. *American Journal of Psychiatry, 154*(Suppl.), 1–63.

Audet, A. M., Greenfield, S., & Field, M. (1999). Medical practice guidelines: Current activities and future directions. *Annals of Internal Medicine, 30,* 709–714.

Berg, A. O., Atkins, D., & Tierney, W. (1997). Clinical practice guidelines in practice and education. *Journal of General Internal Medicine, 12*(Suppl. 2), S25–S33.

Bhandary, A. N., Fernandez, F., Gregory, R. J., et al. (1997). Pharmacotherapy in adults with ADHD. *Psychiatric Annals, 27*(8), 545–555.

Birmaher, B., Brent, D., & Heydl, P. (1999). Childhood-onset depressive disorders. In J. Fawcett, D. J. Stein, & K. O. Jobson (Eds.), *Textbook of treatment algorithms in psychopharmacology* (pp. 135–163). New York: Wiley.

Buscema, C. A., Abbasi, Q. A., Barry, D. J., & Lauve, T. H. (2000). An algorithm for the treatment of schizophrenia in the correctional setting: The forensic algorithm project. *Journal of Clinical Psychiatry, 61*(10), 767–783.

Cabana, M. D., Rand, C. S., Powe, N. R., Wu, A. W., Wilson, M. H., Abboud, P. C., et al. (1999). Why don't physicians follow clinical practice guidelines? A framework for improvement. *Journal of American Medical Association, 282,* 1458–1465.

Canadian Psychiatric Association. (1998). Canadian clinical practice guidelines for the treatment of schizophrenia. *Canadian Journal of Psychiatry, 43*(Suppl. 2), 25S–40S.

Conners, C. K., March, J. S., Frances, A., Wells, K. C., & Ross, R. (2001). The expert consensus guideline series: Treatment of attention-deficit/hyperactivity disorder. *Journal of Attention Disorders, 4*(Suppl. 1).

Coplan, J. D., & Gorman, J. M. (1999). Panic disorder. In J. Fawcett, D. J. Stein, & K. O. Jobson (Eds.), *Textbook of treatment algorithms in psychopharmacology* (pp. 88–89). New York: Wiley.

Crismon, M. L., Trivedi, M. H., Pigott, T. A., Rush, A. J., Hirschfeld, R. M., Kahn, D. A., et al. (1999). The Texas Medication Algorithm Project: Report of the Texas consensus conference panel on medication treatment of major depressive disorder. *Journal of Clinical Psychiatry, 60*, 142–156.

Dantzler, A., & Osser, D. N. (1999). Algorithms for the pharmacotherapy of acute depression in patients with bipolar disorder. *Psychiatric Annals, 29*, 270–284.

Davis, D. A., & Taylor-Vaisey, A. (1997). Translating guidelines into practice: A systematic review of theoretic concepts, practical experience, and research evidence in the adoption of clinical practice guidelines. *Canadian Medical Association Journal, 157*, 408–416.

Davis, D. A., Thomson, M. A., Oxman, A. D., & Haynes, R. B. (1995). Changing physician performance: A systematic review of the effect of continuing medical education strategies. *Journal of American Medical Association, 274*, 700–705.

DeBattista, C., Solvaason, B., Nelson, C., & Schatzberg, A. F. (1999). Major depression and its subtypes. In J. Fawcett, D. J. Stein, & K. O. Jobson (Eds.), *Textbook of treatment algorithms in psychopharmacology* (pp. 38–57). New York: Wiley.

Department of Veterans Affairs. (2000). *The pharmacologic management of major depression in the primary-care setting* [Veterans Health Administration Publication No. 00-0016]. Retrieved September 20, 2003, from www.vapbm.org/PBM/treatment.htm ACCESSED.

Etminan, M., Wright, J. M., & Carleton, B. C. (1998). Evidence-based pharmacotherapy: Review of basic concepts and applications in clinical practice. *Annals of Pharmacotherapy, 32*(11), 1193–1200.

Fishbein, M. (1995). Developing effective behavioral change interventions: Some lessons learned from behavioral research. In *Reviewing the behavioral science knowledge base on technology transfer* (NIDA Research Monograph No. 155). Rockville, MD: National Institute on Drug Abuse.

Foa, E. B., Davidson, J. R. T., & Frances, A. (Eds.). (1999). The expert consensus guideline series: Treatment of posttraumatic stress disorder. *Journal of Clinical Psychiatry, 60*(Suppl. 16).

Foa, E. B., Keane, T. M., & Friedman, M. J. (2000). Guidelines for treatment of PTSD. *Journal of Traumatic Stress, 13*, 539–588.

Frances, A., Kahn, D., Carpenter, D., Frances, C., & Docherty, J. (1998, July). A new method of developing expert consensus practice guidelines. *American Journal of Managed Care* (7), 1023–1029.

Gilbert, D. A., Altshuler, K. Z., Rago, W. V., Shon, S. P., Crismon, M. L., & Toprac, M. G. (1998). Texas Medication Algorithm Project: Definitions, rationale, and methods to develop medication algorithms. *Journal of Clinical Psychiatry, 59*, 345–351.

Greco, P. J., & Eisenberg, J. M. (1993). Changing physician practices. *New England Journal of Medicine, 329*, 1271–1274.

Guyatt, G. H. (1992). Evidence-based medicine: A new approach to teaching the practice of medicine. Evidence-Based Medicine Working Group. *Journal of American Medical Association, 268*(17), 2420–2425.

Hayes, R. B., Devereaux, P. J., & Guyatt, G. H. (2002). Physicians and patients choices in evidence-based practice. *British Medical Journal, 324,* 1350.

Hughes, C. W., Emslie, G. J., Crismon, M. L., Wagner, K. D., Birmaher, B., Geller, B., et al. (1999). The Texas Children's Medication Algorithm Project: Report of the Texas consensus conference panel on medication treatment of childhood major depressive disorder. *Journal of the American Academy of Child and Adolescent Psychiatry, 38,* 1442–1454.

Institute of Medicine. (1990). In M. J. Field & K. N. Lohr (Eds.), *Clinical practice guidelines: Directions of a new program.* Washington, DC: National Academy Press.

Institute of Medicine. (2001). *Crossing the quality chasm: A new health system for the 21st century.* Washington, DC: National Academy Press.

Kashner, M. T., Rush, J. A., & Altshuler, K. Z. (1999, September). Measuring costs of guideline-driven mental health care: The Texas Medication Algorithm Project. *Journal of Mental Health Policy Economics, 2*(3), 111–121.

Kosecoff, J., Kanouse, D. E., Rogers, W. H., McCloskey, L., Winslow, C. M., & Brook, R. H. (1987). Effects of the National Institutes of Health consensus development program on physician practice. *Journal of American Medical Association, 258,* 2708–2713.

Lomas, J. (1991). Words without action? The production, dissemination, and impact of consensus recommendations. *Annual Review of Public Health, 12,* 41–65.

Lomas, J., Anderson, G. M., Domnick-Pierre, K., Vayda, E., Enkin, M. W., & Hannah, W. J. (1989). Do practice guidelines practice? The effect of a consensus statement on the practice of physicians. *New England Journal of Medicine, 321,* 1306–1311.

March, J. S., Frances, A., Kahn, D. A., & Carpenter, D. (Eds.). (1997). The expert consensus guideline series: Treatment of obsessive-compulsive disorder. *Journal of Clinical Psychiatry, 58*(Suppl. 4).

Marshall, R. D., & Schneier, F. R. (1996). An algorithm for the pharmacotherapy of social phobia. *Psychiatric Annals, 26*(4), 210–216.

McEvoy, J. P., Scheifler, P. L., & Frances, A. (Eds.). (1999). The expert consensus guideline series: Treatment of schizophrenia 1999. *Journal of Clinical Psychiatry, 60*(Suppl. 11).

Mellman, T. A., Miller, A. L., Weissman, E. M., Crismon, M. L., Essock, S. M., & Marder, S. R. (2001). Evidence-based pharmacologic treatment for people with severe mental illness: A focus on guidelines and algorithms. *Psychiatric Services, 52,* 619–625.

Mikkelsen, E. J., & McKenna, L. (1999). Psychopharmacologic algorithms for adults with developmental disabilities and difficult-to-diagnose behavioral disorders. *Psychiatric Annals, 29*(5), 302–314.

Miller, A. L., Chiles, J. A., Chiles, J. K., Crismon, M. L., Shon, S. P., & Rush, A. J. (1999). The Texas Medication Algorithm Project (TMAP) schizophrenia algorithms. *Journal of Clinical Psychiatry, 60,* 649–657.

Milner, K., & Valenstein, M. (2002). A Comparison of Guidelines for the Treatment of Schizophrenia. *Psychiatric Services, 53,* 888–890.

Mulsant, B. H., Alexopoulos, G. S., Reynolds, C. F., III, Katz, I. R., Abrams, R., Oslin, D., et al. (2001). Pharmacological treatment of depression in older primary care patients: The PROSPECT algorithm [International]. *Journal of Geriatric Psychiatry, 16,* 585–592.

National Guideline Clearinghouse. Retrieved May 24, 2004, from www.guideline.gov.

Osser, D. N., & Patterson, R. D. (1998). Algorithms for the pharmacotherapy of depression, part one (unipolar, dysthymia), part two (psychotic, treatment-refractory, comorbid). *Directions in Psychiatry, 18,* 303–333.

Osser, D. N., Renner, J. A., & Bayog, R. (1999). Algorithms for the pharmacotherapy of anxiety disorders in patients with chemical abuse and dependence. *Psychiatric Annals, 29*(5), 285–301.

Osser, D. N., & Sigadel, R. (2001). Short-term inpatient pharmacotherapy of schizophrenia. *Harvard Review of Psychiatry, 9,* 89–104.

Osser, D. N., & Zarate, C. A. (1999). The Harvard Psychopharmacology Algorithm Project: Consultant for the pharmacotherapy of schizophrenia. *Psychiatric Annals, 29,* 252–267.

Phillips, K. A. (2000). Pharmacotherapy of body dysmorphic disorder: A review of empirical evidence and a proposed treatment algorithm. *Psychiatric Clinics of North America Annals of Drug Therapy, 7,* 59–82.

Pliszka, S. R., Greenhill, L. L., Crismon, M. L., Sedillo, A., Carlson, C., Conners, C. K., et al. (2000). The Texas Children's Medication Algorithm Project: Report of the Texas Consensus Conference Panel on Medication Treatment of Childhood Attention-Deficit/Hyperactivity Disorder: I. Attention-deficit/hyperactivity disorder. *Journal of American Academy of Child and Adolescent Psychiatry, 39*(7), 908–919.

Post, R. M., Denicoff, K. D., Frye, M. A., & Leverich, G. S. (1997). Algorithms for bipolar mania. In A. J. Rush (Ed.), *Mood disorders: Systematic medication management* (pp. 114–145). Basel, Switzerland: Karger.

Rosenbaum, J. F., Pollack, M. H., & Friedman, S. J. (1998). The pharmacotherapy of panic disorder. In J. F. Rosenbaum & M. H. Pollack (Eds.), *Panic disorder and its treatment* (pp. 153–180). New York: Marcel Dekker.

Rush, A. J., Crismon, M. L., Toprac, M. G., Shon, S. P., Rago, W. V., Miller, A. L., et al. (1999). Implementing guidelines and systems of care: Experiences with the Texas Medication Algorithm Project (TMAP). *Journal of Practical Psychiatry and Behavioral Health, 5,* 75–86.

Rush, A. J., & Frances, A. (2000). The expert consensus guideline series: Treatment of psychiatric and behavioral problems in mental retardation. *American Journal on Mental Retardation, 105* 159–228.

Sachs, G. S., Printz, D. J., Kahn, D. A., Carpenter, D., & Docherty, J. P. (2000). *The expert consensus guideline series: Medication treatment of bipolar disorder* [A postgraduate medicine special report]. New York: McGraw-Hill.

Schatzburg, A. F., DeBattista, C., Zarate, C., & Ketter, T. (n.d.) *The Stanford Algorithm Project—Treatment of psychotic major depression 2002.* Retrieved September 2, 2003, from http://stagehand.stanford.edu/pmd.

Soloff, P. H. (1998). Algorithms for pharmacological treatment of personality dimensions: Symptom-specific treatment for cognitive-perceptual, affective, and impulsive-behavioral dysregulation. *Bulletin of the Menninger Clinic, 62*(2), 195–214.

Soloff, P. H. (2000). Psychopharmacology of borderline personality disorder. *Psychiatric Clinics of North America, 23*(1), 169–192.

Stein, D. J., Kasper, S., Matsunaga, H., Osser, D. N., Stein, M. B., van Ameringen, M., et al. (2001). Pharmacotherapy of social anxiety disorder: An algorithm for primary care. *Primary Care Psychiatry, 7*(3), 107–110.

Stuart, G. W., Rush, A. J., & Morris, J. A. (2002). Practice guidelines in mental health and addiction services: Contributions from the American College of Mental Health Administration. *Administration and Policy in Mental Health, 30*(1), 21–33.

Suppes, T., Dennehy, E. B., Swann, A. C., Bowden, C. L., Calabrese, J. R., Hirschfeld, R. M., et al. (2002). Report of the Texas Consensus Conference Panel on Medication Treatment of Bipolar Disorder 2000. *Journal of Clinical Psychiatry, 63,* 288–299.

Sutherland, S. M., & Davidson, J. R. T. (1999). Social phobia. In J. Fawcett, D. J. Stein, & K. O. Jobson (Eds.), *Textbook of treatment algorithms in psychopharmacology* (pp. 107–118). New York: Wiley.

Toprac, M. G., Rush, A. J., Conner, T. M., Crismon, M. L., Dees, M., Hopkins, C., et al. (2000). The Texas Medication Algorithm Project patient and family education program: A consumer-guided initiative. *Journal of Clinical Psychiatry, 61,* 477–486.

Trivedi, M. H. (2002). Algorithms in clinical psychiatry: A stepped approach toward the path to recovery. *Psychopharmacology Bulletin, 36*(Suppl. 2), 142–149.

Trivedi, M. H. (2003). Using treatment algorithms to bring patients to remission. *Journal of Clinical Psychiatry, 64*(Suppl. 2), 8–13.

Wolf, F. M. (2000). Lessons to be learned from evidence-based medicine: Practice and promise of evidence-based medicine and evidence-based education. *Medical Teacher, 22*(3), 251–259.

CHAPTER 6

Psychosocial Rehabilitation

James H. Zahniser

Services for people diagnosed with serious mental illnesses have entered a new era of recovery, in which the expectations for what people can achieve, despite their diagnoses, have increased (Ahern & Fisher, 2001; Anthony, 1993; Hogan, 2003). Although psychosocial rehabilitation (PSR) once was perceived as ancillary to the "real" treatment delivered by clinicians, it is now more often seen as integral to services because of its direct relevance to recovery goals (Anthony, Cohen, Farkas, & Gagne, 2002). A palpable sense of optimism can be detected at conferences and in the literature, as innovations continue to emerge, the range of PSR services expands, and the research base for PSR continues to build. The growing confidence that recovery can and does happen (Anthony et al., 2002; Harding & Zahniser, 1997) and that PSR can play a major role in the recovery process seems to be stimulating innovation and research. This new optimism also is related to the increase in involvement and influence of consumers and survivors in the field over the past couple of decades (see, e.g., Ahern. & Fisher, 2001; Chamberlin, 1990; Fisher, 1994).

The field of PSR now has several different models that have been developed for a variety of purposes and that have been demonstrated and researched for effectiveness. Vocational rehabilitation has often been seen as the heart of PSR (Anthony et al., 2002), and several different models have been developed, including supported employment (Anthony et al., 2002; Drake & Becker, 1996), the clubhouse/transitional employment model (Beard, Propst, & Malamud, 1982; Macias, Jackson, Schroeder, & Wang, 1999), and diversified placement models (Dincin, 1995; Starks, Zahniser, Maas, & McGuirk, 2000). But PSR includes more than vocational rehabilitation, and in this chapter supported education, skills training, illness management, and consumer/peer-delivered service models are reviewed.

Some PSR models have been researched more extensively than others. For example, the individual placement and support model of supported employment (SE) has been experimentally tested in more than one setting with diverse populations (see Bond, Drake, Becker, & Mueser, 1999; Bond, Becker, et al., 2001, for reviews). Likewise, illness management and skill training approaches have been examined in controlled studies over the course of the past 2 decades (Kopelowicz, Liberman, & Zarate, 2002; Mueser et al.,

I would like to thank Cassie Morgan for her assistance in conducting background research and providing editorial assistance in preparing the manuscript for publication.

2002). Many other promising programs do not have as long a history of research. Nevertheless, vocational models other than SE, supported education, and consumer-operated/ consumer-involved programs, have evidenced good outcomes in less-controlled, but often well-conceived, quasi-experimental and outcome evaluation studies and in the few randomized, controlled studies completed to date. Indeed, as Table 6.1 shows, many of these programs hold great promise for the ultimate outcomes of recovery and empowerment and are important to include in PSR programming.

This chapter also addresses the important issue of evidence-based *processes.* Anthony (2003) argued recently that rehabilitation *processes* are as central to the achievement of recovery outcomes as are rehabilitation *practices* (programs and models). While PSR models in many cases have addressed processes (see, e.g., Anthony et al., 2002; Bellack, Mueser, Gingerich, & Agresta, 1997; Kingdon & Turkington, 1994; Liberman, 1988; Mowbray, Brown, Furlong-Norman, & Soydan, 2002; Pratt, Gill, Barrett, & Roberts, 1999), the research on which evidence-based practice is based has tended to focus more on establishing the efficacy and/or effectiveness of whole PSR programs than on elucidating critical service process ingredients. For the practitioner who is interested in providing evidence-based services, there is also a need for information on evidence-based processes because provision of services to real people in the real world is too complex for providers to rely on evidence-based *practices* only, at least as they are identified or defined currently.

The few formal practice guidelines that exist in PSR do address issues of process, as well as issues of practice (International Association of Psychosocial Rehabilitation Services [IAPSRS], 1997). In this chapter, practice guidelines and their implications for the development of PSR programming are reviewed following each description of contemporary PSR program or intervention. The review of guidelines is followed by a discussion of outcomes and fidelity assessment, training issues, and a closing summary/discussion of the PSR service domain. The chapter concludes with a discussion of future directions for the field.

REVIEW OF EMPIRICALLY SUPPORTED PSYCHOSOCIAL REHABILITATION SERVICES AND TOOLS FOR IMPLEMENTATION

The ultimate goal for contemporary PSR services is *recovery*—people once identified as having psychiatric disabilities* participating actively and meaningfully in the roles and communities of their choice and having a sense of hope and optimism for their lives and their futures. The "vision of recovery" (Anthony, 1993) was given impetus by longitudinal research showing that people with psychiatric disabilities often fully or substantially recover (DeSisto, Harding, McCormick, Ashikaga, & Gautman, 1995; Harding, Brooks, Ashikaga, Strauss, & Breier, 1987; Harding, Zubin, & Strauss, 1992). PSR services aim

---

*The terms *people with psychiatric disabilities* and *consumer* are used frequently in this chapter. In this chapter, both terms refer to people who have been diagnosed with serious mental illness and, as a result, have experienced barriers to full participation in adult life in the community.

Table 6.1 PSR Programs and Their Evidence-Based PSR Outcomes

Psychosocial Rehabilitation Program	PSR Outcome Domains				
	Social Skills and Support	Illness Management Skills	Recovery Beliefs and Attitudes	Role Performance (Work, School, etc.)	Quality of Life
Vocational Rehabilitation					
Supported employment			*Self-esteem**	**Competitive employment**	*Leisure** *Finances**
Diversified placement				*Employment*	
Clubhouse/transitional employment				*Employment*	
Supported education			*Self-esteem* *Empowerment* *School efficacy*	*Employment* *Educational status*	*Income*
Social skills training (Liberman, Bellack, Boston University)	**Social skills** **Problem solving** **Relationship skills**		*Self-esteem* *Empowerment*	*Independent living skills*	
Illness Management					
Psychoeducation		**Medical knowledge**			
Cognitive-behavioral	*Social functioning*	**Medical knowledge** **Medical adherence** **Reduced illness**			

(continued)

Table 6.1 *Continued*

			PSR Outcome Domains		
Psychosocial Rehabilitation Program	Social Skills and Support	Illness Management Skills	Recovery Beliefs and Attitudes	Role Performance (Work, School, etc.)	Quality of Life
Relapse prevention		**Reduced illness**			
Comprehensive and coping skills programs	**Social functioning** *More social contacts*	**Active coping skills**	*Self-esteem Self-confidence*		*Well-being*
Consumer/Peer-Delivered Services					
Mutual/peer support	*Larger social networks Social functioning and adjustment*	*Reduced illness*	*Self-esteem Decision making Hope*	*More social roles Role performance (work, family)*	
Consumer-run services	*Social functioning*	*Reduced illness*		*More social roles Employment*	*Quality of life*
Consumers as individual providers	*Social support*		*Self-image*		*Quality of life*

Note: **Bold** indicates evidence-based outcomes, while *italicized* indicates emerging evidence base for outcomes.
*Based on findings that competitive employment is associated with these outcomes.

to assist consumers in achieving recovery through providing individually tailored services targeted to consumers' chosen recovery goals. Services are delivered in contexts of collaborative partnerships, in which people are treated with respect and encouraged to take increasing control over their lives. PSR approaches eschew an expert-dummy model, in which the professional has all of the expertise and unilaterally uses his or her knowledge and skill to solve the client's problems.

Along with the vision of recovery, there is an increasing emphasis on *empowerment* of people with psychiatric disabilities (Chamberlin, 1997; Fisher, 1994; Salzer, 1997; Zimmerman & Warchausky, 1998). The emergence of empowerment as a partner concept to recovery was inevitable, given that people often were disempowered by the disabilities associated with mental illness and the societal stigma they invariably faced (Corrigan, 2003; Corrigan et al., 2003; Read & Harré, 2001; Read & Law, 1999). The more people are denied opportunities and capacities for having control over their lives, the more crucial it is that they gain or regain self-determination and mastery over the factors influencing their well-being (Rappaport, 1981). The focus on empowerment has added impetus to empowering interventions, such as supported employment, supported education, and peer support, but it also has encouraged the efforts of consumers/survivors and consumer advocates to increase their involvement in the design and monitoring of service systems. There appears to be a growing recognition in PSR that sharing power with consumers promotes recovery and, paradoxically, empowers providers to be more efficacious in their work.

Psychosocial rehabilitation technology has expanded in recent years to better address the recovery- and empowerment-oriented outcomes of interest. Imaginative and carefully designed interventions and programs have helped consumers to attain more meaningful roles and involvement in the communities of their choice. In addition, roles for consumers to partner with providers in the design, delivery, and evaluation of services have expanded (Salzer, 1997). The evidence base for these approaches is solid and growing. However, a lingering problem is the discomfit between the availability of effective programs and the actual delivery of them in "usual care" (Drake, Goldman, et al., 2001; Torrey et al., 2001). Thus, at a systems level, an overarching goal is for PSR programs and technology to be more widely disseminated.

Vocational Rehabilitation Programs

The fundamental goal of PSR, or any recovery-oriented endeavor, is to assist people in obtaining, maintaining, and expanding meaningful social roles in their communities of choice (Ahern & Fisher, 2001; Anthony et al., 2002). Vocational rehabilitation is at the very core of PSR because it helps people to obtain and maintain the role of employee, a most fundamental social role for adults. Adult developmental theorists have long discussed the fact that through *vocation,* most adults define core aspects of self and live productive lives (Erikson, 1963; Fowler, 2000; Vaillant, 2002). Yet, population data indicate extraordinarily high rates of unemployment for persons with psychiatric disabilities (National Institute of Disability and Rehabilitation Research, 1993; E. S. Rogers, Walsh, Masotta, & Danley, 1991; see also McQuilken et al., 2003). Vocational rehabilitation, perhaps more than any other aspect of PSR, helps people restore or develop for the first time meaningful and dignified adult identities. Because Chapter 2 of this volume provides an in-depth discussion of the most evidence-based model of vocational rehabilitation available (supported employment), a cursory overview of vocational rehabilitation models is provided here.*

Supported Employment/Individual Placement and Support

Supported employment (SE) was imported into PSR from other disability fields by innovators and researchers at Boston University (BU) and at the New Hampshire-Dartmouth Psychiatric Research Center (Anthony et al., 2002; Bond, 1998; Drake & Becker, 1996). As the only model of vocational rehabilitation with a body of randomized, controlled studies supporting its effectiveness, SE formally has been identified as an evidence-based practice (see Bond, Becker, et al., 2001). SE helps people obtain competitive employment at much higher rates than are obtained through "usual services" (Bond, Becker, et al., 2001; Bond et al., 1999; see Drake, McHugo, Becker, Anthony, & Clark, 1996; Drake et al., 1999; Lehman et al., 2002, for examples of controlled outcome studies). In addition, an interesting study by Bond and colleagues found that people who gained competitive employment through SE or through a nonspecific vocational program showed greater improvements in quality of life and self-esteem than consumers who were placed in sheltered work or who did not work at all (Bond, Resnick, et al., 2001), reinforcing the SE focus on competitive employment versus sheltered or protected jobs. SE also has been examined for its cost effectiveness (Clark, Xie, Becker, & Drake, 1998; E. S. Rogers, Sciarappa, MacDonald-Wilson, & Danley, 1995).

The empirically supported principles and active ingredients of SE have been reviewed thoroughly by Bond (1998) and are important to note within the context of this chapter. The first principle, according to Bond, is that *competitive employment* is the goal: Supported employment programs help people obtain and maintain community integrated positions, as opposed to sheltered work. Programs starting consumers with sheltered work substitute sheltered work for competitive work and do not prepare people well for integrated employment (p. 13). The second principle argues for a rapid job search, instead of a gradual approach to placement in employment positions. Bond provides a convincing review of research demonstrating the superior outcomes achieved by a rapid search for competitive employment.

An additional SE principle reviewed by Bond is that mental health and vocational rehabilitation services should be *integrated*, rather than provided separately. Otherwise, vocational and other service goals often work at cross-purposes. Drake, Becker, and colleagues reviewed research demonstrating the superiority of integrated versus separately provided services in helping consumers achieve competitive employment and, through a multimethod review of service process data, identified four consistent advantages of integrated services (Drake, Becker, Bond, & Mueser, 2003):

---

*The terms *program, model,* and *intervention* appear to be used interchangeably. However, the intention is to use the terms *program* and *model* when discussing PSR approaches that provide comprehensive and organized sets of interventions based on particular theories or models of how people can best be helped to recover from psychiatric disability. The term *intervention* is intended for use in describing more discrete PSR services that are less comprehensive in nature.

1. Higher rates of retention and engagement in services

2. Better communication between vocational and clinical staff

3. Clinicians' greater understanding and appreciation of employment services

4. Better incorporation and integration of vocational goals and plans into the treatment plan

Another SE principle is that the focus is on *consumers' vocational preferences,* because consumers have greater satisfaction and longer tenure in jobs they have chosen (Becker, Drake, Farabauch, & Bond, 1996). Additionally, assessment of consumer preferences, consumer role performance, and characteristics of the work environment is continuous and comprehensive. Traditional assessments, based on diagnosis, have shown limited utility. Periodic PSR assessments conducted in the environments in which consumers perform their roles, and which focus on personal and environmental assets and needs for enhancement, are crucial to the success of vocational rehabilitation. The final principle reviewed by Bond (1998) is that SE provides support indefinitely, for as long as the person wants it. In summary, SE principles militate against efforts to "protect" consumers by making decisions for them and by cloistering them in "safe" roles. SE principles emphasize collaboration with consumers and the integration of PSR services with clinical services to achieve optimal outcomes.

Clubhouse/Transitional Employment Model

The clubhouse, founded by consumers in New York City nearly a half century ago (see Anderson, 1998; Beard et al., 1982), assists people in adjusting to community living through providing opportunities for membership and belonging in a consumer-run program and through developing skills for community living. The widespread dissemination of the original clubhouse, Fountain House, led to the establishment of an International Center for Clubhouse Development.

Work has been an orienting activity for clubhouse programs, and not long after the establishment of Fountain House in New York City, a *transitional employment* (TE) model of vocational rehabilitation emerged. The TE approach involves the following components. First, clubhouse members participate in clubhouse work units, which, in addition to helping them feel needed and an important part of the club, build members' work skills and confidence (Beard et al., 1982). Once members become acclimated to work and develop core work skills, they are placed in transitional employment positions developed by clubhouse workers in collaboration with community agencies and businesses. TE potentially is a boon to community businesses in that the clubhouse program guarantees someone will fulfill the responsibilities of the job, even if the clubhouse member cannot be at work on a particular day. In addition, because clubhouse programs have a relatively steady stream of members entering TE, vacated positions often can quickly be filled. Because most of the TE positions are entry-level and, therefore, are high-turnover positions, this aspect of TE also can be attractive to employers.

Cathaleene Macias and colleagues provided data related to the employment outcomes of clubhouse members (Macias, 2001; Macias, Boyd, & Members of the Fountain Home Research Unit, 1999; Macias, Harding, Alden, Geertson, & Barreira, 1999;

Macias, Jackson, et al., 1999). In a cross-sectional national survey of clubhouse programs, Macias, Jackson, et al. (1999) found that just under 20% of active members were in TE placements, while 17.5% were in independent competitive employment. (The two categories of TE and independent employment were not mutually exclusive; therefore, it is not clear what percentages were in either TE or independent employment.) Bond and colleagues (1999) reviewed the evidence base for the clubhouse/TE model of vocational rehabilitation and reported rates of employment that were clearly higher than rates in the general population of people with serious mental illness. However, such results are found with many vocational rehabilitation programs, and there were no randomized, controlled studies of the clubhouse/TE model that would allow for a clear comparison of the clubhouse/TE model to other vocational rehabilitation programs.

Diversified Placement Models

This group of vocational rehabilitation approaches attempts to avoid the "single model trap" (IAPSRS, 1998) by offering a variety of vocational rehabilitation program choices to consumers, including SE, TE, "work experiences," and consumer-run businesses. Diversified placement (DP) programs have been developed by large, comprehensive PSR programs in urban/metropolitan areas, serving diverse consumers (Chandler, Levin, & Barry, 1999; Dincin, 1995; Starks et al., 2000). Proponents of this approach argue that a variety of vocational options need to be available because not all consumers want competitive employment or participation in a clubhouse.

The Thresholds program in Chicago is the most researched DP model (Bond et al., 1999). Evaluations of Thresholds have observed good employment outcomes. For example, in 1997, Thresholds assisted 16% of its served clients in achieving individual placements (presumably, representing independent employment), another 16% in obtaining positions in Thresholds-run businesses, and 8% in working in sheltered employment (McCoy, 1998, as cited in Bond et al., 1999). Several other program evaluations yielded positive findings (see Bond et al., 1999). Positive findings also have been reported by Chandler et al. (1999) for the Village program in Long Beach, California, and by Starks et al. (2000) for a program in Denver. Bond and colleagues currently are using a randomized, controlled methodology to compare DP and SE models at the Thresholds program in Chicago (Bond, personal communication, May 29, 2003).

Summary of Vocational Rehabilitation Models

Because Chapter 2 of this volume contains a thorough treatment of these issues as they relate to SE, only a brief summary discussion of the various vocational rehabilitation models is provided here, along with recommendations for program implementation. The practice guidelines issued by the International Association of Psychosocial Rehabilitation Services (IAPSRS, 1997) provide overall direction for the provision of PSR services, within the context of SE or any other type of PSR service. The IAPSRS guidelines were developed by experts in the field of PSR, who comprised a special task force of the Joint Commission on the Accreditation of Healthcare Organizations and the IAPSRS Managed Care Committee. The guidelines are focused on PSR practices that support the recovery of people with psychiatric disabilities and address practice domains such as assessment and planning, psychosocial interventions, management for recovery, cognitive interventions, and substance abuse interventions. The guidelines do not promote specific PSR programs, but they do prescribe categories of PSR programs (e.g., employment, education, and illness management services) and are useful in both planning PSR services and evaluating the comprehensiveness and appropriateness of current PSR programming.

Because numerous consumer surveys have identified work as a primary outcome and community integration goal for consumers (Campbell & Schraiber, 1989; Mallik, Reeves, & Dellario, 1998; McQuilken et al., 2003; E. S. Rogers et al., 1991) and because SE is an evidence-based practice, *comprehensive PSR programs should have a vital, well-staffed SE service that operates using the principles cited earlier.* Furthermore, the evidence base available suggests these SE services should be integrated into ongoing clinical and other PSR services. What *integration* means in a particular setting, or under various circumstances, may vary somewhat—it could involve integration at the service system level (through carefully articulated interagency agreements), at the program level within an agency, or at the direct service delivery level. Drake et al. (2003) noted that integration at the service delivery level is where better outcomes have been documented. However, these outcomes of integrated services often have been documented in the context of intensive, assertive treatment teams. Some consumers who need SE services do not need such an intensive level of clinical care. For this reason, it makes sense to integrate services at the program level, versus at the direct service delivery level, for people needing less intensive levels of care. For example, vocational specialists, working out of an SE or DP program, may collaborate with clinicians to respond to consumer needs for vocational services. The vocational specialists, however, will need to do more than simply "be available" when clinicians seek their services. Rather, at the program level, directors or team leaders should establish agreements concerning regular assessments of needs for vocational services and for integrating service planning and service delivery functions. One approach for this has been developed at the Mental Health Corporation of Denver (see McQuilken et al., 2003; Starks et al., 2000).

The extent to which service systems should contain DP and clubhouse-type programs is an important issue to address. Ideally, all service providers would be equipped with the latest PSR and SE knowledge and skill technology. However, because this is, realistically, a distant reality, it is probably best for service systems to have as part of the service mix a comprehensive PSR/DP type of program to ensure the ongoing availability of vocational services and to provide channels within the service system for greater consumer empowerment and ownership of services (Anthony et al., 2002). However, cautionary notes need to be sounded: First, for consumers in need of intensive clinical services, these comprehensive stand-alone PSR programs should not substitute for an integrated direct service model (as described earlier). Second, program-level integration functions between the clinical/treatment teams, and the vocational/PSR program will need to be carefully and meticulously worked out. Third, the comprehensive PSR/DP program should avoid a focus on prevocational services and training, as these generally have been found to be unhelpful (Bond et al., 1999). Instead, the principles of SE, as outlined by Bond (1998) and as described in the SE Toolkit (Substance Abuse and Mental Health Services Administration [SAMHSA], 2002; www.mentalhealthpractices.org http://www.mentalhealthpractices.org), should be used.

Supported Education Programs

Vocational services are effective in helping many consumers achieve competitive employment goals, but there is much work to be done in assisting consumers to achieve longer tenure in positions that provide enough pay to substantially improve consumers' economic well-being (Baron & Salzer, 2000; Lehman et al., 2002; Mowbray, Collins, & Bybee, 1999). On average, people with psychiatric disabilities are poor and suffer from maladies associated with poverty. Part-time, entry-level competitive employment positions do not necessarily help consumers transcend poverty. It is not surprising that surveys of adults with serious mental illness have found high percentages of respondents wanting more education (McQuilken et al., 2003; E. S. Rogers et al., 1991). In a statewide survey in Massachusetts, Rogers and colleagues found that nearly two-thirds of consumers wanted more education and one-third to half wanted specific educational supports, such as assistance in applying to an education program.

Supported education (SEd) helps consumers develop the resources necessary to obtain better paying jobs and to develop career paths (Mowbray et al., 2002). Anne Sullivan Soydan (2002) described the core purposes of SEd: "Supported education services help students learn the skills, access the supports, and identify and use the academic adjustments necessary to successfully complete a class, course, or degree or training program" (p. 3). Compared with supported employment, SEd is in a more nascent stage of development. Currently, various models are being tested and further refined, and it is too soon to promote one model over another. Nevertheless, successful demonstrations of the SEd approach have prompted the federal Center for Mental Health Services to label it exemplary service (Mowbray & Collins, 2002).

Mowbray et al. (2002) categorized SEd programs into campus-based and off-campus models. Due to space considerations, only campus-based models of SEd are reviewed here. These programs attempt to provide supportive services onsite to maximize social integration and minimize the burden of negotiating multiple service sites. Two of the most well-established campus-based models are the Michigan Supported Education Program and the Boston University SEd program (Collins, Bybee, & Mowbray, 1998; Unger, Anthony, Sciarappa, & Rogers, 1991).

Boston University Model of Supported Education

The Continuing Education Program developed at Boston University's Center for Psychiatric Rehabilitation uses an academic support curriculum in which students participate in a series of classes that are taught at the higher education institution to create a normalizing experience. The classes offer didactic and interactive modules on profiling vocational potential, researching occupational alternatives, career planning, and mobilizing personal skills and resources. Teachers in the original BU demonstration project were two master's-level mental health specialists with experience in classroom-based interventions (Unger et al., 1991). They were assisted by two graduate students, who helped students with extraeducational supports and provided assistance with independent living needs, social security benefits, and recreation. After completing the SEd-based classes, students typically elected to take additional higher education classes, to participate in other types of education or training, or to obtain employment. Students are encouraged to take advantage of ongoing SEd services, including weekly job club and alumni association meetings.

In their original report, Unger et al. (1991) found that two-thirds of the students completed a four-semester curriculum. While 19% of study participants were employed or involved in education at baseline, 42% were involved in employment or higher education after the four-semester intervention. This single group longitudinal design also showed a decline in hospitalization rates and an increase in self-esteem. In a follow-up report by Danley (1997), the educational and employment gains reported by Unger et al. were found to be maintained. More recently, Unger and colleagues again found positive outcomes for SEd sites in Massachusetts, Connecticut, and California (Unger, Pardee, & Shafer, 2000).

The BU group recently expanded on the SEd model by combining supported employment with a computer training educational program (Hutchinson, Anthony, Massaro, Rogers, & Cash, in press). In this Training for the Future (TFTF) program, which represents a partnership with the IBM Corporation, students are taught "industry standard computer and office skills" and to hone the interpersonal resources they need for career success. After completing the program, students participate in a 2-month internship to continue their computer and office training while engaging in a true work experience. The SEd component of the program helps people select and retain employment in jobs that are consistent with career/vocational goals and are higher paying than the entry-level jobs consumers often obtain through vocational rehabilitation programs. Hutchinson et al. are reporting encouraging outcomes from this demonstration, including positive advances in work status and income.

Michigan Supported Education Program

The Michigan Supported Education Program (MSEP) grew out of the efforts of a Detroit-based chapter of the National Alliance for the Mentally Ill to enhance support services on college campuses for persons with psychiatric disabilities (Carey, Duff, & Kean, 2002). The original demonstration/evaluation of the program used a randomized controlled study to examine the outcomes of two different models of campus-based SEd programs—a *classroom model,* patterned after the original BU model, and a *group model,* developed in Michigan—compared with a control group. In the classroom model, adult learning techniques (group exercises and experiential techniques) were used to teach students educational skills in a traditional classroom. The group model was consumer-driven and less structured than the classroom model. Two group leaders, one a consumer, assisted students in identifying and modifying educational resources to achieve their education goals. The group model guided students through four consumer-driven steps:

1. Participating in a structured group to identify environmental resources and to develop skills for making educational/career decisions and navigating the higher education landscape

2. Developing a group curriculum related to the learning goals of group members

3. Working together to pursue and utilize school and community resources

4. Evaluating the group

Collins et al. (1998) reported evidence of the effectiveness of both experimental conditions versus the control group, in which individuals were assigned a staff person to meet their needs for educational support. For both the classroom and the group conditions, a more than doubling of involvement in higher education and employment was found from pre- to postintervention. Students in the group condition had the highest levels of participation, enjoyment, and satisfaction among the three conditions. Students in the classroom model, however, showed the most positive change in empowerment and school efficacy. Attrition from both of the experimental programs was significant, but, as the authors pointed out, not different from attrition in higher education programs, more generally. A follow-up report of longer term outcomes further documented positive outcomes of the SEd models, relative to the control condition (Mowbray et al., 1999). And, in a rather interesting process analysis of a core program ingredient thought to be important to the achievement of high priority SEd outcomes (goal setting/attainment), Collins, Mowbray, and Bybee (1999) found that the group SEd model led to increasingly complex and specific goals over time, especially for highly involved participants. In addition, the authors found that high participation in the program and selecting school as the most important goal was positively associated with later enrollment in higher education.

Practice Guidelines

Psychosocial rehabilitation programs interested in implementing SEd are encouraged to peruse the models available, especially those with good outcomes data that have been implemented more than once, and to follow the program guidelines for the model that best fits the types of resources, expertise, and existing or potential interagency partnerships. The Mowbray et al. (2002) volume contains descriptions of campus-based and off-campus program models. In addition, a forthcoming issue of the journal, *Psychiatric Rehabilitation Skills,* will include descriptions of five SEd programs that have not yet been published (C. Mowbray, personal communication, June 9, 2003).

Description of Guidelines   Mowbray and colleagues have described the major SEd implementation steps (Mowbray & Collins, 2002; Mowbray, Moxley, & Brown, 1993):

1. A strong and diverse coalition of key stakeholder groups, including representatives from mental health, academic, and vocational rehabilitation agencies, as well as consumers and family members, should be established.

2. The coalition needs to become knowledgeable about SEd as an evidence-based practice.

3. An assessment of participants' mental health, rehabilitation/recovery, and educational needs must be conducted to focus the program.

4. Potential policy and resource barriers that might present obstacles to program implementation and success need to be identified.

5. Program values and priorities need to be identified and articulated by the coalition. Often, these values clarify the primary outcome goals of the SEd program (e.g., normalization and integration).

6. Technical assistance for implementing SEd programs should be sought in areas of need.

Where and How Deployed   Program models and implementation guidelines should be used in the context of a PSR program that has established (or is establishing) linkages with the key stakeholder groups outlined earlier. The PSR or mental health agency will need to be the core organization involved in running the SEd program, unless another agency has the necessary staff with expertise in psychiatric rehabilitation to run the program. However, even in the latter instance, strong linkages to a PSR/mental health agency are crucial.

Strengths and Weaknesses   Supported education implementation guidelines are based on the successful experiences of SEd programs from around the country. However, although many SEd programs have significant empirical support for their outcome effectiveness and some research is starting to identify critical ingredients (Collins et al., 1999), more needs to be done to get inside the SEd program's "black box" and explicate empirically verified program ingredients (Mowbray & Collins, 2002).

Contraindications for Use   On average, participants in supported education programs have had higher prior education levels than those found in the population of people with psychiatric disabilities (Mowbray, Bybee, & Shriner, 1996). This suggests that, at least for programs developed to date, a certain level of educational attainment is helpful. However, some programs have included people without high school diplomas or GEDs at program entry and, otherwise, no specific guidelines are available as to who will and will not benefit from SEd.

Fidelity Assessment

No fidelity tools for SEd could be found at the time of this writing, partly because, as Mowbray and Collins (2002) concluded, information about staff to consumer ratios, the necessary content of SEd, and other considerations have not yet been established empirically. However, the program description for an SEd model could be used to construct a fidelity instrument for monitoring program implementation and ongoing service delivery, and an existing fidelity instrument for PSR sister programs, such as the Individual Placement and Support Fidelity Scale (Bond, Becker, Drake, & Vogler, 1997) could be used as a guide.

Outcomes Assessment

An outcomes assessment approach can be extrapolated from the SEd demonstration and research projects that have been published to date. Mowbray and Collins (2002) parsed out outcomes for SEd into five domains:

1. *Educational attainment* outcomes should be assessed for SEd programs. Outcomes include enrollment in higher education programs (by type), number of higher

education courses/credits attempted and completed, grade point averages, and receipt of postsecondary degrees and certificates.

2. *Employment* outcomes should be assessed, including job attainment (broken out by competitive/independent and other types of jobs), tenure in employment, number of hours worked per week, and amount of income. A useful tool for capturing outcomes in the *educational attainment* and *employment* outcome domains is the IAPSRS Toolkit for Measuring Psychosocial Outcomes (Arns, Rogers, Cook, Mowbray, & Members of the IAPSRS Research Committee, 2001; IAPSRS, 1995). The IAPSRS Toolkit has easy-to-use forms for collecting baseline and outcome data pertinent to the educational and employment domains. It also offers guidance for using the data and for setting up a database, and it can be useful for benchmarking.

3. *Self-esteem and other self-perception measures* may be particularly useful in assessing the extent to which the program is empowering for persons psychologically. Instruments that have been used in SEd outcome evaluations include the Rosenberg Self-Esteem scale (Rosenberg, 1979), Lehman's Quality of Life scale (Lehman, 1991), a School Self-Efficacy Scale (Mowbray et al., 1999), and Empowerment (Pearlin & Schooler, 1978; D. Rogers, Chamberlin, Ellison, & Crean, 1997).

4. *Hospitalizations* can be tracked as an outcome of the program, particularly as a means of adding cost-related support for the program.

5. *Consumer satisfaction* should be assessed. Programs assessing consumer satisfaction should ensure that the process is consumer-driven by equipping consumers to take the lead in developing surveys or modifying existing survey questions, administering the survey instrument, interpreting the results, and making recommendations in using them for program quality improvement (McQuilken et al., 2003).

Wherever possible, programs should assess participants' status on outcomes measured pre- and postinvolvement in the program. These data can be tracked over time to monitor program improvement in outcomes performance, as well as to celebrate program successes and market the program to prospective payers (Barrett, Bartsch, Zahniser, & Belanger, 1998). In addition, programs can identify outcome benchmarks, based on the results reported by other, similar SEd programs. The recent review by Mowbray and Collins (2002) could be used, for example, in identifying outcome benchmarks (averages of performance across studies reviewed).

Summary/Discussion of Supported Education

In addition to one randomized, controlled trial, several outcome evaluations and quasi-experimental studies have found support for the relationship between SEd and progress in academic and/or employment outcome domains (Mowbray & Collins, 2002). Furthermore, it is almost inconceivable, even with outstanding supported employment programs in place, that most consumers would be able to develop satisfying and financially rewarding career paths without SEd-type services. Given the face validity of SEd in adding a uniquely important component to recovery-oriented PSR services, the consistently positive findings from studies of SEd, and the fact that no negative outcomes have been observed, it is not surprising that the federal Center for Mental Health Services identified SEd as an important recovery-related service.

The problem with SEd, however, is that it requires skill and ingenuity in collaborating with a diverse array of institutions and in putting financing mechanisms in place (Mowbray et al., 2002; Soydan & Rapp, 2002; Szilvagyi, Madigan, & Holter, 2002). Many of the most prominent models of SEd originally were funded through demonstration projects or collaborations with industry and benefited from the resources of psychiatric rehabilitation research and training centers. How is an ordinary community mental health center to begin thinking about providing such a complex service? The implementation/practice guidelines outlined earlier are helpful, and the volume by Mowbray et al. (2002) provides further descriptions of nearly a dozen different SEd programs, including a consumer-led program (Ekblaw & Zambuto, 2002). This excellent resource from Mowbray and colleagues also contains chapters on financing SEd programs, collaborating between public and private sectors, and the unique roles of the community mental health and vocational rehabilitation service in supported education services.

Social Skills Training and Illness Management Programs

Although no single skill training (SST) or illness management (IM) model is identified as *the* evidence-based practice in PSR, enough controlled experimental studies with consistently positive outcomes have been completed that, as a group, SST and IM PSR interventions are identified as evidence-based practices (Kopelowicz et al., 2002; Mueser et al., 2002). Skills training and illness management approaches are lumped together here because, although their more proximal outcomes are specific personal and interpersonal skills, their ultimate outcome goals include enhanced community participation and role performance. Dilk and Bond (1996), in a review of skills training studies, concluded that these approaches had established effectiveness in improving the proximal outcomes related to skill attainment, but there was less evidence of their effectiveness in helping consumers generalize such skills to enhance role performance. In recent years, increased emphasis has been placed on the generalization and application of skills in social roles. Due to space considerations, SST and IM programs that have been used primarily in outpatient settings are reviewed. The works of Paul, Lentz, Menditto, and others provide information on similar programs developed for inpatient settings (Menditto, Baldwin, O'Neal, & Beck, 1992; Menditto et al., 1996; Paul & Lentz, 1977; Paul & Menditto, 1992; see also Corrigan, 1995; Kopelowicz et al., 2002).

Social Skills Training Programs

Extensive development and research of social skills training interventions have been carried out by Robert Liberman and associates (Liberman, Glynn, Blair, Ross, & Marder, 2002; Liberman & Martin, 2002; Liberman et al., 1993, 1998) by the Boston University Center for Psychiatric Rehabilitation (Anthony et al., 2002) and by Bellack and colleagues (1997). Each of these groups has produced comprehensive, well-delineated treatment manuals for practitioners. As Kopelowicz et al. (2002) have noted, SST can be used in either a group-based format or in individually tailored PSR service delivery. The Liberman program, a portable, easy to adopt program, is highlighted in this chapter.

UCLA Social and Independent Living Skills Modules   The UCLA group, led by Robert Liberman, has developed a precisely defined approach to training people in skills needed to interact with others effectively and to participate in community living. Liberman/UCLA skills training involves instruction, modeling, rehearsal, and reinforcement. It is a behavioral, psychoeducational approach to skills training. Liberman and colleagues have tailored their interventions to the specific needs of people with persistent psychiatric disabilities. Noting the information processing difficulties that people diagnosed with schizophrenia and other mental illnesses sometimes face, they suggest certain modifications to typical skill training interventions. For example, to counteract the attentional problems many participants experience, new information should be presented slowly, repetitively, and consistently; in accounting for memory impairments, material is presented in small chunks of information, with several reviews of the information, combined with reinforcement for recognition and recall; and to cover for difficulties with abstraction, language and activities are used that are familiar to consumers in their own sociocultural environments along with in vivo exercises tailored to participants' living environments. Investigators have developed procedures for adapting SST modules to persons with particularly high levels of thought disorder and distractibility (Kopelowicz, Wallace, & Zarate, 1998) and have begun to incorporate supportive persons in the consumers' own environment as helpers in ensuring skill generalization and maintenance (Tauber, Wallace, & Lecomte, 2000).

Liberman and colleagues have produced several social skills training modules, with accompanying manuals and training videos, many of which have been translated into several languages. They define a module as "a delimited element of service that has an integrated theme, provides patients with information needed to acquire specific knowledge and skills, is streamlined for structured and prescriptive delivery by clinicians, and can fit as a component into a broader treatment and rehabilitation program" (Liberman et al., 1993, p. 48). Within each module is a list of skill areas, along with the behaviors for performing or relating in each. For example, within the medication self-management module, there is a skill area called "negotiating medication issues," which has a group of 11 different requisite behaviors, including "pleasant greeting," and "describe problem specifically." Available skill training modules include, among others, Medication Management, Substance Abuse Management, Basic Conversation Skills, Interpersonal Problem Solving, Friendship and Intimacy, Community Re-entry, Recreation for Leisure, and Symptom Management. Modules are delivered through a series of learning activities involving didactic introduction of the skill, video-assisted modeling, role playing, preparing to use the skills outside the training session, and in vivo exercises.

Research on the skill-training modules has revealed positive outcomes in consumers' skill attainment (Dilk & Bond, 1996; Kopelowicz et al., 2002). Some controlled studies of skills training have found consumers learn and maintain skills even into follow-up, postintervention periods. As mentioned earlier, efforts have focused on the generalization of social skills to real-life settings. A controlled study by Eckman et al. (1992), for example, found that social skills training led to the attainment and maintenance of skills and their use in real-life settings. Similarly, a study by Liberman et al. (1998) found that participants in social skill training versus those randomly assigned to occupational therapy showed greater use of independent living skills in their natural environments. In the latter study, social skills training was administered by paraprofessionals, indicating the ease of use and portability of this social skills training intervention. Finally, Tauber et al. (2000) used "indigenous community supports" (selected by consumers themselves) as skills generalization aides to promote the use of social skills in the community following social skills training. Their findings indicated that interpersonal and community functioning improved even 12 months after the social skills intervention.

Illness Management Interventions

Illness management (IM) includes educational, skill training, and cognitive-behavioral interventions aimed at equipping consumers to take more control of their lives by collaborating effectively with professionals and others to reduce susceptibility to illness and cope effectively with symptoms (Mueser et al., 2002). A variety of approaches have been developed, some more successfully than others, that target outcomes such as greater knowledge of mental illness, better communication of medication and side effects with practitioners, reduced number of recurrences of illness, and enhanced coping. Mueser et al.'s typology of IM approaches is followed fairly closely next.

Psychoeducation Interventions   Psychoeducation involves providing information to consumers about mental illness (e.g., the stress-vulnerability model), controlling symptoms, and treatment. Mueser et al. (2002) reviewed four controlled studies of psychoeducation and found that most of them improved consumers' knowledge about mental illness, but only one study reported better adherence to medical regimens. Other outcome domains of interest to PSR programs do not appear to have been affected.

Medication-Focused Interventions   These interventions, which incorporate psychoeducational and cognitive-behavioral methods, aim to improve collaboration between consumers and practitioners in the area of medication management. Psychoeducation (PE) teaches people about medications, side effects, and strategies for managing side effects to help them make informed decisions about medications. Most studies of PE have found increases in consumers' knowledge about medications, but Mueser et al. reported that most studies have not found improvements in medication adherence. Authors of the one study that used a no-treatment control group reported that, although consumers in the PE condition were more likely to show increases in insight about their illness, they also were more likely than the no-treatment control consumers to discontinue medication and to show increased suicidality (Owens et al., 2001).

Cognitive-Behavioral Programs   Cognitive-behavioral (CBT) programs, on the other hand, have had more success in demonstrating their effectiveness (Mueser et al., 2002). They use a variety of techniques, including behavioral tailoring, simplifying the medication regimen, motivational interviewing, and social skills training to help consumers improve medication management. Behavioral tailoring helps consumers develop ways of incorporating taking their medicine into daily routines (Boczkowski, Zeichner, & DeSanto, 1985). Motivational interviewing techniques are rooted in the approach to substance abuse treatment developed by W. R. Miller and Rollnick (1991), which involves helping people to explore the advantages and disadvantages of taking medication, amplifying positive motivations for responsible medication self-management, and promoting consumer choice and self-determination. Social skills training teaches consumers successful ways of discussing their concerns about medications with practitioners (Eckman et al., 1992).

Cognitive-behavioral approaches also have been applied in recent years more directly to the reduction of symptoms in people who do not seem to be responding to medication treatment. These approaches could just as easily be categorized as clinical services, but they do involve teaching people skills that are oriented toward helping them manage their symptoms and gain control over their psychiatric problems. Across the eight separate controlled studies of CBT, Mueser et al. (2002) reported, "the consistent finding . . . has been that cognitive-behavioral treatment is more effective than supportive counseling or standard care in reducing the severity of psychotic symptoms" (p. 1280). In particular, the positive effects of behavioral tailoring on medication adherence have been well established in several controlled studies. One study of motivational interviewing (Kemp, Kirov, Everitt, Hayward, & David, 1998) and another study of a more comprehensive CBT program (Lecompte & Pele, 1996) found improved medication adherence outcomes. These latter studies also reported improvements in other outcome domains, including decreases in symptoms, hospitalizations, recurrences of illness, and an increase in social functioning. Overall, CBT programs improve outcomes beyond merely increasing consumers' knowledge about mental illness or medications and hold promise for improving illness self-management and social functioning. Comprehensive descriptions and manuals are available for using CBT with people with serious mental illnesses (Kingdon & Turkington, 1994; Newman, Leahy, Beck, Reilly-Harrington, & Gyulai, 2002; see also Gingerich & Mueser, 2002).

Relapse Prevention Programs   These programs overlap with those described earlier, but have slightly different foci, including greater emphases on identifying environmental triggers for symptoms and early signs of symptom recurrence, as well as developing skills for coping with triggers, warning signs, or symptoms. Some of these programs also include a family psychoeducation component. All of the five programs that have been studied in randomized, controlled trials reported reduced rates of illness recurrence and/or hospitalization (Mueser et al., 2002).

The relapse prevention program of Herz and colleagues exemplifies this approach (Herz et al., 2000). Their Program for Relapse for Prevention (PRP) includes five components:

1. Educating consumers and their family members about identifying signs and symptoms of illness.
2. Developing a collaborative approach among consumers, treatment team members, and family members to monitoring prodromal symptoms.
3. Early clinical intervention when prodromal episodes are detected (crisis problem solving, supportive therapy, and medication changes).
4. A group intervention emphasizing improving coping skills, or individual supportive therapy, depending on consumer preference.
5. Multifamily psychoeducation groups.

In a randomized controlled outcome study, Herz et al. found that people in the treatment as usual (TAU) condition had double the rate of relapse and nearly double the rate of rehospitalization than participants in the PRP condition. An analysis of efforts to detect prodromal symptoms early on in the relapse process indicated that, while 35% of people in the TAU group met the criteria for full relapse by the time their increased symptoms were observed, only 4% of PRP participants' episodes met such criteria when recurring symptoms first were identified.

Coping Skills Training and Comprehensive Programs   Coping skills training programs teach people to deal better with stress or persistent symptoms and are consistent in their use of CBT-oriented techniques, but varied in the particular foci or outcome goals for the skills training interventions. Mueser et al.'s (2002) review of controlled studies found that all showed positive results for reducing symptom severity. Other outcomes that were found to be superior in the experimental conditions versus the control conditions included self-esteem, coping skills, number of social contacts, well-being, and self-confidence.

The coping skills intervention developed and researched by Lecomte and colleagues is particularly pertinent because of its incorporation of empowerment approaches as part of the intervention (Lecomte et al., 1999). Within the relatively structured, 12-week group skills training intervention was an individualized approach to facilitating consumers' selection of outcome goals and strategies for achieving them in the areas of self-esteem and coping. Lecomte et al. found that, although no changes were observed in self-esteem, outcome results at postintervention favored the experimental group versus a comparison group on positive symptoms and active coping. These investigators also found that study participants who were in service environments characterized as more supportive of the skills and competencies learned in the experimental group condition had better outcomes.

Comprehensive programs variously include psychoeducation, stress management, promotion of social skills and social integration, problem-solving training, and counseling of family members or significant others in the person's life. Three controlled studies reviewed by Mueser et al. (2002) found positive effects for these programs. For example, Hogarty et al., in their research of a program called Personal Therapy (PT), found increases in social functioning for participants in PT, versus controls, and prevention of relapse in participants who were living with family members at the time (Hogarty, Greenwald, et al., 1997; Hogarty, Kornblith, et al., 1997). Other studies also have demonstrated reduced relapse and/or improved social functioning for comprehensive program participants (Mueser et al., 2002).

Illness Self-Management Approaches   Illness *self*-management has been identified as an IM intervention led by consumers or peers (Mueser et al., 2002). An example of illness self-management is Mary Ellen Copeland's (1997) Wellness Recovery Action Planning (WRAP). Although formal research on this program has not been reported, informal experience with consumers around the country indicates that it is highly regarded. WRAP includes many of the same elements of other illness management approaches, offering a well-structured format for identifying the triggers and warning signs for symptoms, as well as prescribed coping strategies and a process for consumers to identify their own unique coping mechanisms for reducing susceptibility to recurrences of illness and for coping with symptoms. Intensive trainings have been designed and disseminated, and a manual is available (Copeland, 1997).

Practice Guidelines for Single Skill Training and Illness Management Programs

Various manuals and thorough explications of program models are available for SST and IM interventions. Practitioners interested in SST programming should review the manuals of Bellack et al. (1997) and Anthony et al. (2002), the modules of skills training from Liberman and associates (Liberman, 1988; Liberman & Martin, 2002; Liberman et al., 1993), and the toolkit on illness management by Gingerich and Mueser (2002). This latter resource from Gingerich and Mueser is reviewed here because of its comprehensiveness and its utility for practitioners.

History of Development   The Illness Management and Recovery Implementation Resource Kit (IMRIRT) was developed based on a review of the literature and on the input of 20 experts in IM. The Resource Kit, sponsored by the federal Substance Abuse and Mental Health Services Administration (SAMHSA) and the Robert Wood Johnson Foundation, synthesizes illness management techniques and approaches into one comprehensive program. The IMRIRT currently is being used in a pilot study.

Description of Guidelines   The IMRIRT describes a series of weekly sessions that practitioners and consumers use over the course of three to six months. The program can be used either individually or in groups and aims to provide accessible tools for helping people who have experienced psychiatric problems "to develop personalized strategies for managing their mental illness and moving forward in their lives" (Gingerich & Mueser, 2002, p. 4). Practitioner guidelines are provided for IM interventions such as educating consumers about mental illness and the stress-vulnerability model, building social support, using medication effectively, reducing relapses, and coping with stress. The practitioner guidelines for recovery strategies, for example, describe four different goals to be achieved across two to four sessions. Among the goals are "instill hope that the person can accomplish important personal goals" and "help the person develop a specific plan for achieving one or two personal goals." Intervention strategies to be used in addressing the goals are organized into three categories—motivational strategies, educational strategies, and cognitive-behavioral strategies—that guide the practitioner.

In addition to the practical and detailed practitioner guidelines, logistics of program implementation and core IM practice values are described. In the logistics domain, Gingerich and Mueser cover issues such as selection of participants, structuring IM sessions, session length, and guidelines for involving significant others. With respect to IM practice values, the authors assert:

1. Having hope and instilling hope in the consumer is the core ingredient in service delivery.

2. It is important to have the attitude that the service recipient is the expert on his or her experience and goals.

3. Consumer choice is paramount.

4. Practitioners have a collaborative stance toward consumers.

5. Practitioners convey respect to consumers at all times.

Although these values are common among PSR approaches, it is important to iterate them in the context of an educational/skills training approach, in which it is tempting for practitioners to slip into an "expert" role with consumers and dampen their sense of self-determination and control.

Where and How Deployed   Illness management and SST interventions have a lot of flexibility built in and can be deployed in a wide array of settings, from inpatient settings, to outpatient clinics, to PSR program sites. In addition, individual and group formats can be used.

Strengths and Weaknesses   Perhaps the greatest strength of IM and SST interventions is their flexibility. In addition, the guidelines described by Gingerich and Mueser and those presented in other sources cited earlier provide a level of detail that makes these interventions easy to adopt. Although studies increasingly use diverse populations, both demographically and clinically, many use inclusion/exclusion criteria that may limit the generalizability of IM and SST outcomes.

Contraindications for Use   Consumers tend to benefit from IM and SST interventions. However, a medication-focused psychoeducational program researched by Owens et al. (2001) found that it increased insight into illness but also made people more suicidal, suggesting that educational approaches need to be delivered within the context of a broader IM or PSR approach, which provides individualized support and instills a sense of hope for accomplishing personal goals. SST and IM approaches with an overemphasis on the illness aspects of psychiatric disability may not be very hope-inspiring (see Read & Harré, 2001; Read & Law, 1999).

Kopelowicz et al. (2002) emphasized the fact that when people are severely distressed, they often cannot attend to and learn from instruction and practice in social skills training. When working with actively distressed persons, practitioners should use techniques developed to help engage persons in distress (e.g., Kopelowicz et al., 1998).

Fidelity Assessment

A fidelity scale and protocol recently have been developed by Gingerich, Mueser, Bond, and Campbell (2002). This tool specifies different levels of IM program fidelity across 13 domains, including practitioner to consumer ratio for IM sessions, program length and comprehensiveness, involvement of significant others, use of goal setting, and frequency of core IM techniques, including motivational strategies and cognitive-behavioral techniques. The fidelity scales tie into the program guidelines described earlier and provide quantitative measures of guideline adherence. For example, the fidelity scale assesses programs based on their adherence to a practitioner to consumer ratio of less than 15 : 1 in IMR sessions and to a standard program length of at least 3 months. "Illness Management/Recovery Goal Follow-Up" is another domain assessed.

Programs are given the lowest of five possible fidelity ratings if fewer than 20% of persons involved in IMR services have a personal goal listed in their charts, whereas the highest rating is given when more than 90% of consumers have at least one personal goal listed.

Outcomes Assessment

Although no standard outcomes protocol is used, several approaches to outcomes measurement for SST and IM services are available in the literature. The manual by Bellack and colleagues (1997), for example, contains useful scales for measuring consumers' performance, cooperation, and attention in sessions, and a Social Adaptive Functions Scale (SAFE; Harvey et al., 1997), which is particularly useful with older adults. The SAFE contains anchored ratings for each of 19 different social skills areas. Kopelowicz et al. (2002) promote use of the Independent Living Skills Survey (ILSS; Wallace, Liberman, Tauber, & Wallace, 2000), which is handy for treatment planning, monitoring, and outcomes assessment and provides a comprehensive means of tracking basic functional living skills in people receiving SST services. Finally, portions of the consumer-oriented outcomes protocols described next should also be used in assessing outcomes because they address recovery- and empowerment-based outcomes relevant to all PSR services.

Training for Single Skill Training and Illness Management Service Delivery

Gingerich and Mueser (2002) provide a useful description of the qualifications of IM practitioners. The characteristics they describe are more related to the personal qualities and skills possessed by IM practitioners than professional licenses or graduate degrees and include warmth and the ability to establish relationships with people, a "shaping" approach in which the practitioner is able to facilitate and look for small steps toward goal attainment, and the ability to teach skills and structure IM training sessions appropriately. Very similar qualities would be expected in persons using SST interventions, which overlap considerably with IM approaches. In training practitioners, then, a couple of recommendations are in order. First, IM and SST staff should be selected based on evidence that they possess the qualities delineated by Gingerich and Mueser. The ability to use instructional methods, to structure IM sessions, and to apply shaping procedures and approaches in a patient manner is critical for practitioner success. Second, in training staff in IM and SST, emphasis should be placed not only on transferring IM and SST knowledge but also on in vivo practice and feedback for specific intervention skills.

Summary of Social Skill Training and Illness Management Models

Social skill training and IM have much to recommend them in that, together, they are recognized as evidence-based approaches, and they contain a wide variety of interventions for meeting the needs of diverse groups of consumers. In addition, SST and IM are relatively easy to adopt because they can be assimilated into the more clinically oriented paradigms with which most practitioners are familiar. Moreover, because staff can be trained in them and interagency and other types of collaborations are usually not necessary for implementation, SST and IM interventions are relatively inexpensive to adopt. Programs also find it easy to obtain reimbursements for these types of services, at least compared with some other PSR services, such as SEd. This strength, however, should be seen as a potential danger: Because these approaches are easy to adopt, programs may be tempted to orient their PSR programming around them. While SST and IM should be part of any comprehensive PSR program and can help facilitate ultimate PSR outcomes, they should not substitute for programs that more directly assist consumers in obtaining, maintaining, and enhancing social roles in the community.

Peer Support and Consumer-Delivered Services

Psychosocial rehabilitation-type services delivered consumer-to-consumer have become an increasingly visible aspect of the publicly funded mental health services scene. A recent survey of respondents in 28 different states, who had ordered a consumer-developed, recovery-oriented program curriculum from the National Empowerment Center, found a wide variety of mainstream and alternative program representatives developing or currently using consumer-driven service principles (Zahniser, Ahern, & Fisher, in press). A large-scale, multisite demonstration/research evaluation of consumer-delivered services (CDS) is underway, with nearly 2,000 consumers involved as service recipients in seven different programs from geographical locations around the country (the Consumer Operated Services Program [COSP] Multi-site Research Initiative, http://www .cstprogram.org; J. Campbell, personal communication, June 13, 2003). The importance to PSR of consumer-delivered services, which often specifically target PSR outcomes of interest, such as empowerment and recovery, has been emphasized by consumer/survivors (Ahern & Fisher, 1999b, 2001; Davidson et al., 1999; Solomon & Draine, 2001). Several have noted that consumers as service providers have unique capacities to understand other consumers' experiences and can empathize more readily (Deegan, 1993). Adding consumer providers to the system could, therefore, facilitate the delivery of compassionate and skillful services. Second, consumer providers may exemplify hope for recovery for other consumers by virtue of their relevance and attainability as role models (Lockwood & Kunda, 2000). Davidson et al. (1999) quoted a particularly relevant and poignant statement on these issues by Patricia Deegan, a psychologist who was diagnosed with schizophrenia as a teenager:

> To me, mental illness meant Dr. Jekyll and Mr. Hyde, psychopathic serial killers, loony bins, morons, schizos, fruitcakes, nuts, straight jackets, and raving lunatics. They were all I knew about mental illness, and what terrified me was that professionals were saying I was one of them. It would have greatly helped to have had someone come and talk to me about surviving mental illness—as well as the possibility of recovering, of healing, and of building a new life for myself. It would have been good to have role models—people I could look up to who had experienced what I was going through—people who had found a good job, or who were in love, or who had an apartment or a house on their own, or who were making a valuable contribution to society. (p. 165)

The mere presence of consumer providers in the system may raise expectations and hopes for recovery (Davidson et al., 1999). Finally, there are the potential benefits for those consumers hired—taking on the meaningful role of service provider may help in the consumer provider's recovery process (Mowbray, Moxley, Jasper, & Howell, 1997).

Davidson et al. (1999) gave a thorough review of the peer support and consumer-operated services literature and proposed a typology of peer support that included:

1. Mutual support services provided apart from the mental health system
2. Consumer-run services that were originally alternatives to the formal system (but are now in a partnership phase)
3. Consumer providers within clinical and PSR settings

For each of these categories of peer/consumer-oriented approaches, an overview of the empirically based benefits is reviewed.

Mutual Support Programs

Self-help and mutual support groups have proliferated in recent decades. However, only a few—for example, GROW and Recovery Anonymous—have been developed specifically for people with psychiatric disabilities. Davidson and colleagues (1999) defined mutual support as a:

> process by which persons voluntarily come together to help each other address common problems or shared concerns. Participation in such a process reflects an intentional effort to find a social niche in which there are resources and structures available to enhance an individual's ability to address such concerns. (p. 168)

Mutual support can be distinguished from naturally occurring support in that it includes standard procedures, routines, and prescriptions for addressing everyday problems and challenges, in the context of coping with a psychiatric disability. Participants learn new coping strategies and alternative ways of thinking about their condition (for example, as a challenge or spiritual journey), and they often are exposed to successful role models and can benefit from vicarious learning.

Additional benefits of mutual help have been described by Davidson and others. First, sharing life experiences and listening to others' stories, which are often similar or overlapping in content, can reduce social isolation and increase a sense of community. In addition, the structured processes developed by mutual support groups allow for the development of socially valued roles among participants, including those of helping, role modeling, group leadership, and community organizing (Zimmerman et al., 1991). Finally, mutual support groups offer worldviews that help people make sense of their experiences and integrate them into meaningful life narratives (Rappaport, 1993).

GROW is a good example of a mutual support group. This organization, founded by an Australian priest after his unsatisfactory experience as a patient in the mental health system, provides mutual support opportunities for people with psychiatric disabilities (see Rappaport et al., 1985; Salem, Seidman, & Rappaport, 1988). Besides providing ongoing emotional and instrumental support, GROW offers guidance to participants in coping with mental illness and everyday challenges through published literature. GROW also intentionally uses role modeling to demonstrate to newcomers how mental illness can be coped with and to instill hope that people can completely recover from mental illness (Davidson et al., 1999). GROW has positioned itself to receive funding from state agencies to provide mutual support services to people with psychiatric disabilities and has thus moved into an era of partnership with the mental health system (Davidson et al., 1999).

Only one randomized, controlled study of mutual support has been reported to date (Kaufmann, Schulberg, & Schooler, 1994), but additional process and outcome studies of mutual support organizations have documented the outcomes of mutual support involvement. Researchers have examined the effects of mutual support participation on symptoms, hospitalization, recovery-oriented beliefs and attitudes, and social integration. With respect to the traditional, more clinically related outcomes of symptoms and hospitalizations, research has produced a mix of findings. No studies have found negative effects of mutual support group participation. The one controlled study by Kaufmann et al. found no effects on symptoms, but trends from longitudinal studies examining the effects of mutual support groups on symptoms hospitalization have been more positive (Davidson et al., 1999; Roberts et al., 1999). In an interesting quasi-experimental study, Kennedy (cited in Rappaport, 1993) used 12 demographic and clinical indexes to match GROW participants with other consumers receiving formal services. Among the GROW and non-GROW consumers, there were no differences in hospitalizations in the 32-month period before GROW members joined a group. However, Kennedy found that GROW participants' average number of days of hospitalization was reduced from 179 to 49, while non-GROW participants' average number of days of hospitalization changed less significantly, from 175 to 123 days. Qualitative analysis indicated that GROW members tended to use GROW literature for coping while in the hospital and received supportive visits from GROW members. In addition, hospital staff tended to discharge GROW members earlier, because they knew they had the support of GROW after discharge.

Studies of social integration have focused on three areas: developing voluntary relationships, attainment of social roles, and participation in life-enriching activities (Davidson et al., 1999). Cross-sectional studies have reported that long-term participants in mutual support groups have larger social networks than shorter term participants. One study, by Rappaport et al., 1985, lent support to the hypothesis that it was participation level and not consumer characteristics that explained the difference in social network size. Nevertheless, more prospective, controlled studies are needed in this area. Studies that have been conducted on the attainment of social roles have underscored the importance of mutual support in providing opportunities for consumers to assume helping roles and not just receiving roles. A couple of studies have found that consumer-operated programs, in general, tend to create a greater number of formal social roles for consumers than professionally operated programs of the same type. (Carpinello, Knight, & Janis, 1992; see also Davidson et al., 1999). Finally, in the area of life-enriching activities and quality of life, several studies of mutual support, including one controlled study, have found positive effects of mutual support on social functioning, perceptions of self-esteem, and decision making. In one longitudinal study of 186 GROW members, Roberts et al. (1999) found statistically significant positive changes in a measure of role performance that included work, social and leisure activity, family relationships, marital role, and parental role domains. A study by Carpinello et al. (1992) also found that continued participation in mutual support was positively associated with pursuing educational goals and finding employment. Studies of GROW have found that persons who participate in an ongoing way, by their own reports, tend to do so because the mutual support group instilled hope in them and provided them with greater self-understanding (Davidson et al., 1999). Finally, several consumers who have been innovators and/or consistent proponents of mutual help organizations have emphasized the importance of participation in them for empowerment and, in particular, for the political advocacy dimension of empowerment (Chamberlin, 1977; Davidson et al., 1999; Deegan, 1993). Interesting process research of GROW by investigators at the University of Illinois found that the positive climate of mutual support meetings may be particularly important in contributing to outcomes in this domain. Toro, Rappaport, and Seidman (1987) and Roberts et al. (1991) both presented data indicating that interactions and statements from one member to another tended to be overwhelmingly positive, supportive, and helping in character and that group norms tended to discourage negative interactions. In a rigorous process study, Roberts et al. (1999) found that giving help, in particular, giving guidance to others, was associated with positive growth in social adjustment/role performance.

Consumer-Run Services

Another category of consumer-driven services is made up of consumer-run PSR programs, including drop-in centers, residential programs, and vocational programs (Chamberlin, 1990). Like some mutual support groups, consumer-run services originally were developed as alternatives to the mental health system, but, as they have become established, some have entered into partnership with the formal system (Davidson et al., 1999). Thus, this category of programs includes those that are entirely run by consumers, but which vary in their levels of connection to the mental health system. All programs, however, are characterized by consumer-driven and controlled decision making about the core aspects of program operation, even if nonconsumers are involved in some capacities (Solomon & Draine, 2001). A nonexhaustive list of consumer-run services includes a team of consumers who visits other consumers in the hospital and assists with discharge planning and follow-up (Mowbray, Chamberlain, Jennings, & Reed, 1988), consumer-run drop-in centers (e.g., Chamberlin, Rogers, & Ellison, 1996), programs to train consumers in advocacy work (COSP; http://www.cstprogram.org), supported education (Ekblaw & Zambuto, 2002), leadership development (Jasper, 1997), personal assistance in community existence (PACE; Ahern & Fisher, 2001), and vocational programs (e.g., Kaufmann, 1995; L. Miller & Miller, 1997). Mowbray et al.'s (1997) edited volume describes consumer-operated programs around the country.

Outcome studies of consumer-run services generally reveal high levels of satisfaction and other consumer-perceived benefits (Davidson et al., 1999; Solomon & Draine, 2001). Controlled studies have also revealed positive results in a variety of outcome domains. Miller and Miller (1997) reported high rates of closure of vocational rehabilitation services and employment tenure for persons receiving services from a consumer-operated supported employment program. Herinckx, Kinney, Clarke, and Paulson (1997) randomly assigned consumers to a consumer-run assertive community treatment (ACT) team, or a nonconsumer-run ACT team, or "usual care." They found no statistically significant differences between the ACT teams in any outcome areas after 2 years of program operations. (Incidentally, both ACT teams had higher rates of retention in services but also higher hospitalization rates.) Similarly, a randomized, controlled study by Solomon and Draine (1995) comparing consumer-operated and nonconsumer-operated intensive case management teams found no outcome differences. Process analyses found that consumers provided more face-to-face services and services outside the office setting than nonconsumer providers. Finally, a quasi-experimental study by Klein, Cnaan, and Whitecraft (1998) examined the outcomes of people with mental illness and substance use problems receiving peer social support on top of their case management services, compared with those of a matched group receiving case management only. Klein et al. found decreases in crisis events and hospitalizations, improved social functioning, a reduction in substance use, and higher quality of life for people in the experimental condition.

Consumers as Individual Providers of Psychosocial Rehabilitation Services

Finally, consumers can provide peer services by assuming regular clinical or PSR positions in mental health and PSR agencies. Often, these positions, such as case manager aide or peer specialist, extend services provided by nonconsumer professionals (Felton et al., 1995). However, consumers can also fill core clinical, case management, and PSR positions and studies of consumers as core providers generally have yielded positive findings (Davidson et al., 1999; Solomon & Draine, 2001). In a quasi-experimental study, Felton et al. (1995) found that the addition of peer specialists to intensive case management (ICM) teams enhanced outcomes for consumers with histories of homelessness and heavy use of emergency services. These investigators found that consumers served by teams enhanced by peer specialists had fewer life problems, greater gains in quality of life, and greater gains in self-image and social support, versus people served by ICM teams with no enhanced positions or with additional, nonconsumer assistants. Peer specialists in the study received 8 weeks of training in (1) a peer counseling approach characterized by the sharing of common experiences, practical strategies for recovery and survival, and social and recreational activities; (2) advocacy services; and (3) organizing self-help social clubs.

Because there is also much to be gained for the people who provide peer services, from a PSR perspective other employee roles for consumers within the system are of potential interest. McQuilken et al. (2003), for example, reported on a consumer-led research project, which not only added to the existing knowledge of barriers and facilitating factors involved in consumers obtaining employment, but also led to enhancements of the PSR and clinical programs within which the participatory action project was operating. The evaluation/research partnership between consumers and nonconsumer administrators and PSR programs located within the agency produced paid work experiences for dozens of consumers in the agency, many of whom went on to independent employment afterward (Zahniser, McGuirk, McQuilken, Flaherty, & High, 1999). Others have discussed roles for consumers in mental health systems that do not involve direct service but can empower consumers within the organization (Mowbray et al., 1997; Salzer, 1997).

Practice Guidelines

Mark Salzer and the Mental Health Association of Southeastern Pennsylvania Best Practices Team (2002) issued practice guidelines for consumer-delivered services (CDS). Additional material relevant to a discussion of practice guidelines is available from the National Empowerment Center (NEC) in Lawrence, Massachusetts (Ahern & Fisher, 1999a, 1999b; http://www.power2u.org), the National Mental Health Consumers' Self-Help Clearinghouse (http://www.mhselfhelp.org), and others. The Salzer et al. material is reviewed here because it was crafted with practice guidelines specifically in mind.

History of Development   Salzer and colleagues based their practice guidelines development on a review of the CDS literature and discussions among CDS leaders at the Mental Health Association of Southeastern Pennsylvania. The guidelines focus more on program characteristics unique to CDS, versus issues related to consumers filling traditional clinical and PSR service roles.

Description of Guidelines   First, with respect to CDS involvement or "dosing" guidelines, the guiding force should be consumer choice. There are no general guidelines for the amount of involvement consumers should have in CDS programs. Rather, consumers should be assisted in participating "at their own pace" (Ahern & Fisher, 2001). Second, there should be ongoing monitoring of consumer progress and problems, analogous to the monitoring of side effects medication management best practice. CDS programs, even those that are somewhat informal, such as drop-in centers or mutual support groups, should make provisions for providing increased support to participants who appear to be struggling. This should be done respectfully and without coercion to maintain the voluntary nature of CDS. Third, CDS, like other PSR programs, should attend carefully to gender and cultural issues. Especially within programs that involve one-to-one peer support or mentoring between consumers, attention should be paid to fit. Finally, in relationship to gender/cultural issues, because many self-help groups have been predominantly White, culturally appropriate and inviting marketing materials should be used and support group processes that appeal to a diverse array of participants should be developed.

The seven remaining guidelines from Salzer et al. all pertain to CDS that involve paid consumer-providers. These guidelines address issues of hiring, training, supervision, dual relationships, role conflicts/confusion, confidentiality, and creating a positive CDS environment. Because of space considerations, hiring, training, dual relationships, and creating a positive CDS environment are reviewed in this chapter.

Hiring

A consumer-provider who would be an excellent fit for an open position should not be inappropriately excluded from eligibility. For most paid positions, a high school education is required for workers to be able to complete the necessary paperwork and so on. However, where reimbursement is at least partially contingent on the credentials of the consumer-providers employed, programs often can find ways to support consumers in obtaining necessary credentialing certificates, or they can cover consumer-providers with the licenses of supervisors.

Dual Relationships

Supervisors also will need to be proactive in addressing issues of dual relationships, confidentiality, role conflicts, and other issues that need to have special consideration in the context of CDS. Dual relationships, according to Salzer et al. (2002), refer to "the existence of more than one relationship, either professional, social, personal, business, or financial, between an individual and another individual or organization" (p. 17). Dual relationships concerns can arise when consumer-provider positions are filled by people who currently are receiving services in the PSR program or mental health agency in which they are being hired. Salzer and colleagues suggest that programs wanting to enjoy the role-modeling and other benefits of hiring consumer-providers from within should ensure that the person who conducts personnel matters for a consumer-provider is one who does not have a dual relationship with that person. See Salzer et al. (2002) for discussion of additional dual relationship issues, including consumer-provider dual relationships with other providers and issues related to intimate relationships.

Creating a Positive Consumer-Delivered Services Environment

It is important to create an environment that supports and celebrates the unique contributions that CDS make to the PSR program. This can be done through training of nonconsumer staff in the benefits associated with CDS and through creating opportunities where honest, frank discussion can take place. In addition, making available consumer mentors from other programs outside the CDS program or its larger agency can help create a positive experience for consumer-providers.

Where and How Deployed   Implementation steps can be discussed separately for consumer-operated programs, such as self-help programs run entirely by consumers, and for programs that are operated by PSR programs employing consumers. With respect to CDS that are more independent of formal systems, implementation is often not a direct concern, in that consumers/survivors often already have developed programs. Nonconsumer professionals and PSR program leaders can play important roles, however, in establishing mechanisms for referring consumers to these programs, helping to organize groups, and providing space for groups to meet. In addition, progressive PSR programs can promote CDS by developing contracts for services.

For CDS provided within the mental health system, nonconsumer professionals' involvement can provide support and collaboration that recognizes and values the unique contributions of CDS. Salzer et al. (2002) note that it is important for the unique critical ingredients of CDS programs to be acknowledged and protected throughout any collaborative relationships between consumers and program administrators. Ongoing communication that addresses these issues is important to maintaining the specific and unique contributions of CDS.

Strengths and Weaknesses   Although the Salzer et al. guidelines cover important areas, provide a nice overview of the issues involved in CDS, and offer several solutions to those issues, there still is a need for the development of more precise guidelines for a variety of different CDS and for separate guidelines for the categories of CDS identified by Davidson et al. (1999).

Contraindications for Use   There are no identifiable subgroups of consumers found to be harmed by CDS (Salzer et al., 2002). However, mutual support does not appear to be of universal appeal to consumers. Studies have shown that a minority of consumers choose to attend mutual support (Kaufmann et al., 1994) and that two-thirds continue to attend for at least 3 months (Luke, Roberts, & Rappaport., 1993). Salzer et al. argue that *choice* is the criterion to be used in determining who receives CDS. As with other services, those not desiring CDS often will not adhere to the intervention.

Fidelity Assessment

Jean Campbell and colleagues produced the Fidelity Assessment Common Ingredients Tool (FACIT) for use across different types of CDS. Similar to other state-of-the-art fidelity instruments, the FACIT includes operational criteria for program fidelity. Within each fidelity domain, the FACIT defines the critical program ingredients, the questions that should be asked of key program staff to obtain information on each ingredient, and anchored scales for rating the program (Campbell & Johnsen, 2001). Fidelity domains include Program Structure, Environment, Belief Systems, Empowerment, Peer Support, Crisis Prevention, Education, and Advocacy. The FACIT was developed through a rigorous, 2-year process of obtaining consumer input into the critical ingredients of CDS and through pilot testing and reliability analysis. The FACIT is accompanied by a detailed protocol (Campbell & Johnsen, 2001).

Outcomes Assessment

Both the Consumer Operated Services Program (COSP) outcomes protocol and the Peer Outcomes Protocol (POP) are comprehensive tools developed by consumer researchers that incorporate multidimensional outcome measures field tested for reliability and validity (Campbell & Einspahr, 2002; http://www.cstprogram.org). The COSP includes outcome measures from nearly 20 different recovery-related outcome domains, including, for example, Finances and Entitlements, Housing, Satisfaction, Consumer Perceptions of Outcomes, Lifetime Service Use, Side Effects from Medications, Substance Use, Empowerment, Social Inclusion, Social Acceptance, Discrimination, Recovery, Religion/Spirituality, and Hope. PSR programs would find it nearly impossible to use the whole COSP tool on an ongoing basis. Rather, it is recommended as a resource for selecting validated, consumer-oriented instruments for ongoing and targeted use in CDS and other PSR programs. Similarly, the POP covers several outcome domains of interest to CDS but is not as comprehensive in its coverage. The POP provides a structured format for obtaining data on demographics, Employment, Quality of Life, Well-Being, Program Satisfaction, Service Use, and Housing/Community Life.

Training for Consumer-Delivered Services

Training for CDS includes two facets: training consumer-providers and training nonconsumer staff to work in a supportive, collaborative, and effective manner with consumer providers. As with any other program, CDS should have specific training procedures that cover the program's mission, vision, and philosophy, as well as specific skills and knowledge needed to perform each role/position in the program. Salzer et al. recommend that specific training topics capitalize on the unique benefits of consumer-provider services, for example, using personal experiences to build empathy with program participants. Although topics such as dual relationships and confidentiality are staple components of any new employee training program, these areas should be covered thoroughly with consumer-providers, some of whom may not have been exposed to these training areas in prior educational programs.

Salzer et al. note that the areas of confidentiality and dual relationships also will need to be addressed in training nonconsumer staff working with consumer-providers for the first time. In addition, nonconsumer staff will need training in relating skillfully and supportively to consumers as they make the transition to the provider role. They will need guidance in learning how to treat consumers as colleagues and avoid assuming a therapist role with the consumer.

Summary and Discussion of Consumer and Peer-Delivered Services as Psychosocial Rehabilitation

There is a relatively strong evidence base for CDS in producing the outcomes of greatest relevance to PSR. Almost none of the many longitudinal and quasi-experimental studies to date have found negative outcomes for consumer-operated and peer support services, and most have documented positive changes over time in PSR outcomes. Second, consumer accounts of recovery from mental illness consistently point to the importance of peer support (Ahern & Fisher, 1999a, 1999b, 2001; Kanapaux, 2003). Finally, the randomized, controlled studies conducted to date have revealed positive outcomes for CDS and that common service programs staffed by consumers are not inferior to those services staffed by nonconsumer professionals.

What is needed in the area of CDS is a framework that incorporates and organizes the available CDS programs and approaches. The National Empowerment Center (NEC), a federally funded Consumer Technical Assistance Center, has developed a personal assistance in community existence model (the PACE/Recovery Program) that attempts to do this. PACE articulates the core principles of recovery, as identified by consumers themselves who have recovered (Fisher, Deegan, & Ahern, 1999) as well as the CDS that are essential to any mental health system or comprehensive recovery effort. See Ahern and Fisher (1999a, 1999b, 2001) for further descriptions and emerging evidence for this program. Currently, the NEC is developing a PACE/Recovery Program Implementation Manual.

FUTURE DIRECTIONS IN PSYCHOSOCIAL REHABILITATION

Despite the explosive growth in PSR services, important issues remain concerning evidence-based practice. This section reviews issues that must be attended to if PSR services are to receive the level of policy and funding support they need to thrive. The section concludes with a discussion of exciting growth areas that are pregnant with possibility.

Getting the Psychosocial Rehabilitation House in Order

For PSR to sustain its growth, researchers, innovators, practitioners, and administrators will need to collaborate in better explicating practice guidelines, generating effective dissemination and adoption strategies, demonstrating the "recovery significance" of program results, and developing more integrated models of delivering PSR services.

Fortunately, recent work on manuals, fidelity scales, workbooks/toolkits, and integrated PSR models has moved the field toward accomplishing these goals.

Better Explication of Practice Guidelines

For some programs, such as supported education, diversified placement models of vocational services, and consumer-delivered services, practice guidelines, per se, are either not available or need to become more precise. Research on the critical ingredients of these programs, as well as their optimal settings and service participants, should help elucidate practice guidelines (Anthony, 2003). The study by Collins et al. (1999), cited earlier, provides a good example of researchers and program developers connecting a core ingredient of program theory (in this case, goal setting in SEd) to participant outcomes. Roberts' study on mutual help processes, cited earlier, is another excellent example (Roberts et al., 1999).

Generating Effective Dissemination and Adoption Strategies

Given the evidence base for PSR services, far too few consumers have access to them (Drake, Goldman, et al., 2001; Torrey et al., 2001). Corrigan, Steiner, McCracken, Blaser, and Barr (2001) identified two broad barriers to dissemination of evidence-based practices (EBPs): (1) lack of service provider's knowledge and skill in assimilating the innovation into practice and (2) organizational dynamics that interfere with implementation. Corrigan et al. suggested three sets of strategies for overcoming these barriers and for successfully implementing EBPs: (1) packaging EBPs such that they are more accessible and user-friendly for service providers, (2) educating and training providers about knowledge and skills, and (3) addressing organizational dynamics that interfere with implementation. The Gingerich and Mueser (2002) IMR workbook and toolkit is an example of an accessible and user-friendly tool for adopting an EBP. A fourth suggestion is to advocate for the adequate funding of PSR services with state and local mental health authorities. Such advocacy may be especially important in increasing access to PSR for persons of color.

One system-level strategy for disseminating EBPs is to develop academic-state mental health authority collaborations to improve training for the core professions. Graduate programs can collaborate with state mental health authorities to train students (tomorrow's providers) in EBPs, while also encouraging students' participation in developing innovations relevant to recovery and empowerment outcomes (Coursey, Gearon, et al., 2000). Descriptions of core provider competencies (see Coursey et al., 2000a, 2000b) are increasingly available and can help guide training. Another way to enhance dissemination is to involve consumers as trainers. Cook, Jonikas, and Razzano (1995) showed that consumers' involvement in training staff can enhance training outcomes. These authors examined the effects on training for existing mental health staff, but consumer involvement also can be useful in training students (Coursey, 1994).

Finally, examples of converting services based on weaker programs into EBPs have emerged in the literature and provide clues for systems changes. Drake, Becker, and colleagues, in studying the conversion of day treatment programs in New Hampshire into supported employment programs, found that SE produced much better outcomes but that some consumers missed social aspects of day treatment (Drake et al., 1994).

The development of self-help groups helped obviate the problems associated with that unintended negative consequence. Examples like this produce wisdom narratives that PSR advocates can share with program leaders, policymakers, consumers, and family members concerned about making changes in service delivery.

Demonstrating the Recovery Significance of Psychosocial Rehabilitation Services

More than a decade ago, Jacobson and Truax (1991) challenged clinical researchers by advocating for measures of the "clinical significance" of treatment. At this juncture, it would seem appropriate to develop approaches to assessing the "recovery significance" of PSR services. For example, a study might reveal a statistically significant, higher rate of employment for participants in the experimental condition of a vocational services program, relative to those in a control condition. However, even with a dramatic difference between the experimental and the control groups in this hypothetical study, the extent to which outcomes in financial, role performance, quality of life, and empowerment domains are experienced as significant by the person and lead to persistently higher levels of goal attainment in those areas may not be quantifiable unless new measures are developed. The use of recovery significance measures should be accessible and interpretable for a wide variety of stakeholders, and they should simultaneously help programs improve their fidelity to known EBP models and PSR innovators develop services and supports that can increase the recovery significance of outcome results.

Developing More Integrated Models of Psychosocial Rehabilitation

Models are needed that allow for the development of comprehensive, yet integrated, PSR services. Various authors have presented comprehensive analyses and programming for PSR services (e.g., Anthony et al., 2002; Carling, 1995), but Patrick Corrigan's (2003) recent treatment of this issue is particularly pertinent in the current context. Corrigan suggests that one way to develop an integrated, structural model of PSR is to locate PSR service programs and interventions within four key structures—goals, strategies, settings, and roles. Programs can select a mix of PSR services, based on the factors operating for them in each of the four structural domains. For example, a rural community mental health center might have as its primary goals to help consumers become more integrated into the community and to have a strong support network. The preceding *goals* might be bolstered by the *strategies* of providing supported employment services, independent living services, and developing support groups for consumers and family members. The *settings* for these activities might include the mental health center and local businesses for the SE work, the local housing authority and consumers' apartments or homes for the independent living services, and local congregations for the mutual support and family support groups. Finally, *roles* might include administrators, professional rehabilitation providers, consumers and family members, paid consumer leaders, and community collaborators. Agencies and programs can use the basic structure suggested by Corrigan in designing services and in helping to identify resources that might not previously have been considered for achieving PSR outcome goals.

As to integration at the service-delivery level, it may also be helpful for integrated programs, in which PSR specialists are working closely with clinical staff, to ensure that all staff are trained in and using the basic PSR techniques of identifying consumer-driven goals, building competencies, and so forth. At the same time, specific PSR interventions could be parsed out in a teamlike way, depending on areas of expertise. More clinically oriented practitioners and more skill training-oriented PSR staff may use the social skills and IM approaches, whereas vocational specialists and consumer-oriented staff may be involved with the SE, SEd, and consumer-operated services approaches.

Psychosocial Rehabilitation Home Remodeling and Expansion Projects

There are important issues for PSR that have not been fully addressed by extant programs. Two of these issues, spirituality and attitudinal aspects of recovery, have been selected for brief discussion here.

Spirituality and Recovery

Russinova, Wewiorski, and Cash (2002), in a study of alternative healthcare usage among 157 adults diagnosed with serious mental illness, found that 85% used some form of alternative healthcare practice in their recovery efforts. The two most prevalent alternatives identified by respondents included the use of traditional religious practices, such as prayer and attendance at religious services, and meditation. Other investigators have observed that significant percentages of persons with psychiatric disabilities, not unlike the general population, see religion and spirituality as integral to their coping and well-being (Fallot, 1998; Lindgren & Coursey, 1997). Yet, mental health and PSR programs often shy away from addressing spirituality, and especially religion, for a variety of reasons, including their own skepticism, concerns about reinforcing delusional thoughts, or concerns about having undue influence on persons' privately held religious beliefs (Fallot, 1998). Lindgren and Coursey developed a short-term, structured PSR group for people with psychiatric disabilities and have shown positive outcomes. However, this effort is relatively rare in the PSR services literature. Given the level of interest among consumers, PSR programs should consider developing and demonstrating models of PSR services that can increase opportunities for recovery in the religious/spiritual domain. In addition, churches, synagogues, and other religious institutions offer opportunities for social integration and assuming meaningful social roles (Pargament & Maton, 2000), and PSR programs should explore collaborative ventures with these institutions, just as they have with community businesses in the delivery of vocational services.

Attitudinal Aspects of Recovery and Empowerment

Consumer/survivor writers emphasize the importance of attitudes, such as hope, as well as positive expectations for the recovery process (Ahern & Fisher, 2001; Deegan, 1997; Lovejoy, 1982). Efforts in this area are not quite as lacking as in the spirituality domain, as PSR program developers and researchers increasingly have targeted outcomes of hope, well-being, and psychological empowerment. Indeed, the COSP Multi-site Research Initiative cited earlier is examining peer support and consumer-delivered services models that target this domain and is using a comprehensive outcome assessment that incorporates attitudinal measures of recovery and empowerment. Still, it should be routine that PSR programs would assess their effects on consumers' senses of hope and empowerment.

CONCLUSION

In this chapter, major programs and interventions in psychosocial rehabilitation services for people with psychiatric disabilities have been reviewed. The field has gained in diversity and strength over the past couple of decades and is poised to achieve a status, perhaps, equal to that of clinical services. Attending to important issues that can help to further increase the relevance and effectiveness of PSR services will enable policymakers, administrators, practitioners, and other stakeholders to embrace PSR in a way only heretofore dreamt of.

REFERENCES

Ahern, L., & Fisher, D. (1999a). *Personal assistance in community existence: A recovery curriculum.* Lawrence, MA: National Empowerment Center.

Ahern, L., & Fisher, D. (1999b). *Personal assistance in community assistance: A recovery guide.* Lawrence, MA: National Empowerment Center.

Ahern, L., & Fisher, D. (2001). Recovery at your own PACE (Personal Assistance in Community Existence). *Journal of Psychosocial Nursing and Mental Health Services, 39*(4), 22–32.

Anderson, S. B. (1998). *We are not alone: Fountain House and the development of clubhouse culture.* New York: Fountain House.

Anthony, W. A. (1993). Recovery from mental illness: The guiding vision of the mental health service system in the 1990's. *Psychosocial Rehabilitation Journal, 16*(4), 11–23.

Anthony, W. A. (2003). At issue: Studying evidence-based processes, not practices. *Psychiatric Services, 54*(1), 7.

Anthony, W. A., Cohen, M. R., Farkas, M. D., & Gagne, C. (2002). *Psychiatric rehabilitation* (2nd ed.). Boston: Boston University, Center for Psychiatric Rehabilitation.

Arns, P., Rogers, E. S., Cook, J., Mowbray, C., & Members of the IAPSRS Research Committee. (2001). The IAPSRS Toolkit: Development, utility, and relation to other performance measurement systems. *Psychiatric Rehabilitation Journal, 25*(1), 43–52.

Baron, R. C., & Salzer, M. S. (2000). The career patterns of persons with serious mental illness: Generating a new vision of lifetime careers for those in recovery. *Psychiatric Rehabilitation Skills, 4,* 136–156.

Barrett, T. J., Bartsch, D. A., Zahniser, J. H., & Belanger, S. (1998). Implementing and evaluating outcome indicators of performance for mental health agencies. *Journal for Healthcare Quality, 20*(3), 6–13.

Beard, J. H., Propst, R. N., & Malamud, T. J. (1982). The Fountain House model of psychiatric rehabilitation. *Psychosocial Rehabilitation Journal, 5*(1), 48–53.

Becker, D. R., Drake, R. E., Farabauch, A., & Bond, G. R. (1996). Job preferences of clients with severe psychiatric disorders participating in supported employment programs. *Psychiatric Services, 47,* 1223–1226.

Bellack, A. S., Mueser, K. T., Gingerich, S., & Agresta, J. (1997). *Social skills training for schizophrenia: A step-by-step guide.* New York: Guilford Press.

Boczkowski, J., Zeichner, A., & DeSanto, N. (1985). Neuroleptic compliance among chronic schizophrenic outpatients: An intervention outcome report. *Journal of Consulting and Clinical Psychology, 53,* 666–671.

Bond, G. R. (1998). Principles of the individual placement and support model: Empirical support. *Psychiatric Rehabilitation Journal, 22*(1), 11–21.

Bond, G. R., Becker, D. R., Drake, R. E., Rapp, C. A., Meisler, N., Lehman, A. F., et al. (2001). Implementing supported employment as an evidence-based practice. *Psychiatric Services, 52,* 313–322.

Bond, G. R., Becker, D. R., Drake, R. E., & Vogler, K. M. (1997). A fidelity scale for the individual placement and support model of supported employment. *Rehabilitation Counseling Bulletin, 40,* 265–284.

Bond, G. R., Drake, R. E., Becker, D. R., & Mueser, K. T. (1999). Effectiveness of psychiatric rehabilitation approaches for employment of people with severe mental illness. *Journal of Disability Policy Studies, 10*(1), 18–52.

Bond, G. R., Resnick, S. G., Drake, R. E., Xie, H., McHugo, G. J., & Bebout, R. R. (2001). Does competitive employment improve nonvocational outcomes for people with severe mental illness? *Journal of Consulting and Clinical Psychology, 69*(3), 489–501.

Campbell, J., & Einspahr, K. (2002, May). *New studies and tools for consumer-operated programs.* Washington, DC: National Conference on Mental Health Statistics.

Campbell, J., & Johnsen, M. (2001). *FACIT protocol.* Available from the Consumer Operated Services Program Multi-site Research Initiative, http://www.cst.program.org.

Campbell, J., & Schraiber, R. (1989). *The well-being project: Mental health clients speak for themselves.* Sacramento: California Department of Mental Health.

Carey, M., Duff, S., & Kean, L. R. (2002). Michigan Supported Education Program. In C. T. Mowbray, K. S. Brown, K. Furlong-Norman, & A. S. Soydan (Eds.), *Supported education and psychiatric rehabilitation: Models and methods* (pp. 89–98). Columbia, MD: International Association of Psychosocial Rehabilitation Services.

Carling, P. J. (1995). *Return to community: Building support systems for people with psychiatric disabilities.* New York: Guilford Press.

Carpinello, S. E., Knight, E. L., & Janis, L. (1992, July). *A study of the meaning of self-help, self-help group processes, and outcomes.* Paper presented at the annual meeting of the National Association of State Mental Health Program Directors (NASMHPD), Arlington, VA.

Chamberlin, J. (1977). *On our own* (2nd ed.). Lawrence, MA: National Empowerment Center.

Chamberlin, J. (1990). The expatients movement: Where we've been and where we're going. *Journal of Mind and Behavior, 11,* 323–336.

Chamberlin, J. (1997). A working definition of empowerment. *Psychiatric Rehabilitation Journal, 20*(4), 43–46.

Chamberlin, J., Rogers, E. S., & Ellison, M. L. (1996). Self-help programs: A description of their characteristics and their members. *Psychiatric Rehabilitation Journal, 19,* 33–42.

Chandler, D., Levin, S., & Barry, P. (1999). The menu approach to employment services: Philosophy and five-year outcomes. *Psychiatric Rehabilitation Journal, 23*(1), 24–33.

Clark, R. E., Xie, H., Becker, D. R., & Drake, R. E. (1998). Benefits and costs of supported employment from three perspectives. *Journal of Behavioral Health Services and Research, 25*(1), 22–33.

Collins, M. E., Bybee, D., & Mowbray, C. T. (1998). Effectiveness of supported education for individuals with psychiatric disabilities: Results from an experimental study. *Community Mental Health Journal, 34*(6), 595–613.

Collins, M. E., Mowbray, C. T., & Bybee, D. (1999). Establishing individualized goals in a supported education intervention: Program influences on goal-setting and attainment. *Research on Social Work Practice, 9*(4), 485–507.

Cook, J. A., Jonikas, J. A., & Razzano, L. A. (1995). A randomized evaluation of consumer versus nonconsumer training of state mental health service providers. *Community Mental Health Journal, 31,* 229–238.

Copeland, M. E. (1997). *Wellness recovery action plan.* Brattleboro, VT: Peach Press.

Corrigan, P. W. (1995). Use of a token economy with seriously mentally ill patients: Criticisms and misconceptions. *Psychiatric Services, 46*(12), 1258–1263.

Corrigan, P. W. (2003). Towards an integrated, structural model of psychiatric rehabilitation. *Psychiatric Rehabilitation Journal, 26*(4), 346–358.

Corrigan, P. W., Steiner, L., McCracken, S. G., Blaser, B., & Barr, M. (2001). Strategies for disseminating evidence-based practices to staff who treat people with serious mental illness. *Psychiatric Services, 52*(12), 1598–1606.

Corrigan, P. W., Thompson, V., Lambert, D., Sangster, Y., Noel, J. G., & Campbell, J. (2003). Perceptions of discrimination among persons with serious mental illness. *Psychiatric Services, 54*(8), 1105–1110.

Coursey, R. D. (1994). Serious mental illness: The paradigm shift involved in providing services and training students. In D. T. Marsh (Ed.), *New directions in the psychological treatment of serious mental illness* (pp. 123–140). New York: Praeger.

Coursey, R. D., Curtis, L., Marsh, D. T., Campbell, J., Harding, C., Spaniol, L., et al. (2000a). Competencies for direct service staff members who work with adults with severe mental illness in outpatient public mental health/managed care systems. *Psychiatric Rehabilitation Journal, 23*(4), 370–377.

Coursey, R. D., Curtis, L., Marsh, D. T., Campbell, J., Harding, C., Spaniol, L., et al. (2000b). Competencies for direct service staff members who work with adults with severe mental illness: Specific knowledge, attitudes, skills, and bibliography. *Psychiatric Rehabilitation Journal, 23*(4), 378–392.

Coursey, R., Gearon, J., Bradmiller, A., Ritscher, J., Keller, A., & Selby, P. (2000). A psychological view of people with serious mental illness. *New Directions for Mental Health Services, 88,* 61.72.

Danley, K. S. (1997). *Long-term outcomes of participants in a career educational program for young adults who have psychiatric disabilities* (Briefing Paper No. 1 of 3). Boston: Boston University, Center for Psychiatric Rehabilitation.

Davidson, L., Chinman, M., Kloos, B., Weingarten, R., Stayner, D., & Tebes, J. K. (1999). Peer support among individuals with severe mental illness: A review of the evidence. *Clinical Psychology: Science and Practice, 6*(2), 165–187.

Deegan, P. E. (1993). Recovering our sense of value after being labeled mentally ill. *Journal of Psychosocial Nursing, 31,* 7–11.

Deegan, P. E. (1997). Recovery as a journey of the heart. In L. Spaniol, C. Gagne, & M. Koehler (Eds.), *Psychological and social aspects of psychiatric disability (pp. 74–83).* Boston: Boston University, Center for Psychiatric Rehabilitation.

DeSisto, M. J., Harding, C. M., McCormick, R. V., Ashikaga, T., & Gautman, S. (1995). The Maine-Vermont three decades studies of serious mental illness: Longitudinal course of comparisons. *British Journal of Psychiatry, 167,* 338–342.

Dilk, M. N., & Bond, G. R. (1996). Meta-analytic evaluation of skills training research for individuals with severe mental illness. *Journal of Consulting and Clinical Psychology, 64*(6), 1337–1346.

Dincin, J. (1995). Core programs in the Thresholds approach. *New Directions for Mental Health Services, 68,* 33–54.

Drake, R. E., & Becker, D. R. (1996). The individual placement and support model of supported employment. *Psychiatric Services, 47,* 1125–1127.

Drake, R. E., Becker, D. R., Biesanz, J. C., Torrey, W. C., McHugo, G. J., & Wyzik, P. F. (1994). Rehabilitation day treatment vs. supported employment: I. Vocational outcomes. *Community Mental Health Journal, 30,* 519–532.

Drake, R. E., Becker, D. R., Bond, G. R., & Mueser, K. T. (2003). A process analysis of integrated and non-integrated approaches to supported employment. *Journal of Vocational Rehabilitation, 18*(1), 51–58.

Drake, R. E., Essock, S. M., Shaner, A., Carey, K. B., Minkoff, K., Kola, L., et al. (2001). Implementing dual diagnosis services for clients with severe mental illness. *Psychiatric Services, 52*(4), 469–476.

Drake, R. E., Goldman, H. H., Leff, H. S., Lehman, A. F., Dixon, L. B., Mueser, K. T., et al. (2001). Implementing evidence-based practices in routine mental health service settings. *Psychiatric Services, 52*(2), 179–182.

Drake, R. E., McHugo, G. J., Bebout, R. R., Becker, D. R., Harris, M., Bond, G. R., et al. (1999). A randomized clinical trial of supported employment for inner-city patients with severe mental illness. *Archives of General Psychiatry, 56,* 627–633.

Drake, R. E., McHugo, G. J., Becker, D. R., Anthony, W. A., & Clark, R. E. (1996). The New Hampshire study of supported employment for people with severe mental illness. *Journal of Consulting and Clinical Psychology, 64*(2), 391–399.

Eckman, T. A., Wirshing, W. C., Marder, S. R., Liberman, R. P., Johnston-Cronk, K., Zimmerman, K., et al. (1992). Technology for training schizophrenia patients in illness self-management: A controlled trial. *American Journal of Psychiatry, 149,* 1549–1555.

Ekblaw, E. B., & Zambuto, F. (2002). CAUSE: A grass-roots program. In C. T. Mowbray, K. S. Brown, K. Furlong-Norman, & A. S. Soydan (Eds.), *Supported education and psychiatric rehabilitation: Models and methods* (pp. 155–162). Columbia, MD: International Association of Psychosocial Rehabilitation Services.

Erikson, E. H. (1963). *Childhood and society* (2nd ed.). New York: Norton.

Fallot, R. (Ed.). (1998). *Spirituality and religion in recovery from mental illness.* San Francisco: Jossey-Bass.

Felton, C. J., Stastny, P., Shern, D. L., Blanch, A., Donahue, S. A., Knight, E., et al. (1995). Consumers as peer specialists. *Psychiatric Services, 46*(10), 1037–1044.

Fisher, D. B. (1994). Health care reform based on an empowerment model of recovery by people with psychiatric disabilities. *Hospital and Community Psychiatry, 45,* 913–915.

Fisher, D. B., Deegan, P., & Ahern, L. (1999). *Final report of recovery project.* Lawrence, MA: National Empowerment Center. Available from http://www.power2u.org.

Fowler, J. W. (2000). *Becoming adult, becoming Christian* (Rev. ed.). San Francisco: Jossey-Bass.

Gingerich, S., & Mueser, K. T. (2002). *Illness management and recovery implementation resource kit.* Rockville, MD: Substance Abuse and Mental Health Services Administration.

Gingerich, S., Mueser, K. T., Bond, G. R., & Campbell, K. (2002). *Illness management/recovery fidelity scale and protocol.* Available from jim.zahniser@empx.greenville.edu; mailto:jim.zahniser@empx.greenville.edu for information on the IMR fidelity scale's availability.

Harding, C. M., Brooks, G. W., Ashikaga, T., Strauss, J. S., & Breier, A. (1987). The Vermont longitudinal study of persons with severe mental illness: II. Long-term outcomes of subjects who retrospectively met *DSM-III* criteria for schizophrenia. *American Journal of Psychiatry, 144,* 727–735.

Harding, C. M., & Zahniser, J. H. (1997). Empirical correction of seven myths about schizophrenia with implications for treatment. *Acta Psychiatrica Scandinavica, 90*(Suppl. 384), 140–146.

Harding, C. M., Zubin, J., & Strauss, J. S. (1992). Chronicity in schizophrenia: Revisited. *British Journal of Psychiatry, 161*(Suppl. 18), 27–37.

Harvey, P. D., Davidson, M., Mueser, K. T., Parrella, M., White, L., & Powchik, P. (1997). The Social-Adaptive Functioning Evaluation (SAFE): A rating scale for geriatric psychiatric patients. *Schizophrenia Bulletin, 23,* 131–145.

Herinckx, H. A., Kinney, R. F., Clarke, G. N., & Paulson, R. I. (1997). Assertive community treatment versus usual care in engaging and retaining clients with severe mental illness. *Psychiatric Services, 48,* 1297–1306.

Herz, M. I., Lambert, S., Mintz, J., Scott, R., O'Dell, S. P., McCartan, L., et al. (2000). A program for relapse prevention in schizophrenia. *Archives of General Psychiatry, 57,* 277–283.

Hogan, M. F. (2003). Recovery from mental illness to gain new attention. *National Psychologist, 12*(3), 1–3.

Hogarty, G. E., Greenwald, D., Ulrich, R. F., Kornblith, S. J., DiBarry, A. L., Cooley, S., et al. (1997). Three year trials of personal therapy among schizophrenic patients living with or independent of family: II. Effects of adjustment on patients. *American Journal of Psychiatry, 154,* 1514–1524.

Hogarty, G. E., Kornblith, S. J., Greenwald, D., DiBarry, A. L., Cooley, S., Ulrich, R. F., et al. (1997). Three year trials of personal therapy among schizophrenic patients living with or independent of family: I. Description of study and effects on relapse rates. *American Journal of Psychiatry, 154,* 1504–1513.

Hutchinson, D., Anthony, W. A., Massaro, J. M., Rogers, E. S., & Cash, D. (in press). *Evaluation of a combined supported education and employment computer training program for persons with psychiatric disabilities.*

International Association of Psychosocial Rehabilitation Services. (1995). *Toolkit for measuring psychosocial outcomes.* Columbia, MD: Author. Available from the Evaluation Center at HSRI.

International Association of Psychosocial Rehabilitation Services. (1997). *Practice guidelines for the psychiatric rehabilitation of persons with severe and persistent mental illness in a managed care environment.* Columbia, MD: Author.

International Association of Psychosocial Rehabilitation Services. (1998). *The single model trap* [IAPSRS position paper]. Columbia, MD: Author.

Jacobson, N. S., & Truax, P. (1991). Clinical significance: A statistical approach to defining meaningful change in psychotherapy research. *Journal of Consulting and Clinical Psychology, 59,* 12–19.

Jasper, C. A. (1997). Moving forward: Consumer initiatives through leadership development. In C. T. Mowbray, D. P. Moxley, C. A. Jasper, & L. L. Howell (Eds.), *Consumers as providers in psychiatric rehabilitation* (pp. 209–219). Columbia, MD: International Association of Psychosocial Rehabilitation Services.

Kanapaux, W. (2003). We are the evidence: Consumers seek shift in research focus. *Behavioral Healthcare Tomorrow,* 25–27.

Kaufmann, C. L. (1995). The self help employment center: Some outcomes form the first year. *Psychosocial Rehabilitation Journal, 18*(4), 145–162.

Kaufmann, C. L., Schulberg, H. C., & Schooler, N. R. (1994). Self-help group participation among people with severe mental illness. *Prevention in Human Services, 11*(2), 315–331.

Kemp, R., Kirov, G., Everitt, B., Hayward, P., & David, A. (1998). Randomised controlled trial of compliance therapy: 18-month follow-up. *British Journal of Psychiatry, 173,* 271–272.

Kingdon, D. G., & Turkington, D. (1994). *Cognitive-behavioral therapy of schizophrenia.* New York: Guilford Press.

Klein, A., Cnaan, R., & Whitecraft, J. (1998). Significance of peer social support for dually-diagnosed clients: Findings from a pilot study. *Research on Social Work Practice, 8,* 529–551.

Kopelowicz, A., Liberman, R. P., & Zarate, R. (2002). Psychosocial treatments for schizophrenia. In N. P. Gorman (Ed.), *Treatments that work in psychiatric disorders* (2nd ed., pp. 234–257). New York: Oxford University Press.

Kopelowicz, A., Wallace, C. J., & Zarate, R. (1998). Teaching psychiatric inpatients to re-enter the community: A brief method of improving the continuity of care. *Psychiatric Services, 49,* 1313–1316.

Lecompte, D., & Pele, I. (1996). A cognitive-behavioral program to improve compliance with medication in patients with schizophrenia. *International Journal of Mental Health, 25,* 51–56.

Lecomte, T., Cyr, M., Lesage, A. D., Wilde, J., Leclerc, C., & Ricard, N. (1999). Efficacy of a self-esteem module in the empowerment of individuals with schizophrenia. *Journal of Nervous and Mental Diseases, 187*(7), 406–413.

Lehman, A. F. (1991). *Quality of Life Interview.* Baltimore: University of Maryland School of Medicine, Center for Mental Health Services Research.

Lehman, A. F., Goldberg, R. W., Dixon, L. B., McNary, S. W., Postrado, L., Hackman, A., et al. (2002). Improving employment outcomes for persons with severe mental illnesses. *Archives of General Psychiatry, 59,* 165–172.

Liberman, R. P. (1988). *Psychiatric rehabilitation of chronic mental patients.* Washington, DC: American Psychiatric Press.

Liberman, R. P., Glynn, S., Blair, K. E., Ross, D., & Marder, S. R. (2002). In vivo amplified skills training: Promoting generalization of independent living skills for clients with schizophrenia. *Psychiatry, 65*(2), 137–155.

Liberman, R. P., & Martin, T. (2002). *Social skills training.* Available from Behavioral Recovery Management web site: http://www.bhrm.org/guidelines/mhguidelines.htm.

Liberman, R. P., Wallace, C. J., Blackwell, G., Eckman, T. A., Vaccaro, J. V., & Kuehnel, T. G. (1993). Innovations in skills training for the seriously mentally ill: The UCLA social and independent living skills modules. *Innovations and Research, 2*(2), 43–59.

Liberman, R. P., Wallace, C. J., Blackwell, G., Kopelowicz, A., Vaccaro, J., & Mintz, J. (1998). Skills training versus psychosocial occupational therapy for persons with persistent schizophrenia. *American Journal of Psychiatry, 155*(8), 1087–1091.

Lindgren, K. N., & Coursey, R. D. (1997). Spirituality and serious mental illness. In L. Spaniol, C. Gagne, & M. Koehler (Eds.), *Psychological and social aspects of psychiatric disability* (pp. 156–170). Boston: Boston University, Center for Psychiatric Rehabilitation.

Lockwood, P., & Kunda, Z. (2000). Outstanding role models: Do they inspire or demoralize us. In A. Tesser, R. B. Felson, & J. M. Suls (Eds.), *Psychological perspectives on self and identity* (pp. 147–172). Washington, DC: American Psychological Association.

Lovejoy, M. (1982). Expectations and the recovery process. *Schizophrenia Bulletin, 8*(4), 605–609.

Luke, D. A., Roberts, L., & Rappaport, J. (1993). Individual, group context, and individual-group fit predictors of self-help group attendance. *Journal of Applied Behavioral Science, 29,* 216–238.

Macias, C. (2001). *Massachusetts Employment Demonstration Intervention Project: An experimental comparison of PACT and clubhouse* [Final report]. Retrieved June, 25, 2003, from http://www.fountainhouse.org/pdfs/samhsa_final.pdf.

Macias, C., Boyd, J., & Members of the Fountain House Research Unit. (1999). *Benchmarks of clubhouse excellence: A guide for evaluating clubhouse organizational performance.* New York: International Center for Clubhouse Development.

Macias, C., Harding, C., Alden, M., Geertson, D., & Barreira, P. (1999). The value of program certification for performance contracting: The example of ICCD clubhouse certification. *Journal of Administration and Policy in Mental Health, 26*(5), 345–360.

Macias, C., Jackson, R., Schroeder, C., & Wang, Q. (1999). What is a clubhouse? Report on the ICCD 1996 survey of USA clubhouses. *Community Mental Health Journal, 35,* 181–190.

Mallik, K., Reeves, R. J., & Dellario, D. J. (1998). Barriers to community integration for people with severe and persistent psychiatric disabilities. *Psychiatric Rehabilitation Journal, 22*(2), 175–180.

McQuilken, M., Zahniser, J. H., Novak, J., Starks, R. D., Olmos, A., & Bond, G. R. (2003). The Work Project Survey: Consumers perspectives on work. *Journal of Vocational Rehabilitation, 18*(1), 59–68.

Menditto, A. A., Baldwin, L. J., O'Neal, L. G., & Beck, N. C. (1992). Social-learning procedures for increasing attention and improving basic skills in severely regressed institutionalized patients. *Journal of Behavior Therapy and Experimental Psychiatry, 22*(4), 265–269.

Menditto, A. A., Beck, N. C., Stuve, P., Fisher, J. A., Stacy, M., Logue, M. B., et al. (1996). Effectiveness of clozapine and a social learning program for severely disabled psychiatric inpatients. *Psychiatric Services, 47*(1), 46–51.

Miller, L., & Miller, L. (1997). A.N.G.E.L.S. Inc: Consumer-run supported employment agency. *Psychiatric Rehabilitation Journal, 21,* 160–163.

Miller, W. R., & Rollnick, S. (1991). *Motivational interviewing: Preparing people to change addictive behavior.* New York: Guilford Press.

Mowbray, C. T., Brown, K. S., Furlong-Norman, K., & Soydan, A. S. (2002). *Supported education and psychiatric rehabilitation: Models and methods.* Columbia, MD: International Association of Psychosocial Rehabilitation Services.

Mowbray, C. T., Bybee, D., & Shriner, W. (1996). Characteristics of participants in a supported education program for adults with psychiatric disabilities. *Psychiatric Services, 47*(12), 1371–1377.

Mowbray, C. T., Chamberlain, P., Jennings, M., & Reed, C. (1988). Consumer-run mental health services: Results from five demonstration projects. *Community Mental Health Journal, 24,* 151–156.

Mowbray, C. T., & Collins, M. (2002). The effectiveness of supported education: Current research findings. In C. T. Mowbray, K. S. Brown, K. Furlong-Norman, & A. S. Soydan (Eds.), *Supported education and psychiatric rehabilitation: Models and methods.* Columbia, MD: International Association of Psychosocial Rehabilitation Services.

Mowbray, C. T., Collins, M., & Bybee, D. (1999). Supported education for individuals with psychiatric disabilities: Long-term outcomes from an experimental study. *Social Work Research, 23*(2), 89–104.

Mowbray, C. T., Moxley, D. P., & Brown, K. S. (1993). A framework for initiating supported education programs. *Psychosocial Rehabilitation Journal, 17*(1), 129–149.

Mowbray, C. T., Moxley, D. P., Jasper, C. A., & Howell, L. L. (Eds.). (1997). *Consumers as providers in psychiatric rehabilitation.* Columbia, MD: International Associations of Psychosocial Rehabilitation Services.

Mueser, K. T., Corrigan, P. W., Hilton, D. W., Tanzman, B., Schaub, A., Gingerich, S., et al. (2002). Illness management and recovery: A review of the research. *Psychiatric Services, 53*(10), 1272–1284.

National Institute of Disability and Rehabilitation Research. (1993). Strategies to secure and maintain employment for people with long-term mental illness. *Rehab Brief: Bringing Research into Effective Focus, 15*(10), 1–4.

National Mental Health Consumers' Self-Help Clearinghouse. Available from http://www.mhselfhelp.org.

Newman, C. F., Leahy, R. L., Beck, A. T., Reilly-Harrington, N. A., & Gyulai, L. (2002). *Bipolar disorder: A cognitive therapy approach.* Washington, DC: American Psychological Association.

Owens, D. G. C., Carroll, A., Fattah, S., Clyde, Z., Coffey, I., Johnstone, E. C., et al. (2001). A randomized controlled trial of a brief intervention package for schizophrenic outpatients. *Acta Psychiatrica Scandinavica, 103,* 362–369.

Pargament, K. I., & Maton, K. I. (2000). Religion in American life: A community psychology perspective. In J. Rappaport & E. Seidman (Eds.), *Handbook of community psychology* (pp. 495–521). New York: Kluwer Academic/Plenum.

Paul, G. L., & Lentz, R. J. (1977). *Psychosocial treatment of chronic mental patients: Milieu versus social learning programs.* Cambridge, MA: Harvard University Press.

Paul, G. L., & Menditto, A. A. (1992). Effectiveness of inpatient treatment programs for mentally ill adults in public psychiatric facilities. *Applied and Preventive Psychology, 1,* 41–63.

Pearlin, L. I., & Schooler, M. (1978). The structure of coping. *Journal of Health and Social Behavior, 19,* 2–21.

Pratt, C. W., Gill, K. J., Barrett, N. M., & Roberts, M. M. (1999). *Psychiatric rehabilitation.* San Diego, CA: Academic Press.

Rappaport, J. (1981). In praise of paradox: A social policy of empowerment over prevention. *American Journal of Community Psychology, 9,* 1–25.

Rappaport, J. (1993). Narrative studies, personal stories, and identity transformation in the mutual help context. *Journal of Applied Behavioral Science, 29,* 239–256.

Rappaport, J., Seidman, E., Toro, P. A., McFadden, L. S., Reischl, R. M., Roberts, L. J., et al. (1985). Collaborative research with a mutual help organization. *Social Policy, 15,* 12–24.

Read, J., & Harré, N. (2001). The role of biological and genetic causal beliefs in the stigmatization of "mental patients." *Journal of Mental Health, 10*(2), 223–235.

Read, J., & Law, A. (1999). The relationship of causal beliefs and contact with users of mental health services to attitudes to the "mentally ill." *International Journal of Social Psychiatry, 45*(3), 216–229.

Roberts, L. J., Luke, D. A., Rappaport, J., Seidman, E., Toro, P. A., & Reischl, T. M. (1991). Charting uncharted terrain: A behavioral observation system for mutual help groups. *American Journal of Community Psychology, 19,* 715–737.

Roberts, L. J., Salem, D., Rappaport, J., Toro, P. A., Luke, D. A., & Seidman, E. (1999). Giving and receiving help: Interpersonal transactions in mutual-help meetings and psychosocial adjustment of members. *American Journal of Community Psychology, 27*(6), 841–868.

Rogers, D., Chamberlin, J., Ellison, M. L., & Crean, T. (1997). A consumer-constructed scale to measure empowerment among users of mental health services. *Psychiatric Services, 48,* 1042–1047.

Rogers, E. S., Sciarappa, K., MacDonald-Wilson, K., & Danley, K. S. (1995). A benefit-cost analysis of a supported employment model for persons with psychiatric disabilities. *Evaluation and Program Planning, 18*(2), 105–115.

Rogers, E. S., Walsh, D., Masotta, L., & Danley, K. S. (1991). *Massachusetts survey of client preferences for community support services.* [Final report]. Boston: Boston University, Center for Psychiatric Rehabilitation.

Rosenberg, M. (1979). *Conceiving the self.* New York: Basic Books.

Russinova, Z., Wewiorski, N. J., & Cash, D. (2002). Use of alternative health care practices by persons with serious mental illness: Perceived benefits. *American Journal of Public Health, 92*(10), 1600–1603.

Salem, D. A., Seidman, E., & Rappaport, J. (1988, Fall). Community treatment of the mentally ill: The promise of mutual help organizations. *Social Work,* 403–408.

Salzer, M. S. (1997). Consumer empowerment in mental health organizations: Concept, benefits, and impediments. *Administration and Policy in Mental Health, 24*(5), 425–434.

Salzer, M. S., & Mental Health Association of Southeastern Pennsylvania Best Practices Team. (2002). *Best practice guidelines for consumer-delivered services.* Available from Behavioral Recovery Management web site: http://www.bhrm.org/guidelines/mhguidelines.htm.

Solomon, P., & Draine, J. (1995). The efficacy of a consumer case management team: Two year outcomes of a randomized trial. *Journal of Mental Health Administration, 22,* 135–146.

Solomon, P., & Draine, J. (2001). The state of knowledge of the effectiveness of consumer provided services. *Psychiatric Rehabilitation Journal, 25*(1), 20–27.

Soydan, A. S. (2002). An overview of supported education. In C. T. Mowbray, K. S. Brown, K. Furlong-Norman, & A. S. Soydan (Eds.), *Supported education and psychiatric rehabilitation: Models and methods.* Columbia, MD: International Association of Psychosocial Rehabilitation Services.

Soydan, A. S., & Rapp, J. (2002). Getting supported education started: A collaboration between public and private sectors. In C. T. Mowbray, K. S. Brown, K. Furlong-Norman, & A. S. Soydan (Eds.), *Supported education and psychiatric rehabilitation: Models and methods* (pp. 215–222). Columbia, MD: International Association of Psychosocial Rehabilitation Services.

Starks, R. D., Zahniser, J. H., Maas, D., & McGuirk, F. D. (2000). The Denver approach to rehabilitation services. *Psychiatric Rehabilitation Journal, 24*(1), 59–64.

Substance Abuse and Mental Health Services Administration. (2002). *Supported Employment Implementation Resource Kit* (Draft version). Washington, DC: U.S. Department of Health and Human Services.

Szilvagyi, S., Madigan, S., & Holter, M. (2002). Supported education: Costs and funding sources. In C. T. Mowbray, K. S. Brown, K. Furlong-Norman, & A. S. Soydan (Eds.), *Supported education and psychiatric rehabilitation: Models and methods* (pp. 223–230). Columbia, MD: International Association of Psychosocial Rehabilitation Services.

Tauber, R., Wallace, C. J., & Lecomte, T. (2000). Enlisting indigenous community supporters in skills training programs for persons with severe mental illness. *Psychiatric Services, 51*(11), 1428–1432.

Toro, P. A., Rappaport, J., & Seidman, E. (1987). The social climate of mutual help and psychotherapy groups. *Journal of Consulting and Clinical Psychology, 55,* 430–431.

Torrey, W. C., Drake, R. E., Dixon, L. B., Burns, B. J., Flynn, L., Rush, A. J., et al. (2001). Implementing evidence-based practices for persons with severe mental illnesses. *Psychiatric Services, 52*(1), 45–50.

Unger, K. V., Anthony, W. A., Sciarappa, K., & Rogers, E. S. (1991). A supported education program for young adults with long-term mental illness. *Hospital and Community Psychiatry, 42*(8), 838–842.

Unger, K. V., Pardee, R., & Shafer, M. S. (2000). Outcomes of postsecondary supported education programs for people with psychiatric disabilities. *Journal of Vocational Rehabilitation, 14,* 195–199.

Vaillant, G. E. (2002). *Aging well.* New York: Little, Brown.

Wallace, C. J., Liberman, R. P., Tauber, R., & Wallace, J. (2000). The Independent Living Skills Survey: A comprehensive measure of the community functioning of severely and persistently mentally ill individuals. *Schizophrenia Bulletin, 26,* 631–658.

Zahniser, J. H., Ahern, L., & Fisher, D. B. (in press). How the PACE Program builds a recovery-oriented mental health system: Results from a national survey. *Psychiatric Rehabilitation Journal.*

Zahniser, J. H., McGuirk, F. D., McQuilken, M., Flaherty, M. J., & High, J. (1999, February). *Outcome evaluation of the Goebel Program: Multiple stakeholders, multiple methods.* Alexandria, VA: National Association of State Mental Health Program Directors Research Institute.

Zimmerman, M. A., Reischl, T. M., Seidman, E., Rappaport, J., Toro, P. A., & Salem, D. A. (1991). Expansion strategies for a mutual help organization. *American Journal of Community Psychology, 19,* 251–278.

Zimmerman, M. A., & Warchausky, S. (1998). Empowerment theory for rehabilitation research: Conceptual and methodological issues. *Rehabilitation Psychology, 43*(1), 3–16.

CHAPTER 7

Evidence-Based Practices for People with Serious Mental Illness and Substance Abuse Disorders

Patrick W. Corrigan, Stanley G. McCracken, and Catherine McNeilly

Since the 1980s, service providers and researchers have acknowledged that substance abuse-related problems are the rule rather than the exception for people with serious mental illnesses such as schizophrenia or bipolar disorder. The relatively independent development of services for people with substance abuse disorders and programs for people with serious mental illnesses over the preceding 50-plus years has offered perhaps the greatest challenge to treatment of people with these dual disorders, that is, the lack of integrated services. Common was the experience of people with dual disorders having their psychiatric symptoms misunderstood in substance abuse programs or their substance abuse problems ignored at mental health centers. Essential to the evidence-based prescription for people with dual disorders is the provision of comprehensive services that simultaneously address the breadth and depth of problems that emerge from being challenged by serious mental illness *and* substance abuse; no priority is given to one set of disorders over the other. Before reviewing the guidelines that have emerged from the evidence base, we first provide a brief summary of the problems related to dual disorders. The chapter also includes recommendations about assessing processes and outcomes as well as training strategies. We end with a brief case study that illustrates the special challenges of dual disorders and the ways in which evidence-based practices help people challenged by these combined problems.

For the past 5 years, the University of Chicago Center for Psychiatric Rehabilitation has been home to the Illinois Mental Illness Substance Abuse (MISA) Institute (http://www.illinoismisainstitute.org). The Institute provides training and technical support to mental health and substance abuse providers in five Illinois consortiums. In the process, faculty and staff of the Institute have learned several practical lessons about transposing the ideals of evidence-based training to real-world settings. Pearls gleaned from these lessons are woven into our chapter.

OVERVIEW OF THE PROBLEM

Dual disorders have been described in many ways: from the perspective of a primary mental illness with substance abuse arising secondarily as a coping mechanism, as a primary substance abuse disorder with mental illness resulting from prolonged abuse, or some mix thereof (Drake & Wallach, 2000; Lehman, Myers, & Corty, 1989). The primacy argument has led to assertions that treatment should focus on substance abuse (if practice guidelines were written by the community of substance abuse providers) or mental illness (if mental health providers authored the guidelines). This work views the problem in a manner consistent with guidelines written by experts on dual disorders (Drake et al., 2001); namely, what came first—the mental illness or the substance abuse disorder—is largely a red herring. People with dual disorders are best served when common etiology, risk factors, and treatments are assumed for the combined syndrome. This chapter specifically focuses on people with serious mental illness (e.g., schizophrenia or bipolar disorder) who also abuse substances.

Epidemiological evidence suggests that dual disorders are a fairly common pattern. Findings from the Epidemiological Catchment Area (ECA) study, for example, found that people with serious mental illness had a lifetime prevalence for substance abuse disorders of about 50% (Regier, Narrow, & Rae, 1990). People with schizophrenia were four times more likely to have a substance abuse disorder in their lifetime than the general population; the prevalence rate for people with bipolar disorder was nearly five times higher than the general population. Mueser and colleagues (1990) summarized findings from 22 other prevalence studies on dual disorders and concluded that, although studies vary widely in terms of the prevalence of substance abuse in people with schizophrenia, it is a formidable problem that challenges at least a third of the population.

Research has also examined whether people with serious mental illness use specific drugs at a higher rate than the rest of the population. The self-medication hypothesis dominated this trend in research; namely, people with serious mental illness use street drugs to control the upsetting symptoms of the illness. If this hypothesis is correct, it would suggest that people with serious mental illness would abuse sedating drugs more frequently than others. Research has sometimes suggested the opposite, however; two studies have shown that people with mental illness abuse stimulants at a higher rate than other drugs (Mueser et al., 1990; Schneier & Siris, 1987). Contrary to the self-medication hypothesis, people with mental illness seem to be using the street drug that would exacerbate their symptoms. However, these findings have not been replicated on large national samples (Kessler et al., 1996; Regier et al., 1990). Instead, evidence suggests that availability of street drugs, rather than their subjective effects, is the best predictor of which specific substances are abused (Mueser, Yarnold, & Bellack, 1992). Of more importance, research has failed to suggest that regular abuse of any one substance leads to a worse outcome than another. In other words, combining substance abuse with mental illness yields harmful outcomes regardless of the substance of choice.

Impact of Dual Disorders

Research suggests that the problems of comorbid serious mental illness and substance abuse disorder are greater than what is typically experienced by either disorder alone

(Drake, Osher, & Wallach, 1989; Linszen et al., 1994; Osher et al., 1994). Table 7.1 summarizes the negative impact of dual disorders across several life domains as well as the research sources that report the evidence supporting these areas as being problematic. Research suggests the course of the disorder is more severe for people with mental illness who abuse drugs and alcohol (e.g., Swofford, Kasckow, Scheller-Gilkey, & Inderbitzin, 1996). People in this group experience more frequent and severe exacerbations in psychosis, depression, mood swings, and anxiety. As a result, this group will more likely experience a significant relapse that requires rehospitalization, usually for longer than typical lengths of stay (Haywood et al., 1995).

Given that people with dual disorders have a more serious illness course, it seems logical that they would show greater benefits from pharmacological and psychosocial treatment. Unfortunately, research suggests that people with dual disorders are less likely to seek out or remain in appropriate services. People in this group show less awareness of their illness and endorse attitudes that are unrealistic in terms of their illness or appropriate treatment (Alterman & McLellan, 1981; Tsuang, Simpson, & Krofol, 1982). Given their higher rates of symptoms and diminished social skills, people in this group are difficult to engage or to help participate in a regular, therapeutic relationship. As a result of problems like these, research suggests people with dual disorders are less likely to adhere to treatment prescriptions (F. Miller & Tanenbaum, 1989).

A worse disease course also undermines the life goals of many people with dual disorders. People with mental illness who abuse substances have a worse work history; they are less likely to be hired into competitive jobs or hold on to them once they are begun (Perkins, Simpson, & Tsuang, 1986). Similarly, the housing situations of people with dual disorders are less stable with an inordinate number of individuals from this group ending on the streets (Bartels & Drake, 1996; Blankertz & Cnaan, 1993). People with dual disorders are also more likely to be involved in the criminal justice system. They show a higher rate of violence than people with single disorders (e.g., Scott et al.,

Table 7.1   Negative Impacts of Dual Disorders

Negative Impact	Cities Providing Empirical Support
More frequent/severe psychiatric symptoms	McLellan, Woody, & O'Brien, 1979; Perkins, Simpson, & Tsuang, 1986; Swofford, Kasckow, Scheller-Gilkey, & Inderbitzin, 1996; Tsuang, Simpson, & Kronfol, 1982
More frequent hospitalization	Haywood et al., 1995
Less able to participate in treatment	Alterman & McLellan, 1981; Tsuang, Simpson, & Kronfol, 1982; McCarrick, Manderscheid, & Bertolucci, 1985; F. Miller & Tanebaum, 1989
Worse work history	Perkins, Simpson, & Tsuang, 1986
More likely to be homeless	Bartels & Drake, 1996; Blankertz & Cnaan, 1993; Caton et al., 1994
Greater rates of violence	Cuffel, Shumway, Choulijian, & Macdonald, 1994; Kay, Kalathara, & Meinzer, 1989; Raesaenen, Tiihonen, Isohanni, Rantakallio, Lehtonen, & Moring, 1998; Scott et al., 1998
Greater rates of incarceration	Abram & Teplin, 1991; Schuckit, 1985
More frequent infections	Koegel & Burnam, 1988; Rosenberg et al., 2001

1998). Greater dangerousness, combined with a higher rate of homelessness, leads to more frequent incarceration and involvement with the police and the courts.

Finally, dual disorders lead to greater rates of infectious diseases (Rosenberg et al., 2001). Some of these diseases—such as AIDS and hepatitis C—are directly related to drug use. Others—such as pneumonia—result from poor nutrition and other diminished lifestyle issues that are commensurate with homelessness. Recuperation after the onset of an illness is typically much slower and more likely to leave residual symptoms.

SUMMARY OF THE EVIDENCE-BASED PRACTICE GUIDELINES

Although most professional associations with interest in clinical services have voiced the need for evidence-based practice guidelines for people with dual disorders, we have found only two sets of consensus guidelines: the consensus report of the Managed Care Initiative coordinated by the University of Pennsylvania Center for Mental Health Policy and Services Research (the MCI report; Minkoff, 2001) and the summary of services generated by researchers especially supported for this project by the Substance Abuse and Mental Health Administration and the Robert Woods Johnson Foundation (the SAMHSA-RWJ report; Drake et al., 2001). Although there are some differences between these two sets of guidelines, many principles, practices, and assessment strategies are common to both. These commonalities are the basis of our summary.

Basic Principles

The MCI report authored by Minkoff (2001) does a nice job of summarizing eight principles to guide services for people with dual disorders. Many of the principles correspond with the nature of the problem as outlined earlier:

1. *Comorbidity should be expected; people with these disorders are not exceptions.* Hence, the system of care should be set up and ready for the difficult treatment needs posed by people with these disorders. They should not be pieced together in an ad hoc manner from mental health and substance abuse services that traditionally work with only one disorder.

2. *When coexisting disorders are observed, both psychiatric and substance abuse disorders should be considered as primary.* All aspects of service need to target both aspects of the duality aggressively from the beginning of care.

3. *Individuals within the population of treatment consumers currently served by any single program are likely to be in all the various stages of change.* Hence, the program needs to provide treatments that address the various stages. Stages of change are discussed more thoroughly later in the chapter.

4. *When possible, services for people with dual disorders should be provided by individuals, teams, and programs who are expert in treating both mental illness and substance abuse.* Piecing together a dual disorders program from the practice of individual mental health and substance abuse centers is likely to be less effective.

5. *Services should be longitudinal and continuous.* Teams and programs should expect that services for people with dual disorders will require months and years of continuous intervention. Long-term intervention is more likely to be successful when the person with dual disorders builds lasting relationships with the same set of providers.

6. *Beware admission criteria that exclude people from participating in a program.* Teams and programs should expect people with dual disorders to have multiple and significant problems including serious physical health problems, homelessness, involvement with the criminal justice system, continued drug abuse, and family physical abuse. None of these issues should be grounds for excluding people from a dual disorders program or for dismissing them from treatment if they recur.

7. *There should be no formal boundaries to dual disorders treatment beyond which services do not occur.* The traditional model of 50-minute hours in the therapist's office is not suitable to address the multitiered problems of people with dual disorders. Teams and programs must seek and serve people with dual disorders in sites that are most convenient and timely to the consumer. Seeing the person in the locale in which problems recur helps the service provider better understand the problem as well as makes interventions more potent.

8. *Fiscal and administrative operations of the program need to yield integrated and effective programs.* The evolution of most public systems has produced independently functioning mental health and substance abuse treatment programs. As a result, people with dual disorders have been served poorly by both. Illinois, like several other states, has attempted to resolve this problem in four steps. First, the state agencies that traditionally served substance abuse (the Illinois Office of Alcohol and Substance Abuse) and mental illness (the Illinois Office of Mental Health) pooled funds from their respective budgets for integrated and/or coordinated programs that specifically served dual disorders. Second, because agencies with this specific specialty did not already exist, the state set up consortia of mental health and substance abuse services in five locations (three in the Chicago area, one in Rockford, and one in East St. Louis). An executive committee made up of leaders from participating programs was charged with developing a comprehensive and integrated program for people with dual disorders using the funds allocated by the state to the consortium.

  Third, the state set up a staff training and technical support program—the Illinois MISA Institute—to work with consortium executive committees. Jointly, the training institute and executive committees identified training needs and brought in necessary experts to educate staff. Rather than an upfront, one-time process, training was meant to continue indefinitely. More information about our training approach and the Illinois MISA Institute is provided later in this chapter. Fourth, impact of system change needed to be assessed. The state, consortia, and Illinois MISA Institute jointly set up annual benchmarks that assess process and outcome enhancements that result from their work. They also identify indicators that represent these benchmarks and user-friendly systems for tracking the benchmarks. This evaluation program is also discussed later in the chapter.

Specific Practices

After reviewing the empirical literature, investigators who authored the SAMHSA-RWJ report identified five practices that were critical for effective dual disorder services (Drake et al., 2001). They augmented these services with three additional practice issues needed for effective programs.

Staged Interventions

People with dual disorders vary in their readiness to change behaviors related to both mental health and substance abuse problems. Hence, services need to be staged so they reflect the key priorities represented by the individual's readiness for change. Two stage models have evolved to guide this process. The first model evolved from clinical experience with people with dual disorders and represents the necessary steps programs must take to move people with dual disorders from the fringe of services to active treatment and relapse prevention (Minkoff, 1991; Ridgely, 1991). Program steps include engagement (forming a trusting and continuous relationship), persuasion (helping the person develop motivation to seek help), active treatment (acquiring skills and supports so the problems that result from dual disorders diminish), and relapse prevention (identifying strategies while symptoms have remitted for how to effectively cope with them if and when they return).

The second approach—called the *transtheoretical model*—maps stages individuals pass through as they seek to change specific behaviors. This model was quickly adapted from change related to substance abuse (Prochaska, DiClemente, & Norcross, 1992) and has been applied to dual disorders (Bellack & DiClemente, 1999; Zuckoff & Daley, 2001). The transtheoretical model has evolved since its inception with the number of stages varying depending on the iteration. The six-stage model is summarized in Table 7.2 where behavior change is represented as a longitudinal process. Progression through these stages depends on the person's identification and relative assessment of the costs and benefits of changing a behavior. Movement through latter stages depends on whether the person is participating in activities to foster change.

These stages have been illustrated with the example of a person considering whether to give up use of alcohol. *Precontemplation* is the first stage; as the name suggests, persons in this stage have not yet considered changing the specified behavior. The individual perceives no benefits to the new behavior (e.g., "My life won't improve by stopping

Table 7.2 Stages of Changing Behaviors

Stage	Cost versus Benefits	Activities in Which the Person Engages to Change Behaviors
Precontemplation	No benefits, many costs	No engagement in activities
Contemplation	Costs >> benefits	No engagement in activities
Determination	Benefits > costs	No engagement in activities
Action	Benefits > costs	Participating in activities for 6 months or *less*
Maintenance	Benefits > costs	Participating in activities for 6 months or *more*
Relapse	Benefits > costs	Participation in activities interrupted by slips and relapses

Note: Stages here represent the costs and benefits of changing a specific behavior.

my beer") and several costs (e.g., "I'll lose my good time and all my drinking buddies"). Hence, persons in the precontemplation stage perceive no reason to participate in substance abuse services. Persons in the *contemplation* stage recognize some benefits to the new behavior (e.g., "My mom will stop nagging me about drinking too much") but still believe the costs are far greater. Hence, although ambivalent, persons in the contemplation stage are unlikely to pursue any services that will change their status. Persons in the *determination* stage (also called the *preparation* stage in this literature; Prochaska et al., 1992) recognize that benefits of the new behavior outweigh costs. Although not yet participating in any active service, persons in this stage are now ready to pursue alcohol abuse treatment as a goal.

Persons in the *action* stage, recognizing more benefits than costs to giving up alcohol, have begun to participate in substance abuse services to achieve their goals. Persons in the *maintenance* stage have been actively involved in the pursuit of their goal for 6 months or more. Researchers recognize that the course to personal goals is fraught with hurdles, especially for persons with severe mental illness (Anthony & Liberman, 1992); many persons get derailed from the services that help them achieve their behavioral goals. The *relapse* stage represents the slips that may, for example, undermine a person's efforts to stay sober. The therapeutic goal of this stage is to help people who relapse become quickly reinvolved in rehabilitation efforts.

Note that the stage of change is specific to the behavior, not the person. Hence, it is common to see a person in one stage for problem A ("Snorting coke is getting me in too much trouble with the law; I have to stop it") but in another stage for problem B ("But there is no need for me to quit drinking; everybody I know has a couple of beers"). In this case, the person might be easily persuaded to participate in a substance abuse program for cocaine but will not understand why an alcohol abuse program is needed. Note that the transtheoretical model also applies to mental health and disability-related problems (Corrigan, McCracken, & Holmes, 2001). For example, people with vocational needs may vary on their readiness to seek competitive work.

Motivational Interventions

A review of the transtheoretical model in Table 7.2 suggests that persons are not ready to participate in active services until they have moved beyond the determination stage. Traditional substance abuse treatment for persons in the precontemplation and contemplation stages will have little impact. Persons in these stages do not believe they have a need to change the status quo. Motivational interventions help persons with dual disorders decide to pursue an individual goal. A variety of strategies may help accomplish this goal (Drake et al., 2001). Key among these is motivational interviewing developed by W. Miller and Rollnick (2002). Motivational interviewing combines the fundamentals of behavior analysis with principles from Rogerian therapy (Miller & Rollnick, 2002). Behavior analysis is an assessment strategy in which the clinician identifies rewards (i.e., advantages) and punishers (disadvantages) that affect a specific behavior. The list of rewards describes reasons that the person might take on the effort of a new behavior.

In motivational interviewing, clinicians help the person identify the profile of rewards and punishers that affect the specific behavioral goal. The list of rewards and punishers defines a decisional balance sheet. If the advantages of behavior change outweigh the disadvantages, the person will engage in activities that overcome barriers to change. If, however, the disadvantages outweigh the advantages, the person will not be motivated to change. The decisional balance also suggests ways in which the person might move toward adopting a behavioral goal. Remember that the disadvantages outlined in a motivational interview are the barriers to adopting that behavior. Strategies that diminish these costs will predispose the person to pursue the goal.

Practitioners might mistakenly assume the purpose of motivational interviewing is to use the list of advantages and disadvantages to *logically* prove that the client's goal is attainable. Clinicians with this perception might unwittingly take a heavy hand, forcefully listing advantages when the person is unable to identify them ("C'mon, Paul. You know that living on the streets is only going to get you killed!"). Unfortunately, motivational interviewing has now become confrontational and suffers significant pitfalls as a result. W. Miller and Rollnick (2002) believed the value of motivational interviewing lies in persons *discovering* the advantages and disadvantages for themselves. Therefore, they outlined five principles to make sure the client's perceptions of a goal are obtained:

1. *Express empathy.* Clinicians use the Rogerian skill of reflective listening to help clarify the person's experience of advantages and disadvantages. This method communicates acceptance of clients that frees them from having to rationalize their reluctance to make change.

2. *Develop discrepancy.* Clinicians help clients understand how failing to change behavior blocks important personal goals. An attitude of discovery is encouraged rather than a confrontational approach.

3. *Avoid argumentation.* Even when using a nondirective approach such as motivational interviewing, consumers are going to continue to deny the importance of behavior change. Clinicians need to avoid these traps and not engage the person in an argument about whether something is really a disadvantage.

4. *Roll with resistance.* Resistance is an indication that the clinician is addressing issues that the client does not perceive to be relevant or important. Miller and Rollnick remind the clinician that the client is an excellent resource for determining how to get back to barriers to change. Have the client solve this kind of difficulty using his or her own resources.

5. *Support self-efficacy.* The consumer is responsible for deciding to change. Clinicians should have confidence that their consumers will decide to change when ready. Only then are persons able to participate in a program to successfully reach their goals.

Counseling

The SAMHSA-RWJ group identified a range of individual, group, and family therapies that are helpful to people in the action stage and maintenance stages of change. They admit that research is not conclusive here but that interventions that target behavioral, cognitive, and interpersonal skills and supports will help people with dual disorders better manage their problems (Barrowclough, 2000; Barrowclough, Haddock, Tarrier, Moring, & Lewis, 2000; Carey, 1996; Roberts, Shaner, & Eckman, 1999). These interventions may include social skills training to address interpersonal pressures that exacerbate mental illness and substance abuse or collaborative cognitive reframing to help people with dual disorders deal with the kind of self-statements that undermine their progress.

Marlatt and colleagues (Marlatt & Gordon, 1985; see also Marlatt, Baer, & Quigley, 1995) developed a counseling strategy that has proved useful for the problems specific to the relapse stage of change. Called *relapse prevention,* the approach is based on the assumption that slips and relapses are the rule rather than the exception and, hence, therapy goals are to either decrease the chance of future relapses or keep one small slip from regressing into a total loss of therapeutic gain. This is called the *abstinence violation effect* (AVE) and exemplified by Harry, who, after 1 year of sobriety, gets high after work, feels he is a loser, and ends up back on the street. Relapse prevention includes recognizing situations where relapse is more likely to occur and developing either an escape plan to get out of those situations or a coping plan for places the person cannot avoid. Relapse prevention also incorporates an action plan so that if a slip occurs, the person has skills and supports to avoid the AVE.

Social Support

An important goal of counseling is to improve social support. In fact, the SAMHSA-RWJ group expanded on this issue as a separate critical component of dual disorder programs. Families are an important source of support for many people. Unfortunately, the problems that arise from dual disorders often alienate many people from their parents, siblings, and other relatives. Family therapy is an especially important strategy to rebuild some of these connections (Clark, 1994). Specific components of family therapy may include training on communication and problem-solving skills so the group is armed with the ability to deal with recurrent problems.

Twelve-step and other self-help programs may be another source of support for people with dual disorders (Davidson et al., 1999; McCrady & Delaney, 1995; Solomon & Draine, 1998). Among the many benefits of groups like these are acceptance by peers and a place where people can develop a social support system that does not reinforce drug or other antisocial practices. Although AA is the prototype of these kinds of programs, anecdote suggests that sometimes these groups are ill-prepared for people with dual disorders. Alternatively, a range of other consumer-led programs may be better equipped for the problems of people with dual disorders.

Assertive Outreach

Many of the preceding interventions take linkage between persons with dual disorder and treatment program as a given. However, research suggests that many, if not most, people with dual disorders are reluctant to become linked with services. In those instances, assertive outreach programs are essential. Effective outreach includes intensive case management and meetings in the person's home (Ho et al., 1999; Mercer-McFadden, Drake, Brown, & Fox, 1997). Typically, the focus is on practical matters such as housing, finances, and the courts. These kinds of community-based strategies help people with dual disorders benefit from services they would otherwise miss if case managers stayed in their offices. Moreover, practical efforts may segue into more therapeutic issues when the person builds a trusting and lasting relationship with his or her case manager in the streets.

Additional Practice Issues

The SAMHSA-RWJ team identified three additional issues that are essential for effective practices. First, services must be *comprehensive*. As previously repeated in this chapter, the problems that result from dual disorders are multileveled and many. People with these disorders are involved with various manifestations of the mental health system (e.g., inpatient settings, outpatient clinics, sustaining care, residential and vocational rehabilitation), the substance abuse system (e.g., detox programs, active treatment, and residential programs), plus a variety of other systems (e.g., criminal justice, public welfare, schools, and public health). Although individual programs might be disconnected and administratively separate, a single person with dual disorders may travel through many of them. Ideally, one service system has all of these programs under its umbrella and can, therefore, develop all components of the path in and out of these services. More than likely, however, people with dual disorders will be traveling in and out of independent programs. In this case, the dual disorders service system needs to be able to open doors to help people get into needed programs, serve as a monitor to make sure individual services are sensitive to the goals of people with dual disorders, and, most importantly, be actively present as the person leaves or otherwise seeks additional programs.

Second, services must be for the *long term*. This parallels one of the eight principles outlined in the MCI report and challenges one of the assumptions that plagues treatments for people with chronic disorders; that is, treatments should be time limited with a discharge goal date. As we discussed earlier, the problems of dual disorders are typically of such breadth and severity that significant time is required for engaging, persuading, and treating people with these problems. Moreover, navigating the service system takes months and years to accomplish successfully. Hence, rather than setting up a system that is attempting to fix someone of his or her problems, effective dual disorders programs are set up more in the rehab model; engineer the social system so the barriers to life problems that result from dual disorders can be overcome. Engineering systems is a never-ending process.

Third, the services team must be *culturally sensitive and competent*. The nature of a set of disorders, as well as the service system developed to treat those disorders, is moderated by the culture of its participants. Research has specifically shown that the effectiveness of critical components of dual disorder programs is affected by the ethnic background of consumers (Mercer-McFadden et al., 1997). The bad news is that ignoring issues of diversity will significantly undermine the success of the service program. The good news is that people of color, as well as individuals from other underserved groups such as farm workers, homeless people, inner-city residents, and people in rural areas, can be effectively engaged and served in dual disorders programs when issues of culture and diversity are strategically implemented in the program (Drake et al., 2001). At a minimum, this means providing the program in the person's community rather than requiring him or her to travel elsewhere. Hiring a diverse staff will significantly enhance the cultural competence of providers. Finally, staff need to be actively engaged in education and discussions about issues of cultural sensitivity and competence.

Useful Assessments

Given the complexity of problems challenging people with dual disorders and of the corresponding range of interventions, effective interventions hinge on comprehensive and longitudinal assessment. Two principles underlie assessment of individuals with dual disorders—specificity and integration (Mueser & Fox, 2001). *Specificity* refers to the need to obtain sufficient behavioral details to allow the team to develop and implement a treatment plan. An *integrated* assessment provides details about how one disorder influences the other, once again suggesting possible interventions. For example, an individual may find that boredom is a trigger for using cocaine; thus participation in a leisure skills group might be recommended to help reduce boredom. Alternatively, a person might find that smoking marijuana increases feelings of depression, leading to a recommendation that the treatment plan include training in coping skills to reduce urges to smoke marijuana. It is recommended that individuals have a comprehensive assessment of mental health and substance abuse that is updated annually (Mueser et al., 2002). The elements to be included in these comprehensive assessments are shown in Table 7.3.

Successful assessments must define the variety of problems in a manner that is phenomenologically consistent with the person's experience and in a way that suggests specific interventions for specific problems. Moreover, regular assessment needs to assess the status of the problem and whether treatment efforts have helped the person better

Table 7.3   Elements of a Comprehensive Assessment of Mental Health and Substance Abuse

Mental Health Assessment	Substance Abuse Assessment
Psychosocial history	History of substance use and abuse
Symptoms	Treatment history
Psychiatric hospitalization and use of other emergency/crisis services	Current/recent use of alcohol and specific drugs (including patterns and amounts)
Social and vocational functioning	Social context of substance abuse
Leisure and recreational activities	Motives for substance use
Family contact and other social support contacts	Consequences of substance use
Housing	Insight
Safety	Motivation to address substance abuse
Independent living skills	
Medical needs	
Insight and understanding of mental illness	

Source: The Dual Disorders Integrated Treatment Fidelity Scale. From "Illness Management and Recovery: A Review of the Research," by K. T. Mueser et al., 2002, *Psychiatric Services, 53*(10), pp. 1272–1284.

deal with it. Assessments need to focus not only on pathology. Of equal importance is understanding the person's life goals across the breadth of life domains (e.g., vocation, housing, relationships, recreation, spirituality) and understand how problems that emerge from dual disorders keep the person from accomplishing his or her goals. Drake, Osher, and Bartels (1996) sorted the various information sources relevant to the goals of dual disorder assessment into several categories and then summarized the strengths and weaknesses of each group. We summarize three of these categories here: self-report, lab tests, and information from collateral sources. Note that assessment can be a labor-intensive process, which, although important for the design of services, may take time away from other intervention processes. Hence, treatment programs need to decide which specific assessment strategies to incorporate into its armamentarium given the strengths and limitations outlined here.

Self-Report

Face-to-face interviews make sense as the place to begin understanding people and their problems. These assessments should start with a summary of the person's needs as well as resources on which he or she can rely (Corrigan, Buican, & McCracken, 1995; Marshall, Hogg, Gath, & Lockwood, 1995; Phelan et al., 1995). The profile of needs and resources should be augmented with assessments that frame related disease processes. Recommended domains of investigation include psychiatric diagnosis that can reliably be obtained by using a structured clinical interview (Spitzer & Levinson, 1988). Level of current symptoms also needs to be evaluated using a semistructured interview such as the Brief Psychiatric Rating Scale (Lukoff, Liberman, & Nuechterlein, 1986). A calendar method helps to document patterns of substance use and abuse (Sobell, Maisto, Sobell, & Cooper, 1979). The range of problems that results from substance use and abuse—including important and practical issues such as involvement in the criminal justice system, problems with housing and employment, and finances—can be assessed using the Addiction Severity Index (McLellan, Luborsky, Cacciola, & Griffith, 1985).

Perhaps the most significant benefit to self-report measures is systematically obtaining the person's perspectives on his or her problems. This perspective can reflect current issues as well as a lifetime profile of concerns. Disadvantages to self-report measures include diminished reliability, especially when denying or minimizing substance use yields secondary gains or when the person may be cognitively disabled during acute exacerbations of his or her disorder.

Lab Tests

Many experts recommend using regular screens for drug and alcohol use (Shaner et al., 1993; Stone, Greenstein, Gamble, & McLellan, 1993). Although blood tests offer the most reliable and sensitive forms of these treatments, the cost and pain involved with regular collection of this data are typically prohibitive. Alternatively, several drug companies have developed urine screens that can be cheaply administered with little physical pain to the consumer. For example, OnTrak (Roche Diagnostic Systems) is an inexpensive urinalysis system that can be used in the clinical setting to test for the presence of drug metabolites. The counselor collects a sample of urine, places a drop of urine and a drop of reagent on the slide, and determines whether the test spot is positive or negative. The process, which is similar to a home pregnancy test, takes about 10 minutes. As with any other assessment procedure, use of on-site testing should be integrated into other aspects of the counseling. For example, while gathering and preparing the sample, the counselor could ask the individual, "What is the test going to indicate?" The counseling could start before the results are even read.

Perhaps the greatest strength of lab tests is that they can be used to validate self-reports. Use of lab tests can change the counseling process and content. We have found, for example, that validating self-report with lab tests may change the focus of counseling from how well the individual is doing in recovery (based on self-report) to how to deal with and prevent relapse (based on more accurate self-report reinforced with testing). Lab tests provide a highly sensitive measure of recent use across the spectrum of drugs. Unfortunately, lab tests are limited in specifying frequency and amount of drug use. Moreover, lab tests are limited in their temporal range; for example, lab tests will not be sensitive to most drugs that were used more than 72 hours before the assessment. Finally, drug testing may conceivably undermine the quality of the therapeutic relationship, especially when consumers perceive drug monitoring to be the goal of the treatment team and not theirs. In using office-based monitoring programs such as On-Trak, therapists and consumers typically agree that this kind of self-monitoring is a useful strategy to keep the consumer honest as he or she seeks prolonged abstinence.

Collateral Sources

People who know the consumer well provide an additional set of information that helps consumer and treatment team better understand problems resulting from dual disorders. Collateral sources may include family members who are still regularly in contact with the person, case managers who provide ongoing in vivo support, and therapists (Clark, 1994; Drake et al., 1990; Osher & Kofoed, 1989; Ryglewicz, 1991). Collateral information can be obtained informally, or a standardized instrument to obtain information might be applied. For example, the Alcohol Use Scale and the Drug Use Scale were developed to obtain this kind of information from case managers in a systematic and comprehensive manner (Drake, Mueser, & McHugo, 1996).

Collateral sources are beneficial because they provide a different view of dual disorder-related problems. In particular, they may provide useful information about the person's substance use and abuse that the consumer is hesitant to admit. Moreover, collateral sources may become useful partners with the consumer and treatment team in helping the person monitor important treatment goals.

Collateral information is limited by the family member or case manager's exposure to the problem. Hence, treatment teams should not expect the amount of information available from collateral sources to be exhaustive. Moreover, the treatment team needs to use collateral sources as *partners* in the service plan. The effectiveness of collateral resources will be significantly limited if the consumer perceives family members or case managers as spying on them.

ASSESSING PROCESSES AND OUTCOMES

It is important to consider both process and outcomes in evaluating MISA programs. One way of viewing program evaluation is to look at process and outcome with respect to consumer, staff, and program/organizational variables. For staff, the process question is whether they are implementing interventions correctly (e.g., are staff using motivational interviewing techniques or falling back on confrontation), and the outcome question is whether implementation of the intervention leads to improved staff job satisfaction, reduced burnout, and a greater sense of accomplishment. For the consumer, the process question is whether consumers are participating in the services, and the outcome question is whether the lives and functioning of consumers improve as the result of participating in these services. (See Corrigan, Luchins, Malan, & Harris, 1994, for a detailed discussion of staff and consumer measures.)

For the organization, the outcome question is whether the program is fulfilling its mission, meeting service delivery goals, and remaining fiscally sound. In addition to data from financial reports and quarterly or annual reports to stakeholders, organizational outcomes can use an aggregate of consumer outcomes, such as those discussed in the MCI report (Minkoff, 2001), the Substance Abuse Treatment Scale (McHugo, Drake, Burton, & Ackerson, 1995), or the Addiction Severity Index (McLellan et al., 1985). An important organizational process question is the degree to which the program maintains fidelity to a particular treatment model. The remainder of this discussion focuses on program fidelity to the dual disorder integrated treatment model (Drake et al., 2001).

Historically, assessment of process at the organizational level focused on the quantity of service, such as numbers of clients seen and number of hours of client contact. More recently, there has been a shift in focus to include assessment of program fidelity in both service delivery (Bond, Evans, Salyers, & Kim, 2000) and in research (Bond, Evans, Salyers, Williams, & Kim, 2000; Wallace, Liberman, MacKain, Blackwell, & Eckman, 1992). *Fidelity* refers to the degree to which a program adheres to a particular program model—in this case, the dual disorders integrated treatment model (Drake et al., 2001). The 21-item Dual Disorders Integrated Treatment Fidelity Scale (DDITFS; Mueser & Fox, 2001) is the standard instrument for assessing fidelity to this model. The DDITFS is designed to assess the adequacy of implementation of evidence-based practices for treatment of individuals with dual disorders (Mueser et al., 2002). The items on the scale rate current behavior and activities (not intended or planned behavior) at the clinical level, rather than at the level of the individual practitioner or team. The DDITFS is organized around six principles of integrated treatment (integration, comprehensiveness, assertive outreach, long-term perspective, harm reduction, and provision of interventions tailored to the population; Drake et al., 2001). The current version of the DDITFS includes an administration guide and a rating sheet (Mueser et al., 2002). The administration guide provides directions about how to engage and prepare the organization for the fidelity assessment. It describes the protocol for gathering data from charts, interviews, and observation of team meetings and groups. For example, there are sets of probe questions for most of the items as well as decision rules to help with scoring. Finally, the administration guide includes a cover sheet on which to record information about the site and a score sheet for recording scores on individual items and a total score for the visit. The rating sheet is a grid with anchors for scoring each item.

The DDITFS may be administered either by internal reviewers (e.g., as a quality improvement activity) or by external reviewers. Because it is important that the ratings be made objectively, there should be at least two reviewers who have experience and training in interviewing and collecting data, who are independent yet familiar with the agency, and who understand the ingredients of integrated MISA treatment (Mueser et al., 2002). We would also recommend, based on our experience using the DDITFS with programs in Illinois, that when using external reviewers, someone from the assessment site (preferably a mid-level administrator, such as a clinical services coordinator) also conduct the assessment. This activity serves two functions. First, it provides an excellent mechanism for training an on-site evaluator who can then, either independently or with the assistance of an external reviewer, conduct follow-up assessments to monitor progress. Second, involving an on-site evaluator helps program staff and administrators better understand how ratings were derived and reasons for specific program recommendations. When we evaluate a site, we also ask that the on-site evaluator write the site evaluation, and we provide feedback for the evaluation. We believe that this provides an additional opportunity for someone onsite to integrate and have ownership for the results of the site evaluation.

The Illinois MISA Institute has used the DDITFS to facilitate discussion with program administrators about priorities for program implementation, staff training, and technical assistance. We have found the chart review portion of the DDITFS provides a useful context for clinical consultation, particularly since an onsite evaluator is present and is also gathering data from charts. While we recognize that fidelity assessment has the potential to generate considerable anxiety or defensiveness among program administrators and staff, we have found that this can be reduced by doing three things:

1. Evaluators should emphasize the learning aspect of program fidelity assessment.
2. Involve someone from the clinic or agency as an evaluator.
3. Use motivational interviewing techniques in providing feedback and recommendations.

TRAINING ISSUES

Clinical staff report that training, at all levels, is the most critical factor for embedding new treatment technologies into existing program structure (SAMHSA-NCCBH Report, 2003). Staff are particularly ready to acquire new skills when they are faced with difficult consumers, with multiple problems, who are not responsive to existing treatment strategies. When staff feel ineffective or when they are faced with broad consumer demand for specific services, they are likely to be motivated to learn new skills. Much like clinicians' attempt to promote behavior change in consumers, program administrators are now recognizing that the same processes apply to teaching staff members new skills drawn from evidence-based research and practice. A number of factors that impact program change have been identified. As a general rule, programs are more likely to be successful when all major participants, including administrators, clinicians, family members, and consumers, are involved in the design and implementation of new services (Torrey et al., 2002). In addition, these authors identify three stages of change in implementing integrated dual diagnosis treatment programs: *motivating* efforts that educate staff so that they want to work for change, *enacting* the practice by creating an environment in which care can be given in a new way, and *sustaining* the changes by reinforcing the effective practice over time.

As programs commit to using evidence-based practices, a number of factors must be addressed before training is initiated to achieve the desired outcome. Research shows that education alone does not strongly influence practice behaviors of treatment staff (Davis, Thomson, Oxman, & Haynes, 1995; Lin et al., 1997; Oxman, Thomson, Davis, & Haynes, 1995). Additional efforts are vital if change is to occur. These can include financial incentives or penalties, changes in administrative rules and procedures, and providing specific supervision related to practice implementations. For example, one dual diagnosis program in Illinois solicited input from supervisors and managers on the most effective way to distribute salary bonuses. After discussion with staff, the supervisors recommended that bonuses be distributed based on how willing and able staff were to use motivational therapy and stage of change process in working with consumers. Interest in and commitment to change was enhanced using this method.

Research also indicates that the intensity of the training effort is directly related to success in practice change (Davis, Thomson, Oxman, & Haynes, 1992; Schulberg, Katon, Simon, & Rush, 1998; Torrey et al., 2001). Sustained change requires that training be an ongoing process that permits staff to apply their new knowledge and skills in a supportive environment that is tolerant of the time needed for new systems to evolve.

Effective training incorporates many tools and strategies, and each program needs to select from training "menus" those activities that are most suited to their program needs. Training is enhanced when there is a strong commitment from senior leaders to this process. When this commitment is absent, training becomes little more than a day away from regular clinical activities and is seldom seen as being embedded in the agency framework. Training must include a wide range of activities such as shaping attitudes and values, providing for knowledge acquisition and skill building, and developing systems standards and practice guidelines as well as specific competencies in evidence-based practice (Minkoff, 2001; SAMHSA-NCCBH Report, 2003). In addition, learning styles of staff must be addressed to elicit the broadest possible support for this process. Clinicians themselves indicate that they need to be convinced that a new process is worth learning for training to be effective. They need the opportunity to learn the techniques through observation as well as lectures, and they need to receive ongoing supervision and feedback on their work (Torrey et al., 2001). As trainers, we have had staff question the utility of learning new practices related to dual diagnosis. They realize that current treatments are not as effective as they should be. But trainees are hesitant to learn new practices without a commitment from their agencies to use the new learning. Questions of relevance and importance are common. Staff are not willing to learn a new practice if they feel it will be quickly replaced by another new "best" intervention.

Use of a variety of training media improves acceptance of the new practice. These can include classroom lectures, videotapes of the new practice, workbooks, textbooks and articles, Web-based learning, and observing programs that implemented the new practice. Clinicians report that they benefit most from seeing a practice in action, rather than reading about it. They also prefer practical workbooks, with training vignettes, definitions, and clear examples. Finally, training workbooks should be designed to be taught in brief modules that provide an opportunity to try the new practice before adding additional steps (Torrey et al., 2001). The Dual Diagnosis Toolkit was designed with these perspectives in mind (SAMHSA, 2002).

Current Practice

Even though research has demonstrated that a variety of training techniques and activities improve integration of new practice, current practice largely uses classroom-style approaches to educate staff on evidence-based practice. The MCI report (Minkoff, 2001) outlines one methodology for dual diagnosis curriculum development, which includes these steps:

- Develop curricula that reflects the needs and resources of the particular system in which it is to be used.
- Define specific competencies as learning objectives.
- Use a consistent format to deliver content.

The training module should list the topic or competency to be covered, its learning goals and objectives, and the activities involved in each module. There are a growing number of curricula designed to teach staff about dual disorders. They range from courses designed for staff who work with specific populations, such as criminal justice consumers or trauma survivors, to general information on treatment needs of dually disordered clients. The SAMHSA-NCCBH (2002) lists approximately 30 different training programs that are available to train staff to treat this population. The entire list can be accessed at http://www.nccbh.org-cooccurringreport.pdf.

Challenges to Providing Training in Evidence-Based Practices

Agencies often feel that basic training is never ending and uses a disproportionate share of training dollars. Hence, the cost of training is a major barrier to agencies. Not all providers have their own training resources. Therefore, administrators must often pay for staff to obtain training, as well as lose billable services hours when staff are not available. Another issue for administrators is related to the cost of collecting clinical outcome data and measuring fidelity over time. We provide training in motivational interviewing and other evidence-based strategies at little or no cost to agencies licensed and funded by the state of Illinois. Nevertheless, we are often asked how much additional paperwork, data collection, and quality assurance costs will result from implementing what is learned in training. A final challenge is that there is little empirical research on the effectiveness of staff training in promoting improved outcome for dually diagnosed individuals.

Next Steps

Training staff in evidence-based practice can be enhanced both by short-term and long-term modifications in treatment programs. Our experience has been that standalone, classroom-style training is effective in motivating staff to evaluate attitudes and beliefs about dually diagnosed individuals and to understand the concepts underlying stage of change and motivational interventions. This is akin to working with clients who are in precontemplation and contemplation. As staff begin to understand and accept these concepts, training needs to move to a more agency-specific and focused on-site activity. We have found that it is critical to support supervisors in developing these skills before they can help staff implement new practices on a daily basis. When supervisors are not comfortable with their skill level, they are reluctant to coach staff in these skills. A local agency that is committed to implementing evidence-based practice trained supervisors to use stage of change and motivational interventions for all supervisory sessions. Administrators were also trained in using this practice.

A long-term response to having staff trained in evidence-based practice would be to focus on these practices at the preprofessional level. Community colleges, graduate schools of social work, and professional schools that provide training in addictions and mental disorders seldom incorporate evidence-based practice in their curricula. As a result, much practical training in treating dually disordered individuals is done by agencies. Our experience has been that agencies that are implementing evidence-based practices prefer to hire less experienced staff to more easily integrate them into the new culture. Many agencies report that experienced staff members are often the most reluctant to employ new learning and that extensive staff training still results in little actual change in practice.

Case Study

This case study indicates how evidence-based practices can be applied to effect change with even the most difficult clients. Steve is a 42-year-old African American male with diagnoses of schizoaffective disorder and alcohol dependence. He also has a history of seizures, especially in withdrawal, and many years of homelessness. Steve was engaged by agency outreach workers at a neighborhood shelter and referred to the agency's Transitional Housing. Steve met with the agency psychiatrist and was willing to engage in treatment for his schizoaffective disorder. Having participated in psychiatric treatment in the past, he understood his medication regimen and was comfortable with the action stage of change concerning his mental illness. Steve was also in the action stage as to his seizure disorder, for which he was treated with medication provided through the agency's primary healthcare services. Staff conducted daily medication monitoring with Steve, especially helping him understand the relationship between his drinking and his seizures.

Steve's feelings about making changes related to his alcohol use were much less settled. Steve recognized that his alcohol use had caused him some serious problems, including a current legal case about which he was significantly anxious. In fact, Steve had made several attempts at quitting in the past but always resumed drinking soon after detoxification. Moreover, given his history of seizures, Steve had a strong negative association with the detox process. Initially, Steve was in the contemplation stage of the change process concerning his use of alcohol.

Steve's move from contemplation to determination was like a pendulum swinging back and forth between the stages—sometimes even wildly. At one point, Steve went into a detox program only to leave after about a day. On his return to Transitional Housing, he was in great physical and emotional distress and was linked with emergency medical attention. Steve would occasionally binge on alcohol and sometimes try to quit on his own. The binges caused him serious problems with his girlfriend, and the attempts at abstinence brought on seizures and significant discomfort.

The Transitional Housing staff worked with Steve from a harm reduction perspective. That is, rather than jump on his intermittent (and fleeting) interest in abstinence, the staff tried to help Steve focus on managing current alcohol use. To this end, staff members encouraged him to budget his money to ensure regular alcohol intake and to avoid binge drinking. Talk of detox was minimized, especially in light of his difficulty enduring it. As a result, Steve had longer periods between binges, though he drank daily, and experienced fewer seizures.

Finally, Steve and his girlfriend had a major argument. Steve was highly inebriated at the time, and his girlfriend became scared. She called off their relationship, stating that his drinking was too unpredictable for her and she feared for her safety. Steve was distraught and became determined to quit drinking for good. Steve discussed his intention with both the staff and his psychiatrist and developed a collaborative plan to help him detoxify safely from alcohol within the Transitional Housing program. Once detoxed, Steve used Revia for a few months to help him avoid alcohol. Steve and his girlfriend were reunited. He strongly emphasized that 12-step support was not for him but, to manage his spare time, became an avid paint-by-numbers enthusiast. After a year of abstinence from alcohol, virtually seizure free, Steve and his girlfriend moved in together. He stays in touch with Transitional Housing staff members and continues to stay the course with his goals.

This example comes from an agency that decided, in order to work with persons who were homeless and suffered from addictions and mental illness, that the entire agency must use evidence-based treatment. The agency spent about a year training administrators, clinical staff, and paraprofessionals in theories of harm reduction, the stages of change model, and motivational interventions. Staff attended training offered by the Illinois MISA Institute, participated in train-the-trainer programs, and modified intake and treatment planning protocols to ensure that staff were consistent in implementing the new treatment models. The agency modified staffing procedures so that consumers were described in terms of stage of change across multiple dimensions, not just mental illness and substance abuse. Primary healthcare, commitment to stable housing, family relationships, and interest in employment are some areas that are included. Staff participate in regular in-house training, as well as specialized MISA Institute training related to evidence-based practice. The agency has worked with us to complete agency self-evaluations using the Integrated Dual Disorders Treatment Fidelity Scale (Mueser & Fox, 2001).

CONCLUSION

Evidence-based treatments offer the potential to standardize quality care across a variety of service systems for the breadth of clinical problems. Central to successful treatment for people with dual disorders is integration of services across provider systems. In this chapter, we illustrated some of the specific tools that providers might adopt to help people with dual disorders accomplish their goals. When systems are integrated in their use of these tools, the prognosis for people with dual disorders is greatly enhanced.

REFERENCES

Abram, K., & Teplin, L. (1991). Co-occurring disorders among mentally ill jail detainees: Implications for public policy. *American Psychologist, 46*(10), 1036–1045.

Alterman, A., & McLellan, T. (1981). A framework for refining the diagnostic categorization of substance abusers. *Addictive Behaviors, 6*(1), 23–27.

Anthony, W. A., & Liberman, R. P. (1992). Principles and practice of psychiatric rehabilitation. In R. Liberman, A. Goldstein, & L. Krasner (Eds.), *Handbook of psychiatric rehabilitation* (pp. 1–29). Los Angeles: UCLA School of Medicine, Brentwood (Psychiatric) Division of the West Los Angeles V.A. Medical Center, Camarillo State Hospital.

Barrowclough, C. (2000). Cognitive behavioral intervention for clients with severe mental illness who have a substance misuse problem. *Psychiatric Rehabilitation Skills, 4*(2), 216–233.

Barrowclough, C., Haddock, G., Tarrier, N., Moring, J., & Lewis, S. (2000). Cognitive behavioral intervention for individuals with severe mental illness who have a substance misuse problem. *Psychiatric Rehabilitation Skills, 4*(2), 216–233.

Bartels, S., & Drake, R. (1996). A pilot study of residential treatment for dual diagnosis. *Journal of Nervous and Mental Diseases, 184*(6), 379–381.

Bellack, A., & DiClemente, C. (1999). Treating substance abuse among patients with schizophrenia. *Psychiatric Services, 50*(1), 75–80.

Blankertz, L., & Cnaan, R. (1993). Serving the dually diagnosed homeless: Program development and interventions. *Journal of Mental Health Administration, 20*(2), 100–112.

Bond, G. R., Evans, L., Salyers, M., & Kim, H. W. (2000). *Psychiatric Rehabilitation Fidelity Toolkit.* Cambridge, MA: Human Services Research Institute.

Bond, G. R., Evans, L., Salyers, M., Williams, J., & Kim, H. (2000). Measurement of fidelity in psychiatric rehabilitation. *Mental Health Services Research, 2*(2), 75–87.

Carey, G. (1996). Family and genetic epidemiology of aggressive and antisocial behavior. In D. Stoff & R. Cairns (Eds.), *Aggression and violence: Genetic, neurobiological, and biosocial perspectives* (pp. 3–21). Boulder: University of Colorado, Institute for Behavioral Genetics.

Caton, C., Shrout, P., Eagle, P., Opler, L., Felix, A., & Dominguez, B. (1994). Risk factors for homelessness among schizophrenic men: A case-control study. *American Journal of Public Health, 84*(2), 265–270.

Clark, R. E. (1994). Family costs associated with severe mental illness and substance use. *Hospital and Community Psychiatry, 45*(8), 808–813.

Corrigan, P. W., Buican, B., & McCracken, S. G. (1995). The needs and resources assessment interview for severely mentally ill adults. *Psychiatric Services, 46*(5), 504–505.

Corrigan, P. W., Luchins, D., Malan, R., & Harris, J. (1994). User-friendly continuous quality improvement for the mental health team. *Medical Interface, 7*(12), 89–95.

Corrigan, P. W., McCracken, S. G., & Holmes, E. (2001). Motivational interviews as goal assessment for persons with psychiatric disability. *Community Mental Health Journal, 37*(2), 113–122.

Cuffel, B., Shumway, M., Chouljian, T., & Macdonald, T. (1994). A longitudinal study of substance use and community violence in schizophrenia. *Journal of Nervous and Mental Diseases, 182*(12), 704–708.

Davidson, L., Chinman, M., Kloos, B., Weingarten, R., Stayner, D., & Tebes, J. (1999). Peer support among individuals with severe mental illness: A review of the evidence. *Clinical Psychology: Science and Practice, 6*(2), 165–187.

Davis, D. A., Thomson, M. A., Oxman, A. D., & Haynes, R. B. (1992). Evidence for the effectiveness of CME: A review of 50 randomized control trials. *Journal of the American Medical Association, 268*(9), 1111–1117.

Davis, D. A., Thomson, M. A., Oxman, A. D., & Haynes, R. B. (1995). Changing physician performance: A systematic review of the effect of continuing medical education strategies. *Journal of the American Medical Association, 274*(9), 700–705.

Drake, R. E., Essock, S., Shaner, A., Carey, K., Minkoff, K., Kola, L., et al. (2001). Implementing dual diagnosis services for clients with severe mental illness. *Psychiatric Services, 52*(4), 469–476.

Drake, R. E., Mueser, K. T., & McHugo, G. J. (1996). "Using clinician rating scales to assess substance abuse among persons with severe mental disorders." In L. Sederer & B. Dickey (Eds.), *Outcomes assessment in clinical practice* (pp. 294–324). Baltimore: Williams & Wilkins.

Drake, R. E., Osher, F., & Bartels, S. (1996). The "dually diagnosed." In W. Breakey (Ed.), *Integrated mental health services: Modern community psychiatry* (pp. 339–352). Hanover, NH: Dartmouth Medical School, New Hampshire Dartmouth Psychiatric Research Center.

Drake, R. E., Osher, F., Noordsy, D., Hurlbut, S., Teague, G. B., & Beaudett, M. S. (1990). Diagnosis of alcohol use disorders in schizophrenia. *Schizophrenia Bulletin, 16*(1), 57–67.

Drake, R. E., Osher, F., & Wallach, M. (1989). Alcohol use and abuse in schizophrenia: A prospective community study. *Journal of Nervous and Mental Diseases, 177*(7), 408–414.

Drake, R. E., & Wallach, M. (2000). Dual diagnosis: 15 years of progress. *Psychiatric Services, 51*(9), 1126–1129.

Haywood, T., Kravitz, H., Grossman, L., Cavanaugh, J., Davis, J., & Lewis, D. (1995). Predicting the "revolving door" phenomenon among patients with schizophrenic, schizoaffective, and affective disorders. *American Journal of Psychiatry, 152*(6), 856–861.

Ho, A., Tsuang, J., Liberman, R. P., Wang, R., Wilkins, J., Eckman, T., et al. (1999). Achieving effective treatment of patients with chronic psychotic illness and comorbid substance dependence. *American Journal of Psychiatry, 156*(11), 1765–1770.

Kay, S., Kalathara, M., & Meinzer, A. (1989). Diagnostic and behavioral characteristics of psychiatric patients who abuse substances. *Hospital and Community Psychiatry, 40*(10), 1062–1064.

Kessler, R., Nelson, C., McGonagle, K., Edlund, M., Frank, R., & Leaf, P. (1996). The epidemiology of co-occurring addictive and mental disorders: Implications for prevention and service utilization. *American Journal of Orthopsychiatry, 66*(1), 17–31.

Koegel, P., & Burnam, M. (1988). Alcoholism among homeless adults in the inner city of Los Angeles. *Archives of General Psychiatry, 45*(11), 1011–1018.

Lehman, A., Myers, C., & Corty, E. (1989). Assessment and classification of patients with psychiatric and substance abuse syndromes. *Hospital and Community Psychiatry, 40*(10), 1019–1025.

Lin, E., Katon, W., Simon, G., Von Korff, M., Bush, T., Rutter, C., et al. (1997). Achieving guidelines for the treatment of depression in primary care: Is physician education enough? *Medical Care, 35*(8), 831–842.

Linszen, D., Dingemans, P., Lenior, M., Nugter, M., Scholte, W. F., & Van der Does, A. J. (1994). Relapse criteria in schizophrenic disorders: Different perspectives. *Psychiatry Research, 54*(3), 273–281.

Lukoff, D., Liberman, R. P., & Nuechterlein, K. (1986). Symptom monitoring in the rehabilitation of schizophrenia patients. *Schizophrenia Bulletin, 12*(4), 578–593.

Marlatt, G., Baer, J., & Quigley, L. (1995). Self-efficacy and addictive behavior. In A. Bandura (Ed.), *Self-efficacy in changing societies* (pp. 289–315). Seattle: University of Washington, Department of Psychology.

Marlatt, G., & Gordon, J. H. (Eds.). (1985). *Relapse prevention.* New York: Guilford Press.

Marshall, M., Hogg, L., Gath, D., & Lockwood, A. (1995). The Cardinal Needs Schedule: A modified version of the MRC Needs for Care Assessment Schedule. *Psychological Medicine, 25,* 603–617.

McCarrick, A., Manderscheid, R., & Bertolucci, D. (1985). Correlates of acting-out behaviors among young adult chronic patients. *Hospital and Community Psychiatry, 40*(8), 847–849.

McCrady, B., & Delaney, S. (1995). Self-help groups. In R. Hester & W. Miller (Eds.), *Handbook of alcoholism treatment approaches: Effective alternatives* (2nd ed., pp. 160–175). New Brunswick, NJ: Rutgers University, Center of Alcohol Studies.

McHugo, G. J., Drake, R. E., Burton, H., & Ackerson, T. (1995). A scale for assessing the stage of substance abuse treatment in persons with severe mental illness. *Journal of Nervous and Mental Diseases, 183*(12), 762–767.

McLellan, T. A., Luborsky, L., Cacciola, J. S., & Griffith, J. E. (1985). New data from the Addiction Severity Index: Reliability and validity in three centers. *Journal of Nervous and Mental Diseases, 173*(7), 412–423.

McLellan, T. A., Woody, G., & O'Brien, C. (1979). Development of psychiatric illness in drug abusers. *New England Journal of Medicine, 301*(24), 1310–1314.

Mercer-McFadden, C., Drake, R. E., Brown, N., & Fox, R. (1997). The community support program demonstrations of services for young adults with severe mental illness and substance use disorders, 1987–1991. *Psychiatric Rehabilitation Journal, 20*(3), 13–24.

Miller, F., & Tanenbaum, J. (1989). Drug abuse in schizophrenia. *Hospital and Community Psychiatry, 40*(8), 847–849.

Miller, W. R., & Rollnick, S. (2002). *Motivational interviewing: Preparing people for change* (2nd ed.). New York: Guilford Press.

Minkoff, K. (1991). Program components of a comprehensive integrated care system for serious mentally ill patients with substance disorders. *New Directions for Mental Health Services, 50,* 13–27.

Minkoff, K. (2001). Developing standards of care for individuals with co-occurring psychiatric and substance use disorders. *Psychiatric Services, 52*(5), 597–599.

Mueser, K. T., Corrigan, P. W., Hilton, D. W., Tanzman, B., Schaub, A., Gingerich, S., et al. (2002). Illness management and recovery: A review of the research. *Psychiatric Services, 53*(10), 1272–1284.

Mueser, K. T., & Fox, L. (2001). *Dual Diagnosis Fidelity Scale.* Concord, NH: Dartmouth Psychiatric Research Center.

Mueser, K. T., Yarnold, P. R., & Bellack, A. (1992). Diagnostic and demographic correlates of substance abuse in schizophrenia and major affective disorder. *Acta Psychiatrica Scandinavica, 85*(1), 48–55.

Mueser, K. T., Yarnold, P. R., Levinson, D. F., Singh, H., Bellack, A. S., Kee, K., et al. (1990). Prevalence of substance abuse in schizophrenia: Demographic and clinical correlates. *Schizophrenia Bulletin, 16*(1), 31–56.

Osher, F. C., Drake, R. E., Noordsy, D., Teague, G., Hurlbut, S. C., Biesanz, J. C., et al. (1994). Correlates and outcomes of alcohol use disorder among rural outpatients with schizophrenia. *Journal of Clinical Psychiatry, 55*(3), 109–113.

Osher, F. C., & Kofoed, L. (1989). Treatment of patients with psychiatric and psychoactive substance abuse disorders. *Hospital and Community Psychiatry, 40*(10), 1025–1030.

Oxman, A., Thomson, M., Davis, D., & Haynes, R. (1995). No magic bullets: A systematic review of 102 trials of interventions to improve professional practice. *Canadian Medical Association Journal, 153,* 142–143.

Perkins, K., Simpson, J., & Tsuang, M. (1986). Ten-year follow-up of drug abusers with acute or chronic psychosis. *Hospital and Community Psychiatry, 37*(5), 481–484.

Phelan, M., Slade, M., Thornicroft, G., Dunn, G., Holloway, F., Wykes, T., et al. (1995). The Camberwell Assessment of Need: The validity and reliability of an instrument to assess the needs of people with severe mental illness. *British Journal of Psychiatry, 167,* 589–595.

Prochaska, J., DiClemente, C., & Norcross, J. (1992). In search of how people change: Applications to addictive behaviors. *American Psychologist, 47*(9), 1102–1114.

Raesaenen, P., Tiihonen, J., Isohanni, M., Rantakallio, P., Lehtonen, J., & Moring, J. (1998). Schizophrenia, alcohol abuse, and violent behavior: A 26-year follow-up study of an unselected birth cohort. *Schizophrenia Bulletin, 24*(3), 437–441.

Regier, D., Narrow, W., & Rae, D. (1990). The epidemiology of anxiety disorders: The epidemiologic catchment area (ECA) experience. *Journal of Psychiatric Research, 24,* 3–14.

Ridgely, M. (1991). Creating integrated programs for severely mentally ill persons with substance disorders. *New Directions for Mental Health Services, 50,* 29–41.

Roberts, L., Shaner, A., & Eckman, T. (1999). *Overcoming addictions: Skills training for people with schizophrenia.* Seattle: University of Washington, Center for Clinical Research.

Rosenberg, S., Goodman, L., Osher, F., Swartz, M., Essock, S., Butterfield, M., et al. (2001). Prevalence of HIV, hepatitis, B., and hepatitis C in people with severe mental illness. *American Journal of Public Health, 91*(1), 31–37.

Ryglewicz, H. (1991). Psychoeducation for clients and families: A way in, out, and through in working with people with dual disorders. *Psychosocial Rehabilitation Journal, 15*(2), 79–89.

Schneier, F., & Siris, S. (1987). A review of psychoactive substance use and abuse in schizophrenia: Patterns of drug choice. *Journal of Nervous and Mental Diseases, 175*(11), 641–652.

Schuckit, M. (1985). The clinical implications of primary diagnostic groups among alcoholics. *Archives of General Psychiatry, 42*(11), 1043–1049.

Schulberg, H., Katon, W., Simon, G., & Rush, A. (1998). Treating major depression in primary care practice: An update of the Agency for Health Care Policy and Research practice guidelines. *Archives of General Psychiatry, 55*(12), 1121–1127.

Scott, H., Johnson, S., Menezes, P., Thornicroft, G., Marshall, J., Bindman, J., et al. (1998). Substance misuse and risk of aggression and offending among the severely mentally ill. *British Journal of Psychiatry, 172,* 345–350.

Shaner, A., Khalsa, M., Roberts, L., Wilkins, J., Anglin, D., & Hsieh, S. C. (1993). Unrecognized cocaine use among schizophrenic patients. *American Journal of Psychiatry, 150*(5), 758–762.

Sobell, L., Maisto, S., Sobell, M., & Cooper, A. (1979). Reliability of alcohol abusers' self-reports of drinking behavior. *Behaviour Research and Therapy, 17*(2), 157–160.

Solomon, P., & Draine, J. (1998). Consumers as providers in psychiatric rehabilitation. *New Directions for Mental Health Services, 79,* 65–77.

Spitzer, D., & Levinson, E. (1988). A review of selected vocational interest inventories for use by school psychologists. *School Psychology Review, 17*(4), 578–593.

Stone, A., Greenstein, R., Gamble, G., & McLellan, A. (1993). Cocaine use by schizophrenic outpatients who receive depot neuroleptic medication. *Hospital and Community Psychiatry, 44*(2), 176–177.

Substance Abuse and Mental Health Service Administration. (2002). *Co-occurring disorders: Integrated Dual Disorders Treatment Implementation Resource Kit.* Unpublished Manuscript.

Substance Abuse and Mental Health Service Administration. (2003). *Strategies for developing treatment programs for people with co-occurring substance abuse and mental disorders* (SAMHSA Publication No. 3782). Rockville, MD: Author.

Swofford, C., Kasckow, J., Scheller-Gilkey, G., & Inderbitzin, L. (1996). Substance use: A powerful predictor of relapse in schizophrenia. *Schizophrenia Research, 20*(1/2), 145–151.

Torrey, W. C., Drake, R. E., Cohen, M., Fox, L., Lynde, D., Gorman, P., et al. (2002). The challenge of implementing and sustaining integrated dual disorders treatment programs. *Community Mental Health Journal, 38*(6), 507–521.

Torrey, W. C., Drake, R. E., Dixon, L. B., Burns, B., Flynn, L., Rush, A., et al. (2001). Implementing evidence-based practices for persons with severe mental illnesses. *Psychiatric Services, 52*(1), 45–50.

Tsuang, M. T., Simpson, J., & Kronfol, Z. (1982). Subtypes of drug abuse with psychosis: Demographics characteristics, clinical features, and family history. *Archives of General Psychiatry, 39*(2), 141–147.

Wallace, C., Liberman, R. P., MacKain, S., Blackwell, G., & Eckman, T. (1992). Effectiveness and replicability of modules for teaching social and instrumental skills to the severely mentally ill. *American Journal of Psychiatry, 149*(5), 654–658.

Zuckoff, A., & Daley, D. (2001). Engagement and adherence issues in treating persons with non-psychosis dual disorders. *Psychiatric Rehabilitation Skills, 5*(1), 131–162.

CHAPTER 8

Evidence-Based Treatments for Children and Adolescents

John S. Lyons and Purva H. Rawal

Historically, behavioral health services for children and adolescents have lagged behind adult services both in development of service systems and funding of research. However, the past 2 decades have seen an explosion of interest in child and adolescent services. This increased interest has been fueled by a number of factors including the changing demographics of the baby boom generation, high-profile tragedies involving school-age children, and provocative observations and findings concerning the status of the existing service system (Knitzer, 1982).

As a result of efforts over the past 20 years, several evidence-based treatment approaches have been identified for children and adolescents. These treatments can be divided into those that are provided as office-based outpatient services and those that involve providing services in the home and community. Initially, we review treatments that are designed for administration as outpatient services. Following this review, two home- and community-based practices—multisystemic treatment and wraparound—are reviewed.

OUTPATIENT TREATMENT

Outpatient treatment is the most widely used mental health service and is a common referral in response to a wide range of problems, including depression, anxiety, oppositional behavior, and attention deficit and impulse control problems. While breakthroughs in pharmacotherapy have led to an increase in the number of medication options for children and adolescents (Jensen et al., 1999), forms of psychotherapy remain the foundation of the treatment approach in outpatient behavioral health settings for children and adolescents. Psychotherapy has come under significant scrutiny and question over the past few decades with both adults and children (e.g., Andrade, Lambert, & Bickman, 2000).

GUIDELINES FOR TREATMENT

Many youth are referred to clinics; however, few families are able to follow through and complete treatment. Dropout rates from outpatient treatment have been found to be as great as 40% (Armbruster & Schwab-Stone, 1994; Pelkonen, Marttunen, Laippala, & Lonnqvist, 2000). Thus, it is difficult for service providers to engage families and maintain them in the treatment setting.

Research has demonstrated that predictors of dropout from treatment include the following: having low socioeconomic status, having membership in a minority group, being younger, having single-parent households, engaging in harsh child-rearing practices, having low levels of family cohesion, living in an urban residence, being a minority, having Medicaid funding, and having parents with histories of antisocial behavior in their childhoods (Armbruster & Schwab-Stone, 1994; Kazdin, 1979; Pelkonen, Marttunen, Laippala, & Lonnqvist, 2000). Families are most likely to drop out during the intake and evaluation phases of treatment (Armbruster & Schwab-Stone, 1994).

Barriers to remaining engaged in services also play a factor in premature treatment termination. A 4-year study examined the role of barriers in treatment attrition (Kazdin, Holland, & Crowley, 1997). The study included 242 youth and their families referred for treatment to an outpatient clinic. Perceived barriers to participation in treatment were associated with early termination. The negative association between barriers and premature termination was not better accounted for by more well-established factors related to attrition (e.g., socioeconomic, child, or family characteristics). There was a positive correlation between increasing barriers and increased risk of dropping out in families at risk for dropping out due to other variables, and having few perceived barriers served as a protective factor in continuing treatment. In addition to demographic characteristics, which have received a significant amount of research attention, perceived barriers to treatment provide important information on treatment attrition and are possible targets of intervention.

ASSESSING OUTCOMES AND EFFICACY

Despite the significant number of families that cannot remain engaged in treatment, there is considerable evidence that children who stay in treatment benefit from psychotherapy. Numerous meta-analyses and reviews indicate positive effects related to child and adolescent psychotherapy (Kazdin, 2000; Kazdin, Bass, Ayers, & Rodgers, 1990; Kutash & Rivera, 1996; Weisz, Weiss, Han, Granger, & Morton, 1995). Effect sizes in the literature range from .50 to .70, which are generally regarded as medium to large (Weisz, Weiss, et al., 1995). These effect sizes are regarded as validating the positive effects of child and adolescent psychotherapy.

One of the most significant obstacles to clearly establishing the effectiveness of psychotherapy in children is the substantial difference between psychotherapy conducted in research versus that conducted in community or clinic settings. Research has demonstrated that outpatient psychotherapy in children and adolescents is most effective when administered in a research setting versus a community setting. The effectiveness of treatment decreases greatly in community settings for three reasons:

1. Research settings usually use cognitive behavioral therapies that have higher levels of effectiveness with children and adolescents (Hoagwood et al., 2001; Weiss, 1995; Weisz, Donenberg, Han, & Kauneckis, 1995). There is little evidence

supporting the use of nonbehavioral psychotherapeutic interventions, and they are not current evidence-based practices (Hoagwood et al. 2001). Thus, results of many studies indicate that behavioral treatments have greater overall success with children and adolescents, and their use in research settings is one of the primary contributing factors to the greater effectiveness of research versus community child psychotherapy.

2. The greater use of specific and focused psychotherapeutic interventions in research settings provides clearer treatment goals over the more eclectic approaches often used in clinic settings (Kutash & Rivera, 1996; Weisz, Donenberg, Han, & Kauneckis, 1995; Weisz, Weiss, et al., 1995). Goals that are more strictly targeted during the course of treatment increase the likelihood of achieving positive outcomes. It is unclear what therapeutic orientations are employed in many community settings; most describe eclectic treatment approaches in which it is difficult to measure treatment goals and corresponding outcomes. Treatment attrition may be higher in clinical settings where theoretically varied approaches are used. Thus, the use of specific and focused treatment approaches in research settings probably contributes to achieving more positive outcomes.

3. Adhering to a specific treatment modality, as is common in research settings, usually results in an emphasis on structure that is associated with positive treatment outcomes. Structure is created in psychotherapy through various mechanisms, the most common being treatment manuals and monitoring techniques, such as supervision. The increased structure may also lead to enhanced fidelity to treatment plans in research settings (Weisz, Donenberg, Han, & Kauneckis, 1995).

Examples of child and adolescent psychotherapies that are specific and structured are increasingly common. One clinical trial used attachment-based family therapy (ABFT), which is based on a treatment manual and uses an adherence measure. The study, conducted with youth with major depressive disorder, found that 81% of ABFT youth no longer met criteria for major depressive disorder at follow-up, compared to only 47% of youth on a waiting list. However, the results have limited generalizability since they are based on a small sample primarily composed of African American females in a low-income urban setting (Diamond, Reis, Diamond, Siqueland, & Isaacs, 2002). Treatments such as ABFT are based on a cognitive-behavioral orientation, are structured, and when administered in research settings have high likelihoods of producing positive results (Kutash & Rivera, 1996; Weisz, Donenberg, Han, & Kauneckis, 1995).

Child outpatient therapy service providers and researchers are paying increasing attention to establishing empirically validated treatments (Kazdin & Weisz, 1998). Treatment fidelity plays a key role in the effort to produce empirically validated treatments because it allows clinicians and researchers to assess quality assurance. Specifically, manualized treatments facilitate developing specific treatment foci, evaluating the integrity of a treatment, codifying results from clinical trials, and replicating treatment procedures for clinical and research settings (Kazdin, 2000). The literature indicates that having a specific therapeutic approach, namely behavioral or cognitive-behavioral, predicts treatment effectiveness in children and adolescents. Structure in treatment and enhanced adherence to treatment plans in research settings may contribute to more positive outcomes than in clinic settings where there is often a lack of structure and treatment fidelity in psychotherapy.

COGNITIVE-BEHAVIORAL INTERVENTIONS

Overall, behavioral or cognitive-behavioral treatment (CBT) in research settings has shown the most promise to date. CBT is a structured, time-limited therapy that is based on the assumption that individuals' thoughts, feelings, and behaviors are based on the way they perceive and process their surroundings (Kendall & Warman, 1996). CBT attempts to integrate cognitive components into behavioral theory to effect therapeutic change (Kendall, 1993). CBT is an active therapy that uses cognitive and behavioral interventions to produce positive changes in cognition, emotion, and behavior. An effort is made to understand behavior in its natural context, the social learning processes in the child's environment, the child's unique information processing style, and the role of each in the development and maintenance of the psychopathology.

Meta-analyses of CBT have resulted in larger effect sizes than nonbehavioral therapies with children and adolescents (Hoagwood et al., 2001; Reinecke, Ryan, & Dubois, 1998; Weiss, 1995). Some have suggested that the differences in effect sizes are artifactual and due to differences in methodological quality of behavioral and nonbehavioral treatments. Weiss and Weisz (1995) conducted a large meta-analysis of 105 studies of behavioral versus nonbehavioral psychotherapy in children and adolescents to determine whether the two differ in methodological quality and whether these potential differences account for varying effect sizes between the two. Results suggested that larger effect sizes associated with behavioral treatments are not due to methodological differences, providing further evidence for the greater effectiveness of CBT techniques with children and adolescents.

Much of the CBT child psychotherapy literature focuses on depression. Child and adolescent depression is characterized by cognitive distortions concerning self-attribution, self-evaluation, and perceptions of events; by a tendency to have an external locus of control; and by having more depressogenic attributions (Kendall, 1993; Kendall & Warman, 1996). Reinecke et al. (1998) examined six studies of cognitive-behavioral therapy for children and adolescents with depressive symptoms. The posttest effect size was −1.20 (95% CI = −1.23 to −.81), suggesting that CBT is effective in alleviating depressive symptoms. The effect size at follow-up was calculated to be −.61 (95% CI = −.88 to −.35), suggesting that treatment gains are maintained over time.

Reynolds and Coats (1986) randomly assigned 30 youth with depressive symptoms to a CBT with relaxation training condition and a waiting-list control condition. The CBT and relaxation training interventions were associated with a significant decrease in self-report and clinical ratings of depressive symptoms at posttest; these gains were maintained at 5-week follow-up and included decreases in anxiety and improved academic self-concept. One of the most significant studies included 24 children in CBT versus a traditional therapy condition (Stark, Rouse, & Livingston, 1991). The CBT condition targeted self-control, social skills, and cognitive restructuring and was associated with significantly greater improvement than the traditional therapy condition at posttest.

These studies are simply two examples of the early success of CBT in treating child and adolescent depression.

Individual CBT is often used to treat anxiety symptoms as well. Recently, a 6-year follow-up of CBT with children and adolescents with anxiety disorders was completed (Barrett, Duffy, Dadds, & Rapee, 2001). Fifty-two participants were included to assess the hypothesis that there would be no significant differences in anxiety symptoms between the 12-month and 6-year follow-up. Results found no significant differences in clinical status at long-term follow-up, indicating CBT gains are maintained at long-term follow-up for treating anxiety disorders.

Behavioral therapies have also shown some preliminary promise with youth with conduct disorder problems in outpatient settings (LeCroy & Jose, 1992). Research efforts on psychotherapy in children and adolescents should focus on the onset, maintenance, termination, and relapse of psychiatric problems; on the mechanisms of change in psychotherapy; on the continued manualization of psychotherapeutic approaches and conduction of outcome studies; on moderating characteristics affecting outcomes (e.g., therapist, family, child); on the generalizability of psychotherapy effects to other settings and populations (Kazdin, 2000; Kazdin & Weisz, 1998); and on understanding the effectiveness of psychotherapy with different subgroups to help inform decisions about treatment use.

Methods of Assessing Fidelity

In 1990, only 19% of all child and adolescent treatment studies measured treatment adherence and fidelity factors (Kazdin et al., 1990). Since then, these issues have been receiving increasing attention. However, assessing fidelity in child and adolescent psychotherapeutic interventions is largely confined to research settings, in which clinician training and treatment fidelity monitoring are considered integral to achieving positive outcomes (Weisz, Donenberg, Han, & Kauneckis, 1995; Weisz, Donenberg, Han, & Weiss, 1995). Studies of therapist adherence, competence, and fidelity in the adult psychotherapy literature have indicated positive relationships between fidelity and outcomes (Miller & Binder, 2002). Adult psychotherapy studies suggest that manual-based training is associated with higher levels of adherence to a therapy model (Miller & Binder). However, little work has been done, even in the adult psychotherapy research, concerning the relationship between manual-based training or treatment adherence and therapy outcomes; furthermore, the results on studies of treatment fidelity and outcomes are also contradictory (Miller & Binder). Thus, a great deal of work remains in establishing ways to measure therapist and treatment adherence in child psychotherapy so that eventually the relationship of therapist adherence and overall treatment fidelity to individual outcomes can be understood.

Future Directions

Larger sample sizes, reliance on self-report measures, increased use of standardized measurement instruments, increased comparison conditions, and long-term follow-ups are needed in child psychotherapy studies (Kendall & Warman, 1996). Translating research-based treatment to clinical settings is also a challenge. In addition, examining treatment fidelity in clinical settings is required.

MULTISYSTEMIC THERAPY

Over the past 20 years, Scott Henggeler and colleagues have developed multisystemic therapy (MST) to treat psychosocial problems in juvenile-justice involved youth. Today, the target population has expanded to families with youth with serious antisocial, emotional, and/or behavioral problems that are at risk for out-of-home placement.

Guidelines for Treatment

Multisystemic therapy was developed in response to the weaknesses of older family therapy treatments. These treatments were unable to give sufficient consideration to the role of individual characteristics and systems outside the family that play significant parts in the development and maintenance of maladaptive behavior. In addition, they were unable to integrate important child development research. Family therapists had a lack of expertise with nonsystemic treatment orientations, such as cognitive-behavioral therapy (Henggeler & Borduin, 1990).

Multisystemic therapy builds a more comprehensive perspective on the adolescent's difficulties than other family therapies because it is able to address community and developmental issues within the framework of the treatment (Schleser & Rodick, 1982). The major systems integrated into MST, other than the most salient—the family—are the youth's peer group, school, and the neighborhood. Even if the family is the most influential system, change can be affected by intervening in any of the other systems as well (Schleser & Rodick). MST adheres to a systems perspective that views symptoms as part of a circular relationship with several causes, not simply as products of a linear individual mental illness (Henggeler & Borduin, 1990). Thus, MST assumes that maladaptive behaviors are closely related to familial patterns of interaction, often resulting from poorly managed life stress and developmental transitions, and that they have a functional purpose (Henggeler & Borduin). MST is based on the family preservation model, where the ultimate purpose is to maintain intact families.

A compelling aspect of MST is the extent to which it is grounded in clinical theory and empirically validated by research demonstrating the systemic influences and determinants of maladaptive behaviors (Schoenwald, Borduin, & Henggeler, 1998). MST has its foundation in systems theory and social ecology, which is rooted in social development, cognitive development, childhood psychopathology, family therapy models, and community mental health (Henggeler, 1982). Henggeler based his treatment on Urie Bronfenbrenner's (1979) work on the ecology of human development that proposes an individual is embedded within a community of interconnected systems. The social ecology model proposes that behavior is best understood when seen in its natural context, and to maximize the likelihood of affecting change, treatments must be able to address multiple factors contributing to the development and maintenance of the problems (Bronfenbrenner, 1979; Schoenwald, Brown, & Henggeler, 2000). Thus, adolescent behaviors are affected by the systems in which they are nested (Henggeler, 1982).

In addition to being grounded in clinical theory, MST integrates empirically based psychological interventions into treatment. Validated treatments are utilized within its treatment protocols, such as cognitive-behavioral therapy, behavioral parent training, and strategic and functional family therapy. These empirically based treatments have traditionally targeted specific aspects of the youth's problems (i.e., individual cognitions, parenting styles); however, when these treatments are integrated into MST, their application is broadened because the treatments are incorporated into the family and youth's larger ecology. Biological factors are also considered, and pharmacological or other medical interventions are included as needed. The foundation of clinical theory, supplemented by empirically validated treatments, limits the use of eclectic treatment approaches that constitute clinical practice in most community-based interventions (Schoenwald, Borduin, et al., 1998).

In the MST model, individual behavior can be changed by interacting environmental systems, and modifying behavior can change the surrounding ecology (Bronfenbrenner, 1979; Burns, Schoenwald, Burchard, Faw, & Santos, 2000). The treatment philosophy relies heavily on empirically validated research demonstrating the systemic influences and determinants of antisocial behavior; thus, the intervention targets the systemic issues (e.g., family, peers, school) maintaining maladaptive behavior (Schoenwald, Borduin, et al., 1998).

The primary goals of MST are to help troubled youth and their families gain clinical skills to function more effectively in their natural environments and to support these changes in their natural ecology. Parents as well as children receive treatment to address any barriers to effective parenting, such as substance abuse or stress (Burns et al., 2000).

Assessing Outcomes and Efficacy

Several randomized clinical trials, uncontrolled studies, and quasi-experimental designs have been conducted of MST. It is one of the most validated children's mental health services in the nation.

A comparison of MST and parent training in treating child abuse and neglect found both groups demonstrated reliable improvement, but parents in the MST condition demonstrated improved parent-child relations over the parent-training condition (Brunk, Henggeler, & Whelan, 1987).

An early, randomized controlled trial of youth with serious juvenile offenses in MST versus usual treatment services was conducted with positive results observed for the MST condition. At over 1 year postreferral, youth in the MST condition had approximately half the arrests of youth in the usual treatment condition (Henggeler, Melton, & Smith, 1992). Family cohesion was higher, and peer aggression was lower in the MST condition than in the comparison. Effect sizes for incarceration, rearrests, family cohesion, and peer aggression ranged from .34 to .62, indicating significant improvement. MST significantly reduced the number of institutional placements and levels of criminal activity in youth with serious juvenile offenses.

A 4-year randomized controlled follow-up study was conducted for the Missouri Delinquency Project comparing the effectiveness of MST to individual therapy in a group of adolescents with juvenile offense records. Results indicated that MST is effective in this population. The recidivism rate for arrests at 4-year follow-up for the MST condition was less than one-third the overall arrest rate for youth in the individual therapy condition (Schoenwald, Borduin, et al., 1998). Adolescents in the MST condition committed fewer and less serious crimes, and there were significantly fewer arrests for violent crimes than with youth in the individual therapy condition. Even parents of youth with MST demonstrated decreases in their own symptoms and greater levels of family cohesion and adaptability from pre- to posttreatment than parents and families in the individual therapy condition (Borduin et al., 1995; Schoenwald, Borduin, et al., 1998). The randomized controlled trial demonstrated the effectiveness of MST by reducing the incidence and severity of criminal acts and improving family outcomes.

Multisystemic therapy has also been used with youth at risk for psychiatric hospitalization. A sample of 113 adolescents qualifying for psychiatric hospitalization was randomized to an MST condition or a hospitalization condition; the purpose of the study was to examine the effectiveness of MST in providing a community-based treatment option in lieu of psychiatric hospitalization (Henggeler, Rowland, & Randall, 1999). The MST protocol was modified to address the needs of seriously emotionally disturbed youth who were in danger of harming themselves or others. Data were collected at entry into treatment, at release from hospitalization (MST youth were assessed at the same time), and at leaving MST services (hospitalized youth were assessed at the same time). Results suggested that MST was more effective at decreasing externalizing behaviors at the third assessment, MST youth spent significantly fewer days out of school and reported higher levels of treatment satisfaction than those in the hospitalization condition, and MST families had become more structured and reported significantly higher levels of family cohesion. Thus, MST appears to be at least as effective, if not more effective, than psychiatric hospitalization in seriously emotionally disturbed youths.

A randomized controlled trial of MST versus out-of-home placement for youths at risk of psychiatric hospitalization with placement rates at 4 months postreferral also demonstrated positive results for the MST condition. MST prevented hospitalization in 75% of the referred cases, whereas 100% of youth in the out-of-home placement condition were hospitalized (Schoenwald, Ward, Henggeler, & Rowland, 2000). In the 25% of cases that were hospitalized, youth spent a mean 2.2 days on the unit, which was significantly less than the approximately 6 days youth in the comparison condition were hospitalized. The decreased use of hospitalization by youth in the MST condition was maintained at 4-month postreferral. Youth participating in MST exhibited greater placement stability and fewer moves to restrictive placements than youth in the out-of-home placement condition. Thus, MST youth were not only less likely to be hospitalized but also less likely to be placed in other restrictive placements.

Multisystemic therapy has also shown positive outcomes with youth with substance abuse problems. A 4-year follow-up was conducted of MST with substance abusing and dependent juvenile-justice involved youth. Sixty-eight percent of the original sample consented to participation in the follow-up; the average age was 19.6 years, 76% male, 60% African American, and 40% Caucasian (Henggeler, Clingempeel, & Brondino, 2002). Those who had received MST services showed a 75% decrease in convictions for aggressive crimes since the age of 17 years and reported committing significantly fewer aggressive crimes than the usual services condition. MST youth had significantly higher rates of marijuana abstinence, similar rates of cocaine abstinence, and nonsignificant differences in internalizing and externalizing problems. Thus, MST successfully achieved positive criminal behavior outcomes and some positive substance abuse outcomes. MST has also demonstrated positive effects on decreasing behavior problems and improving family relations in inner-city youths, decreasing rearrests for sexual and nonsexual crimes in sexually aggressive adolescents, and reducing out-of-home placements, drug use, and rates of incarceration in youth with substance abuse issues (Burns et al., 2000).

Multisystemic therapy is a promising treatment model for youths with a number of serious behavioral problems. One of the goals is to continue to replicate randomized controlled studies with different research groups to confirm the robustness of findings. MST provides children's mental health services a prototype of theory-driven, community-based, and family-centered treatment.

Methods of Training

Multisystemic therapy is an intensive intervention, lasting 3 to 5 months, with therapists working as much as daily with families. They are available around the clock to families, which is dramatically different from traditional office-based psychological interventions (e.g., family therapy). Clinicians work in the family's natural environment, such as the neighborhood, home, and/or school. Due to the intense clinical contact, MST therapists have low caseloads of three to five families. Therapists usually work with families daily initially, but face-to-face time usually decreases as the family continues in treatment (Schoenwald, Borduin, et al., 1998).

The following nine principles dictate assessment and intervention:

1. The purpose of assessment is to understand the fit between problems and the systemic context.
2. Therapeutic interventions emphasize the positive, and systems strengths are used as vehicles for change.
3. Interventions should be designed to increase responsible behavior and decrease irresponsible behaviors in family members.
4. Treatment is focused on the present and is action-oriented, with specific targets.
5. Behavioral sequences within and between systems that maintain maladaptive behavior are targeted.
6. Interventions must be developmentally appropriate.
7. Daily to weekly attempts by family members are required.
8. MST effectiveness is evaluated from multiple perspectives, and providers assume responsibility for failure to overcome barriers to achieve successful outcomes.
9. Interventions should promote lasting and generalizable change by empowering families to address needs across systems (Burns et al., 2000; Schoenwald, Ward, et al., 2000).

First, therapists must affirm the parents' authority while also gathering each family member's perspective on the situation. Second, the therapist must build an understanding of the systemic context the family's problems are maintained in. Following assessment stages, the therapist must identify and build on the family's natural strengths and must help families develop new strengths that can promote behavioral change (Henggeler & Borduin, 1990). Even though MST families have multiple needs, they are viewed as resources to MST and collaborative partners in the treatment. Therapists work with families by empowering them to build on existing resources or on developing family, community, and other resources to help cement lasting changes even when the treatment ends (Schoenwald et al.). The therapist, the family, and the youth create an infrastructure to help families continue to keep troubled children at home and to address inevitable problems that will arise following treatment.

Methods of Assessing Fidelity

Multisystemic therapy has done some of the most impressive work in children's services on measuring and improving treatment adherence. The goal of treatment adherence research is to assess if a therapy occurred as intended. However, few adherence studies are conducted on children's mental health and those that are, vary widely. The first step to ensure treatment adherence in MST providers is to provide direct supervision and/or consultation to new providers from the original treatment developers. A brief MST Adherence Scale was developed to measure therapists' adherence to MST principles during treatment sessions (Schoenwald, Henggeler, Brondino, & Rowland, 2000).

A few studies have been completed using the scale indicating that higher levels of adherence were related to more positive outcomes. In a randomized study of MST with substance-abusing juvenile-justice involved youth, higher therapist adherence scores were associated with decreased criminal activity and fewer out-of-home placements. Further analyses of adherence studies indicated that less productive sessions were associated with poorer family relations, and when families and therapists problem solve together, parental monitoring is more adequate. Fidelity to the MST model was also assessed in an alternative to hospitalization study in which an adherence monitoring protocol was implemented involving weekly feedback on audiotaped sessions. The study suggested that treatment fidelity varied among therapists, but all were able to achieve fidelity targets within 3 to 4 months of initiating the adherence monitoring protocol (Schoenwald, Henggeler, et al.). Thus, the developers of MST have been able to improve overall treatment fidelity and measure treatment adherence, which has been related to positive child and family outcomes.

Future Directions

Studies of MST, including randomized controlled trials, need to be replicated in research groups other than the original developers (Burns et al., 2000). MST has provided an excellent example of what children's mental health services can do to measure and improve therapist adherence and fidelity to a specific treatment. Thus, work to continue to develop new methods and modify existing methods of measuring treatment adherence and fidelity are integral to improving the quality of mental healthcare provided to children and adolescents.

WRAPAROUND SERVICES

Wraparound services provide children and youth with serious emotional disturbances (SED) with a comprehensive array of individualized services to meet their changing needs and to develop their strengths (Burchard & Clarke, 1991). Children with SED are defined as those between the ages of 0 and 18 years who at any time in the past 12 months have had or currently have a diagnosable mental, emotional, or behavioral disorder of sufficient duration to meet the *DSM-III-R* (American Psychiatric Association, 1987) criteria for significant school, family, or community functional impairment (Costello et al., 1996). Typically, children and adolescents with SED have multiple psychiatric diagnoses and experience severe impairment in multiple life domains. Their needs extend beyond adolescence with services being required well into adulthood. Given their high level of need, youth with SED require flexible and individualized services.

Wraparound services have gained increasing popularity in response to a national call for child- and family-centered, community-based mental health treatments (Stroul, 1988a, 1988b). These services have been increasingly implemented across the country with services today provided in more than 40 U.S. states and territories in mental health, education, social service, and juvenile justice service sectors (Burns et al., 2000). Wraparound care has two primary goals: to reduce the likelihood of out-of-home and unnecessarily restrictive placements and to improve behavioral and emotional functioning. These goals are achieved by designing individualized services to meet the unique needs of youth with SED with a combination of case management and flexible funding. Thus, case management and flexible funds that can be used for changing treatment needs are the primary mechanisms through which services are administered (Clark et al., 1998).

There are four principles that characterize wraparound programs. First, strengths are emphasized in assessment, planning, and treatment phases (Clark et al., 1998). Identifying existing strengths and recognizing potential strengths for development are mechanisms for therapeutic change and are integral to service planning (Clark et al., 1998; Grundle, 2002). Strengths-based treatment is a primary focus of wraparound services instead of largely deficit-based treatment models. Second, life-domain planning must involve regular meetings that include not only service providers, but all the important adults in the child's life (e.g., caregivers, teachers, relatives, siblings, mentors; Clark et al., 1998). The treatment design meetings play a key role in revising service planning given the changing needs, strengths, interests, and competencies of youth with SED and their family (Clark et al., 1998; Grundle, 2002). Many traditional services hold treatment planning meetings that do not accommodate and involve the adults that play important roles in the child's life; thus, wraparound services make a commitment to involving families and other important adults in treatment planning from the outset.

Third, clinical case management, one of the primary mechanisms of change in wraparound services, plays a vital role in service provision. Clinical case managers coordinate all necessary services, provide individualized supports tailored to each family's needs, and act as advocates for the child and family (Clark et al., 1998). Children with SED have varying levels of needs, with varying levels of service restrictiveness necessary to meet these needs. At times, low-intensity outpatient psychotherapy may be all that is needed by a youth; or family preservation or crisis services may be necessary in more acute situations to maintain children at home (Grundle, 2002). These services are coordinated by case managers who also use flexible funding, the second primary component of wraparound services (e.g., using funding to provide music lessons or a tutor for schoolwork; Clark et al., 1998; Grundle, 2002). Last, wraparound services seek to foster the development of natural supports to enable families to be their own service advocates (Clark et al., 1998). Wraparound services do not have a prescribed termination and are unconditionally provided (Grundle, 2002); however, there is an assumption that effective wraparound implementation leads to substantive changes in the child, family, and community and presents a natural conclusion when needs are sufficiently resolved and strengths development has progressed (Burns et al., 2000). These four aspects of wraparound services make them unique because they have the capacity to provide comprehensive, long-term services in the child and family's natural context.

Assessing Outcomes and Efficacy

Wraparound programs are focused on outcomes assessment (Clark et al., 1998). Overall, wraparound care has generated positive outcomes with youth with SED at risk for restrictive placements. The Kaleidoscope Program in Chicago, Wraparound Milwaukee, and the states of Alaska and Vermont started some of the first and most successful programs around the country.

Wraparound Milwaukee is one of the best examples of a program that has demonstrated significant reductions in institutional placements and a restructuring of a community service delivery system. Wraparound Milwaukee successfully developed an integrated and coordinated system of care in the local community. Youth involved in Wraparound Milwaukee have more than 70 services by a network of 200 providers available to meet their emotional and behavioral needs that place them at risk for out-of-home placements. The success of the program is due in large part to its ability to pool funds across service sectors and its swift assessment and delivery of crisis services to deflect institutional placements. Outcomes of youth involved in Wraparound Milwaukee have resulted in a 65% reduction in the use of residential and inpatient treatments and significant decreases in legal offenses and adjudications with many of these positive outcomes sustained over time (Grundle, 2002).

In 1985, the Alaska Youth Initiative (AYI) was established to improve the quality of mental health services statewide. As part of the initiative, wraparound services were used to return youth in out-of-state residential care back to their local communities (Burns et al., 2000; VanDenBerg, 1993). The initiative has been described as, ". . . one of the most comprehensive examples of individualized care to date" (Kutash & Rivera, 1996). The initiative resulted in two primary outcomes: First, it prevented youth from receiving institutional treatment outside Alaska and, second, it transitioned numerous youth back into Alaskan communities (VanDenBerg, 1993). The state demonstrated that SED youth can be served in their local communities with existing service systems and do not have to be placed in restrictive residential placements far from their natural environments (VanDenBerg, 1993). Qualitative analyses on 9 of 10 youth served by AYI wraparound services concluded that it was a successful alternative to residential treatment (Burchard & Clarke, 1991). AYI was one of the first instances of a successful statewide implementation of wraparound services.

Several randomized and quasi-experimental studies of wraparound services have also been conducted. In a randomized controlled study of foster children in a Fostering

Individualized Assistance Program (FIAP), wraparound youth eloped for fewer days and had more stable placements than youth in the nonwraparound condition. Gains were maintained at 3.5-year follow-up and suggested a higher likelihood for permanent placement than youth not receiving wraparound services (Clark, Lee, Prange, & McDonald, 1996; Clark et al., 1998). Overall, the study found lower rates of externalizing behavior and conduct-disordered behavior among males compared to youth in the standard foster care condition.

A study of 106 children and adolescents in wraparound and nonwraparound conditions compared youth on mental health, school, and legal outcomes. Investigators found that youth involved in wraparound services experienced less restrictive placements and were more involved in community activities. Wraparound youth also attended school and/or work more regularly than youth not receiving wraparound care (Hyde, Burchard, & Woodworth, 1996). Significant declines in behavior problems and higher levels of adjustment were also observed in the wraparound sample (Hyde et al., 1996; Yoe, Santarcangelo, Atkins, & Burchard, 1996). One strength of the study was that 2 years after services were initiated, almost 50% of wraparound youth were living in the community or were attending school or work regularly; however, the youth in the nonwraparound condition did not constitute a randomized control group, limiting the conclusions of the study (Hyde et al., 1996).

A second randomized controlled trial compared wraparound services using intensive case management that coordinated services to treatment foster care in the state of New York. Family-centered intensive case management (FCICM) wraparound condition is an intensive child-centered case management service conducted in home, school, and community settings with SED youth to maintain them in their natural environments (Evans, Armstrong, Kuppinger, Huz, & McNulty, 1998). Despite both groups generally improving over time, children in the FCICM condition demonstrated improved behavior toward self and others, improved mood and emotions, fewer thought-disordered problems, fewer somatic complaints, and lower rates of delinquency. Unfortunately, families in the FCICM condition did not experience greater levels of family cohesion or adaptability; the observed lack of nonsignificant differences in family variables is unknown. The results suggested that youth in the FCICM condition could be maintained at home instead of being placed in treatment foster care, and the negative effects of remaining at home were not observed for these youth.

In one study, children at risk for out-of-home placement were randomized to the FIAP wraparound condition or the standard practice (SP) foster care control group (Clark et al., 1998). The study consisted of 131 youth in a foster care system, of whom over 60% were male, 62% were Caucasian, and 34% were African American. Younger children in the FIAP and SP conditions each spent approximately 50% of their time in permanent home settings during the posttreatment period. However, at the same 3.5-year follow-up period, older youth in the FIAP condition spent 50% of their time in permanent settings compared to same-age counterparts in the SP condition, who spent only about 20% of their time in permanent home settings. For those youth incarcerated, FIAP youth spent fewer days in incarceration than youth in the SP condition. Females in the FIAP condition reported significantly higher rates of conduct disorder than females in the standard foster care condition; this finding was opposite in male FIAP participants.

Perhaps wraparound programs such as FIAP may work best in reducing externalizing and conduct disorder behaviors in males and in achieving greater placement stability in older youths. A reason for differential gender effects in the FIAP condition may be that more than 75% of females have sexual abuse histories; thus, more specific therapeutic interventions may be necessary to meet their unique needs. These studies indicate that wraparound models of care help SED youth by assisting families and service systems to work more efficiently together with the unique needs of each child at the forefront.

Measuring Fidelity

Assessing fidelity to treatment protocols is important in establishing the effectiveness of interventions (Bruns & Burchard, 2000).

The Annie E. Casey Foundation provided the Kaleidoscope Program in Chicago with a grant to evaluate its child and adolescent wraparound program. One piece of the evaluation was to develop and assess a wraparound fidelity measure, the Wraparound Observation Form (WOF). The WOF is a 34-item instrument measuring the following eight elements of wraparound:

1. Providing community-based services
2. Providing individualized services
3. Involving family members in the treatment process
4. Encouraging interagency collaboration
5. Providing unconditional care
6. Measuring treatment outcomes
7. Including key participants in meetings
8. Fostering cooperation among team members (Epstein et al., 1998)

The mean interrater reliability across reviewers was 95.3%. None of the items had a reliability less than 70%, and the median agreement on items was 100% (Epstein et al.). Thus, there is a growing interest in and commitment to understanding the processes of wraparound care and increasing fidelity to wraparound principles.

Future Directions

In addition to the need for long-term follow-up, further research is needed on using wraparound services with other populations, such as juvenile sex offenders (Grundle, 2002). To date, there are approximately 14 published studies on wraparound programs (Burns et al., 2000). Few randomized controlled studies have been completed, which could provide valuable information on the viability and effectiveness of wraparound services. Wraparound services are gaining much attention and support and are being implemented variably across the nation (Burns et al., 2000). Thus, fidelity models and standards for wraparound services are being created and investigated. Given these factors and the mounting evidence in favor of wraparound care, more randomized controlled trials are needed to establish it as an evidence-based practice.

FAMILY PRESERVATION

Family preservation (FP) has its roots early in the twentieth century. One of the first places where the concept of FP was formally introduced was at the First White House Conference on Children in 1909 (Morton, 1993; Schuerman, Rzepnicki, & Littell, 1994). There was a tremendous increase in the use of foster care and institutional placements in the late nineteenth and early twentieth centuries, bringing the idea of FP to bear in children's services (Schuerman et al., 1994). The growing realization that there is a significant degree of overlap between the child welfare and child mental systems also spurred the growth of interest in family preservation because of the potential for ameliorating the problems of the larger familial context (Yelton & Friedman, 1991). The appeal of FP services is their emphasis on keeping the nuclear family intact, on providing services in the least restrictive setting, and on providing cost-effective treatment (Biegel & Wells, 1991; Schuerman et al., 1994). Today, there are more than 200 FP programs in almost all 50 states, which usually target families who are at risk for a child being placed in out-of-home placement (Morton, 1993; Schuerman et al., 1994).

Programs vary widely from one to the next on several dimensions, such as treatment approaches, organizational differences, and program size and capacity. However, some hallmark features have been identified (Schuerman et al., 1994):

1. Services should be family-centered and should seek to increase family functioning as a whole.
2. Services should be delivered in the home, as opposed to an office-based setting.
3. Services should be initiated when a crisis is identified, and they should be intensive and time-limited, thereby taking advantage of the crisis to promote change.
4. Services should empower families and build on strengths.
5. Services should encourage the use of formal and informal community-based resources.
6. Case management should be used to obtain, coordinate, and monitor service use.

Thus, FP makes a commitment to providing family-centered, community-based care that focuses on strengths to prevent out-of-home placement in the short term and to foster family empowerment in the long term.

The children's mental health system is increasingly complex, and the role of newer services that vary from one program to the next can be difficult to discern. Thus, researchers have outlined four primary roles of FP programs within the context of the larger mental health system:

1. Ensuring the protection and safety of clients
2. Conducting ecologically valid assessment in the family's natural environment to get a comprehensive view of their needs and strengths
3. Providing treatment that defuses the initial crisis, builds a treatment plan with the help of the family, and monitors and supports their progress

4. Linking the family to services that will empower the family to continue fostering natural supports and to seek formal services long after the FP intervention has ended (Yelton & Friedman, 1991)

The proliferation of FP programs has been one of the most important developments in the movement to provide family-centered and community-based treatment to children and their families (Yelton & Friedman, 1991). They have been able to provide in-home services that prevent costly institutional placements for families and youth that are regarded as "unworkable." Thus, the role of FP extends beyond deflecting inpatient and residential placements (Yelton & Friedman, 1991).

Assessing Outcomes and Efficacy

One of the earliest FP programs was the Homebuilders Program in Tacoma, Washington. Since its inception, the Homebuilders model is probably one of the most widely implemented programs around the country. Homebuilders emphasizes the intensive and short-term nature of FP services, with low caseloads of no more than two families and clinicians being available 24 hours per day, 7 days per week for 4 to 6 weeks (Schuerman et al., 1994).

In 1985, Hennepin County, in Minnesota, implemented FP services for the first time to reduce the high numbers of youth in residential treatment (Schwartz, AuClaire, & Harris, 1991). Schwartz et al. conducted a study to assess how successful their FP program was as an alternative to out-of-home placements. A total of 116 cases were included in the sample, with 55 receiving FP services and the remainder serving as a comparison group. Fifty-four percent of the sample was male, more than two-thirds were Caucasian, and the majority were referred to residential treatment whether they were in the FP or the comparison group. Follow-up was conducted for 1 year from entry into the program. Clients in the comparison group were placed almost twice as many times as FP clients (76 in the FP group and 134 in the comparison group), and they experienced almost three times as many days in placement (4,777 in the FP group and 12,037 in the comparison group); however, there were nonsignificant differences in the mean number of placements (2.45 in the FP group and 2.3 in the comparison group). There were also 31 youth in the FP condition that were placed, suggesting that subsets of youth may benefit differentially from FP services. The Hennepin County study suggests that families receiving FP services are more likely to maintain children at home and to use fewer days of restrictive placements when placed.

Families that were more involved in goal-setting and the treatment process were also more likely to achieve positive outcomes (Schwartz et al., 1991). Families that treatment teams judged as achieving significant goal progress used only 5% of placement days, as opposed to 25% for families judged as not achieving goal progress. Thus, the degree of family involvement in the treatment model is associated with the likelihood of out-of-home placement.

In 1987, New Jersey's Department of Youth and Family Services (DYFS) piloted an FP program modeled after the Homebuilders program (Feldman, 1991). A total of 183 families were randomly assigned to an FP condition ($N = 96$) or to traditional community services (TC; included less intensive counseling, mental health agencies, family courts) condition ($N = 87$). More than half of all youth were reported to display "out-of-control" behavior. At 1-year follow-up, significantly fewer number of youth in the FP condition, 45.8%, were in placement compared to the 57.7% of youth in placement in the TC condition; families in the FP condition also had a significantly slower time to entry into placement, 4.3 months, compared to TC condition, 2.4 months. There were nonsignificant differences in the level of placement restrictiveness, placement types, total number of placement events, or total time in placement up to the 12-month follow-up (Feldman). The New Jersey DYFS program appeared to prevent and delay short-term placement for youth in the FP condition; however, the long-term effectiveness of the FP program is unclear.

The National Resource Center on Family Based Services and the Regional Research Institute for Human Services at Portland State University carried out a 2-year exploratory study of 11 FP programs around the country (Nelson, 1991). The study sought to answer the questions: (1) Are placement rates in FP programs due to selection (i.e., are families with less severe or with fewer needs more likely to avoid placement)? and (2) What factors differentiate placement and nonplacement cases? Five FP programs and 248 families were examined. The study design used a mental health and juvenile-justice sample as a point of comparison. Across programs, families receiving FP services had more problems than those in the comparison group, suggesting that lower placement rates in FP samples is not due to selection. Families with higher levels of substance abuse, concurrent mental health service involvement, and a lack of care-giver cooperation tended to be associated with an increased risk for placement. FP is a viable community-based alternative that produces positive outcomes and allows for the provision of mental health services in a community setting.

Measuring Fidelity

Limited work has been conducted on treatment fidelity in FP programs. One attempt at measuring treatment fidelity was made by the New Jersey DYFS FP program. They assessed basic program characteristics, including mean number of weeks of involvement with families, level of intensity provision, and the selected goals, and used interventions to assess adherence to the Homebuilders model (Feldman, 1991). Based on these surface characteristics, the New Jersey DYFS FP program appeared to adhere to the Homebuilders model. However, little other work has been published on FP treatment fidelity.

Future Directions

More randomized controlled trials of FP programs are necessary to establish it as an evidence-based practice. Multisite, large sample studies are needed to generalize the early successes of FP to other settings and populations. Little is known about fidelity to FP principles from one program to another, which is essential in understanding and maintaining the effectiveness of the treatment.

CONCLUSIONS

Considerable progress has been made over the past several years in identifying evidence-based treatments for children and adolescents. Despite this progress, serious deficiencies remain. There is little known about the context of evidence-based treatments in congregate care settings. While the system of care philosophy emphasizes treatment in the community, residential treatment remains the single largest investment in the children's system (Barker, 1998; Frensch & Cameron, 2002). The efficacy and effectiveness of specific forms of crisis intervention, including psychiatric hospitalization and its alternatives, are not well established (Kiesler, 1993). In-home crisis intervention is a promising practice, but the findings to date are insufficient to be called evidence-based (Mosier et al., 2001).

Perhaps even more urgent than the identification of evidence-based treatment in crisis settings and congregate care is the reality that despite the identification of evidence-based treatments in outpatient and intensive community care, the actual implementation of these approaches is spotty at best. Despite evidence to suggest an improved approach to treatment, clinicians serving children and adolescents around the country continue to use treatment approaches for which scant evidence of effectiveness exists. While many states and third-party payers have initiated programs to encourage the adoption of evidence-based treatments, it is unclear the degree to which these initiatives are having an impact on practice. Solving the challenge of successfully disseminating treatment innovations should be a priority.

In addition, investment in the infrastructure of the children's service system to support the ongoing collection of reliable, valid, and meaningful outcomes data is critical to the long-term success of the movement toward evidence-based treatments (Lyons, 2004). Without the ongoing ability to monitor outcomes and treatment fidelity in the service delivery system, it will be difficult to assess the effectiveness of treatment. It will also be difficult to identify which promising new approaches to subject to more rigorous scientific scrutiny to establish new evidence-based treatments.

The recent interest in children's mental health has stimulated a great deal of progress in identifying treatment approaches that work. However, much work remains both to continue to identify approaches that fit across the range of services in the full array of a system of care and to implement identified treatments within the existing system. By maintaining a focus on the best interests of children and families through the use of outcomes in the service system and rigorous research in laboratory settings, these gaps can and must be bridged.

REFERENCES

American Psychiatric Association. (1987). *Diagnostic and statistical manual of mental disorders* (3rd ed., rev.). Washington, DC: Author.

Andrade, A. R., Lambert, E. W., & Bickman, L. (2000). Dose effect in child psychotherapy: Outcomes associated with negligible treatment. *Journal of the American Academy of Child and Adolescent Psychiatry, 39,* 161–168.

Armbruster, P., & Fallon, T. (1994). Clinical, sociodemographic, and systems risk factors for attrition in a children's mental health clinic. *American Journal of Orthopsychiatry, 64*(4), 577–585.

Armbruster, P., & Schwab-Stone, M. (1994). Sociodemographic characteristics of dropouts from a child guidance clinic. *Hospital and Community Psychiatry, 45*(8), 804–808.

Barker, P. (1998). The future of residential treatment for children. In C. Schaefer & A. Swanson (Eds.), *Children in residential care: Critical Issues in treatment* (pp. 1–16). New York: Van Nostrand Reinhold.

Barrett, P. M., Duffy, A. L., Dadds, M. R., & Rapee, R. M. (2001). Cognitive-behavioral treatment of anxiety disorders in children: Long-term (6-year) follow-up. *Journal of Consulting and Clinical Psychology, 69*(1), 135–141.

Biegel, D. E., & Wells, K. (1991). Introduction. In D. E. Biegel & K. Wells (Eds.), *Family preservation services: Research and evaluation* (pp. 1–29). Newbury Park, CA: Sage.

Borduin, C. M., Mann, B. J., Cone, L. T., Henggeler, S. W., Fucci, B. R., Blaske, D. M., et al. (1995). Multisystemic therapy of serious juvenile offenders: Long-term prevention of criminality and violence. *Journal of Consulting and Clinical Psychology, 63*(4), 569–578.

Bronfenbrenner, U. (1979). *The ecology of human development: Experiments by nature and design.* Cambridge, MA: Harvard University Press.

Brunk, M., Henggeler, S. W., & Whelan, J. P. (1987). Comparison of multisystemic therapy and parent training in the brief treatment of child abuse and neglect. *Journal of Consulting and Clinical Psychology, 55*(2), 171–178.

Bruns, E. J., & Burchard, J. D. (2000). Impact of respite care services for families with children experiencing emotional and behavioral problems and their families. *Children's Services: Social Policy, Research and Practice, 3,* 39–61.

Burchard, J. D., & Clarke, R. T. (1991). The role of individualized care in a service delivery system for children and adolescents with severely maladjusted behavior. *Journal of Mental Health Administration, 17,* 48–60.

Burns, B. J., Schoenwald, S. K., Burchard, J. D., Faw, L., & Santos, A. B. (2000). Comprehensive community-based interventions for youth with severe emotional disorders: Multisystemic therapy and the wraparound process. *Journal of Child and Family Studies, 9*(3), 283–314.

Clark, H. B., Lee, B., Prange, M. E., & McDonald, B. A. (1996). Children lost within the foster care system: Can wraparound service strategies improve placement outcomes? *Journal of Child and Family Studies, 5*(1), 39–54.

Clark, H. B., Prange, M., Lee, B., Stewart, E. S., McDonald, B. A., & Boyd, L. A. (1998). An individualized wraparound process for children in foster care with emotional/behavioral disturbances: Follow-up findings and implications from a controlled study. In R. Friedman (Ed.), *Outcomes for children and youth with emotional and behavioral disorders and their families: Programs and evaluation best practices.* Austin, TX: ProEd.

Costello, E. J., Angold, A., Burns, B. J., Erkanli, A., Stangl, D. K., & Tweed, D. L. (1996). The great Smoky Mountains study of youth: Functional impairment and serious emotional disturbance. *Archives of General Psychiatry, 53*(12), 1137–1143.

Diamond, G. S., Reis, B. F., Diamond, G. M., Siqueland, L., & Isaacs, L. (2002). Attachment-based family therapy for depressed adolescents: A treatment development study. *Journal of American Academy of Child and Adolescent Psychiatry, 41*(10), 1190–1196.

Epstein, M. H., Jayanthi, M., McKelvey, J., Frankenberry, E., Hardy, R., Dennis, K., et al. (1998). Reliability of the wraparound observation form: An instrument to measure the wraparound process. *Journal of Child and Family Studies, 7*(2), 161–170.

Evans, M. E., Armstrong, M. I., Kuppinger, A. D., Huz, S., & McNulty, T. L. (1998). Preliminary outcomes of an experimental study comparing treatment foster care and family-centered intensive case management. In A. Duchnowski (Ed.), *Outcomes for children and youth with emotional and behavioral disorders and their families: Programs and evaluation best practices* (pp. 543–580). Austin, TX: ProEd.

Feldman, L. H. (1991). Evaluating the impact of intensive family preservation services in New Jersey. In D. E. Biegel & K. Wells (Eds.), *Family preservation services: Research and evaluation* (pp. 127–168). Newbury Park, CA: Sage.

Frensch, K. M., & Cameron, G. (2002). Treatment of choice or a last resort? A review of residential mental health placements for children and youth. *Child and Family Youth Care Forum, 31*(5), 307–339.

Grundle, T. J. (2002). Wraparound care. In D. T. Marsh & M. A. Fristad (Eds.), *Handbook of serious emotional disturbance in children and adolescents* (pp. 323–333). New York: Wiley.

Henggeler, S. W. (1982). The family-ecological systems theory. In S. W. Henggeler (Ed.), *Delinquency and psychopathology: A family-ecological systems approach* (pp. 1–10). Boston: John Wright PSG.

Henggeler, S. W., & Borduin, C. M. (1990). *Family therapy and beyond: A multisystemic approach to treating the behavior problems of children and adolescents.* Pacific Grove, CA: Brooks/Cole.

Henggeler, S. W., Clingempeel, W. G., & Brondino, M. J. (2002). Four-year follow-up of multisystemic therapy with substance-abusing and substance-dependent juvenile offenders. *Journal of the American Academy of Child and Adolescent Psychiatry, 41*(7), 868–874.

Henggeler, S. W., Melton, G. B., & Smith, L. A. (1992). Family preservation using multisystemic therapy: An effective alternative to incarcerating serious juvenile offenders. *Journal of Consulting and Clinical Psychology, 60*(6), 953–961.

Henggeler, S. W., Rowland, M. D., & Randall, J. (1999). Home-based multisystemic therapy as an alternative to the hospitalization of youths in psychiatric crisis: Clinical outcomes. *Journal of the American Academy of Child and Adolescent Psychiatry, 38*(11), 1331–1339.

Hoagwood, K., Burns, B. J., Kiser, L., Ringeisen, H., & Schoenwald, S. K. (2001). Evidence-based practices in child and adolescent mental health services. *Psychiatric Services, 52,* 1179–1189.

Hyde, K. L., Burchard, J. D., & Woodworth, K. (1996). Wrapping services in an urban setting. *Journal of Child and Family Studies, 5*(1), 67–82.

Jensen, P. S., Bhatara, V. S., Vitiello, B., Hoagwood, K., Feil, M., & Burke, L. B. (1999). Psychoactive medication prescribing practices for U.S. children: Gaps between research and clinical practice. *Journal of the American Academy of Child and Adolescent Psychiatry, 38,* 557–565.

Kazdin, A. E. (2000). Developing a research agenda for child and adolescent psychotherapy. *Archives of General Psychiatry, 57*(9), 829–835.

Kazdin, A. E., Bass, D., Ayers, W. A., & Rodgers, A. (1990). Empirical and clinical focus of child and adolescent psychotherapy research. *Journal of Consulting and Clinical Psychology, 58*(6), 729–740.

Kazdin, A. E., Holland, L., & Crowley, M. (1997). Family experience of barriers to treatment and premature termination from child therapy. *Journal of Consulting and Clinical Psychology, 65*(3), 453–463.

Kazdin, A. E., & Weisz, J. R. (1998). Identifying and developing empirically supported child and adolescent treatments. *Journal of Consulting and Clinical Psychology, 66,* 19–36.

Kendall, P. C. (1993). Cognitive-behavioral therapies with youth: Guiding theory, current status, and emerging developments. *Journal of Consulting and Clinical Psychology, 61*(2), 235–247.

Kendall, P. C., & Warman, M. J. (1996). Emotional disorders in youth. In P. M. Salkovskis (Ed.), *Frontiers of cognitive therapy* (pp. 509–530). New York: Guilford Press.

Kiesler, C. A. (1993). Mental health policy and the psychiatric inpatient care of children. *Applied and Preventive Psychology, 2,* 91–99.

Knitzer, J. (1982). *Unclaimed children: The failure of public responsibility to children and adolescents in need of mental health services.* Washington, DC: Children's Defense Fund.

Kutash, K., & Rivera, V. R. (1996). *What works in children's mental health services? Uncovering answers to critical questions.* Baltimore: Paul H. Brookes.

LeCroy, C. W. A., & Jose, B. (1992). Children's mental health: Current findings and research directions. *Social Work Research and Abstracts, 28*(1), 13–20.

Lyons, J. S. (2004). *Redressing the emperor: Evolving the children's public mental health service system.* Westport, CT: Praeger.

Miller, S. J., & Binder, J. L. (2002). The effects of manual-based training on treatment fidelity and outcome: A review of the literature on adult individual psychotherapy. *Psychotherapy: Theory, Research, Practice and Training, 39*(2), 184–198.

Mosier, J., Burlingame, G. M., Wells, M. G., Ferre, R., Latkowski, M., Johansen, J., et al. (2001). In-home, family-centered psychiatric treatment for high-risk children and youth. *Children's Services: Social Policy, Research, and Practice, 4,* 51–68.

Morton, E. S. (1993). The evolution of family preservation. In E. S. Morton & R. K. Grigsby (Eds.), *Advancing family preservation practice* (pp. 98–124). Newbury Park, CA: Sage.

Nelson, K. E. (1991). Populations and outcomes in five family preservation programs. In D. E. Biegel & K. Wells (Eds.), *Family preservation services: Research and evaluation* (pp. 59–97). Newbury Park, CA: Sage.

Pelkonen, M., Marttunen, M., Laippala, P., & Lonnqvist, J. (2000). Factors associated with early dropout from adolescent psychiatric outpatient treatment. *Journal of the American Academy of Child and Adolescent Psychiatry, 39*(3), 329–335.

Reinecke, M. A., Ryan, N. E., & Dubois, D. L. (1998). Cognitive-behavioral therapy of depression and depressive symptoms during adolescence: A review and meta-analysis. *Journal of the American Academy of Child and Adolescent Psychiatry, 37*(1), 26–34.

Reynolds, W., & Coats, K. (1986). A comparison of cognitive-behavior therapy and relaxation training for the treatment of depression in adolescents. *Journal of Consulting and Clinical Psychology, 54,* 653–660.

Schleser, R., & Rodick, J. D. (1982). A comparison of traditional family therapy models and the family-ecological systems approach. In S. W. Henggeler (Ed.), *Delinquency and psychopathology: A family-ecological systems approach* (pp. 11–26). Boston: John Wright PSG.

Schoenwald, S. K., Borduin, C. M., & Henggeler, S. W. (1998). Multisystemic therapy: Changing the natural and service ecologies of adolescents and their families. In M. Epstein, K. Kutash, & A. J. Duchnowski (Eds.), *Outcomes for children and youth with emotional and behavioral disorders and their families: Programs and evaluation best practices* (pp. 485–512). Austin, TX: ProEd.

Schoenwald, S. K., Brown, T. L., & Henggeler, S. W. (2000). Inside multisystemic therapy: Therapist, supervisory, and program practices. *Journal of Emotional and Behavioral Disorders, 8*(2), 113–128.

Schoenwald, S. K., Henggeler, S. W., Brondino, M. J., & Rowland, M. D. (1998). Multisystemic therapy: Monitoring treatment fidelity. *Family Process, 39*(1), 83–103.

Schoenwald, S. K., Ward, D. M., Henggeler, S. W., & Rowland, M. D. (2000). Multisystemic therapy versus hospitalization for crisis stabilization of youth: Placement outcomes 4 months post-referral. *Mental Health Services Research, 2*(1), 3–12.

Schuerman, J. R., Rzepnicki, T. L., & Littell, J. H. (1994). *Putting families first: An experiment in family preservation.* Hawthorne, NY: Aldine de Gruyter.

Schwartz, I. M., AuClaire, P., & Harris, L. J. (1991). Family preservation services as an alternative to the out-of-home placements of adolescents: The Hennepin County experience. In D. E. Biegel & K. Wells (Eds.), *Family preservation services: Research and evaluation* (pp. 202–231). Newbury Park, CA: Sage.

Stark, K. D., Rouse, L. W., & Livingston, R. (1991). Treatment of depression during childhood and adolescence: Cognitive-behavioral procedures for the individual and family. In P. C. Kendall (Ed.), *Child and adolescent therapy: Cognitive-behavioral procedures* (pp. 165–206). New York: Guilford Press.

Stroul, B. A. F. (1988a, July/August). Principle for a system of care. *Children Today,* 11–14.

Stroul, B. A. F. (1988b, July/August). Putting principles into practice. *Children Today,* 15–17.

VanDenBerg, J. E. (1993). Integration of individualized mental health services into the system of care for children and adolescents. *Administration and Policy in Mental Health, 20*(4), 247–257.

Weiss, B. W., Jr. (1995). Relative effectiveness of behavioral versus nonbehavioral child psychotherapy. *Journal of Consulting and Clinical Psychology, 63*(2), 317–320.

Weiss, B. W., Jr., & Weisz, J. R. (1995). Effectiveness of psychotherapy. *Journal of the American Academy of Child and Adolescent Psychiatry, 34,* 971–972.

Weisz, J. R., Donenberg, G. R., Han, S. S., & Kauneckis, D. (1995). Child and adolescent psychotherapy outcomes in experiments versus clinics: Why the disparity? *Journal of Abnormal Child Psychology, 23*(1), 83–106.

Weisz, J. R., Donenberg, G. R., Han, S. S., & Weiss, B. (1995). Bridging the gap between laboratory and clinic in child and adolescent psychiatry. *Journal of Consulting and Clinical Psychology, 63*(5), 688–701.

Weisz, J. R., Weiss, B., Han, S. S., Granger, D. A., & Morton, T. (1995). Effects of psychotherapy with children and adolescents revisited: A meta-analysis of treatment outcome studies. *Psychological Bulletin, 117*(3), 450–468.

Yelton, S. W., & Friedman, R. M. (1991). Family preservation services: Their role within the children's mental health system. In D. E. Biegel & K. Wells (Eds.), *Family preservation services: Research and evaluation* (pp. 35–71). Newbury Park, CA: Sage.

Yoe, J. T., Santarcangelo, S., Atkins, M., & Burchard, J. D. (1996). Wraparound care in Vermont: Program development, implementation, and evaluation of a statewide system of individualized services. *Journal of Child and Family Studies, 5*(1), 23–39.

CHAPTER 9

Recovery from Severe Mental Illnesses and Evidence-Based Practice Research

E. Sally Rogers, Marianne Farkas, and William A. Anthony

The term *recovery* was largely absent from the past century's diagnostic nomenclature (American Psychiatric Association, 1987), mental health programs, and interventions (Bachrach, 1976; Grob, 1983; New Freedom Commission on Mental Health, 2003). Despite its more recent and widespread use to denote a severely mentally ill person's ability to grow and heal, the concept of recovery remains poorly understood and is frequently used in policy and political statements rather than as an empirically based and operationally defined concept. We argue in this chapter that a consensus about the meaning of recovery is beginning to develop through various empirical investigations and anecdotal writings on the topic, but the term is critically in need of a multifaceted theoretical model informed by both mental health and behavioral science research.

This chapter first reviews the current status of research on the concept of recovery and suggests a multidimensional model of recovery. The second part of the chapter focuses on the limits of current evidence-based research on recovery processes and outcomes and outlines ways in which research can be additive and compatible with recovery-oriented programs and systems.

RECOVERY FROM SEVERE MENTAL ILLNESSES

Within the past decade, state mental health systems and, by implication, program administrators and clinicians who work in these systems have witnessed a major shift in the conceptualization of how mental healthcare should be delivered. The long-term

The authors would like to acknowledge funding support to the Center for Psychiatric Rehabilitation, which has made it possible over the past several years to advance our understanding of recovery. This support includes The National Institute of Mental Health through a research infrastructure award, the Center for Mental Health Services within the Substance Abuse and Mental Health Services Administration, and the National Institute on Disability and Rehabilitation Research. The ideas and opinions in this chapter, while developed with funding from the agencies mentioned, do not necessarily represent their views and are wholly the views of the authors. We would also like to thank Erin Dunn for her assistance with manuscript preparation. Staff of the Center for Psychiatric Rehabilitation, through their conceptual understanding and various research projects on recovery, helped to lay the groundwork for this chapter.

course of severe mental illnesses is no longer viewed as wholly deteriorative (DeSisto, Harding, McCormick, Ashikaga, & Brooks, 1995; Harding, Brooks, Ashikaga, Strauss, & Breier, 1987; Harrison, Hopper, Craig, Laska, & Siegel, 2001; Sartorius, Gulbinat, Harrison, Laska, & Siegel, 1996), yet the mental health system developed over the past century has been built on the assumption that serious mental illness (SMI) is almost universally associated with a poor prognosis for recovery (APA, 1987; New Freedom Commission on Mental Health, 2003). Thus, until recently service systems have tended to focus on symptom reduction and stabilization, rather than on interventions that promote growth and recovery. To align mental health policies, practices, and services, the field needs a better understanding of the processes and outcomes of recovery.

As mentioned earlier, the term *recovery* is increasingly being used to denote a severely mentally ill person's potential for growth and healing (Deegan, 1996; Liberman, Kopelowicz, Ventura, & Gutkind, 2002; Ralph, 2000; Ridgway, 2001; Spaniol, Wewiorski, Gagne, & Anthony, 2002). Despite its more recent widespread use in mental health systems, the concept of recovery until recently has been poorly understood and poorly operationalized. More recently, there has been a convergence of thinking about the meaning of the term recovery and its definition. Our preliminary conceptualization of recovery is based on current literature and research in the field, as well as initial studies done by our colleagues at the Center for Psychiatric Rehabilitation at Boston University. Taken together, these sources of information suggest that the *process* of recovery should be viewed as a long-term, almost continuous one; as a multidimensional process that must be defined both objectively and subjectively; along a continuum (rather than as recovered versus not recovered); and involving interdependent domains of functioning (including living, working, and social domains). Additionally, our preliminary conceptualization of the outcomes of *recovery* suggests that it involves psychosocial adjustment to the disability itself, achievement of subjective well-being, some degree of remission and/or stability of the signs and symptoms of the illness, and improvement in instrumental role functioning (Harding & Strauss, 1984; Liberman et al., 2002; Livneh, 2001; Ridgway, 2001).

Use of the Term Recovery

A review of systems-level literature and mental health policy statements suggests that even though there is no explicit consensus about the meaning of the term recovery, the term is now guiding policies and practice in many state mental health systems (see, e.g., Beale & Lambric, 1995; Jacobson & Curtis, 2000; Legislative Summer Study Committee of the State of Vermont Division of Mental Health, 1996; New Freedom Commission on Mental Health, 2003; State of Nebraska Recovery Work Team, 1997; State of Wisconsin Blue Ribbon Commission on Mental Health, 1997), as well as in entire countries such as New Zealand (O'Hagan, 2001). The following example taken from the Connecticut Commissioner's Policy Statement (2003) provides an excellent illustration of this trend:

> [T]he concept of recovery shall be the guiding principle and operational framework for the system of care provided by the partnership of state and private agencies and consumer-run services that comprise the Department's healthcare system. . . . The Department shall

create new and make necessary revisions to existing policies, procedures, programs and services and shall ensure that all new initiatives are consistent with a recovery-oriented services system.

Consumer groups have examined how systems can facilitate or hinder recovery and how this can be measured through system performance indicators (Onken, Dumont, Ridgway, Dornan, & Ralph, 2002). Further, recovery is listed as a performance indicator to monitor and improve the outcomes of clients served by state mental health systems, and several other indicators are recommended that measure initiatives consistent with a recovery mission (NASHMPD, 2001).

In addition to the use of the term in state mental health systems, recovery has also entered the lexicon of federal planning documents. The notion of recovery has found its way into the *Surgeon General's Report on Mental Health* (U.S. Department of Health and Human Services, 1999) and in the president's *New Freedom Commission* (2003), which began its report to the president with the following words: "We envision a future when everyone with a mental illness will recover . . ." (p. 1). In the letter to the president accompanying the report, the Chair of the Commission recommended a transformation of the nation's approach to mental healthcare, so as to ensure ". . . that mental health services and supports actively facilitate recovery. . . . Too often, today's system simply manages symptoms and accepts long term disability."

While the notion that individuals with a diagnosis of severe mental illness can regain premorbid levels of functioning and/or improve substantially over time has been introduced in government reports and state and local planning documents, many clinicians, program administrators, and system planners are uncertain about how to incorporate this knowledge into their clinical practice and program structures. Rather than used as window dressing, recovery needs to be effectively incorporated into service systems and practice. Therefore, we need more knowledge about how, why, and under what circumstances people recover. At the same time, we need to understand the implications of this concept for the design of new treatment interventions and for the development of evidence-based practices that will facilitate recovery outcomes.

Two principles appear basic to our future understanding of recovery. First, the complexity of the concept of recovery requires a multidisciplinary approach. To implement this principle, the study of recovery must emanate from the knowledge accumulated from collaboration among prominent scholars in the areas of psychology, sociology, rehabilitation, psychiatry, public health, social work, nursing, and others. Special attention must be paid as well to translation of cutting-edge behavioral science research into enhancing our understanding of recovery (National Institute of Mental Health [NIMH], 2003). Second, research into the processes and outcomes of recovery must be based on the principle of *participatory action research* (Rogers & Palmer-Erbs, 1994; Whyte, 1991), which requires individuals with severe mental illness to be actively involved in the design and implementation of such research. Participatory methods have been used in sociological and anthropological research for decades, but only recently have those methods gained more acceptability in the mental health field. Given the subjective nature of recovery and the importance of it to persons with severe mental illness, it is critical that they be involved in its understanding, definition, and research.

Development of the Concept of Recovery

It appears that several disparate bodies of knowledge converged in the 1980s and paved the way for the concept of recovery. One source of knowledge is the writing of people with SMI (e.g., Ralph, 2000), another source of evidence is the long-term outcome studies reviewed by Harding (1994; in press), and the final source is the research evidence suggesting that substantial improvements can be effected through mental health interventions (Bond, Becker, et al., 2001; Cook & Razzano, 2000; Drake, McHugo, Becker, Anthony, & Clark, 1996; Drake, Becker, et al., 1999; Mueser, Corrigan, Hilton, Tanzman, & Schaub, 2002). Based on these bodies of knowledge, working definitions of *recovery outcome* have emerged. One definition suggests that it involves the development of new meaning and purpose in life as a person grows beyond the effects of mental illness (Anthony, 1993). Other authors have developed criterion-based definitions (see, e.g., Liberman et al., 2002; Sullivan, 1994) involving instrumental role functioning across several domains such as work, social functioning, and living independence as well as reduced symptomatology. Like other mental health terms, there is no one consensual, operational definition of recovery outcomes. There remains disagreement about the extent to which being symptom free is a requisite for recovery outcome (cf. Deegan, 1988) or whether the need for treatment, medications, or hospitalizations should factor into the definition. For example, in the Vermont follow-up study reported by Harding and Zahniser (1994), the authors used the following definition of recovery from schizophrenia: "no signs or symptoms of mental illness, no current medications, work, relating well to family and friends, integrated into the community . . ." (p. 140). A further complication of the use of the term recovery is that some researchers and authors refer to recovery as an outcome (Liberman et al., 2002; Sullivan, 1994) while others refer to recovery as a process. As is illustrated in the recovery model proposed later in this chapter, we attempt to differentiate recovery processes and outcomes.

Research Related to Recovery Processes and Outcomes

Recently, a number of investigations have attempted to further our understanding of the processes and outcomes of recovery. Given the historical lack of clarity noted earlier surrounding the term recovery and its operational definition, it is somewhat difficult to classify the research that has a direct bearing on this concept. Several threads of research appear to have laid the groundwork for the concept of recovery. Here we review briefly these major categories of literature: the long-term follow-up studies of individuals with schizophrenia and major mental illness, the qualitative studies and first-person narratives of individuals reporting to have recovered from severe mental illness, and the research suggesting that mental health interventions can substantially improve the role functioning of people with SMI. We deliberately exclude a review of psychopharmacological interventions because of their intention to focus more narrowly on remission of symptoms, as well as the literature on psychotherapy, as most individuals with severe mental illness do not traditionally receive courses of psychotherapy as interventions (Malmberg & Fenton, 2001). We also review several recent mental health interventions that focus on instrumental role functioning, subjective, objective, and multidimensional outcomes of individuals with serious mental illness, including self-esteem and quality of life. Our goal in this section is to examine some of the literature that bears directly on the processes and outcomes of recovery; uses functional, objective, and subjective criteria to examine outcomes; and views outcomes from a multidimensional perspective.

Long-Term Outcomes

Numerous national and international longitudinal studies designed to examine the long-term outcome from schizophrenia have been reported in the literature over the past few decades. These include studies from Switzerland (Bleuler, 1972; Ciompi & Muller, 1976), Germany (Huber, Gross, & Schuttler, 1975), Japan (Ogawa et al., 1987), and the United States (DeSisto et al., 1995; Harding et al., 1987; Tsuang, Woolson, & Fleming, 1979). In addition, the World Health Organization conducted a multinational study in which outcomes among numerous diverse cultural groups were examined (Harrison et al., 2001). The follow-up period in these studies ranged from 22 to 37 years with sample sizes ranging from 186 to 269 and consisting mainly of individuals hospitalized with diagnoses of schizophrenia, generally considered the diagnosis with the poorest prognosis.

Results of these studies have been summarized by Harding (in press). They suggested that in the majority of samples, at least half and sometimes up to two-thirds of the sample was reported as significantly improved or recovered using the definition of recovery cited earlier (Harding & Zahniser, 1994). Some studies, which included individuals with varying diagnoses, found that individuals with schizophrenia or other psychotic disorders faired slightly worse in their long-term outcomes (Tsuang et al., 1979). Contrary to the long-term studies that found largely favorable outcomes are two long-term studies and one meta-analysis that found slightly less favorable outcomes: the Cologne study (Marneros, Deister, Rohde, Steinmeyer, & Junemann, 1989), the Chestnut Hill Lodge study (McGlashan, 1984), and a meta-analysis of 320 studies on schizophrenia from 1895 to 1992. This latter study suggested that somewhat less than one-half of patients diagnosed with schizophrenia show substantial clinical improvement after an average follow-up of 6 years (Hegarty, Baldessarini, Tohen, Waternaux, & Oepen, 1995). Differing definitions of what constitutes improvement, different treatments, varied sociocultural environments, and differing samples may account for some of the observed differences in outcomes. Nevertheless, it is clear from these studies that a substantial portion of individuals with severe mental illnesses do experience significant improvement over time.

Qualitative Studies

Unlike the longitudinal studies of individuals with severe mental disorders, the majority of studies in this category are based on observation, anecdotal information, qualitative interviews, and analyses or syntheses of personal narratives or accounts. These studies also tend to focus on the process of coping with a severe mental illness.

Some of the earliest qualitative studies of individuals' adjustment to SMI were conducted by Strauss at Yale University. Davidson and Strauss (1992), for example, reviewed self-reports of individuals with severe psychiatric disabilities and deduced four basic processes:

1. Discovering a more active sense of self
2. Taking stock of strengths and weaknesses of the self
3. Putting the self into action
4. Appealing to the self

Williams and Collins (1999) examined the experiences of 15 individuals diagnosed with schizophrenia for varying lengths of time. These authors describe the struggle of individuals to prevent relapse, to redefine themselves and their social identity, and to reconnect with a community. Young and Ensing (1999) studied 18 individuals with severe mental illness using open-ended interviews and focus groups. They categorized the processes of recovery as:

1. Overcoming "stuckness"
2. Discovering and fostering self-empowerment
3. Learning and self-redefinition
4. Returning to basic functioning
5. Improving quality of life

Spaniol and his colleagues (Spaniol, Gagne, & Koehler, 2003), in a qualitative study of 19 individuals recovering from mental illness, found that individuals with psychiatric disabilities often must cope with a loss of sense of self, a loss of interpersonal connectedness, a loss of power and self-efficacy, a loss of valued roles (such as worker, parent, citizen), and a loss of a sense of hope as a result of their illness.

Three researchers have recently conducted meta-analyses of first-person accounts of the process of recovery (Jacobson, 2001; Ralph, 2000; Ridgway, 2001). Jacobson (2001) examined 30 narratives and determined that individuals view their own recovery at least in part based on their explanatory framework for understanding the cause of the illness (i.e., whether it is caused by environment, trauma, biology). She identified four processes in recovery:

1. Recognizing the problem
2. Transforming the self
3. Reconciling the system
4. Reaching out to others

Ralph (2000) examined first-hand accounts of individuals with SMI and found the following factors frequently mentioned in their coping and adaptation:

1. Personal factors such as insight and determination
2. External factors such as social supports and family support
3. Self-managed care, that is, the extent to which the individual can participate in his or her own mental healthcare
4. Empowerment or a sense of self-efficacy and control

Similarly, Ridgway (2001) analyzed personal narratives of four well-known individuals whose writings appeared in the 1980s. She found the following themes recurring during the process of adjustment:

1. Reawakening of hope
2. Achieving understanding and acceptance of the disability
3. Engagement and active participation in life
4. Active coping
5. Reclaiming a positive sense of self
6. Regaining a sense of meaning and purpose

She concludes that the process of recovery is complex and nonlinear and that it cannot be accomplished without social support.

Studies of Vocational Improvement

In the past two decades, there has been a growing empirical base of information about the effects of particular vocational models on the role functioning of persons diagnosed with severe mental illness, including the interpersonal placement and support model (IPS; Drake, Becker, Clark, & Mueser, 1999; Drake et al., 1996; Drake, McHugo, et al., 1999), general vocational rehabilitation services (Cook & Razzano, 2000), and supported employment interventions (Crowther, Marshall, Bond, & Huxley, 2001). Experimental studies of IPS have found that it dramatically increases the percentage of persons employed. The authors examined the effects of IPS on outcomes more relevant to recovery (e.g., self-esteem and quality of life) and found that the effects of IPS on these outcomes were inconsistent and need further study (Bond, Resnick, et al., 2001). Supported employment improves vocational role functioning, including amount of earnings and hours worked (Crowther et al., 2001) but has not consistently shown an improvement in other more subjective outcomes related to recovery. Furthermore, in a review of vocational interventions for people with severe psychiatric disabilities, Cook and Razzano (2000) found that while individuals with schizophrenia experience poorer outcomes from vocational rehabilitation services, they do experience improvements in functioning.

Summary

The foregoing literature suggests that recovery is long term and almost continuous (Deegan, 1988), it is multidimensional (defined both objectively and subjectively; Bond, Resnick, et al., 2001; Ralph, 2000), it should be viewed along a continuum rather than as a dichotomous variable (Ridgway, 2001), it involves interdependent domains of functioning (including employment, residential, social, and educational domains; Harding & Zahniser, 1994; Liberman et al., 2002; Spaniol et al., 2003), and more study is needed as to how mental health services can bring about recovery outcomes (Drake, Goldman, et al., 2001; Mueser et al., 2002; Twamley, Jeste, & Lehman, 2003).

Based on the research reviewed in this section, it is possible to suggest a working definition of recovery outcome that can serve as a guide for research that targets recovery outcomes and that can be modified and refined over time. Aware that these terms may overlap in their meaning and our understanding of them, we suggest that recovery outcomes target the following domains: instrumental role functioning, symptomatology, subjective well-being, self-esteem, meaning in life, psychosocial adjustment, health status, and quality of life. The measures used to assess these domains are numerous, and consensus has not been reached about which measures are most relevant, reliable, and valid. Our review of current literature suggests that there is greater consensus about the outcomes of recovery than there is about the processes by which recovery is achieved.

Recovery and Its Parallels to Positive Psychology and Physical Medicine

The finding that people with severe mental illnesses can achieve positive outcomes, despite having a seemingly deteriorative disease, is consistent with the emergence of positive psychology (Seligman & Csikszentmihalyi, 2000). Positive psychology emphasizes growth, personal accomplishments, and success in valued roles. Individuals are not seen as passive vessels responding to internal and external stimuli, but as decision makers, with the capacity to choose and become efficacious (Bandura, 1986; Seligman, 1992). While the zeitgeist of positive psychologists is to study how "normal people flourish" (Seligman & Csikszentmihalyi, 2000), we argue that the dimensions and processes they postulate are equally important for people with serious mental illness, especially variables such as self-determination, subjective well-being, optimism, and hope (Ryan & Deci, 2000). The field has made significant advances in understanding the factors related to optimal mental health in the general population. Yet rarely are these advances brought to bear to understand how individuals reconstruct their lives and achieve recovery. We contend that this research and knowledge is useful and highly relevant for understanding the recovery processes and outcomes of people with severe mental illness.

In addition to the parallel with positive psychology, an analogy about recovery from mental illness can be drawn to recovery in physical medicine. That is, there are numerous disabilities and conditions that until recently have had a poor prognosis for survival and recovery (e.g., high-level spinal cord injury and very low birth-weight infants). Until the past decade or so, the focus has been on the treatment of individuals with such physical conditions to reduce mortality. Now that the survival rate for high-level spinal cord injury and very low birth-weight infants has improved dramatically, medicine is turning to understanding the processes involved in assisting those individuals to regain (or attain) functioning in a variety of roles and improve their quality of life (Pharoah, Stevenson, & West, 2003; Tate & Forchheimer, 2002). Similarly, since we now know that individuals with severe mental illnesses can and do improve, it is necessary to widen our research agenda and practice repertoire to encompass those processes and dimensions that affect such improvement and recovery.

Recovery Processes and Outcomes and Current Behavioral Science Research

Behavioral and social science research conducted with the general population in the areas of self-esteem, self-regulation, self-judgment, and subjective well-being is all pertinent to recovery but has rarely been brought to bear on our understanding of it. In our examination of this literature, it seems that the work of behavioral scientists is especially relevant. Crocker (1998), for example, is studying contingencies of self-worth

(CSW) and how to measure them. Her research has a special focus on stigma, which can influence outcomes experienced by people with SMI. More recently, Crocker has worked on the risks of pursuing self-esteem goals (Crocker & Park, 2004) and the specific domains of self-worth. We wonder if and how these contingencies of self-worth may shift during the recovery process. Higgins (1990) is investigating approach/avoidance motivations (promoting gains versus preventing losses) and how they affect adaptive and maladaptive self-regulation. Of particular interest to the recovery concept is whether, as people progress toward recovery, their motivation strategies shift from preventing losses to promoting gains. Diener's (2001) work focusing on understanding the individual, cultural, and situational effects on subjective well-being is particularly relevant to recovery. Gross (1998) is studying different forms of emotion regulation: reappraisal (reinterpreting situations to reduce emotional reactions before they begin) and suppression (inhibiting emotions that have already developed strong response tendencies). Self-regulation is an important skill for successful role functioning and psychological adjustment; Gross's concepts help inform our thinking about healthy forms of self-regulation that promote the process of recovery and how self-regulation might be measured. While this list of relevant literature is not meant to be exhaustive, it is instructive for us to look beyond the typical arenas for empirical investigations and conceptual developments that may assist us in better understanding the processes and outcomes of recovery. The behavioral sciences have much to offer in this regard.

The Center for Psychiatric Rehabilitation and Recovery

Over the course of 30 years of research, Anthony and his associates at the Boston University Center for Psychiatric Rehabilitation (CPR) have been building a research base that has provided groundwork for the study of recovery processes and outcomes. The CPR has developed, demonstrated, disseminated, and promoted utilization of psychiatric rehabilitation knowledge and technology (Anthony, 1979; Anthony, Cohen, & Farkas, 1990; Anthony, Cohen, Farkas, & Gagne, 2002; Farkas & Anthony, 1989). While we primarily studied increases in role performance, we were struck by the fact that many individuals who were involved in state-of-the-art rehabilitation interventions experienced improvements not only in role performance but also reported improvements on subjective outcomes such as self-esteem, subjective well-being, and overall quality of life. Anecdotally, it seemed that a certain number of people were rebuilding their lives in very profound and meaningful ways after a diagnosis of severe mental illness.

More recently, the CPR has embarked on several studies relevant to recovery from severe mental illness. CPR researchers are using surveys and qualitative studies to build (1) an initial understanding of the processes as well as the factors that promote, hinder, or mediate recovery; (2) factors that might specifically affect recovery in the vocational domain; and (3) notions about mental health practices that affect recovery outcomes. Knowledge gained from these ongoing studies is being used to refine our model of the factors that influence recovery process and outcomes (Ellison & Russinova, 1999; Russinova & Wewiorski, 2002; Russinova, Wewiorski, & Cash, 2002; Russinova, Wewiorski, & Legere, 2001; Spaniol et al., 2002). In addition, anecdotal findings from the CPR's service provision, coupled with our initial research, have

Table 9.1   Assumptions about Recovery from Severe Mental Illnesses

1. Recovery can occur without professional intervention. Professionals do not hold the key to recovery; the individual does. The task of professionals is to facilitate recovery; the task of people with the disability is to recover. Recovery may be facilitated by the person's natural support system. After all, if recovery is a common human condition experienced by us all, then people who are in touch with their own recovery can help others through the process. Self-help groups, families, and friends are the best examples of this phenomenon. It is important for mental health providers to recognize that what promotes recovery is not simply the array of mental health services. Also essential to recovery are non-mental health activities and organizations (e.g., sports, clubs, adult education, and churches). There are many paths to recovery including choosing not to be involved in the mental health system.

2. A common denominator of recovery is the presence of people who believe in and stand by the person in need of recovery. Seemingly universal in the recovery concept is the notion that critical to one's recovery is a person or persons in whom one can trust to "be there" in times of need. People who are recovering talk about the people who believed in them when they did not even believe in themselves, who encouraged their recovery but did not force it, who tried to listen and understand when nothing seemed to be making sense. Recovery is a deeply human experience, facilitated by the deeply human responses of others. Recovery can be facilitated by any one person. Recovery can be everybody's business.

3. A recovery vision is not related to one's theory about the causes of mental illnesses. Whether the causes of mental illnesses are viewed as biological and/or psychosocial generates considerable controversy among professionals, advocates, and people with psychiatric disabilities. Adopting a recovery vision does not commit one to either position on this debate, nor on the use or nonuse of medical or alternative interventions. Recovery may occur whether one views the illnesses as biological or not. People with other disabilities (e.g., blindness, quadriplegia) can recover even though the physical nature of the disability is unchanged or even worsens.

4. Recovery can occur even though symptoms reoccur. The episodic nature of severe mental illnesses does not prevent recovery. People with other illnesses that might be episodic (e.g., rheumatoid arthritis, multiple sclerosis) can still recover. Individuals who experience intense psychiatric symptoms episodically can also recover. Others may recover and not experience psychiatric symptoms again.

5. Recovery changes the frequency and duration of symptoms. People who are recovering and experience symptom exacerbation may have a level of symptom intensity as difficult as or even worse than previously experienced. As one recovers, the symptom frequency and duration appear to have been changed for the better. That is, symptoms interfere with functioning less often and for briefer periods of time. More of one's life is lived symptom-free. Symptom recurrence becomes less of a threat to one's recovery, and return to previous levels occurs more quickly after exacerbation.

6. Recovery is not a linear process. Recovery involves growth and setbacks, periods of rapid change and little change. While the overall trend may be upward, the moment-to-moment experience does not feel so "directionful." Intense feelings may overwhelm one unexpectedly. Periods of insight or growth happen unexpectedly. The recovery process feels anything but systematic and planned.

7. Recovery from the consequences of the illness is sometimes more difficult than recovering from the illness itself. Issues of dysfunction, disability, and disadvantage are often more difficult than impairment issues. An inability to perform valued tasks and roles, and the resultant loss of self-esteem, are significant barriers to recovery. The barriers brought about by being placed in a discriminatory category can be overwhelming. These disadvantages include loss of rights and equal opportunities, and discrimination in employment and living, as well as barriers created by the system's attempts at helping (e.g., lack of opportunities for self-determination, disempowering treatment practices). These disabilities and disadvantages can combine to limit a person's recovery even though one has become predominantly asymptomatic.

Adapted from *Psychiatric Rehabilitation* (pp. 99–101), by W. A. Anthony, M. R. Cohen, M. Farkas, and C. Gagne, 2002, Boston: Boston University Center for Psychiatric Rehabilitation.

suggested a series of assumptions about recovery (Anthony et al., 2002, pp. 99–101), which is reproduced in Table 9.1.

Taken together, these studies and assumptions form the basis of our initial conceptual framework and model of recovery, described next.

Initial Conceptual Framework and Model of Recovery Processes and Outcomes

Based on the long-term research, the first-person accounts of people with severe mental illness, mental health services research, and the research of behavioral scientists outside the field of severe mental illness, we propose a preliminary conceptual model of the processes and outcomes of recovery and the factors that influence it (see Figure 9.1). Our model also draws from a contextual model for clinical mental health effectiveness research advanced by Hohmann (1999) and a model of psychosocial adaptation to chronic illness and disability proposed by Livneh (2001).

This conceptual model guides our understanding of the complexities of recovery in a way that encourages both dialogue about recovery and a research agenda that is

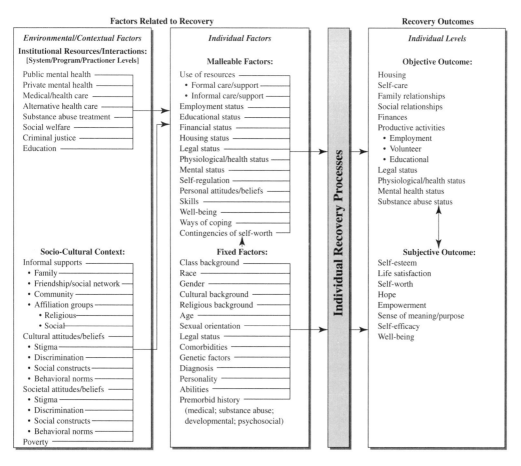

Figure 9.1   A conceptual model of the factors related to recovery.

compatible with the notion of recovery. As a heuristic model, it provides direction that is flexible rather than fixed and is based on the relevant literature. The proposed conceptual model suggests that the processes and outcomes of recovery are influenced by a variety of factors, many of which researchers would consider extraneous variables (Hohmann, 1999). We continue to revise this model using a multidisciplinary perspective, incorporating research conducted both inside and outside the field of severe mental illness. This recovery model mandates that we look beyond established measures of pathology and treatment to examine what recovery means, why some people recover and under what circumstances, and what the characteristics are of those who recover. Directed by this evolving model, which is based on extant literature, the particular outcomes studied expand dramatically and include both subjective dimensions (e.g., self-esteem, self-efficacy, subjective well-being, hope) and objective dimensions (e.g., instrumental role functioning). The central construct in the model is that there are environmental, sociocultural, and individual factors that affect both the processes and outcomes of recovery. Mental health system factors affect outcomes and include, in addition to the obvious ingredients of the intervention or program model itself, factors such as the treatment environment and the interpersonal relationship between the practitioner and consumer.

RECOVERY AND RESEARCH ON EVIDENCE-BASED PRACTICES

Existing mental health research, while extremely important and additive, is wanting with respect to the emerging concept of recovery. This deficiency is understandable in that much of the existing evidence-based practice (EBP) research was conceived and/or implemented before or concurrent with attempts to examine the concept of recovery. Using the conceptual model of recovery (Figure 9.1) and drawing from a previous analysis of EBP in the recovery era (Anthony, Rogers, & Farkas, 2003), this section first critiques the relevance of current EBP research to the recovery literature. Following this critique, we suggest a research direction that builds on and is additive to existing EBP research and is guided by the conceptual model of recovery.

Limitations of Existing Evidence-Based Practice Research

1. *Outcomes are often not consumer outcomes but rather system outcomes.* The variables most often used as outcomes in randomized clinical trials are variations on inpatient hospitalization, typically recidivism, hospital days or days in the community, and, in some studies, employment rates. In an era embracing recovery, these outcomes may be less important than measures related to consumers' goals. Simple counts of employment or hospitalization status alone are insufficient to measure the construct of recovery.

2. *Recovery-related outcomes are relatively rarely reported to be positively affected by evidence-based practices.* In contrast to the plethora of positive impacts on days of hospitalization and days employed, evidence-based practice research has focused less on outcomes such as meaningful work, quality of life, self-esteem, empowerment, freedom, safety, privacy, and the like. When these dimensions are measured, the impact of best practices is currently much less convincing (e.g., Bond, Resnick, et al., 2001).

3. *Subjective outcomes have not been perceived as important outcomes in current evidence-based practice research.* Data suggest that there are many paths to recovery and that the paths to recovery are as numerous as the number of people recovering (Deegan, 1988; Spaniol et al., 2002). This is not to deny the possibility that there may be typical dimensions that are more objective and that cut across individuals. Historically, however, evidence-based practice research has paid insufficient attention to qualitative or subjective measures of outcome that may be gathered through interview and narrative.

4. *Evidence-based practice research using program models focuses on replicating the entire model.* A notable example of the focus on entire program models is the evidence-based practice research on assertive community treatment (ACT). It appears that arguments are being made about the importance of fidelity to all the identified ingredients of the model, even when the research itself suggests that some ingredients may be more important than others. In fact, one of the studies widely cited as indicative of the evidence that all the components of the ACT program model should be implemented if the expected outcomes are to occur found that not to be the case (McHugo, Drake, Teague, & Xie, 1999). In this study, certain ACT program ingredients (team approach, small caseload size, high-intensity services, and collaboration with support system) did not distinguish between programs that produced good versus poor outcomes.

5. *Evidence-based practice program models have neglected to study the helper/ consumer relationship, which appears to be an important component of recovery.* First-person accounts of recovery repeatedly mention the relationship of the person recovering to another person(s) who was close and believed in him or her. Studies from psychiatric rehabilitation, case management, substance abuse, and education all point to the rather obvious conclusion that people are helped and learn best from other people with whom they have a positive relationship. For the most part, this basic dimension of helping and learning is not addressed in the evidence-based practice literature.

6. *Evidence-based practice research does not make full use of findings from nonexperimental research.* Guidelines suggest that the evidence-based practices that can be practiced with the most confidence are from randomized clinical trials. Implied to some is that anything less does not make an important contribution to our knowledge. Yet it was the nonexperimental research showing the relationship to outcomes of practices such as goal setting, skill teaching, providing support and accommodations, and establishing an alliance with the client that has formed the basis of the psychosocial interventions that are now the subject of evidence-based research. "The absence of excellent evidence does not make evidence-based decision making impossible: in this situation, what is required is the best evidence available, not the best evidence possible" (Muir Gray, 1997, p. 61). We need all types of evidence, which means at many times the best evidence available and not just clinical trial evidence. Certainly at this period in our field's development, evidence-based research founded on rigorous, experimental research is limited. Under these circumstances, program administrators, system planners, and clinicians must act on all varieties of evidence currently available.

These conclusions lead us to recommend guidelines for the conduct of future research into evidence-based practices.

Suggestions to Make Evidence-Based Practice Research More Recovery Compatible

1. *Outcomes in evidence-based practice research should focus on those that consumers believe are most critical in addition to the outcomes currently studied.* Much of the evidence-based practice research conducted to date was conceived and implemented before widespread adoption of the concept of recovery. As a result, evidence-based research has emphasized and demonstrated a positive impact on measures that reflect a different view of what is possible for people with mental illness. The subjective experiences and perceptions of consumers may carry equal weight with outcomes such as hospitalization, participation in mental health services, employment rates, and number of skills. Meaningful work, feelings of self-determination and self-efficacy, reduced discrimination, minimal iatrogenic impacts, decent housing, and enrollment in school may be examples of outcome dimensions more commensurate with those reflecting recovery.

2. *Qualitative measures of outcome must assume greater credibility and utilization.* While randomized clinical trials allow for a causative interpretation of ingredients that bring about change, it is only through qualitative study that we can obtain participants' understanding of the tolerability of an intervention, the likelihood of engaging in such an intervention outside a clinical trial, the participants' perception of the elements of the intervention that were potent, and their views of the relevance of the outcomes themselves. Through various qualitative analyses, the researcher can find out if there was one element of the intervention that seemed most causative from the participants' perspectives or if the intervention may have stimulated some other perceived causative factor. The point is not whether qualitative or quantitative measures are better; rather, they are complementary and not duplicative. Qualitative research will enrich the power and usability of data derived from clinical trials.

3. *Research on evidence-based practices should attempt to identify principles and practices that transcend program models.* Similar to research on nonspecific factors in psychotherapy that cut across therapist orientation and are responsible for positive outcomes, there is a need to identify the principles and practices that may be common to many program models and have a salutary effect on recovery. Not all of the learning in such an endeavor is likely to come from randomized clinical trials. One recent attempt at such an approach in supported employment is highly instructive (Bond, Becker, et al., 2001). We applaud this effort at mining all types of research and wish to emphasize that correlational research and quasi-experimental research are excellent sources of data pertinent to the development of evidence-based principles of practice. In fact, it was this type of research that formed the basis of the evidence for psychiatric rehabilitation principles such as self-determination and skill and support development that are now capable of being researched in clinical trials (Lovell & Cohn, 1998; Shern, Trochim, & LaComb, 1995; Shern et al., 2000).

4. *Evidence-based practice research on program models should attempt to unbundle the model to identify specific practices rather than entire programs that are responsible for positive outcomes.* The logical next step is to research which specific components of a program model account for its positive impact. Because various program models, such as ACT (McHugo et al., 1999), IPS (Drake, Becker, et al., 1999), clubhouse (Macias,

Jackson, Schroeder, & Wang, 1999), and Choose-Get-Keep (Anthony et al., 2002), have enumerated specific program components, they are in a position to do this next level of evidence-based practice research. Because of its lengthy record of empirical studies, ACT in particular can immediately embark on this endeavor. One recent review (Anthony et al., 2002) of this type of ACT research hypothesized various critical therapeutic ingredients of ACT, including the helper/service recipient relationship.

5. *Evidence-based practice research should examine dimensions related to the field's underlying values.* Proponents are quick to point out that nothing about evidence-based practices contradicts the importance of client-centered values in clinical practice (Drake et al., 2001). The humanistic values of behavioral healthcare are not called into question by evidence-based practice research. Yet, often these values are implicit in programs and not explicit. Making them explicit has value for the field and enables these values, such as self-determination and growth, to be researched. An example of research that targets values might include what techniques work best to help individuals make choices about engaging in services (Farkas, Sullivan-Soydan, & Gagne, 2000). Evidence-based practice research at this level will provide data that transcends program models and service types to operationalize the values of behavioral healthcare and make them researchable.

6. *Research on evidence-based practices must take into account the possible impact of non-mental health system factors in people's recovery.* As illustrated in Figure 9.1, sociocultural factors such as family, friendships, discrimination, and poverty are hypothesized to affect recovery. In addition, other public systems, such as the welfare system, the vocational rehabilitation system, and the like, can influence recovery outcomes. Researchers must be open to investigations that examine whether and how these factors play a role in people's recovery and how mental health services might affect non-mental health factors, which then may be linked to recovery outcomes. These non-mental health factors can and should be included and measured in research on evidence-based practices.

FUTURE DIRECTIONS

A number of key principles are inherent in the notion of recovery from severe mental illnesses. One of the most fundamental principles is that of "people first"; that is, people with mental illnesses are people before they are cases, diagnoses, or patients. They should not be primarily defined and governed by their symptoms and their diagnoses. Rather, the principle of "people first" assumes that people with severe mental illnesses can (or can be assisted to) direct their own lives as do their nondiagnosed brethren. That is, much like the "nondisabled" population, they are influenced by their relationships with others, their own goals, their hopes and dreams, interests, and so forth.

While at first blush this principle may look straightforward, its adoption has major implications for how the field will continue to develop in this era of recovery. By incorporating this principle of "people first" into the field of severe mental illnesses, what constitutes evidence will be expanded dramatically. For example, given the model and the guidelines we espouse, research should consider the potential impact of the non-mental health environment on people's recovery, the use of qualitative measures along with quantitative assessments to estimate recovery outcomes, and the reasons for recovery.

Furthermore, behavioral sciences research on the processes that bring about positive changes in all types of people (who typically do not have severe mental illnesses) are relevant and should be brought to bear on the evidence-based practice initiative in mental health. By definition, evidence-based practice integrates ". . . individual clinical expertise with the best available external clinical evidence from systematic research. . . . By best available external clinical evidence we mean clinically relevant research . . ." (Sackett, Rosenberg, Muir Gray, Haynes, & Richardson, 1996, p. 71). With respect to the field of severe mental illness, "clinically relevant research" has often been confined to studies in the mental health services research arena. Yet the research literature on how people change and grow, not just people with severe mental illnesses but all people, is what is relevant under a "people first" principle. The behavioral science literature, supported at times by mental health services research, has identified certain human interactive processes that help people change and grow, including:

- Experiencing a positive relationship with the people providing help
- Setting their own goals
- Being taught new skills
- Being encouraged to have positive expectancies and hope for change
- Developing self-awareness about aspects of their own behavior

Without compromising fidelity to a program model, evidence-based practices can promote a positive relationship between providers and recipients, help people set their own goals, teach skills, engender hope for change, and promote self-awareness. It is these evidence-based processes that can occur within any program model and that all types of research suggest can add outcome variance to evidence-based practices.

REFERENCES

American Psychiatric Association. (1987). *Diagnostic and statistical manual of mental disorders* (3rd ed., rev.). Washington, DC: Author.

Anthony, W. A. (1979). *The principles of psychiatric rehabilitation.* Baltimore: University Park Press.

Anthony, W. A. (1993). Recovery from mental illness: The guiding vision of the mental health service system in the 1990s. *Psychosocial Rehabilitation Journal, 16*(4), 11–23.

Anthony, W. A., Cohen, M. R., & Farkas, M. D. (1990). *Psychiatric rehabilitation.* Boston: Boston University, Center for Psychiatric Rehabilitation.

Anthony, W. A., Cohen, M. R., Farkas, M. D., & Gagne, C. (2002). *Psychiatric rehabilitation* (2nd ed.). Boston: Boston University Center for Psychiatric Rehabilitation.

Anthony, W. A., Rogers, E. S., & Farkas, M. D. (2003). Research on evidence-based practices: Future directions in an era of recovery. *Community Mental Health Journal, 39*(2), 101–114.

Bachrach, L. L. (1976). *Deinstitutionalization: An analytical review and sociological perspective.* Rockville, MD: National Institute of Mental Health.

Bandura, A. (1986). *Social foundations of thoughts and action.* Englewood Cliffs, NJ: Prentice-Hall.

Beale, V., & Lambric, T. (1995). *The recovery concept: Implementation in the mental health system* (Report by the Community Support Program Advisory Committee). Columbus: Ohio Department of Mental Health.

Bleuler, M. (1972). *Die schizophrenen geistesstorungen im lichte langjahriger kranken und familiengeschichten* [The Schizophrenic disorders: Long-term patient and family studies] (S. M. Clemens, Trans.). Stuttgart, Germany: Georg Thieme.

Bond, G. R., Becker, D. R., Drake, R. E., Rapp, C., Meisler, N., Lehman, A., et al. (2001). Implementing supported employment as an evidence-based practice. *Psychiatric Services, 52*(3), 313–322.

Bond, G. R., Resnick, S. G., Drake, R. E., Xie, H., McHugo, G. J., & Bebout, R. R. (2001). Does competitive employment improve nonvocational outcomes for people with severe mental illness? *Journal of Consulting and Clinical Psychology, 69*(3), 489–501.

Ciompi, L., & Muller, C. (1976). *Lebensweg und Alter der Schizophrenen: Eine katamnestische Longzeitstudie bis ins senium.* Berlin, Germany: Springer-Verlag.

Cook, J. A., & Razzano, L. A. (2000). Vocational rehabilitation for persons with schizophrenia: Recent research and implications for practice. *Schizophrenia Bulletin, 26*(1), 87–103.

Crocker, J. K. (1998). *Contingencies of self esteem* (NIMH Grant 5R01MH058869). Ann Arbor: University of Michigan.

Crocker, J. K., & Park, L. E. (2004). The costly pursuit of self-esteem. *Psychological Bulletin, 130*(3), 392–414.

Crowther, R. E., Marshall, M., Bond, G. R., & Huxley, P. (2001). Helping people with severe mental illness to obtain work: Systematic review. *British Medical Journal, 322*(7280), 204–208.

Davidson, L., & Strauss, J. S. (1992). Sense of self in recovery from severe mental illness. *British Journal of Medical Psychology, 65*(2), 131–145.

Deegan, P. E. (1988). Recovery: The lived experience of persons as they accept and overcome the challenge of the disability. *Journal of the California Alliance for the Mentally Ill, 11,* 11–19.

Deegan, P. E. (1996). Recovery as a journey of the heart. *Psychiatric Rehabilitation Journal, 19*(3), 91–97.

DeSisto, M. J., Harding, C. M., McCormick, R. V., Ashikaga, T., & Brooks, G. W. (1995). The Maine and Vermont three-decade studies of serious mental illness: I. Matched comparisons of cross-sectional outcome. *British Journal of Psychiatry, 167,* 331–338.

Diener, E. F. (2001). *Cultural differences in self reports of well-being* (NIMH Grant 5R01MH060849). Champaign: University of Illinois.

Drake, R. E., Becker, D. R., Clark, R. E., & Mueser, K. T. (1999). Research on the individual placement and support model of supported employment. *Psychiatric Quarterly, 70,* 289–301.

Drake, R. E., Goldman, H. H., Leff, H. S., Lehman, A. F., Dixon, L., Mueser, K. T., et al. (2001). Implementing evidence-based practices in routine mental health service settings. *Psychiatric Services, 52*(1), 179–182.

Drake, R. E., McHugo, G. J., Bebout, R. R., Becker, D. R., Harris, M., Bond, G. R., et al. (1999). A randomized clinical trial of supported employment for inner-city patients with severe mental disorders. *Archives of General Psychiatry, 56*(7), 627–633.

Drake, R. E., McHugo, G., Becker, D. R., Anthony, W. A., & Clark, R. E. (1996). The New Hampshire study of supported employment for people with severe mental illness. *Journal of Consulting and Clinical Psychology, 64*(2), 391–399.

Ellison, M. L., & Russinova, Z. (1999, May 10–14). *Professional achievements of people with psychiatric disabilities.* Workshop presented at the 24th IPSRS Conference, Minneapolis.

Farkas, M. D., & Anthony, W. A. (Eds.). (1989). *Psychiatric rehabilitation programs: Putting theory into practice.* Baltimore: Johns Hopkins University Press.

Farkas, M. D., Sullivan-Soydan, A., & Gagne, C. (2000). *Introduction to rehabilitation readiness.* Boston: Boston University Center for Psychiatric Rehabilitation.

Grob, S. (1983). Psychosocial rehabilitation centers: Old wine in a new bottle. In I. Barofsky & R. D. Budson (Eds.), *The chronic psychiatric patient in the community: Principles of treatment* (pp. 265–280). Jamaica, NY: Spectrum.

Gross, J. J. (1998). *Emotion regulation and its consequences* (NIMH Grant 5R29MH058147). Palo Alto, CA: Stanford University.

Harding, C. M. (1994). An examination of the complexities in the measurement of recovery in severe psychiatric disorders. In R. J. Ancill, D. Holliday, & G. W. MacEwan (Eds.), *Schizophrenia: Exploring the spectrum of psychosis* (pp. 153–169). Chichester, England: Wiley.

Harding, C. M. (in press). Overcoming the persistent resistance of professionals within the helping professions ideas of recovery in serious mental illness. In P. Ridgway & P. E. Deegan (Eds.), *Deepening the mental health recovery paradigm: Defining implications for practice.* Lawrence: University of Kansas Press.

Harding, C. M., Brooks, G. W., Ashikaga, T., Strauss, J. S., & Breier, A. (1987). The Vermont longitudinal study of persons with severe mental illness: II. Long-term outcome of subjects who retrospectively met *DSM-III* criteria for schizophrenia. *American Journal of Psychiatry, 144*(6), 727–735.

Harding, C. M., & Strauss, J. S. (1984). How serious is schizophrenia? Comments on prognosis. *Biological Psychiatry, 19*(12), 1597–1600.

Harding, C. M., & Zahniser, J. H. (1994). Empirical correction of seven myths about schizophrenia with implications for treatment. *Acta Psychiatrica Scandinavica Supplementum, 90*(384, Suppl.), 140–146.

Harrison, G., Hopper, K., Craig, T., Laska, E., & Siegel, C. (2001). Recovery from psychotic illness: A 15- and 25-year international follow-up study. *British Journal of Psychiatry, 178,* 506–517.

Hegarty, J., Baldessarini, R., Tohen, M., Waternaux, C., & Oepen, G. (1995). One hundred years of schizophrenia: A meta-analysis of the outcome literature. *American Journal of Psychiatry, 151*(10), 1409–1416.

Higgins, E. T. (1990). *Approach/avoidance orientations and operations* (NIMH Grant 5R01MH039429). New York: Columbia University.

Hohmann, A. (1999). A contextual model for clinical mental health effectiveness research. *Mental Health Services Research, 1,* 83–91.

Huber, G., Gross, G., & Schuttler, R. (1975). A long-term follow-up study of schizophrenia: Psychiatric course of illness and prognosis. *Acta Psychiatrica Scandinavica, 52*(1), 49–57.

Jacobson, N. S. (2001). Experiencing recovery: A dimensional analysis of consumers' recovery narratives. *Psychiatric Rehabilitation Journal, 24*(3), 248–256.

Jacobson, N. S., & Curtis, L. (2000). Recovery as policy in mental health services: Strategies emerging from the states. *Psychiatric Rehabilitation Journal, 23*(4), 333–341.

Legislative Summer Study Committee of the State of Vermont Division of Mental Health. (1996). *A position paper on recovery and psychiatric disability.* Waterbury: Vermont Development Disability and Mental Health Services.

Liberman, R. P., Kopelowicz, A., Ventura, J., & Gutkind, D. (2002). Operational criteria and factors related to recovery from schizophrenia. *International Review of Psychiatry, 14,* 256–272.

Livneh, H. (2001). Psychosocial adaptation to chronic illness and disability: A conceptual framework. *Rehabilitation Counseling Bulletin, 44*(3), 151–160.

Lovell, A. M., & Cohn, S. (1998). The elaboration of "choice" in a program for homeless persons labeled psychiatrically disabled. *Human Organization, 57*(1), 8–20.

Macias, C., Jackson, R., Schroeder, C., & Wang, Q. (1999). What is a clubhouse? Report on the ICCD 1996 Survey of USA Clubhouses. *Community Mental Health Journal, 35*(2), 181–190.

Malmberg, L., & Fenton, M. (2001). Individual psychodynamic psychotherapy and psychoanalysis for schizophrenia and severe mental illness. *Cochrane Database of Systematic Reviews* (3) CD001360.

Marneros, A., Deister, A., Rohde, A., Steinmeyer, E. M., & Junemann, H. (1989). Long-term outcome of schizoaffective and schizophrenic disorders, a comparative study: I. Definitions, methods, psychopathological, and social outcome. *European Archives of Psychiatry and Neurological Sciences, 238,* 118–125.

McGlashan, T. H. (1984). The Chestnut Lodge follow-up study: II. Long-term outcomes of schizophrenia and the affective disorders. *Archives of General Psychiatry, 41,* 586–601.

McHugo, G. J., Drake, R. E., Teague, G. B., & Xie, H. (1999). Fidelity to assertive community treatment and client outcomes in New Hampshire dual disorders study. *Psychiatric Services, 50*(6), 818–824.

Mueser, K. T., Corrigan, P. W., Hilton, D. W., Tanzman, B., & Schaub, A. (2002). Illness management and recovery: A review of the research. *Psychiatric Services, 53*(10), 1272–1284.

Muir Gray, J. A. (1997). *Evidence based healthcare: How to make policy and management decisions.* London: Churchill Livingston.

National Institute of Mental Health. (2003). *Priority areas for behavioral translation research.* Available from http://www.nimh.nih.gov/tbsia/priority.cfm.

National State Mental Health Program Directors. (2001). *Recommended operational definitions and measures to implement the NASMHPD framework of mental health performance indicators* (Technical Workgroup on Performance Indicators. Report submitted to the NASMHPD President's Task Force on Performance Measures).

New Freedom Commission on Mental Health. (2003). *Achieving the promise: Transforming mental health care in America* (Final report. DHHS Publication No. SMA-03-3832). Rockville, MD: Author.

Ogawa, K., Miya, M., Watarai, A., Nakazawa, Yuasa, S., & Utena, H. (1987). A long-term follow-up study of schizophrenia in Japan-with special reference to the course of social adjustment. *British Journal of Psychiatry, 151,* 758–765.

O'Hagan, M. (2001, March). *Recovery competencies for New Zealand Mental Health Workers: Pupu Whakaaro Mental Health Commission* (New Zealand). New Zealand. Available from www.MHC.govt.NZ/publications/2001/Recovery_Competencies

Onken, S. J., Dumont, J., Ridgway, P., Dornan, D., & Ralph, R. (2002). *Mental health recovery: What helps and what hinders? A national research project for the development of recovery facilitating system performance indicators* Available from http://www/NASMPHD.org/generalfiles.

Pharoah, P. O., Stevenson, C. J., & West, C. R. (2003). General certificate of secondary education performance in very low birthweight infants. *Archives of Disabled Children, 88*(4), 295–298.

Ralph, R. (2000). Recovery. *Psychiatric Rehabilitation Skills, 4,* 480–517.

Ridgway, P. A. (2001). Re-storying psychiatric disability: Learning from first person recovery narratives. *Psychiatric Rehabilitation Journal, 24*(4), 335–343.

Rogers, E. S., & Palmer-Erbs, V. K. (1994). Participatory action research: Implications for research and evaluation in psychiatric rehabilitation. *Psychosocial Rehabilitation Journal, 18*(2), 3–12.

Russinova, Z., & Wewiorski, N. J. (2002, October 24–26). *Interim findings from the sustained employment study: Stigma at the workplace.* Paper presented in the workshop: Employment outcomes: Results of various studies and initiatives at the CPR. Innovations in recovery and rehabilitation conference, Boston.

Russinova, Z., Wewiorski, N. J., & Cash, D. J. (2002). Use of alternative health care practices by persons with serious mental illness: Perceived benefits. *American Journal of Public Health, 92*(10), 1600–1603.

Russinova, Z., Wewiorski, N. J., & Legere, L. (2001, May 9–11). *Sustained employment outcomes of people with psychiatric disabilities.* Workshop presented at the 26th annual IAPSRS Conference, Houston.

Ryan, R. M., & Deci, E. L. (2000). Self-determination theory and the facilitation of intrinsic motivation, social development, and well-being. *American Psychologist, 55,* 68–78.

Sackett, D. L., Rosenberg, W. M. C., Muir Gray, J. A., Haynes, R. B., & Richardson, W. S. (1996). Evidence based medicine: What it is and what it isn't. *British Medical Journal, 312,* 71–72.

Sartorius, N., Gulbinat, W., Harrison, G., Laska, E., & Siegel, C. (1996). Long-term follow-up of schizophrenia in 16 countries: A description of the International Study of Schizophrenia conducted by the World Health Organization. *Social Psychiatry and Psychiatric Epidemiology, 31,* 249–258.

Seligman, M. E. P. (1992). *Helplessness: On depression, development, and death.* New York: Freeman.

Seligman, M. E. P., & Csikszentmihalyi, M. (2000). Positive psychology. *American Psychologist, 55*(1), 5–14.

Shern, D. L., Trochim, W. M. K., & LaComb, C. A. (1995). The use of concept mapping for assessing fidelity of model transfer: An example from psychiatric rehabilitation. *Evaluation and Program Planning, 18*(2), 143–153.

Shern, D. L., Tsemberis, S., Anthony, W., Lovell, A. M., Richmond, L., Felton, C. J., et al. (2000). Serving street-dwelling individuals with psychiatric disabilities: Outcomes of a psychiatric rehabilitation clinical trial. *American Journal of Public Health, 90,* 1873–1878.

Spaniol, L., Gagne, C., & Koehler, M. (2003). The recovery framework in rehabilitation and mental health. In D. Moxley & J. R. Finch (Eds.), *Sourcebook of rehabilitation and mental health practice* (pp. 37–50). Boston: Kluwer Academic/Plenum Press.

Spaniol, L., Wewiorski, N., Gagne, C., & Anthony, W. A. (2002). The process of recovery from schizophrenia. *International Review of Psychiatry, 14*(4), 327–336.

State of Connecticut Department of Mental Health and Addiction Services. (2003). *Commissioner's Policy Statement Number 83: Promoting a Recovery-Oriented Service System.* Available from http://www.nimh.nih.gov/tbsia/priority.cfm.

State of Nebraska Recovery Work Team. (1997). *Recovery: A guiding vision for consumers and providers of mental health services in Nebraska.* Omaha, NE: Author.

State of Wisconsin Blue Ribbon Commission on Mental Health. (1997). *Final report.* Madison: Department of Health and Family Services.

Sullivan, W. P. (1994). A long and winding road: The process of recovery from severe mental illness. *Innovations and Research, 3*(3), 19–27.

Tate, D., & Forchheimer, M. (2002). Contributions from the model systems programs to spinal cord injury research. *Journal of Spinal Cord Medicine, 25*(4), 316–330.

Tsuang, M. T., Woolson, R. F., & Fleming, J. A. (1979). Long-term outcome of major psychoses: I. Schizophrenia and affective disorders compared with psychiatrically symptom free surgical conditions. *Archives of General Psychiatry, 36,* 1295–1131.

Twamley, E. W., Jeste, D. V., & Lehman, A. F. (2003). Vocational rehabilitation in schizophrenia and other psychotic disorders: A literature review and meta-analysis of randomized controlled trials. *Journal of Nervous and Mental Diseases, 191*(8), 515–523.

U.S. Department of Health and Human Service. (1999). *Mental health: A Report of the Surgeon General.* Rockville, MD: Author.

Whyte, W. F. (1991). *Participatory action research.* Newbury Park, CA: Sage.

Williams, C. C., & Collins, A. A. (1999). Defining frameworks for psychosocial intervention. *Psychiatry: Interpersonal and Biological Processes, 62*(1), 61–78.

Young, S. L., & Ensing, D. S. (1999). Exploring recovery from the perspective of people with psychiatric disabilities. *Psychiatric Rehabilitation Journal, 22*(3), 219–231.

CHAPTER 10

Evidence-Based Psychosocial Practices: Past, Present, and Future

Timothy J. Bruce and William C. Sanderson

The past decade has witnessed efforts to bring findings from clinical research on psychosocial interventions into everyday clinical practice. These efforts have sought to identify treatments for specific diagnoses that have shown efficacy through empirical study. The identified treatments have sequentially been termed *empirically validated, empirically supported,* and *evidence-based practices* (EBPs). The interventions described in this volume are a few of the products of this effort. Several groups including government agencies, professional experts, and healthcare organizations have designated certain treatments as EBPs, but their means and rationale for doing so are not often clear.

In this chapter, we review how EBPs have been identified by the primary professional groups involved, including the criteria used and key scientific concepts underpinning them. We examine how these criteria compare to criteria for best practice treatment guidelines. And we explore some of the prominent controversies and criticisms of the EBP movement. Future directions of the movement—known and speculative—conclude the chapter. Despite the controversy it has created, the movement to identify and disseminate EBPs will continue; providers, consumers, and payers of mental health services will influence its course. Understanding the processes through which EBPs are identified, their strengths and weaknesses, and the types of questions being raised by the process informs decisions about their appropriate role in quality mental health service delivery.

IDENTIFYING EVIDENCE-BASED PRACTICES

The initial, and perhaps the most influential, effort to identify EBPs was undertaken by members of The Society of Clinical Psychology (Division 12) of the American Psychological Association (APA). In 1993, then-president David H. Barlow, PhD organized the Task Force on Promotion and Dissemination of Psychological Procedures to review comprehensively the empirical literature in search of psychosocial interventions that had proven efficacy. Using sets of criteria reflecting different levels of empirical support, this group has published three reports of its efforts (available at http://pantheon.yale.edu /~tat22/empirically_supported_treatments.htm). The first of these reports (Task Force, 1995) described the criteria used to select EBPs and a working list of 25 treatments, primarily for adult populations, that met those criteria. As of the last of the other two reports (Chambless et al., 1996, 1998), 71 EBPs had been identified. In addition, the task force published a series in the Division 12 journal, *The Clinical Psychologist.* In it, experts describe the EBPs, the models underpinning them, the empirical work supporting them, and information on protocols and training (Sanderson & Woody, 1995; Woody & Sanderson, 1998). Division 12 has also disseminated this information to state psychological associations and psychology training programs. The task force was transformed into a standing committee of the Division in 1999 (i.e., the Committee on Science and Practice) and continues its efforts today.

Other professional efforts to identify EBPs have since been undertaken. For example, another task force within Division 12, "The Task Force on Effective Psychosocial Interventions: A Lifespan Perspective," identified EBPs and prevention programs for children. Results can be found in Spirito (1999). The Division also commissioned a book, *A Guide to Treatments that Work,* now in its second edition (Nathan & Gorman, 1998, 2002). In these edited volumes, various content experts review and identify psychosocial and pharmacological EBPs. In a special section of the *Journal of Consulting and Clinical Psychology,* Kendall and Chambless (1998) report results of EBP reviews for adults, children, marital, and family therapies. In addition, EBPs for problems common to the elderly have been offered by Gatz and colleagues (1998), as have those for treatment of chronic pain conditions (J. Wilson & Gil, 1996). Outside the United States, EBP reviews have taken place in England (Roth & Fonagy, 1996) and Canada (Hunsley, Dobson, Johnston, & Mikail, 1999). Chambless and Ollendick (2001) review the results of each of these efforts, the criteria used to make their determinations, and address putative concerns raised by the efforts.

THE CLINICAL RESEARCH PROCESS

Any assessment of the strengths and weaknesses of the EBP identification process is informed by an understanding of the scientific processes that promising treatments undergo before being designated as evidence-based. More than 2 decades ago, Agras and Berkowitz (1980), updating Agras, Kazdin, and Wilson (1979), offered a model of applied research that clarifies the processes used to develop and evaluate promising treatments (Figure 10.1).

As shown in this model, most eventual EBPs originate from a clinical innovation, a new theoretical advance, or basic research findings that have clinical implications. After a promising intervention is developed sufficiently for use, often involving initial case studies, it is typically tested in a small group comparison to a no-treatment control condition. This kind of study addresses the question of whether the treatment works better than simply leaving the condition to run its natural course. It is possible that a problem seemingly responding to treatment is in fact remitting on its own. A comparison to a no-treatment control rules out this alternative explanation. At this early stage of treatment development, other studies may be conducted to identify what aspects of the treatment are contributing to its outcome (e.g., a dismantling study). Adjunctive procedures or parametric changes may be made to improve outcome. Later, the critical step of conducting comparative studies with a nonspecific or attention-control condition is needed

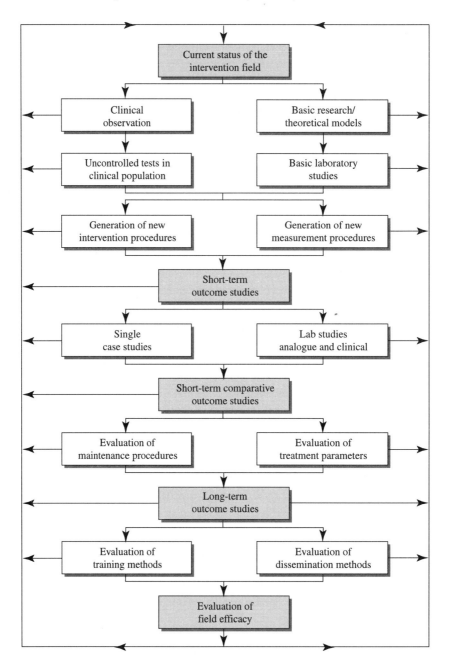

Figure 10.1 A progressive model of clinical research. Reprinted with permission from W. S. Agras and R. Berkowitz, 1980, *Behavior Therapy, 11,* pp. 472–487.

to determine whether aspects unique to the new treatment significantly contribute to therapeutic outcome over and above the contributions made by variables common to all psychotherapies such as attention, psychoeducation, and the like. Comparative studies with established treatments may be conducted at these stages as well. Initially, these studies are usually restricted to investigating the effects of active therapy (i.e., pretreatment to posttreatment comparisons). Studies of the treatment's long-term effects typically follow. Last, Agras and Berkowitz indicated that studies should be conducted to determine if the beneficial results observed in previous studies generalize to real-world applications.

The controlled comparative studies designed to test whether a treatment works as a result of its unique or specific ingredients have been termed *efficacy studies*. Studies designed to test whether an already efficacious treatment works in real-world applications have been termed *effectiveness studies* (Hoagwood, Hibbs, Brent, & Jensen, 1995; Moras, 1998). In addition to differences in their purpose, efficacy and effectiveness studies often differ in experimental design and in the types of conclusions that can be drawn from their results.

Designs used to establish a treatment's efficacy place a strong emphasis on maximizing *internal validity*, the degree to which a design rules out alternative explanations of results. Features of designs that increase internal validity include random assignment, nonspecific or attention controls, large samples, blind and independent assessment of outcome on psychometrically sound measures, and measures of whether the experimental and comparison treatments were delivered distinctively and with treatment integrity and fidelity (generally referring to the idea that they were delivered as intended). Efficacy studies often use specific inclusion and exclusion criteria for enrollment of participants, in part so that the target of the treatment's efforts is consistently represented across individuals and the problem(s) for which a benefit was derived can be specified. Independent replication of results is desirable to rule out an allegiance effect, the possibility that the benefit observed is specific to one or a few settings or providers such as experts or advocates of the treatment.

The ideal single efficacy study would compare the experimental treatment to a nonspecific control treatment that duplicates all but the hypothesized active ingredients of the experimental intervention (a psychological placebo). Participants would be randomly assigned to groups to distribute any other factors that might influence outcome. If the placebo group fails to perform as well as the experimental treatment group, confidence is increased in the conclusion that the active ingredients of the experimental treatment were responsible for the outcome. The closest realization of this ideal is the randomized controlled trial (RCT). Alternatively, a large-scale clinical replication series using controlled single-subject designs is also capable of producing this type of evidence as well (see Barlow, Hayes, & Nelson, 1984). Within the Agras and Berkowitz model, efficacy studies fall under the general rubric of outcome studies. It is important that a treatment that has not been subjected to efficacy evaluation may be producing its beneficial effects through factors other than those unique to it, or only on specific or biased measures of outcome, or result from other uncontrolled factors.

Effectiveness studies, on the other hand, ask the question of whether the efficacy a treatment has previously demonstrated will transfer to real-world applications. The designs of effectiveness studies usually differ from those used to evaluate efficacy in that they place high value on maximizing external or ecological validity. *External validity* refers to the extent to which experimental results can be generalized to the larger population from which a client sample was drawn, including different settings, providers, more complicated clinical presentations, and the like. To a large degree, design features of effectiveness studies attempt to mimic real-world applications. For example, random assignment, a cardinal feature of efficacy studies, may be omitted from an effectiveness study because patients in the real world are not randomly assigned to treatment options (see Seligman, 1995). These studies may have clients participate in only one treatment, as opposed to some efficacy studies that have them cross over into comparison treatments. Inclusion and exclusion criteria of effectiveness studies may be broader than some efficacy studies so they can capture the complexities seen in real-world settings.

We cannot draw the conclusion from the typical effectiveness study that the outcome observed is due to the unique effects of the treatment, because it typically lacks the controls needed to rule out alternative explanations of the results. We can determine, however, whether a treatment's benefits witnessed in previous efficacy studies did or did not generalize to the particular application tested. In interpreting the results of uncontrolled effectiveness studies, it is assumed that the observed benefits are due to the treatment in question because that treatment has previously demonstrated efficacy in controlled comparisons. Common threats to external validity can be found in Kazdin (2003). Considerations for balancing the internal and external validity of applied research designs can be found in Miklowitz and Clarkin (1999).

BEST PRACTICE TREATMENT GUIDELINES

Understanding the types of studies involved in treatment development and the types of questions they ask and can answer informs evaluation of how EBPs are identified. Accordingly, knowing the types of criteria recommended for best practice treatment guidelines can inform an evaluator of how well current EBP criteria conform to these standards and how well the literature supporting a particular EBP conforms as well. Treatment guidelines can be thought of as a specific form of best practice recommendations. They recommend treatment options available to patients that are likely to maximize their chances for recovery. Ideally, they are informed by the best empirical evidence and by expert clinical consensus.

Despite the proliferation of treatment guidelines by various groups, only recently has there been offered a comprehensive set of criteria for judging how guideline authors should evaluate the treatment options they recommend. This was undertaken by a collaborative task force within the APA representing the Board of Professional Affairs, the Board of Scientific Affairs, and the Committee for the Advancement of Professional Practice within the organization. This group has published what is recognized as a comprehensive and rigorous set of criteria for constructing or evaluating treatment guidelines (APA, 2000). Although most relevant to psychosocial interventions, these recommendations are applicable to healthcare interventions broadly.

This task group's criteria for guidelines are organized around two fundamental dimensions of evaluation that should now ring familiar to readers: treatment efficacy and clinical utility. *Treatment efficacy* refers to essentially the same concept discussed earlier, "the systematic and scientific evaluation of whether a treatment works" (p. 4). *Clinical utility* is a concept similar to effectiveness as described earlier, but broader. It refers to "the applicability, feasibility, and usefulness of the intervention in the local or specific setting where it is to be offered." It includes a "determination of the generalizability of an intervention whose efficacy has been established" (p. 4) as well as cost considerations.

The value placed on the demonstration of efficacy in these guideline recommendations is evident in several of the criteria. For example, guideline crafters are urged to base their recommendations on a broad and comprehensive evaluation of the empirical literature supporting any treatment. They are urged to consider the rigor of the methodology used, including the quality of comparison/control groups and the quality and specificity of outcome assessments. The authors emphasize that without controlled evidence of efficacy, providers are forced to rely exclusively on their direct experience, which risks erroneous conclusions when used as a sole source of knowledge.

An example of the benefit of scientifically establishing efficacy is found in the history of the development of systematic desensitization (SD), an EBP for specific phobias identified by all independent review panels. Systematic desensitization originally contained several procedures that were later found to be unnecessary in reducing phobic fear and avoidance (see Barlow, 2002; Bruce & Sanderson, 1998). For example, the original version of SD involved first teaching participants to relax deeply. This relaxed state was then repeatedly paired with exposure to imagined phobic stimuli until no significant distress was elicited upon exposure. Patients would systematically repeat this process moving from low-fear to high-fear stimuli. This pairing procedure was based on the theoretical notions of reciprocal inhibition and counterconditioning. The originator of SD, Joseph Wolpe (1958), hypothesized that phobic stimuli had been conditioned to sympathetic nervous system arousal (e.g., increased heart rate, respiration, and tension). The treatment was designed to countercondition those phobic stimuli through systematic, repeated, and exclusive pairing with a response that would minimize sympathetic arousal, in this case, the (reciprocally inhibitory) parasympathetically based relaxation response. Subsequent controlled studies found, however, that this pairing was not a necessary condition for phobic fear reduction and that exposure alone was sufficient. Other studies showed, for example, that the hierarchical presentation of stimuli, although more tolerable to more patients, was not a necessary condition for fear reduction as well. These studies not only helped identify key therapeutic procedures, but also advanced the profession's understanding of the mechanisms of fear reduction. Without the controlled studies leading to the establishment of efficacy, these developments may not have taken place. The APA guideline authors cite other more serious consequences of excluding efficacy evaluation such as popular treatments once believed to be effective but later shown to be ineffective or even harmful.

In addition to this emphasis on efficacy, guideline criteria stress consideration of the utility of interventions. This value is reflected in several recommendations. For example, the task group recommends consideration of a breadth of patient variables that could influence outcome, including age, gender, race, and cultural background. They advise consideration of the complexities of clinical presentations, such as comorbidity and severity. Feasibility is reflected in recommendations to consider data on the effect of a practitioner's training, skill, and experience and the evaluation of costs, to the patient and to the healthcare system, is underscored as well.

The degree to which an empirical literature supportive of an EBP meets these criteria depends on how advanced it is along the clinical research process. Empirical literatures certainly vary in this regard. For example, the empirical support for identified EBPs for depression has advanced to where efficacy has been strongly demonstrated and initial effectiveness studies support their generalizability. On the other hand, the literature supporting identified EBPs for substance abuse and dependence have not clearly established efficacy (see Chambless & Ollendick, 2001). Factors such as the complexity of the target problem(s), the type of intervention under study, funding priorities, and the like can influence the degree to which an empirical literature advances. To address this variability and fill the gaps left by the absence of empirical data, the APA group encourages guideline developers to "consider clinical opinion, observation, and consensus of experts representing the range of views in the field" (p. 5). Accordingly, the relative degree to which empirical evidence or clinical opinion informs a treatment recommendation will depend on the problem area and treatment in question.

THE EVIDENCE-BASED PRACTICE IDENTIFICATION CRITERIA

The criteria developed originally by the Division 12 task group has served as a model for EBP criteria. Those criteria, the criteria used in other reviews, and how they compare to each other is shown in Table 10.1.

The Division 12 group categorized their criteria into different levels of evidence based on the rigor and volume of the empirical studies supporting a particular treatment. The categories are termed well-established, probably efficacious, and experimental. A close examination of the criteria for the highest level of evidence, "well-established," reflects the degree to which they value both efficacy and utility. The first criterion emphasizes the internal validity of designs used to test the efficacy of the treatment in question. It requires that treatments have shown either equivalence in outcome to an already established treatment or superiority to a pill or psychotherapy placebo condition using a "good between-groups design" in at least two separate studies. Alternatively, Criterion II allows acceptance of a large-scale, rigorously conducted clinical replication series (i.e., multiple single case design studies) involving a treatment comparison.

Criterion III requires the use of manuals in the delivery of the treatment or an equivalent clear description of treatment, a criterion that has met with praise (e.g., see G. Wilson, 1998) and criticism (e.g., see Bohart, O'Hara, & Leitner, 1998). This criterion has been explained in a manner that emphasizes the generalizability of efficacy study results. For example, Chambless and Ollendick (2001) state, ". . . in terms of generalizable knowledge, it is meaningless to say that a treatment works without being able to say what that treatment is" (p. 701). But some critics have argued that manual use overly restricts necessary therapeutic flexibility (e.g., Lambert, 1998; Silverman, 1996) or may limit the likelihood of generalizability because therapists in the field do not use them (Seligman, 1995). A survey of therapists on this topic found that, indeed, many report not using manuals, but it also found that many therapists do not know that EBP manuals

Table 10.1   Workgroup Criteria for the Identification of Empirically Supported Therapies

Division 12 Task Force Criteria[a]

Well-Established Treatments

  I. At least two good between-group design experiments must demonstrate efficacy one or more of the following ways:

    A. Superiority to pill or psychotherapy placebo, or to other treatment

    B. Equivalence to already established treatment with adequate sample sizes

OR

  II. A large series of single-case design experiments must demonstrate efficacy with:

    A. Use of good experimental design and

    B. Comparison of intervention to another treatment

  III. Experiments must be conducted with treatment manuals or equivalent clear description of treatment.

  IV. Characteristics of samples must be specified.

  V. Effects must be demonstrated by at least two different investigators or teams.

Probably Efficacious Treatments

  I. Two experiments must show that the treatment is superior to waiting-list control group.

OR

  II. One or more experiments must meet well-established criteria IA or IB, III, and above but V is not met.

OR

  III. A small series of single-case design experiments must meet well-established treatment criteria.

Experimental Treatments

Treatment not yet tested in trials meeting task force criteria for methodology.

Special Section of the *Journal of Pediatric Psychology*[b]

Well-Established Treatments
Same as Chambless et al. (1998).

Probably Efficacious Treatments
Same as Chambless et al. (1998).

Promising Interventions

  I. There must be positive support from one well-controlled study and at least one other less-well-controlled study.

OR

  II. There must be positive support from a small number of single-case design experiments.

OR

  III. There must be positive support from two or more well controlled studies by the same investigator.

[a] From "Update on Empirically Validated Therapies: II," by D. L. Chambless et al., 1998, *The Clinical Psychologist, 51*(1), pp. 3–16.
[b] From "Empirically Supported Treatments in Pediatric Psychology" [Special issue], by A. Spirito, Ed., 1999, *Journal of Pediatric Psychology, 24,* pp. 87–174.

(*continued*)

Table 10.1   *Continued*

Special Section of the *Journal of Clinical Child Psychology*[c]

Well-Established Treatments
Same as Chambless et al. (1998).

Probably Efficacious Treatments
Same as Chambless et al. (1998) except there must be at least two, rather than one, group design studies meeting criteria for well-established treatments if conducted by the same investigator.

Special Section of the *Journal of Consulting and Clinical Psychology*[d]

Efficacious and Specific
Same as Chambless et al. (1998) for well-established treatments.

Possibly Efficacious and Specific Treatments
Same as efficacious and specific above except treatment only required to be found superior to rival treatment in one study.

Efficacious and Possibly Specific Treatments
Same as efficacious and specific criteria above except treatment was found superior to wait-list group in one study and superior to rival treatment in another study by a different team.

Efficacious Treatments
Same as Chambless et al. (1998) for well-established treatments except treatment must be demonstrated to be better than no treatment but not been shown to be better than nonspecific intervention, placebo, or rival intervention.

Possibly Efficacious Treatments
Same as Chambless et al. (1998) for probably efficacious treatments.

What Works for Whom?[e]

Clearly Effective Treatments
  I. There must be a replicated demonstration of superiority to a control condition or another treatment condition.

OR

 II. There must be a single high-quality randomized control trial in which:
    A. Therapists followed a clearly described therapeutic method useable as the basis for training.
    B. There is a clearly described patient group.

Promising Limited-Support Treatments
Treatment must be innovative and a promising line of intervention.

OR

Treatment is a widely practiced method with only limited support for effectiveness.

---

[c] From Lonigan, C. J., & Elbert, J. C. (Eds.). "Empirically Supported Psychosocial Interventions for Children," 1998 [Special issue], *Journal of Clinical Child Psychology, 27,* pp. 138–226.
[d] From "Empirically Supported Psychological Therapies" [Special issue], by P. C. Kendall and D. L. Chambless, Eds., 1998, *Journal of Consulting and Clinical Psychology, 66*(3), p. 167.
[e] From *What Works for Whom? A Critical Review of Psychotherapy Research,* by A. D. Roth and P. Fonagy, 1996, New York: Guilford Press.

Table 10.1   *Continued*

A Guide to Treatments That Work[f]

Type 1 Studies
   I. Study must include a randomized prospective clinical trial.

   II. Study must include comparison groups with random assignment, blind assignments, clear inclusion and exclusion criteria, state-of-the-art diagnostic methods, and adequate sample size for power.

   III. There must be clearly described statistical methods.

Type 2 Studies
   Clinical trials must be performed, but some traits of type-1 study were missing (e.g., trial with no double blind or group assignment not randomized).

Type 3 Studies
   I. These are open treatment studies that are aimed at obtaining pilot data.

OR

   II. These are case control studies in which treatment information was obtained retrospectively.

Treatments for Older Adults[g]
Same as Chambless et al. (1998) criteria.

Treatments for Chronic Pain[h]
Same as Chambless et al. (1998) criteria.

[f] From *A guide to treatments that work,* by P. E. Nathan, and J. M. Gorman, Eds., 1998, New York: Oxford University Press.
[g] From "Empirically Validated Psychological Treatments for Older Adults," by M. Gatz, A. Fiske, L. S. Fox, B. Kaskie, J. E. Kasl-Godley, et al., 1998, *Journal of Mental Health and Aging, 41,* pp. 9–46.
[h] From "The Efficacy of Psychological and Pharmacological Interventions for the Treatment of Chronic Disease-Related and Non-Disease-Related Pain," by J. J. Wilson and K. M. Gil, 1996, *Clinical Psychology Review, 16,* pp. 573–597.
Source: From "Empirically Supported Psychological Interventions: Controversies and Evidence," by D. L. Chambless and T. H. Ollendick, 2001, *Annual Reviews of Psychology, 52,* pp. 685–716. Adapted and reprinted with permission.

exist (Addis & Krasnow, 2000). It is interesting that the few effectiveness studies that have used manuals to guide treatment have reported success. It remains an empirical question as to whether manual use will facilitate generalizability for some or all EBPs. It is unclear how many treatments were excluded from consideration by Division 12 because of this requirement.

Although this criterion has been explained in terms of generalizability, it has implications for internal validity as well. Providing a description of the principles and procedures of a treatment, whether through use of a manual or other means, allows the assessment of treatment integrity, fidelity, and distinctiveness of the compared treatments. In other words, it can be used to assess whether treatments compared in efficacy studies were delivered as intended and distinctively from the treatments compared to them. From a design perspective, this is the notion that we cannot conclude that an independent variable, in this case, the EBP, was responsible for the outcome unless it is certain that it has been applied as intended and delivered those elements that distinguish it from the control treatment. Some efficacy studies supportive of EBPs report fidelity data. Others do not.

Criteria IV and V for well-established treatments place value on both internal and external validity. For example, Criterion IV requires that characteristics of study participants are identified. This helps define the dependent variable(s), and it allows consumers of the study to determine for what clients and problems the EBP may apply. Criterion V, which requires independent replication of results, ensures that the results of a study used to support an EBP were not a product of an allegiance effect. This requirement is relevant to internal validity in that it rules out an alternative explanation of the results. It also supports generalizability in strengthening confidence that the benefits of the treatment are transportable to other sites, providers, and circumstances. These examples show that, consistent with its charge, the Division 12 task force placed strong emphasis on the establishment of efficacy in the criteria it used to identify EBPs. Utility is not ignored, nor is definitive demonstration of it required. As shown in Table 10.1, criteria that were used in other reviews have had a similar emphasis on efficacy, although not all used the same categorical breakdown used by Division 12. There are some differences in the detail of criteria used in the reviews cited, discussion of which is beyond the purpose of this chapter. Interested readers are referred to Chambless and Ollendick (2001).

So, how far have the empirical literatures used to support currently identified EBPs advanced through the clinical research process, and how well do they meet the criteria for treatment guidelines recommended by the APA task group discussed earlier (APA, 2000)? At last report, 22% of interventions identified by Division 12 had reached the "well-established" level of evidence, strongly supporting their efficacy. Approximately 60% of these treatments are for anxiety or depressive disorders. Effectiveness studies, the furthest developmental advance in the clinical research process and supportive of clinical utility, have been far fewer in number and published primarily in these areas, particularly in panic disorder and unipolar depression (see Chambless & Ollendick, 2001). The majority of identified EBPs (78%) are supported at less than well-established levels of efficacy, indicating that although data supportive of efficacy exists, they are insufficient to rule out with certainty alternative explanations of results. In many cases, it is an allegiance effect that has not been ruled out, meaning that the studies supporting the EBP have not been independently replicated. Although these treatments may be as they are labeled, "probably efficacious," the lack of independent replication leaves questions about their transportability and generalizability unanswered. Thus, although it appears that psychosocial treatment development and outcome research is well advanced for some identified EBPs, the current status of literatures supporting most EBPs is at levels supporting efficacy, but not yet demonstrating their generalizability, feasibility, and cost-effectiveness in community application.

CONTROVERSIES

The Division 12 task group's interest in identifying EBPs is part of a larger worldwide movement to make findings from applied medical research more available to clinicians in practice, a movement known generally as *evidence-based medicine* (Sackett, Richardson, Rosenberg, & Haynes, 1997). The primary aim of this effort is to improve the quality of patient care by making it easier for practitioners to empirically inform their services. Empirically informed treatment guidelines have been a common means of disseminating this information. And if the APA criteria for evaluating treatment guidelines serve as a model, the criteria used to identify EBPs are consistent with them, particularly concerning the demonstration of efficacy. It is also clear that the degree to which current literatures supportive of EBPs meet these criteria varies and depends on the problem area in question. Even the most advanced bodies of work, those for anxiety and depressive disorders, do not satisfy all recommended guideline criteria. Most have not reached a level of evidence convincingly demonstrating the generalizability, feasibility, and cost-effectiveness of treatment. More effectiveness studies are needed to address these issues, and federal funding priorities acknowledge this need. The next decade will witness a surge in these types of studies and provide more direct evidence of the degree to which EBPs improve the quality of mental healthcare. In the meantime, any mental health service provider that uses an EBP should be prepared to adapt it to clients as needed using its best clinical judgment, a point true of nearly all healthcare interventions. As worthy as the intent of the EBP movement may seem, it, its products, and, in particular, the use of these products have created controversy.

Selection Bias

One criticism of EBPs is the claim that they are essentially products of a specific group of, primarily cognitive-behavioral, clinical researchers whose theoretical model and treatment approaches are more amenable than alternative treatments to the kinds of scientific evaluation being recommended as criteria for EBPs. It is true that cognitive-behavioral clinical researchers were represented on the Division 12 task force, that many cognitive-behavioral therapies (CBTs) have been manualized (a required criterion of some reviewers), and that CBT emphasizes measurable treatment goals. It is also true that therapies based on CBT models appear prominently on EBP lists and have been studied more than other approaches. Yet, several individuals and groups have undertaken the EBP identification task, not all were cognitive-behavioral in orientation, and they have come to similar conclusions concerning appropriate EBP criteria. Further, the APA task group for evaluating treatment guidelines, a group representing diverse professional allegiances, also generated criteria consistent with those of the independent EBP review panels—as have several other prominent guideline authors (e.g., American Psychiatric Association). Although many CBTs for varied problem areas have met EBP criteria, some non-CBT therapies that have been subjected to empirical scrutiny have met them as well (e.g., brief psychodynamic therapy for depression). The "unfairness" of excluding unstudied but practiced therapies from these lists may be more the issue here and is discussed further in a subsequent section.

CAPTURING COMPLEXITY

It has been argued that most studies supportive of EBPs fail to capture the complexity and uniqueness of patients seen in community practice, and by implication their applicability to the community patient is minimal. This argument has taken several forms. For example, it has been said that efficacy studies use criteria to define samples that rely too heavily on the *DSM,* that their selection criteria often exclude common comorbidities, or that they otherwise treated easier-to-treat clients than are found in the community (e.g., Bohart et al., 1998; Henry, 1998; Levant, 2004).

This argument concerning the *DSM* suggests that categorical diagnostics, such as those used in the *DSM,* are inadequate in capturing dimensional complexities with which clients commonly present. Although some task forces, such as Division 12's, used more than *DSM* diagnoses in evaluating studies (e.g., cutoff scores of questionnaires, specific behavioral targets of treatment), by and large the *DSM* has indeed guided most recent treatment outcome research. Of course, a categorical diagnosis does not preclude a treatment plan based on the category's dimensional features. In addition, some *DSM* diagnostic categories do capture complex and difficult clinical presentations (e.g., borderline personality disorders [BPD]), and some identified EBPs have shown promise in treating them (e.g., dialectic behavior therapy for BPD). But the essence of this argument is that the limitations of the *DSM* reduce the applicability of efficacy studies to the community (a point to which we return later).

The study typically used to support the complexity argument is Westen and Morrison (2001), who reported that complexity, defined as syndromal comorbidity, is underrepresented in efficacy studies. These investigators reported that approximately two-thirds of potential participants in treatment studies of depression, panic disorder, and generalized anxiety disorder did not meet inclusion criteria due to comorbidity. Results of this study stand in contrast, however, to studies that have reported a high degree of similarity between samples used in efficacy studies and those drawn from the community, with a trend toward increased complexity in research samples (Lipsey & Wilson, 1993; Shadish, Matt, Navarro, & Phillips, 2000). In interpreting these mixed results, L. E. Beutler (personal communication, November 3, 2003) noted that over time, increased emphasis has been placed on improving the representativeness of research samples. The inclusion of earlier studies in the Westen and Morrison (2001) meta-analysis may explain its results.

An assumption of the complexity argument, which is not a given, is that an EBP focused on one disorder is not applicable or will be ineffective for patients with other comorbidity. This is an empirical question that has received some preliminary study, producing mixed results. The question under study has been whether treating the primary disorder of a comorbid profile (e.g., the most severe or initial) results in improvement in the primary and comorbid conditions. Tsao, Lewin, and Craske (1998) found that symptoms of comorbid social anxiety, generalized anxiety, and posttraumatic stress disorder decreased significantly following the EBP treatment of the primary panic disorder. Borkovec, Abel, and Newman (1995) found similar results in a group of patients with a primary diagnosis of generalized anxiety disorder. McLean, Woody, Taylor, and Koch (1998) found, however, that comorbid depressive symptoms remained relatively unchanged after treatment of the primary panic disorder. Those symptoms predicted impaired treatment response on some measures and warranted further treatment. Brown, Antony, and Barlow (1995) found decreased comorbidity following treatment of a primary panic disorder, but symptoms had returned to pretreatment level by the 2-year follow-up. These mixed results suggest that there may be applications of current EBPs designed for single disorders to certain comorbidity profiles, but some comorbidities will not respond. Further studies inclusive of complex participants will help answer these questions.

Perhaps a more subtle consequence of using the *DSM* is the limited focus on Axes I and II in defining samples. It is fair to say that the concept of Axis IV (psychosocial stress) and its relevance to treatment planning is underdeveloped in the guidance it offers for treatment planning and in its role in defining study samples. This does not negate testing psychosocial interventions related to Axis I or II diagnoses, but indirectly discourages conceptualizing and studying client problems more inclusive than Axis I or II diagnoses.

A final argument concerns the application of EBPs to complex individual clients and is part of a larger criticism on the limitations of the RCT. This argument, too, has taken many forms. For example, it has been suggested that the data analyses commonly used in RCTs place inordinate emphasis on group trends (nomothetic level of analysis) over that of individual patient responses (idiographic analyses). Another version of the argument has been that RCTs favor quantitative research methods over qualitative ones, suggesting the latter of which are more sensitive to individual responses (e.g., Bohart et al., 1998). Within most applied research models, qualitative studies are often seen as a source of hypotheses that may be tested in subsequent controlled studies. A strength of applied qualitative research is that it often provides data rich in individual participants' responses to an intervention. A weakness, though, is that the design often lacks the internal validity sufficient to rule out alternative explanations of the results. Without controlled internally valid designs, it is impossible to ascertain to what any participant is responding.

This emphasis on internal validity and efficacy in most EBP criteria reflects more the value placed on systematic as opposed to unsystematic observation. Yet, it is true that many RCTs have favored designs and data analytic procedures that are largely quantitative and nomothetic. For instance, data from many RCTs are analyzed using traditional f- or t-tests of group by time interactions. These types of analyses are conducted using aggregated (group) data, results of which may not predict a future individual's response to treatment. There is a trend toward describing some RCT results in terms of the percentage of patients who meet varying levels of improvement, often defined multidimensionally. But, idiographic analyses are often not done or reported in RCTs. Recent trends in statistical analyses are addressing these concerns and are discussed more fully under the Future Directions section.

Demonstrating Utility

The need for more effectiveness studies of EBPs has been recognized since the movement to identify EBPs began. In 1999, a special issue of the online journal *Prevention and Treatment* published several excellent articles addressing this need and considerations, theoretical and applied (available at http://journals.apa.org/prevention/volume2). Effectiveness studies are beginning to appear and are likely to continue for some time. What have been the results of studies completed to date? Have EBPs shown promise of utility in the real-world healthcare system? Have they worked in community agencies, with difficult-to-treat clients, multiple demands, and limited resources? Although the body of this research is small, the trend in existing evidence is supportive of generalization, not uniformly, though, and not without some qualifications. For example, Wade, Treat, and Stuart (1998) reported improvements comparable to benchmark efficacy studies in a large broad-based sample of community mental health patients treated for panic disorder with or without agoraphobia using a standard manual-based EBP (Barlow & Craske, 1994). Dropout rates were lower than rates typically observed in this population, but higher than in efficacy studies. Results suggested improvement over standard care but short of complete generalization across indexes. This same treatment was tested with a group of urban, low income, and primarily Latino patients whose pretreatment severity levels were higher than benchmark efficacy studies (Sanderson, Raue, & Wetzler, 1998). Results showed statistically significant improvement, but to posttreatment severity levels that were also higher than posttreatment efficacy benchmarks. In a study of CBT for depression, improvements reaching benchmark levels were achieved, but the number of therapy sessions needed had to be extended over those used in efficacy studies (Persons, Bostrom, & Bertagnolli, 1999).

These examples show the promise of EBPs in producing good outcome, but efficacy benchmarks may not be achieved or EBPs may need some modifications to achieve them. Whether other identified EBPs will show effectiveness in routine practice waits to be seen. What the nature of the outcome will be, whether it will be found throughout the range of patient complexities, what systemic obstacles may arise, and what role is best played by the EBP in the treatment plan are questions awaiting further study. As noted, federal funding agencies are making such studies a priority, and answers to these questions are forthcoming.

Treatment Specificity and Nonspecific Factors

One consequence of the EBP identification movement has been to rekindle a long-running debate about what types of factors produce the therapeutic outcome seen in efficacy studies and whether some therapies do this better than others. The former debate has been focused primarily on the relative contribution to therapeutic outcome of factors specific to the treatment (specific factors) versus those that are common to all psychotherapies (nonspecific factors). Critics have argued that a literature supporting the important role of nonspecific factors has been ignored by the focus on identifying specific treatments for specific disorders.

Perhaps the most concerted effort to identify and disseminate information on the role of nonspecific factors has come from another task force, the Task Force on Empirically Supported Therapy Relationships, formed by members of APA Division 29 (Psychotherapy). This task force summarized a literature investigating factors related to the therapist, the therapeutic relationship, and nondiagnostic patient characteristics. Two reports from that work (i.e., Lambert & Barley, 2001; Norcross, 2001) have been cited by critics of EBP lists because they concluded that factors specific to treatments account for no more than 15% of the variance in therapeutic outcomes, the same percentage accounted for by placebo and expectancy effects. The remaining 70% of variance was due to factors related to patients (15%), therapeutic relationships (40%), and changes outside the therapy (15%). These figures, however, are not consistent with other studies, perhaps because of the way in which they were calculated (L. E. Beutler, personal communication, November 3, 2003). Specifically, Beutler notes that they were not derived from direct calculations of effect size, the preferred method, but from estimates of what the total variance would have been if all the studies used in the analysis had employed analyses of variance statistics in which total variance can be calculated. Studies of relationship variables, for example, that have used direct effect size calculations have yielded correlations ranging from .11 (Stevens, Hynan, & Allen, 2000) to .26 (Horvath & Symonds, 1991) with most falling near .24. When the variance accounted for by these factors is calculated, it shows that relationship and treatment-specific factors make similar contributions to outcome approximating .10. This may be beside the point, however, because these types of studies may be artificially separating factors that may in practice interact in complex and varied ways to influence outcome (Beutler et al., 2003). Alternative approaches to analyzing these interactions hold the promise of capturing this complex interplay and may help depolarize the debate over what factors are the most influential (see Future Directions section).

Even if specific and nonspecific factors interact inextricably to produce outcome, it is possible that certain treatments may still result in better outcomes than others, also known as *treatment specificity*. Chambless and Ollendick (2001) review evidence of treatment specificity and show that it is indeed evident in some literatures, particularly anxiety disorders and childhood depression. It is interesting that in the highly evolved literature on adult depression, evidence supports the conclusion that different psychotherapies (e.g., psychodynamic, interpersonal, and behavioral) can each produce desired outcome. Literatures for other problem areas vary in their capacity to address this question.

Meta-analytic evidence showing that psychotherapy is generally effective is often cited as evidence against treatment specificity (e.g., Shapiro & Shapiro, 1982; Weisz, Weiss, Han, Granger, & Morton, 1995). This type of result, however, does not constitute evidence against the notion that some treatments are more effective than others for particular problems. The most direct evidence comes from direct comparative studies. Unfortunately, these types of studies are typically seen only in the more advanced literatures. Although not every psychotherapy can be tested in comparison to others, it seems that tests of specificity among commonly used interventions may reveal differences in outcome that can inform treatment selection in ways that improve a client's chance of recovery. This is relevant given that several studies are finding that the majority of clients who suffer disorders for which there are well-established EBPs are nevertheless not receiving them and, in many cases, receiving therapies shown to be inferior (Addis & Krasnow, 2000; Goisman, Warshaw, & Keller, 1999; Plante, Andersen, & Boccaccini, 1999; Sanderson, Hiatt, & Schwartz, 2001; Taylor, King, & Margraf, 1989).

Forced Use

Perhaps the most disconcerting consequence of the EBP movement is one that has not to do with the identification process per se, but with the manner in which EBPs are being seen and used by payers of services. For example, some authors (e.g., Seligman & Levant, 1998; Silverman, 1996) point out that managed care and insurance companies are beginning to restrict healthcare coverage to specific EBPs, not acknowledging the absence of data demonstrating their utility. Similar restrictions are emerging through some state and federal funding agencies. Kovacs (1995) warns that this precedent may make practitioners who do not use identified EBPs vulnerable to malpractice lawsuits. A consequence of restricted coverage is that potentially valuable services developed in the community by licensed clinicians are rendered unavailable to clients because they have not been subjected to extensive empirical testing. Levant (2004) has made the point that restricting payment to EBPs over untested alternatives is tantamount to equating the latter with therapies that have demonstrated a lack of efficacy. These points argue against the forced and exclusive use of EBP, whether through funding incentives, legal deterrents, or other means.

Another objection to forced use has been more philosophical. Some therapeutic models differ from others at the level of the worldviews supporting them, worldviews that may derive from contradictory epistemic values. Most experienced mental health professionals practicing today remember being taught psychotherapy in its relation to personality theory and being taught personality theory in its relation to the philosophical schools of thought from which they derive. A scientific worldview and therapies consistent with it, many of which are identified EBPs, were taught as one of many options, others of which may not be bedded in the logical positivism and empiricism of science. It was common that students were instructed to choose a model, in part, based on how consistent it was with their personal worldview. It has been suggested that science is but one of several "faiths" in this sense and that treatments deriving from it should not be forced on practitioners (cf. Levant, 2004).

Counterpoints to these arguments have essentially been practical in nature. They acknowledge that seasoned clinicians may indeed be providing effective services, but that without some demonstration of this, payers have to trust that they are not buying an ineffective approach. In the current atmosphere of increased accountability in healthcare service provision, payers are not likely to offer this trust a priori. To the more philosophical argument, the counterpoints have been similarly practical. Today, the practice of psychotherapy is not treated as a matter of choice in a faith, but as a healthcare treatment option subject to cost and benefit/risk analyses. In this atmosphere, for better or worse, the practitioner's option to choose what he or she offers based on philosophic grounds has become an intellectual luxury not affordable to those seeking third-party reimbursement for their services.

Unfortunately, there are few alternatives to resolving the problem of how to recognize potentially effective yet untested treatments apart from some form of scientific study. It is unlikely that reimbursement policies will return to the days when licensure was sufficient to justify choice of intervention. Practitioners now need to demonstrate outcome. And outcome measurement, indeed, may be a means to addressing several of the concerns raised by the forced use issue. Demonstration of outcome may not only serve to justify reimbursement of services but also holds promise of demonstrating the effectiveness of current clinical practices. Although some therapeutic models may indeed be more difficult to operationalize, their desired outcome is definable and measurable. To date, however, efforts to organize outcome measurement systems for these purposes are not concerted. The task is clearly challenging. Capturing major domains of client progress, such as symptom, function, or quality of life in a reliable, valid, relevant, and least burdensome manner is difficult and resource intensive. Despite its challenges, though, the use of outcome measurement systems to assess the effects of field-delivered interventions may be one of the few ways to preserving choice of interventions while satisfying the demand for accountability to payers.

FUTURE DIRECTIONS

The movement to identify EBPs has potential risks and benefits. Decades of clinical research have led to the development of efficacious psychosocial treatments that have benefited thousands of clients and hold the promise of doing the same for future consumers. Improvement rates for many of these psychosocial treatments rival or exceed those of the primary alternative treatment, state-of-the-art medications (Nathan & Gorman, 2002). Initial studies of how these approaches work in community settings have been promising. Many of the objections to the dissemination of EBPs revolve around the risk of potential misuse by payers and by a legal system that may not appreciate the complexities of addressing community mental health needs and the appropriate roles of EBPs in that effort. The challenge of defining those roles and educating these systems in the appropriate use of EBPs will be ongoing. It is likely to play out in several arenas, including the public mental health system, court systems, funding agency policies, treatment guidelines, EBP toolkits, and the relevant professional literatures.

As noted, several studies have shown that the majority of people seeking mental health treatment are receiving therapeutic approaches of unknown efficacy or of efficacy known to be inferior to EBPs (Addis & Krasnow, 2000; Goisman et al., 1999; Plante et al., 1999; Sanderson et al., 2001; Taylor et al., 1989). Use of EBPs for those clients is likely to improve care, but EBPs are not universally effective with the disorders for which they were developed. Even experienced EBP providers know that some client problems are of a complexity or severity to be unamenable to an unmodified EBP protocol. The nature of these limits to the generalizability of EBPs will be better known as they are subjected to effectiveness studies over the next decade. Advocates and critics agree that EBPs still requires using clinical expertise and sensitivity to the client's needs and wishes.

This chapter highlighted the risk that exclusive use of EBPs may prevent potentially effective, field-developed, or otherwise innovative treatments from being recognized. Science and practice are likely to move toward integration if a means can be found to bring the underrecognized voice of seasoned practitioners into the effort to define and shape best practices. Although there are several means to this end, one option highlighted in this chapter is the growing effort to collect, evaluate, and disseminate outcome data collected on community-based interventions.

Work has begun in this regard, and its continued development may be fruitful. For example, through Practice-Research Networks, standardized outcomes are being collected across selected participating practices (e.g., Borkovec, Echemendia, Ragusea, & Ruiz, 2001). Fishman (1999) has also described a model system for organizing and disseminating case studies of adequate design. The call for the use of standardized measurement systems has been made in clinical research arenas to allow for better comparison of results across empirical studies. It seems equally applicable for demonstration projects of field-developed or EBP therapies. Although efforts like research networks are likely to be used to field test EBPs, field testing current community practices (e.g., between EBPs and treatment as usual) may improve understanding of the relative contributions of each approach. In addition, public payers, such as state divisions of mental health, as well as private insurers are in a position to contribute to this effort if they organize these types of projects and seek funding opportunities. Funding and outlets for the results of efforts are increasing as priorities are shifting toward effectiveness research. It waits to be seen if such efforts will be made.

The EBP movement has rekindled discussion and debate about types of questions that should be asked in treatment outcomes studies. The debate on the relative contributions of the content (specific factors) and the process (nonspecific factors) to therapeutic outcome was highlighted. Efforts to reexplore the integration of these seemingly separate aspects of psychosocial interventions are being witnessed in current research and may have far-reaching consequences for the EBP movement and the field in general. As introduced previously, the conventional design of most RCTs has framed treatment as an independent variable exerting its effects on dependent variables (e.g., the patient/participant). Factors other than those specific to the treatment (the nonspecific factors) are controlled, usually by randomly distributing or duplicating them across all groups under study. Traditionally, outcome has been analyzed in part by isolating the magnitude of change on the dependent variable that is correlated exclusively with the application of the specific factors of the therapy.

This model is enriched when patient and therapist variables traditionally considered nonspecific (e.g., relationship quality, degree of fit between patient and treatment) are studied as potential moderating variables. These kinds of moderated relationships can be explored within traditional RCT designs by employing regression statistics, for example, which allow unique correlational variance to be ascertained. A recent example of this approach was published by Beutler et al. (2003). These investigators analyzed results of an RCT conventionally, evaluating group differences across time on the dependent variable. They also analyzed these same data using a regression analytic strategy that evaluated four sets of variables: (1) patient factors, (2) treatment procedures, (3) relationship quality, and (4) the degree of patient-procedure fit. These four classes of variables each added independent variance to the prediction of outcomes, accounting for from 53% to over 90% of the variance, depending on the outcome variable. Increased use of these types of analyses holds the promise of improving our understanding of the complexity of the mechanisms of therapeutic change, depolarizing the debate between nonspecific and specific factors, and changing the manner in which EBPs are conceptualized.

An organized example of this move toward integration is the current effort by a large task force of the APA that is exploring empirically supported "principles" of therapeutic change, as opposed to lists of specific treatments (Beutler & Castonguay, in press). Four problem areas have been the initial focus of this group: dysphoric disorders, anxiety disorders, personality disorders, and habit disorders (broadly defined to include addictions). The principles under study are reflective of traditional content and process emphases: those related to treatment procedures (specific factors), treatment participants (e.g., the patient and therapist), and the therapeutic relationship. This work represents a shift toward conceptualizing and studying specific and nonspecific factors as intertwined and operating in complex relationships, perhaps differently in different individuals, to produce outcome.

Should efforts such as outcome measurement use and research on specific and nonspecific factors produce results, they are still likely to encounter some challenges in demonstrating accountability to payers. For example, some funding agencies require the demonstration of fidelity of the services they fund (assessments of whether the treatment is being conducted as intended) in addition to demonstrations of outcome. Although adhering to the fidelity of some EBPs seems important to achieving their outcome (e.g., assertive community training), others allow more flexibility as long as the principle of the treatment is honored (e.g., exposure-based therapies). The "principles" approach described earlier is inherently broader and more flexible in application than a specific EBP protocol. Some complex field-developed interventions may be as well. Fidelity requirements would also need to be flexible.

As much as the EBP identification process has stirred controversy and debate, efforts to acknowledge, depolarize, and integrate science and practice perspectives are being seen as a result. Another arena in which this integration is possible is in the development of treatment guidelines. Although a representative task force within the APA has defined criteria for good treatment guidelines, there have been no direct attempts to contribute a set of working treatment guidelines based on them. Whether such an effort will be witnessed in the near future is unknown, but it could advance current conceptualizations of psychosocial treatment beyond the specific treatment approach. Empirically and clinically informed guidelines such as these might be as educational to the systems that might misuse EBPs as they would be practical to interested providers.

Translating evidence-based treatment recommendations into practice requires acceptance and training of practitioners as well as acceptance by patients. As to EBPs, a Division 12 survey of directors of APA-approved clinical training programs revealed that approximately 20% of programs do not teach them at a minimum level of coverage as defined by the survey authors (Crits-Christoph, Frank, Chambless, Brody, & Karp, 1995). Data showing that most patients do not receive EBP treatment suggests, albeit indirectly, that these treatments are a tool not many therapists possess or are willing to use. Weissman and Sanderson (2002) offer an example of a model for training EBPs applicable across disciplines.

As to patient acceptance, recent years have witnessed the adoption of the *recovery model* by advocates of persons with severe mental disorders. This model advances the strong value of placing responsibility and control over the recovery process in the hands of the sufferer of the condition. Accordingly, this places a need on providers to educate consumers about the risks and benefits of various service options available to them. It would seem that EBPs would stand in good stead in this regard, in that their risks and benefits have an empirical base. But, it is not uncommon in recovery circles to view science with suspicion and reject certain services regardless of the evidence supporting their contributions to recovery. An example of one way to close this gap between scientific and recovery model adherents has been offered by Frese, Stanley, Kress, and Vogel-Scibilia (2001). Other efforts are likely to be witnessed as well and will be important to the dissemination effort.

CONCLUSION

In this chapter, we discussed the current status and future directions of the EBP identification movement. We reviewed means used to identify EBPs and key scientific concepts underlying that process. We examined how EBP criteria compare to standards for best practice treatment guidelines and found that those criteria overlap in many ways, particularly concerning efficacy. We reviewed the degree to which literatures supporting particular EBPs have advanced through the clinical research process and found that although most demonstrate efficacy or its promise, few have convincingly demonstrated treatment utility. Effectiveness studies are needed to evaluate utility and are a priority of research funding agencies.

Controversies surrounding EBPs have had many consequences. One perhaps unexpected consequence has been the degree to which this debate has informed research on the role of specific and nonspecific factors in therapy. Innovative and integrative work is being done in this area. Controversy has also revealed problems with the potential misuse of EBPs by purchasers and the legal system. Most critics argue that evidence supportive of EBPs may show efficacy but is limited concerning utility and, as such, is insufficient to warrant their exclusive use, exclusive funding, and legal penalties for nonuse. Unfortunately, the practical and financial motives of payers are not likely to be swayed simply by a risk that efficacious EBPs may not generalize. Options for addressing misuse of EBPs such as applications of outcome assessment and the development treatment guidelines reflecting empirical and clinical input were presented. In the end, demonstration of the strengths and limitations of EBPs will determine the future of the movement, and results of those efforts are what the next decade is likely to witness.

REFERENCES

Addis, M. E., & Krasnow, A. D. (2000). A national survey of practicing psychologists' attitudes toward psychotherapy treatment manuals. *Journal of Consulting and Clinical Psychology, 68,* 331–39.

Agras, W. S., & Berkowitz, R. (1980). Clinical research in behavior therapy: Halfway there? *Behavior Therapy, 11,* 472–487.

Agras, W. S., Kazdin, A. E., & Wilson, G. T. (1979). *Behavior therapy: Toward an applied clinical science.* San Francisco: Freeman.

American Psychological Association. (2000). *Criteria for evaluating treatment guidelines.* Washington, DC: Author.

Barlow, D. H. (2002). *Anxiety and its disorders: The nature and treatment of anxiety and panic.* New York: Guilford Press.

Barlow, D. H., & Craske, M. G. (1994). *Mastery of your anxiety and panic* (Vol. II). Albany, NY: Graywind.

Barlow, D. H., Hayes, S. C., & Nelson, R. O. (1984). *The scientist practitioner: Research and accountability in clinical and educational settings.* New York: Pergamon Press.

Beutler, L. E., & Castonguay, L. G. (Eds.). (in press). *Empirically supported principles of therapy change.* New York: Oxford University Press.

Beutler, L. E., Malik, M., Alimohamed, S., Harwood, T. M., Talebi, H., Noble, S., et al. (2003). Therapist variables. In M. J. Lambert (Ed.), *Handbook of psychotherapy and behavior change* (5th ed., pp. 227–306). New York: Wiley.

Bohart, A. D., O'Hara, M., & Leitner, L. M. (1998). Empirically violated treatments: Disenfranchisement of humanistic and other psychotherapies. *Psychotherapy Research, 8,* 141–157.

Borkovec, T. D., Abel, J. L., & Newman, H. (1995). Effects of psychotherapy on comorbid conditions in generalized anxiety disorder. *Journal of Consulting and Clinical Psychology, 63*(3), 479–483.

Borkovec, T. D., Echemendia, R. J., Ragusea, S. A., & Ruiz, M. (2001). The Pennsylvania Practice Research Network and possibilities for clinically meaningful and scientifically rigorous psychotherapy effectiveness research. *Clinical Psychology: Science and Practice, 8,* 155–167.

Brown, T. A., Antony, M. M., & Barlow, D. H. (1995). Diagnostic comorbidity in panic disorder: Effect on treatment outcome and course of comorbid diagnoses following treatment. *Journal of Consulting and Clinical Psychology, 63*(3), 408–418.

Bruce, T. J., & Sanderson, W. C. (1998). Specific phobias: Clinical applications of evidence-based psychotherapies. NJ: Aronson.

Chambless, D. L., Baker, M. J., Baucom, D., Beutler, L. E., Calhoun, K. S., Crits-Christoph, P., et al. (1998). Update on empirically validated therapies: II. *Clinical Psychologist, 51*(1), 3–16.

Chambless, D. L., & Ollendick, T. H. (2001). Empirically supported psychological interventions: Controversies and evidence. *Annual Review of Psychology, 52,* 685–716.

Chambless, D. L., Sanderson, W. C., Shoham, V., Johnson, S. B., Pope, K., Crits-Christoph, P., et al. (1996). Empirically validated therapies: A project of the division of clinical psychology, american psychological association, task force on psychological interventions. *Clinical Psychologist, 49*(2), 5–15.

Crits-Christoph, P., Frank, E., Chambless, D. L., Brody, C., & Karp, J. F. (1995). Training in empirically-validated treatments: What are clinical psychology students learning? *Professional Psychology: Research and Practice, 26,* 514–522.

Fishman, D. B. (1999). *The case for pragmatic psychology.* New York: New York University Press.

Frese, F. J., Stanley, J., Kress, K., & Vogel-Scibilia, S. (2001). Integrating evidence-based practices and the recovery model. *Psychiatric Services, 52*(11), 1462–1468.

Gatz, M., Fiske, A., Fox, L. S., Kaskie, B., Kasl-Godley, J. E., et al. (1998). Empirically validated psychological treatments for older adults. *Journal of Mental Health and Aging, 41,* 9–46.

Goisman, R. M., Warshaw, M. G., & Keller, M. B. (1999). Psychosocial treatment prescriptions for generalized anxiety disorder, panic disorder, and social phobia, 1991–1996. *American Journal of Psychiatry, 156,* 1819–1821.

Henry, W. P. (1998). Science, politics, and the politics of science: The use and misuse of empirically validated treatments. *Psychotherapy Research, 8,* 126–140.

Hoagwood, K., Hibbs, E., Brent, D., & Jensen, P. (1995). Introduction to the special section: Efficacy and effectiveness in studies of child and adolescent psychotherapy. *Journal of Consulting and Clinical Psychology, 63,* 683–687.

Horvarth, A. O., & Symonds, D. B. (1991). Relationship between working alliance and outcome in psychotherapy: A meta-analysis. *Journal of Counseling Psychology, 38,* 139–149.

Hunsley, J., Dobson, K. S., Johnston, C., & Mikail, S. F. (1999). Empirically supported treatments in psychology: Implications for Canadian professional psychology. *Canadian Psychologist, 40,* 289–302.

Kazdin, A. E. (2003). *Research design in clinical psychology* (4th ed.). Needham Heights, MA: Allyn & Bacon.

Kendall, P. C., & Chambless, D. L. (Eds.). (1998). Empirically supported psychological therapies [Special issue]. *Journal of Consulting and Clinical Psychology, 66*(3), 167.

Kovacs, A. (1995). We have met the enemy and he is us! *Independent Practitioner, 15*(3), 135–137.

Lambert, M. J. (1998). Manual-based treatment and clinical practice: Hangman of life or promising development? *Clinical Psychology: Science and Practice, 5,* 391–395.

Lambert, M. J., & Barley, D. E. (2001). Research summary on the therapeutic relationship and psychotherapy outcome. *Psychotherapy: Theory, Research, Practice and Training, 38,* 357–361.

Levant, R. F. (2004). The empirically-validated treatments movement: A practitioner/educator perspective. *Clinical Psychology: Science and Practice,* 219–224.

Lipsey, M. W., & Wilson, D. B. (1993). The efficacy of psychological, educational, and behavioral treatment: Confirmation from meta-analyses. *American Psychologist, 48,* 1181–1209.

McLean, P. D., Woody, S., Taylor, S., & Koch, W. J. (1998). Comorbid panic disorder and major depression: implications for cognitive-behavioral therapy. *Journal of Consulting and Clinical Psychology, 66*(2), 240–247.

Miklowitz, D. J., & Clarkin, J. F. (1999). Balancing internal and external validity. *Prevention and Treatment, 2,* article 0020004c. Available from http://jurnals.apa.org/prevention/volume2/pre002004c.html.

Moras, K. (1998). Internal and external validity of intervention studies. In A. S. Bellack & M. Hersen (Eds.), *Comprehensive clinical psychology* (pp. 201–224). Oxford, England: Elsevier.

Nathan, P. E., & Gorman, J. M. (Eds.). (1998). *A guide to treatments that work.* New York: Oxford University Press.

Nathan, P. E., & Gorman, J. M. (Eds.). (2002). *A guide to treatments that work* (Vol. II). New York: Oxford University Press.

Norcross, J. C. (2001). Purposes, processes, and products of the task force on empirically supported therapy relationships. *Psychotherapy: Theory, Research, Practice and Training, 38,* 345–356.

Persons, J. B., Bostrom, A., & Bertagnolli, A. (1999). Results of randomized controlled trials of cognitive therapy for depression generalize to private practice. *Cognitive Therapy and Research, 23,* 535–548.

Plante, T. G., Andersen, E. N., & Boccaccini, M. T. (1999). Empirically supported treatments and related contemporary changes in psychotherapy practice: What do clinical ABPPs think. *Clinical Psychologist, 52,* 23–31.

Roth, A. D., & Fonagy, P. (1996). *What works for whom? A critical review of psychotherapy research.* New York: Guilford Press.

Sackett, D. L., Richardson, W. S., Rosenberg, W. M. C., & Haynes, R. B. (1997). *Evidence-based medicine.* New York: Churchill Livingstone.

Sanderson, W. C., Hiatt, D., & Schwartz, J. (2001). *Psychological treatment of panic disorder by managed care providers.* Manuscript submitted for publication.

Sanderson, W. C., Raue, P. J., & Wetzler, S. (1998). The generalizability of cognitive behavior therapy for panic disorder. *Journal of Cognitive Psychotherapy, 12,* 323–330.

Sanderson, W. C., & Woody, S. R. (1995). Manuals for empirically validated treatments: A project of the task force on psychological interventions. *Clinical Psychologist, 48*(4), 7–11.

Seligman, M. E. P. (1995). The effectiveness of psychotherapy: The consumer reports study. *American Psychologist, 50,* 965–974.

Seligman, M. E. P., & Levant, R. (1998). Managed care policies rely on inadequate science. *Professional Psychology: Research and Practice, 29,* 211–212.

Shadish, W. R., Matt, G. E., Navarro, A. M., & Phillips, G. (2000). The effects of psychological therapies under clinically representative conditions: A meta-analysis. *Psychological Bulletin, 126,* 512–529.

Shapiro, D. A., & Shapiro, D. (1982). Meta-analysis of comparative therapy outcome studies: A replication and refinement. *Psychological Bulletin, 92,* 581–604.

Silverman, W. H. (1996). Cookbooks, manuals, and paint-by-numbers: Psychotherapy in the 90's. *Psychotherapy, 33,* 207–215.

Spirito, A. (Ed.). (1999). Empirically supported treatments in pediatric psychology [Special issue]. *Journal of Pediatric Psychology, 24,* 87–174.

Stevens, S. E., Hynan, M. T., & Allen, M. (2000). A meta-analysis of common factor and specific treatment effects across the outcome domains of the phase model of psychotherapy. *Clinical Psychology: Science & Practice, 7*(3), 273–290.

Task Force on Promotion and Dissemination of Psychological Procedures. (1995). Training in and dissemination of empirically-validated psychological treatments. *Clinical Psychologist, 48,* 3–23.

Taylor, C. B., King, R., & Margraf, J. (1989). Use of medication and in vivo exposure in volunteers for panic disorder research. *American Journal of Psychiatry, 146,* 1423–1426.

Tsao, J. C., Lewin, M. R., & Craske, M. G. (1998). The effects of cognitive-behavior therapy for panic disorder on comorbid conditions. *Journal of Anxiety Disorders, 12*(4), 357–371.

Wade, W. A., Treat, T. A., & Stuart, G. L. (1998). Transporting an empirically supported treatment for panic disorder to a service clinic setting: A benchmarking strategy. *Journal of Consulting and Clinical Psychology, 66,* 231–239.

Weissman, M. M., & Sanderson, W. C. (2002). Problems and promises in modern psychotherapy: The need for increased training in evidence based treatments. In B. Hamburg (Ed.), *Modern psychiatry: Challenges in educating health professionals to meet new needs* (pp. 132–160). New York: Josiah Macy Foundation.

Weisz, J. R., Weiss, B., Han, S. S., Granger, D. A., & Morton, T. (1995). Effects of psychotherapy with children and adolescents revisited: A meta-analysis of treatment outcome studies. *Psychological Bulletin, 117,* 450–468.

Westen, D., & Morrison, K. (2001). A multidimensional meta-analysis of treatments for depression, panic, and generalized anxiety disorder: An empirical examination of the status of empirically supported therapies. *Journal of Consulting and Clinical Psychology, 60,* 875–899.

Wilson, G. T. (1998). Manual-based treatment and clinical practice. *Clinical Psychology: Science and Practice, 5,* 363–375.

Wilson, J. J., & Gil, K. M. (1996). The efficacy of psychological and pharmacological interventions for the treatment of chronic disease-related and non-disease-related pain. *Clinical Psychology Review, 16,* 573–597.

Wolpe, J. (1958). *Psychotherapy by reciprocal inhibition.* Stanford, CA: Stanford University Press.

Woody, S. R., & Sanderson, W. C. (1998). Manuals for empirically supported treatments: 1998 update. *Clinical Psychologist, 51*(1), 17–21.

CHAPTER 11

Controversies and Caveats

Chris E. Stout

There is an ever-growing contemporary interest in evidence-based practice (or its variants—evidence-based medicine, evidence-based programs, evidence-based procedure[s], evidence-based treatment[s], and so forth—while all indeed do represent different things, for brevity's sake, we shall simply use the initials EBP. It is probably good that there is such interest and momentum developing.

Like with all things that become popular, there are the dual risks of faddism and of becoming the latest in a series of the "next big thing" or the "procedure du jour." When either of these two things occur, what was initially considered as innovative and promising, quickly devolves into the wastebin of the corny and obsolete (think Sony Betamax or reengineering). It seems to take very little to turn what seems relevant and promising today into the snake oil of tomorrow.

Arguably, EBP has its roots in the area of outcomes management, which was spawned from experimental efficacy research and quasi-experimental effectiveness studies. Eysenck's classic (but flawed) study unsatisfyingly identified the Law of Thirds: One-third of patients got better in treatment, one-third got worse, and one-third didn't appreciably change. By 1986, the Joint Commission on Accreditation of Healthcare Organizations (JCAHO) had gotten into the act, noting that soon it would be expecting hospitals to be able to demonstrate that they were evaluating their patients' outcomes. This is now known as the ORYX initiative.

It is not this author's intent to dissuade the use of EBPs or even practice guidelines—quite the contrary, in general this author has been a strong advocate (if not evangelist) for their rational use—however, readers need to be fully informed as to some issues to consider before the wholesale adoption of any such practice to avoid later disillusionment—or worse.

WHAT'S THE PROBLEM?

Why wouldn't a clinician use an EBP in his or her clinical work? It seems like an obvious approach, so why is there any controversy with using EBPs? This author (Stout, 2001b, p. 8) investigated this question and found such inhibitions have been seen to result from four factors: (1) lack of clinician support; (2) difficulties in converting clinical guidelines into actionable performance measures; (3) poor use of available technologies to gauge the gaps in performance; and (4) inadequate integration of findings into daily operations. This matter and potential responses are discussed later in this chapter.

QUESTION OF IMPACT

Princeton healthcare economist Uwe Reinhard noted in the January 9, 2002 issue of the journal of the American Medical Association (*Medical News Perspective*), concepts from a recent keynote he delivered entitled "What do we mean by quality?" Reinhard noted that if we consider what it is providers of care do is analogous to a production process in the manufacturing of health, then research demonstrates that what healthcare "produces" accounts for only about 10% of health or health outcomes. Seems that it is those "fuzzy" to clinically manage aspects of human existence, like stress levels, environmental exposure, and a patient's general level of healthy habits (or lack thereof), interact complexly with the even harder to alter genetic makeup and this is what is responsible for determining a patient's health or illness.

At one level, this is good (but not new) news for those specializing in health and medical psychology or public health, as well as for those having good genes and habits. But another consideration is the likely obvious question, "If 90% of how healthy someone is has nothing to do with healthcare services (not including the wise and seldom paid for preventative services), then why do we spend so much time, effort, and research on treatments—even EBPs?"

Reinhard then suggested that it is "process that should be paid for, not outcomes!" Which may remind one of the old joke of the surgeon saying that the operation was a success, but the patient died. In behavioral healthcare, this is even murkier. Imagine the following interchange in the future on reconciling such issues vis-a-vis Evidence-Based Practice projects—"Doctor, you sure do provide XYZ-school of psychotherapy well, but for goodness sake, your patients sure don't seem to get any better."

LIABILITY CONCERNS AND "ONE CLINICIAN'S EVIDENCE-BASE IS ANOTHER'S HOG WASH"

Managed care organizations (MCOs) have shown an interest in the adoption of EBPs in conducting case management functions. The issues for concerned clinicians is the fear that the MCO will become prescriptive in a limiting way and tell the clinician that if the patient has "X" diagnosis (e.g., major depression), then the clinician must provide "Y" procedure (e.g., Cognitive-Behavioral Therapy). But what is to be done if the clinician is not a cognitive-behavioral therapist? More contentious "clinical scientists have gone so far as to call for the American Psychological Association and other professional organizations 'to impose stiff sanctions, including expulsion if necessary' (Lohr, Fowler, & Lilienfeld, 2002, p. 8) against practitioners who do not practice empirically-validated assessments and treatments" (Levant, 2004).

Similarly, there are risk management and liability concerns that if someone has a frivolous malpractice suit filled and the clinician (exercising purely good clinical judgment in the choice of treatment modality used, let's say) did not use an EBP, that such would not bode well for the defendant-clinician's defense in the trial proceedings. Of course, this does not mean that the clinician should shun EBPs for this fear—we need to be careful to avoid throwing out the baby with the bathwater. But we need to also be on the lookout for biases and quality differences in what you may choose as an EBP to adopt into your clinical practice.

How do you do so? There are a variety of tools that can help. This author particularly finds the Appraisal of Guidelines for Research and Evaluation (AGREE) Instrument at www.agreecollaboration.org and Critical Appraisal Skills Programme (CASP) "making sense of evidence about clinical effectiveness" at www.phru.org.uk/~casp /index.htm to be helpful resources.

There are additional concerns (that will only be touched on briefly) as to what satisfies the criteria for being evidence-based or empirically supported. Levant (2004) notes that the American Psychological Association's "Task Force came up with lists of 'Well-Established Treatments' and 'Probably Efficacious Treatments.' Not surprisingly, the lists themselves emphasized short-term behavioral and cognitive-behavioral approaches, which lend themselves to manualization; longer term, more complex approaches (e.g., psychodynamic, systemic, feminist, and narrative) were not well represented."

Levant goes on to quote Koocher's (personal communication, July 20, 2003) perspective that "'empirical' is in the eye of the beholder, and sadly many beholders have very narrow lens slits. That is to say, qualitative research [and] case studies . . . have long been a valuable part of the empirical foundation for psychotherapy, but are demeaned or ignored by many for whom 'empirical validation' equates to 'randomized clinical trial' [RCT]. In addition, a randomized clinical trial demands a treatment manual to assure fidelity and integrity of the intervention; however, the real world of patient care demands that the therapist (outside of the research arena) constantly modify approaches to meet the idiopathic needs of the client . . . Slavish attention to 'the manual' assures empathic failure and poor outcome for many patients."

This author co-chaired a subcommittee that is charged with developing the design of the blueprint for the construction of an EBP Clearinghouse of Information on EBPs and Promising Practices for the state of Illinois. This author found in doing the research, it became abundantly obvious that *quality varies*. There are no Good Housekeeping Seals of Approval on a myriad of web sites that exist touting some procedures as being evidence based. And to make matters worse, the *Journal of the American Medical Association* noted that the vast majority of authors of some medication clinical guidelines have some tie to the pharmaceutical industry, Thus, posing potentially awkward biases or conflicts of interest.

In this author's work for the state, the group developed a set of "Guidelines for the Evaluation of Guidelines," based on an amalgam of what is used by the federal-level National Guideline Clearinghouse (NGC) combined with the criteria for Evaluating Treatment Guidelines as adapted from the Template Implementation Work Group of the Board of Professional Affairs, Board of Scientific Affairs, and Committee for the Advancement of Professional Psychology—approved by the American Psychological Association's Council of Representatives, August 2000.

This then provided a tool to weigh an EBP, a promising practice, or a treatment guideline with considerations including clinical utility (i.e., the ability of clinicians to use, and of consumers to accept, the treatment/program/practice under consideration, the range of applicability of that treatment/program/practice, and its cost). This dimension reflects the extent to which the intervention will be effective in the practice setting where it is to be applied, regardless of the efficacy that may have been demonstrated in the clinical research setting. We also considered generalizability—the ability of an EBP to work regardless of the context of application. This would take into consideration characteristics of the consumers, clinicians, and settings along with the interactions among these factors.

Feasibility of an EBP addresses such factors as the applicability of the EBP to real-world settings and the potential consumers, their ability and willingness to comply with the requirements of the EBP, the ease of dissemination of the EBP, and the ease of administration of the EBP. The costs associated with an EBP should also be considered. This includes such things as expense to the consumer, expense to the clinician, the cost of any technology or equipment involved in delivering the EBP and measuring its impact, and the cost of (re)training the clinician as well as the costs of withholding or delaying treatment (e.g., consumer's loss of time from work and/or disability costs).

We also addressed issues of scientific standards, including safety, utility across different diverse populations, ongoing outcome evaluation, fidelity to the EBP, level of credible evidence, criteria with which to judge both supportive and nonsupportive/inconclusive literatures, and about 20 other criterion and categories. Legitimate EBPs, their thoughtful evaluation for applicability to our work, and appropriate practice adoption/incorporation methods can do much to enhance clinical efficacy for our clients. But we must be responsibly cautious in our evaluations and use for them to work.

TRAINING ISSUES AND COST

Another area of concern regarding EBPs is that of training. On the one hand, busy clinicians in private practice or working in agencies frequently find it difficult to "afford" time off from their work to take continuing education workshops (such as leaning /implementing EBPs into clinical work). Client sessions cancelled in order to attend such seminars result in lost productivity and billable hours—which translate into real dollars. Also, such educational activities are not typically free, along with additional costs of travel and possible overnight accommodations. And this presupposes that appropriate workshops would be regionally available in the first place. Such problems conspire to tip the scales in favor of *not* participating in such programs.

But quality improvement experts are quick to point out that not providing healthcare services that are sound is wasteful of time and money, as well as putting clients at risk. Ganju (2003, p. 128) notes "within the mental health system, many EBPs have been shown to be very effective in reducing costly hospitalizations. In mental health systems, however, the cost of ineffective care is borne by other social systems, such as the criminal justice, juvenile justice, or welfare systems. The point is that *not* implementing EBPs may be ultimately a more costly proposition than investing in their implementation" [emphasis in original].

On the other hand, there is a growing call for the initial integration of evidence-based treatment philosophies in graduate training right from the start. Cynthia Belar, executive director for education at the American Psychological Association notes that

". . . the 21st century health-care system requires that (health-service psychologists) have competencies in informatics, interdisciplinary collaboration, quality improvement methods, and evidence-based practice" (2003, p. 57). In some cases there is a challenge of where such courses would fit into already demanding course loads. Some professions' curriculum architects consider EBPs are already residing within their programs. For example, graduate clinical psychology training may actually have a bit of an advantage in that the American Psychological Association already requires that accredited programs "should enable their students to understand the value of science for the practice of psychology and the value of practice for the science of psychology (and that) recognizing that the value of science . . . requires attention to the empirical basis for all methods involved in psychological practice" (Belar, 2003, p. 57).

It would seem that a wise hybrid may include both an integration of the current level of knowledge as to empirically supported methods of treating a particular condition at that point in time (as knowledge and evidence will likely grow, and possibly vary over time), along with the tools of knowing how to evaluate the quality of future developments as they become known in one's professional practice (i.e., assessing quality of the literature and findings, knowing how to critically separate the "wheat from the chaff" as it were). E. O. Wilson's conceptualization of the concept of *consilience* may be a helpful model in consideration of integrating empirically based clinical findings with client-expressed needs/wants, sociocultural context, and so forth.

GENERALIZABILITY OF EVIDENCE

Levant (2004) notes that "empirically-validated treatments on these lists have typically been studied using homogeneous samples of white, middle class clients, and therefore have not often been shown to be efficacious with ethnic minority clients. So . . . suppose we had lists of empirically validated manualized treatments for all *DSM* Axis I diagnoses (which we are actually a long ways away from). We would then have treatments for only 20% of the white, middle class, patients who come to our doors, namely those who meet the diagnostic criteria used in studies that validated these treatments. . . . In order to limit services to only these 20% of the white, middle class, patients who come to us, the average practitioner would have to spend many, many hours, perhaps years, in training to learn these manualized treatments. And if we restricted ourselves to use only these manualized treatments, we would be limiting our role to that of a technician. And, in the end, these treatments would only account for 15% of the variance in therapy outcomes in these patients." Keep in mind that Levant refers to manualized treatments, not all EBPs, per se.

APPROACH "CLASHES" AND THE ROLE OF THE CLIENT

There has been a concern with some schools of clinical procedure that EBPs may exclude their approach. Similarly, there is a parallel concern that a particular approach may not lend itself to examination via the scientific method. In a recent point/counterpoint series of articles in *Clinical Psychology: Science and Practice* (Joiner, Sheldon, Williams, & Pettit, 2003; Schneider, 2003; Sheldon, Joiner, Pettit, & Williams, 2003), such issues were discussed with respect to the aspects of a client's self-determination. Sheldon and his colleagues (2003, p. 318) note "What matters is what *works,* and what works can only be discovered by careful quantitative measurement and by controlled clinical trials. Unfortunately, humanistically oriented clinicians have been reluctant to put their approach to either of these two tests." [emphasis in the original]

This is quite similar to the position that Morrison (Jackim, 2003, p. 21) proffers, "Research comes first . . . there was a time when we didn't know what worked and what didn't and there was no choice other than the clinician's preference. But now we have data that indicate that some treatments are effective and others are not." However, supporters of a recovery approach, feel that "the (mental health) system should be driven by patient preference based on the practitioner's presentation of the evidence, or their own analysis of the evidence, then what drives the decision is what the patient is comfortable doing."

Ganju (2003) notes there maybe a disconnect between what scientists and practitioners consider good outcomes what consumers consider a good outcome in relation to recovery. Per se, recovery has not been the focal point of the development of empirical studies. "However, it could be argued that the outcomes that were used—employment, reduced hospitalization. Independence in community settings, improved quality of life—are indicators of recovery and consistent with a person moving positively over time on a recovery axis" (Ganju, p. 129).

This author was recently at a conference where Scott Miller, PhD, co-founder of the Institute for the Study of Therapeutic Change, and co-author on an investigation of therapeutic effectiveness (Duncan & Miller, 2000), warned of the risk of institutionalizing clinical mythologies. For example, he noted that in a review of 40 years of increasingly sophisticated research, there is little empirical support for:

- The superiority of psychopharmacological treatment for emotional complaints (what he calls the "myth of the magic pill")
- The utility of psychiatric diagnosis in either selecting the course of treatment or predicting the outcome of treatment (the "myth of diagnostic specificity")
- The superiority of any therapeutic approach over any other (the "myth of the silver bullet cure")

To quote from Miller and his colleague Barry Duncan (2000), "Therapists can assign diagnoses, complete treatment plans, use the latest treatment methodologies, and dispense psychoactive drugs from now until doomsday and the overall effectiveness and efficiency of therapy will not improve in the least. These factors are simply not critical to the outcome of therapy. Importantly, this does not mean that therapy does not work" (pp. 8–9). This then begs the question: Where does the point of change seem to lie? Their research indicated the following percentages contributing to positive outcome, regardless of therapist orientation or professional discipline:

- 15% model and technique
- 15% hope and expectancy

- 30% Relationship factors
- 40% Client factors

Indeed, as Ganju (2003, p. 128) notes, many "stakeholders—including consumers, family members, providers, and advocates—are concerned . . . that EBPs will displace—or contaminate—services that, from the stakeholders' perspective, produce the outcome they desire, even though the services may not have the strong evidentiary foundation that EBPs, by definition, have."

Anthony offers an integrative approach of ". . . patient preference, your clinical judgement, and the evidence base" (Jackim, 2003, p. 21). Similarly, Joiner et al. (2003, p. 318) suggest that the important aspects clinical approaches such a humanistic, lie ". . . primarily in the 'how' of therapy, not in the 'what' of therapy. . . . (they) argue that the next 'tier' (of clinical evolution and advancement) involves the marriage of such proven techniques with the humanistically informed motivational prescriptions of self-determination theory."

LIMITATIONS TO INNOVATION AND EVIDENCE VERSUS OUTCOMES

Some fear that the use of EBPs will be a limiting factor to future treatment innovation and clinical advancement. If state payor systems, third-party insurers, or fourth-party managed care organizations are exclusively paying for evidence-based treatment procedures, then where will the new models and methods come from? Solely relying on academic settings for such draws concerns about applicability in the proverbial in vivo, real world, and generalizability across treatment settings (public, private, in- or out-patient, etc.) and venues (urban poor, suburban wealthy, rural, etc.).

There is no easy answer to this concern. One perspective approaches the issue from the view that "it is bad policy and poor economics not to provide services that are known to work" (Ganju, 2003, p. 129). This is the philosophical approach that Illinois adopted. Yet another view is that of Morrison (personal communication, September 30, 2003), who believes that what should really be measured and evaluated is the treatment *outcome,* rather than the *process.* That is, if a clinician is able to have a reasonably comparable, validated treatment outcome with the majority of patients treated, to that of a representative cohort standard, then that is enough. But if the clinician is not doing so well, then it may be helpful to learn of more effective methods. Of course, the methods may involve treatment techniques or other considerations that may have contributory clinical impact (e.g., rapport, client-perceived competence, session management, boundary issues, empathic expression), therefore, a careful examination as to causal factors would need to first be conducted.

FUTURE DIRECTIONS

Physicist Niles Bohr once said "prediction is difficult, especially about the future." So, too, does this author find difficulty in making wise predictions as to the next stages of EBPs. While EBPs are not a panacea, they are a help. At the very least, EBPs help the typically fuzzy-behavioral healthcare field become a bit sharper.

We will always be faced with the inevitable burden of the time lags between what we may practice and developing a sufficient sampling of informational inputs to even begin making sketchy proclamations as to benefit, iatrogenesis, or benign wastes of time in the clinical milieu. Likewise, the opposite problem of in vitro clinical developments gaining widespread enough validatable adoption in various treatment settings to presume generalizability and utility with what kind of population co-varied on what clinical, demographic, sociocultural variables, and biological axes will similarly always be a plague to efficacy research.

Philosophically, we must maintain an openness to new techniques and to surprises. Also, what is developed sometimes needs to become familiar and then its use may become more adaptive to our needs, not the other way around. We can be as creative in the eventual use of something as was the inventor who originated it. However, we also have a responsibility to offer some forethought or foresight as to potential uses or misuses of the new while balancing the good with the limitations.

In today's era of postmodern knowledge management, clinical leaders must be accountable in knowing of the new and evolving capacities offered by advancements in various fields. Technology, while not a magic bullet, may be a definite help in bringing EBP implementation without a Herculean effort for clinicians. Blindly adding computers to solve problems or improve systems is pure fantasy. Technological enhancement of bad systems usually makes them worse (but faster!). There is a paradox of having financially strapped systems, hospitals, practices, and agencies maximize the use of EBPs or clinical outcomes while not alienating the clinician or the client, and do so cost-effectively.

Everyone from the fans of complex science to Zen Buddhists understands the nonlinear causal aspects and interconnectedness of things that may initially seem unrelated. Yet when we think of all the interactive aspects of why behavioral illness may manifest—from genetics to experience to culture to stress to social contacts and so on—we can begin to appreciate the inherent difficulty associated with providing optimal care when needed. With the progression of integrated databases and Electronic Medical Records (EMRs), the proliferation of PDA/notebook/tablet computer input devices along with the ubiquity of Web access, and the growing demand for cost-effective and high-quality services for all, EBP "initiatives" may serve to weave together differential diagnostics and therapeutics with the latest in evidence-based therapies in a way that is robust, individualized, and never obsolete.

Undoubtedly, there will be a development and deployment of various models and methods of EBPs as time passes. And it is expected that EBPs will be always adapting as the science matures, as new treatments come online, and as we simply learn more.

This author developed a model known as "ClinicA" (adapted from Stout, 2001a). It is a concept based on a genetic algorithm used for enhancing clinical decision making. For example, an integrated artificial neural network would make probabilistic assumptions about the provider, the client (demographics and history), the venue of care (clinic, hospital, CMHC, etc.), service availability (based on locality or insurance benefit), assessment data (such as diagnosis and symptom presentation), and the literature relevant to the client's needs in order to trigger the need and/or type of services.

The EBP database would be constantly updated as new knowledge becomes available. Such a database could be queried by a clinical decision-making algorithm that integrates recent client assessment(s) and historic information along with client demographics. (The assessment/history/demographic data would serve as an aid in triage and differential diagnostics as well as establish baseline measures of psychopathology for subsequent evaluation of treatment efficacy and system efficiency.)

The integrated database would algorithmically evaluate available services to best fit the needs of the client. Data inputs could be provided via client self-administered surveys on paper (scanned into the integrated database upon the first office visit), or online via a secure web site, or on a PDA/tablet handheld device in the waiting room, or over the telephone with keypad responses (such as a technology offered by Voxvia) prior to the first visit.

ClinicA is based on a "genetic" algorithm used for clinical decision making. Genetic algorithms are the "DNA" that power artificial intelligence software programs. They enable a complex set of decision rules to be applied to a variety of situations, and they "learn" from the results and incorporate such learning in subsequent responses. These could be built on the EBP literature base. This would develop an artificial neural network (ANN)—a diverse group of nonlinear statistical tools whose strengths lie in their ability to process many variables in a parallel fashion. These tools recognize patterns in complex systems and perform better than more conventional statistical tools, especially when dealing with many interdependent variables.

This network would make probabilistic assumptions about the clinician's expertise, the client's needs, the facility/practice/clinic resources, the clinical diagnosis, the relevant treatment literature, the client's supports and strengths, and symptom presentation variables and suggest the need for and type of (and perhaps level, frequency, or aggressiveness of) active case management and treatment.

The process of training the ANN requires presenting information to the input layer and associating the pattern of inputs with a known output—that is, the EBP literature. The ANN "learns" by adjusting the weight matrix of the intermediate and output layers so that a given input pattern will result in the correct output result. The process of doing this is called "supervised learning" in the Backward Propagating Neural Network paradigm used here. Minor changes in input data can produce substantial changes in output, sometimes called "discontinuities," but this effect can be minimized by increasing the number of neurodes in the intermediate layer and by a variety of techniques using "simulated annealing" and genetic algorithms.

Thanks to faster, more widely available personal computers and the need for parallel processing methods to analyze complex problems, ANNs are finally gaining momentum in many fields of research, including healthcare. With proper precautions, for example, ANN sensitivity to input changes can give early warnings of changing patterns of care in healthcare systems.

Clients who need more, get more; those that don't, don't. The clinician would be provided with probabilistic treatment suggestions to inform the treatment planning and processes. Decision support that is fast, dispassionate, and more likely to be accurate than humans would mean fewer and briefer payor reviews in managed care settings, and more efficient clinician activity in all settings. Costs would be decreased, provider-payor animosities diminished, treatment quality improved, and clinical liability risk reduced.

For ClinicA, the technology is the easy part; such a system could literally be built tomorrow. The challenge lies in orchestrating the leadership to coordinate stakeholders into a shared vision. Remember, EBP has its critics. Technology will likely never be a limiting factor in our becoming better clinicians or scientists in providing better care; the greater problem lies in overcoming parochial, linear models and the resulting, self-imposed boundaries to our imaginations.

An Example

ClinicA could be Web-based and, thus, made available on anyone's desktop—at the clinic, office, or hospital. Let's say that a newly minted social worker, Joe Newbie, moves to Peoria (where he knows absolutely nothing about the available services) to work in a CMHC. Being new to the field, he is also a bit green when it comes to psychodiagnostics and treatment planning.

Ten minutes prior to seeing his first client, he logs into ClinicA, punches in his password and the client's ID, and is able to pull up Carl Client's results from the intake screening survey (given to Carl by the receptionist who then scanned the form into the database for scoring and logging).

Joe then clicks on the screen to "prompt decision making" and is provided with percentage-based recommendations resulting from Carl's elevated scores on depression and anxiety, currently being unemployed, needing child care, and so forth. All this information is synchronized with what is available for him in the local area.

Also, suggestions for a mediation consultation and individual cognitive-behavioral therapy (along with focally special treatment plan recommendations) and resources for employment opportunities that fit Carl's educational and interest backgrounds and that offer on-site day care are provided. When Joe meets with Carl, he is very well prepared, and they get to work in establishing a therapeutic relationship and mutually agreed-upon treatment plan.

This concept is limited by a variety of currently impractical aspects—absent or limited coordination of data input, lack of being able to have data immediately available in order to self-correct and act upon, and so on. An even more difficult shift for some may be away from the opinion that EBP is intrusive and disempowering for the clinician. But the technology will not be the challenge, as artificially intelligent neural networks are self-educating and can offer, test, and recalibrate their own judgments.

CONCLUSION

It is obvious that the wholesale adoption of EBPs without thoughtful and critical prior examination for goodness-of-fit would be counterproductive. But ignoring their value when appropriately utilized is an invitation to mediocrity, or worse. Technology offers both hope and tools for broadening the application, reach, and potential of EBP techniques.

It is the intention of this author, and this book, to help readers become better informed as to their critical examination of what may be helpful tools in their work. It is always good advice to keep your discerning eyes (and mind) wide open.

REFERENCES

Belar, C. (2003). Training for evidence-based practice. *Monitor on Psychology, 57.*

Duncan, B. L., & Miller, S. D. (2000). *The heroic client.* San Francisco: Jossey-Bass.

Ganju, V. (2003). Implementation of evidence-based practices in state mental health systems: Implications for research and effectiveness studies. *Schizophrenia Bulletin, 29*(1), 125–131.

Jackim, L. W. (2003, October). Is all the evidence in? *Behavioral Healthcare Tomorrow,* 21–26.

Joiner, T. E., Sheldon, K. M., Williams, G., & Pettit, J. (2003). The integration of self-determination principles and scientifically informed treatments is the next tier. *Clinical Psychology: Science and Practice, 10,* 318–319.

Levant, R. (2004). The empirically-validated treatments movement: A practitioner/educator perspective. *Clinical Psychology: Science and Practice, 11,* 219–224.

Lohr, J. M., Fowler, K. A., & Lilienfeld, S. O. (2002). The dissemination and promotion of pseudoscience in clinical psychology: The challenge to legitimate clinical science. *Clinical Psychologist, 55,* 4–10.

Schneider, K. J. (2003). A welcome step: Let's climb to the next tier. *Clinical Psychology: Science and Practice, 10,* 316–317.

Sheldon, K. M., Joiner, T. E., Pettit, J., & Williams, G. (2003). Reconciling humanistic ideals and scientific clinical practice. *Clinical Psychology: Science and Practice, 10,* 302–315.

Stout, C. E. (2001a, October). Connecting the dots: Moving to evidence based practice. *Behavioral Healthcare Tomorrow,* 9–12.

Stout, C. E. (2001b, February). *Evidence-based guidelines have a role if addressed realistically.* Behavioral Health Accreditation and Accountability, 8.

CHAPTER 12

Evaluating Readiness to Implement Evidence-Based Practice

Randy A. Hayes

The decision to use evidence-based practices is a long-term commitment by an agency/practice. It is a decision that requires the commitment of agency/practice resources: the staff to research the appropriate evidence-based practices for the agency/practice; the staff to design or modify those practices to fit the needs of the agency/practice; the staff to design and implement the use of those practices within the agency/practice; the staff to train the rest of the staff to use those practices; the staff to collect, aggregate, and report the outcomes of those practices selected; the staff to evaluate the results of the use of the practices to redesign or otherwise further enhance the use of the protocols; the staff to evaluate the direct costs of the use of the practices; and the staff (administrative or management) to evaluate the agency/practice's continued commitment to use the practices based both on the outcomes of their use and the costs to the agency/practice.

To help you fully understand the impact of the decision to use evidence-based practices in your agency/practice, the preceding paragraph is repeated, but with the word *time* after each occurrence of the word *staff:* The decision to use evidence-based practices is a decision that requires: staff time to research the appropriate evidence-based practices for the agency/practice; staff time to design or modify those practices to fit the needs of the agency/practice; staff time to design and implement the use of those practices within the agency/practice; staff time to train the staff to use those practices; staff time to collect, aggregate, and report the outcomes of those practices that have been selected; staff time to evaluate the results of the use of the practices to redesign or otherwise further enhance the use of the protocols; staff time to evaluate the direct costs of the use of the practices; and staff time (administrative or management) to evaluate the continued commitment to use the practices based both on the outcomes of their use and the costs to the agency/practice.

To drive home the impact to the agency/practice, the paragraph is again repeated, this time including the words *and cost* following the words *staff time:* The decision to use evidence-based practices is a decision that requires staff time and costs to research the appropriate evidence-based practices for the agency/practice; staff time and costs to design or modify those practices to fit the needs of the agency/practice; staff time and costs to design and implement the use of those practices within the agency/

practice; staff time and costs to train the staff to use those practices; staff time and costs to collect, aggregate, and report the outcomes of those practices selected; staff time and costs to evaluate the results of the use of the practices to redesign or otherwise further enhance the use of the protocols; staff time and costs to evaluate the direct costs of the use of the practices; and staff time (administrative or management) and costs to evaluate the continued commitment to use the practices based both on the outcomes of their use and the costs to the agency/practice.

The decision to use evidence-based practices is a commitment of more than just staff and staff time. It is a commitment of costs. It is a commitment of both the direct costs associated with actually providing the evidence-based service and a commitment to all of the indirect costs associated with the planning and preparing for the service provision, in addition to the costs associated with analyzing both the effectiveness of the best practice use and analyzing the associated support costs.

THE FIRST STEP

The first step in evaluating the readiness of an agency/practice to begin to use evidence-based practices or best practice protocols is based in the preceding *cost-based* scenario. Is the agency/practice a cost-based entity? That is, is the agency/practice capable of costing-out operational expenses? In this case, *costing-out* does not mean, "Do leaders know if the agency/practice broke even at the end of the funding cycle?" In the current behavioral healthcare industry environment, knowing whether an agency/practice broke even at the end of a funding cycle is insufficient knowledge for continued operations.

Specifically, *costing-out* means: Do leaders know, or can they easily acquire, the total costs associated with the practice or with each of the programs associated with the agency? Do they know which programs are currently losing money for the agency/practice? If the leaders know this, can they easily tell where in the program the loss originates? Is it in direct care staff costs, support care costs, or operations-related costs? Does the loss relate to other human resource-associated staff costs, for example, insurance claims? Would the loss be corrected if the staff were more efficient in their treatment methodologies or more careful with their use of the resources provided to them? Would the program loss be contained if the staff were simply healthier and, thus, had fewer insurance claims? If the leaders do not know the answers to these questions, do they know how to find out the answers? Do leadership, or does anyone in the agency/practice, have the tools and analytical skills necessary to be able to answer these very basic business questions?

And why are these questions important or even a minor consideration in terms of applying evidence-based practices at the agency/practice? Can't the behavioral healthcare industry continue as we have for decades to do "good work" and "help needy people out?" Can't staff just continue to provide what we have assumed to be good practices? Can't administrators just wait for an administration change, either state or national or both, to give us more money so that we can get back to doing our jobs helping people?

Since this book has been chosen, you assuredly know that the answer to all of these questions is no. It is not just that managed care practices have forced behavioral healthcare to become more businesslike. It is not just that cuts in funding at both state and federal levels have caused behavioral healthcare practices to be more sensitive to costs.

It is not just that federal and state mandates have forced greater and greater levels of accountability on us as an industry, although all of these statements are true.

Treatment methods that work are by definition more cost-effective than treatment methods whose effectiveness is unknown. There may have been a time, in some golden age of behavioral healthcare treatment, when effectiveness was less important. However, in this age of reduced funding and tightened budgets, treatment that is known to work, that is known to help people have improved functioning, is of absolute importance. Simply put, the behavioral healthcare industry can no longer afford to use methods that do not work. To know which methods work, industry leadership must be committed to data-based decision making. Staff will continue to provide those treatment methodologies that are known by the evidence to help people improve. However, if agency/practice leadership is in a position that leaders and managers are unable to tell something as simple as how much individual programs cost to run, if leaders and managers do not have the skills (or do not have the desire) to figure this out, how will the leadership ever be able to tell within their agencies what methods help a system as complicated as the human psyche get better?

Thus, the road to applying evidence-based practices or protocols within a behavioral healthcare agency/practice must begin with an inventory of ourselves and our skills as administrators, therapists, case managers, support staff, financial staff, data and information specialists, and statistical process professionals.

EVALUATE THE LEADERSHIP

What type of leadership style exists within the agency/practice or organization? Is it a strictly top-down, no-questions-asked leadership? Is it a leadership that is shared among a trusted few with no other input? Is it a leadership shared among many qualified management staff? Is it a leadership that is shared among so many that it takes forever to get a decision made? Is it a leadership style with decisions sometimes shared and sometimes imposed with no prior warning? Does the leadership in the organization appear to be shared, with input requested and considered—considered, that is, for all except the really "important" decisions that have already been made?

Why does the leadership style make a difference in the decision to implement evidence-based practices? As implied in the introductory discussion of this chapter, the decision for using evidence-based practices requires a commitment to knowing—knowing whether treatments work or not, knowing whether treatments that work are cost-effective, knowing how closely the staff charged with applying the best practices techniques are actually following the treatment protocols. All of these elements need to be in place or need to be able to be in place for evidence-based practice to be effectively initiated or installed within an organization.

Does whatever leadership style is in effect in the organization include *the quest to know?* The quest to know is at the heart of evidence-based practice. The quest to know is also an underlying principle of databased decision making. When applied to leadership styles, the quest to know can be modified into a question: Are decisions within the leadership of the agency/practice based on data or on opinion? Thus, the question in terms of leadership styles for an agency/practice considering embarking on the use of evidence-based practices becomes: Is the style of leadership data driven or opinion driven?

If the agency/practice is data driven, you can further ask: How frequently is the data used in making decisions? Are data always used in making decisions? For example, are data used every time or almost every time data are available for decisions at hand? Or, are data sometimes used to make decisions? For example, data are used if convenient to retrieve, if someone happens to have some data, or if someone happens to think about needing some data for the question at hand. Or, are data used rarely? For example, members of the management staff infrequently think about getting the appropriate data for discussion of any question at hand. Or, are data used only when the data agree with the leader's opinion?

I have seen and experienced all of these data uses in consultations around the United States. Further, I have seen management teams go through these stages (in reverse order as printed) as management teams developed both the desire and the ability to use data to make decisions.

If the agency/practice or organization actually uses data to make decisions, you have to ask another very critical question about its use of data: How frequently are the data used correctly? Far too frequently, organizations that are initiating databased decision making lack the skills necessary to make appropriate decisions based on the data they have in front of them. Databased decision making requires the knowledge and ability to use several statistical analysis skills. Management staff need to be trained in these skills if they are going to be able to make adequate decisions about their data. This applies equally to decisions about the effectiveness of evidence-based practice protocols and to income or staff competency data.

For example, if an organization is going to link consumer satisfaction with pay increases for treatment staff, that organization needs to ensure that a statistically significant number of consumers are interviewed for each staff person. If an organization is going to consider the effectiveness of a treatment protocol, it will likewise have to have adequate outcome measures in place to determine if a statistically significant improvement occurred. If these events do not occur, the probability is very high that any improvement noted is strictly from random variation and not attributable either to the staff person (in terms of the consumer satisfaction survey) or the treatment protocol (in terms of using evidence-based practices).

Further, the theory of statistical process control tells the user that when staff intervene with changes to the system based on an analysis of the data concerning the system, unless the staff know if a system is statistically stable, the intervention may only make the system worse. Use of databased decision making without the knowledge or commitment to use appropriate statistical methodologies is ultimately just opinion-based decision making, dressed up to look like databased decision making. It may be more harmful, ultimately, to the organization, than opinion-based decision making in that the supposed data analysis may carry more weight than the simple opinion.

The Chief Executive Officer's Vision and Evidence-Based Practices

Jason Jennings (2002), in his research on productivity in effective corporations, emphasizes that over and over, it is the vision of the chief executive officer (CEO) that makes the difference in effective and efficient corporations. The CEO's vision concerning the use of evidence-based practices is crucial, especially in terms of the preceding discussions. Will there be sufficient resources to both fund the evidence-based practices and analyze both their effectiveness (Did they work?) and their efficiency (How much did they cost?)? Once we have this data, will we have the skills needed to do this analysis?

If the CEO's vision does not currently include databased decision making, the first step in preparing the agency/practice for initiating evidence-based practices must start there. Initiating evidence-based practices without management having this underpinning is fraught with frustration for both line staff and management. If and when the CEO (and, thus, the agency/practice) has a good understanding and practice of databased decision making, the use of evidence-based practices follows logically. The data, that is, the evidence, indicate the appropriate treatment practices to use.

The Board and Strategic Plan

Once the CEO makes the decision to use databased decision making, the journey toward evidence-based practice must be upward toward the organization's board of directors, thus, the next point of evaluation.

To what extent has the board of directors supported (or will support) the decision to use evidence-based practices? The leadership, guidance, and direction from the board will set the tone for the agency/practice.

One shining example of such board of director leadership comes from The Center for Behavioral Health, Bloomington, Indiana. This board made the decision in 1989 to "operate only those mental health treatments, services and program for which there exists evidence in the professional literature of their efficacy" (Morrison, 2001, slide 17). One of the results of this decision, besides the fact that a significant number of their consumers showed a great improvement in functioning with use of evidence-based practices, was that the organization received the first Joint Commission on the Accreditation of Healthcare Organizations' Ernest A. Codman award in the Behavioral Healthcare category for their pioneering implementation of evidence-based practices.

A second example of board of director leadership comes from my agency. The board of directors of Sinnissippi Centers, Inc., Dixon, Illinois, decided in 1999 to implement an evidence-based practice study on services for the mentally ill substance abuse (MISA) population. This decision was made despite the fact that there was no specific or extra funding for the pilot project for this study; however, the board of directors believed that the study was needed and necessary to improve services for this underserved group. One of the results of the board's decision to implement evidence-based practices was to be awarded an Ernest A. Codman award in Behavioral Healthcare for 2002 for successfully doing so.

EVALUATE THE STANCE

In the early days of community behavioral healthcare, there was a tendency for centers to arrange themselves into what could be thought of as *cooperatives.* Certainly, they were not cooperatives in a formal sense of the word. A cooperative is formally defined as an "enterprise or organization owned by and operated for the benefit of those using its services" (*Webster's Ninth New Collegiate Dictionary,* 1991, p. 288).

The behavioral healthcare cooperatives of the early 1970s were not owned by the clients who were using the services, which would have been a true meaning of the term *cooperative*. As far as I am aware, there have never been any true behavioral healthcare cooperatives, that is, agencies owned and run by those consumers who use the treatment services of such an agency/practice. It has, in fact, taken the past three decades, since the inception of the community mental health movement, for a consumer movement to develop to the point that there is now some growing expectation that there should be consumers on the boards of those community agencies that exist.

No, the early "community mental health centers," as they were called, were not owned by the consumers who used the service, nor were they owned by the behavioral health professionals or practitioners who worked in these centers. In these newly created community agencies with their grant-in-aid funding, there were few requirements in terms of documentation of the services provided by the community mental health professionals. Perhaps due to this very aspect of the community mental health grants, that is, the scarcity of requirements, practitioners were able to act and eventually develop operational habits as though they were owners of the institutions. Documentation requirements were minimal. Treatment practices were based on whatever theory or theories the practitioner had learned in graduate or medical school. Research into the effectiveness of the new psychoactive medications was in its earliest stages. Evidence-based research of the effectiveness of various therapy techniques was also in its infancy.

The process of initiating such centers across the United States started via the Community Mental Health Block Grants in the mid-1970s. The centers were given monies and yearly series of grant monies to fund the provision of services. The consumers who initially used these centers typically had little or no ability to pay for the mental healthcare that they needed, mainly because the large warehouse type of facilities, where these consumers had lived and been cared for, were closed. They found themselves back in communities, still mentally ill and still needing services. These unfortunate (or perhaps fortunate considering the condition of many of the facilities) people were the initial consumers who were to receive the treatment services of the centers and agencies funded across the nation that were given the specific charge to care for those who were then called "the sickest and the poorest."

The clinicians hired into these centers did not have any specific set or sets of requirements from which to work. As many of us who have been in the field since the early days like to laugh and say, "We were doing God's work, caring for the neediest of the needy." We didn't need any direction, or very little direction, to know what we were supposed to do.

These practitioners, hired into and working within this type of directionless or semidirectionless system, functioned in an independent or semi-independent manner. Although they might have been required to work on certain days or certain evenings, they made and kept their own schedules. This practice is still so engrained in what it means to be a therapist in many clinics or agencies that, to this day, it is a major undertaking to effect a change in this behavior that is seen as the "right of a therapist."

There were no specific requirements in terms of documentation of sessions, terms of content, or goals or objectives of the therapeutic session, and certainly not in terms of outcomes. There were no specific limits on the number of sessions a person could have, regardless of diagnosis. In fact, standardization of the diagnosis of mental conditions was in its infancy. There were no specific requirements at any level. We came to work, saw people, and probably or possibly wrote something down about the session, perhaps using some standard format or not, perhaps in some individualistic fashion. We went home and started all over the next day. Once or twice a month, we got paid, with benefits: insurance and sick leave and holidays, perhaps a pension.

The professional treatment staff got paid for doing a professional job for which they had been professionally trained, but for which there were few, if any, specific requirements. There was little, if any, specific accountability, for accountability can come only with requirements—specific requirements for specific activities.

This is not to imply in the least that staff did not act responsibly and did not provide appropriate or adequate service. My experience in the field for the past three decades would indicate that they most certainly did provide appropriate, if not at times excellent, service that helped people in need.

It is, however, to say that this type of system allowed, if not encouraged, the development of a laissez-faire system of professionals. These professionals provided behavioral health services, got paid regularly for this service, but had to provide no specific accountability. For example, they may have had no specific type of clinical documentation required for the service they provided. Or, as still exists in many agencies, they may not have had to work a required number of "billable" hours, that is, hours that the agency/practice is paid for, to receive their paycheck. This system fostered the eventual belief that is lurking in many, if not all, systems of behavioral healthcare, at least among staff who have been around longer than the past 5 years. This is the belief that working for a behavioral healthcare system, especially a behavioral healthcare system that is community supported, is really working as an independent practitioner, who just happens to get a regular paycheck regardless of how much or what quality of work he or she does.

How do we know this belief exists? Attempt to establish centralized scheduling by taking away a clinician's right to control his or her schedule book. See what happens, even among the new clinicians. Begin to talk about establishing evidence-based practices/protocols and see the initial response from clinicians who believe that following their own direction in terms of treatment of "their clients" is their "right."

This is not to imply that this obstacle cannot be dealt with; it most certainly can. However, this is an important evaluation point as you decide the preparedness of your agency/practice in implementing evidence-based practices. What extent does the agency/practice operate as a collective of independent practitioners, as described earlier? To what extent has the agency/practice thrown off the shackles and pitfalls of independent practitionerhood and operated as a business with requirements, standards, accountability, and the reporting thereof?

THE ECONOMIC IMPACT OF EVIDENCE-BASED PRACTICE

As indicated in the preceding discussion, the decision to use evidence-based practices will have an economic impact on the organization. Therefore, the evaluation of the basic business stance is paramount. Once it has been decided that the agency/practice will be run as a business and not as a loose collective of independent practitioners, a number of concerns can affect the success of this decision.

First among the list of concerns is whether the agency/practice has or will have production rates. For the community setting or in the private practice setting, a production rate is the rate of billed service per direct service clinician or practitioner that is needed to meet the budget. In the old days, the days of grants, practitioners seeing clients may have been sufficient to have a successful agency/practice. In the days of service contracts, managed care, and fee for service, it is not. A business cannot be successfully run without some degree of knowing specifically what the deliverable is for most, if not all, staff. The next associated step in building a business stance is the ability to track, aggregate, and analyze the actual production of the rates so that the financial health of the behavioral healthcare business can be known. This gives agency/practice leadership the ability to take appropriate steps for performance improvement should a downward trend in the financial situation be noted.

A second concern is the extent that agency/practice clinicians and staff are aligned in silos or tribes of care. David Lloyd (1998, 2002) provides a complete discussion of this topic. In Lloyd's extensive work with behavioral healthcare agencies, he has found that often staff are divided along lines of care. This division of staff, while making sense clinically, can develop into *silos* or *tribes* of care providers. These silos or tribes can develop into semiautonomous parts of an agency/practice that have their own admission requirements and processes, their own intake documentations, and so on. This division can hamper the agency/practice both clinically and financially. Clinically, such a division hampers the effective use of evidence-based practices, for example, those practices that deal with dual or co-occurring diagnoses. In a tribe type of community behavioral health system, there may be two separate and different intake processes—one for mental health needs and one for addiction needs. Consumers with co-occurring conditions must be able to seamlessly access needed services. The inability to easily access service across tribes, that is, service areas, can affect the decision of the consumer to stay in service. My agency/practice found a 60% dropout rate difference between services that were redesigned to enhance movement through service areas as compared to the nonredesigned services (Hayes et al., 2003). High dropout rates affect the ability of staff to meet production rates.

A second consideration in the examination of silos or tribes of care may make the change to evidence-based practices more difficult than it need be. From a business stance, such a division can and will hamper the dissemination of any, if not most, innovations within the agency/practice because the tribe or silo of care orientation produces a disjointed sense of loyalty. The loyalty is to the service area rather than to the agency/practice/business. Thus, the needs of "my service area" are seen as more important than greater needs of the agency/practice/business on the whole. Further, the silo or tribal stance produces a sense of uniqueness that precludes change: for example, "It might work for them (another service area), but it won't work here. Our clients' service needs won't allow a strict production rate." The existence of silos or tribes within the agency/practice should be evaluated carefully before embarking on the use of evidence-based practices. Staff loyalty must be to the needs of the agency/practice.

This leads to the next consideration: management team stance. Is the management or administrative team a *business* team. That is, do they understand that they are not independent contractors, nor directors of separate businesses within the agency/practice, but part of the larger business that is the agency/practice? For example, is there behavior displayed at the management team meetings that should not be tolerated? Ask this question: Is every member of management on time for the meetings? If the answer is no, you are not running a business. You are trying to run a business with a loose collective of independent practitioners.

One of the common practices of the community behavioral healthcare agencies over the past three decades is that clinicians have been promoted within the agency/practice and are, thus, currently in upper management positions. They have brought with them to their management assignments the bad habits inadvertently learned through their independent practice, as described earlier, within the agency/practice. Therefore, they believe that they have the right, for example, to come when and as they please to the management meetings. They believe, as seen in the behaviors they frequently display, that they have the right to support those decisions with which they agree and can ignore or talk down to their staff the decisions of the agency/practice's management team with which they do not agree.

For an agency/practice to run as a business that will be capable of using evidence-based practices effectively, the management team must function as a business team. This means that each member of the management team must display loyalty first and foremost to the goals of the agency/practice as a business, not to the individual fiefdoms of "my program" or "my division." It will be counterproductive if management members refuse to allow evidence-based practices into "their service area" because the needs of "their consumers" and "their staff" are different, or unique, or any other descriptor used. This means also that members of management must come to the management meetings on time. This means that they must support the agreements made in the meetings. If these three conditions are not met, the agency/practice will not be able to effectively participate in the business of using evidence-based practices. Every manager will be too busy defending and protecting his or her individual turf or fiefdom to fully participate.

If you are a CEO reading these words and recognize your agency/practice's management team in the preceding words, do not lose hope. Things can be changed. But they can be changed only when these behaviors are directly confronted. Begin by explaining to the team that from now on, there will be a few simple rules for each meeting:

- Meetings will start on time. Tardiness will not be tolerated with formal disciplinary write-ups for any further display of tardiness.
- Every meeting will have an agenda with specific time lines for each agenda item. The agenda will be available at least a week before every meeting.
- Anyone on the agenda will be expected to have a written presentation distributed to the team members at least the day before the meeting.
- Everyone on the team will be expected to have read the report and be prepared for an appropriate discussion of the report.

- Sideline or sidebar discussions will not be permitted.
- Taking telephone calls in the meeting will not be permitted.
- Members of the team will not be permitted to leave the meeting early except in preapproved and extenuating circumstances.
- Following the meeting, minutes of the meetings will be distributed to every team member in a timely fashion.
- Every team member will be expected to have read the minutes to be reminded of any assignments or agreements.
- Any decision made in the team, by the team, will be backed by each and every member of the management team. Any example of reneging on a team decision will be met with formal disciplinary action.

The preceding is one set of rules of how a business meeting can be run. For other examples and rules, see Hayes and Nelson (2000). The point is not so much which set of meeting rules are chosen to run the meetings with. The point is that the CEO, as the leader, acts in a true and clear leadership capacity. The CEO has a set of clear expectations for behavior within the management team so that it can function as a business team.

The changes you or the CEO propose to make will come as a shock to many of the management team. They may attempt to dissuade you. They may attempt to steamroller you into changing your mind. (We discuss these staff members and how to deal with them in later sections of this chapter.) However, the course you are about to engage in, implementing evidence-based practices, requires the commitment of every member of the team. It is a costly, time- and resource-consuming commitment. The management team needs to be able to act as a true business team if the time and resources are not going to be wasted. It is the job of the CEO to not let this waste happen.

EVALUATE THE CULTURE

The next step in evaluating the agency/practice's readiness to explore having an evidence-based practice is to evaluate the agency/practice's total culture. The agency/practice culture goes beyond the business culture and the independent practitioner cultures discussed in the preceding paragraphs. The agency/practice culture is more global and pervasive than these two subcultures, although to a larger extent, it contains staff perception of their relationship to these two subcultures, among many other elements.

For example, if the agency/practice is like many behavioral healthcare agencies, it is probable that few staff are involved in any of what might be considered the business aspects of the agency/practice operation. Unless the agency/practice has undertaken some specific performance enhancement projects, the treatment staff may not even be involved in the process of the collection of payment for the services they have just rendered.

More important to the initiation of evidence-based practices, the treatment staff may have a set of beliefs that were either carried over from the old days or disseminated to them, if they are younger staff, through the more senior staff. This set of beliefs probably includes a specific set of ideas about the relationship between the therapist and the consumer. Some of these ideas and beliefs are helpful and appropriate. Some, however, may be counterproductive to both running the agency/practice as a business and to initiating evidence-based practices.

This set of beliefs, for example, may include a specific set of instructions about the appropriateness of clinicians asking clients for payment, that is, for money. This belief will be associated with the staff's own personal belief system about the appropriateness of discussing money issues with other people. The personal belief may serve to either strengthen or loosen the clinical culture belief system about client payment and clinicians that is operating within the agency/practice. If the clinical staff believes that they are not supposed to be talking to consumers about payment, they will believe that these discussions are strictly within the purview of the business staff. They will not then view themselves as part, albeit perhaps a small part, of the business culture of the agency/practice. It is, therefore, this lack of awareness of the clinical staff of their potential to be a part of the business operations of the agency/practice that is then one aspect of the overall agency/practice culture. Indeed, if clinical staff has not been considered as part of the overall business culture of the agency/practice, it seems highly probable that the aforementioned is one aspect of the agency/practice culture.

Another set of beliefs that is part of the agency/practice culture that may be in operation within the agency/practice harkens back to our earlier discussion of the agency/practice as a collective of independent practitioners. A hallmark of the independent practitioner's belief set centers around the meaning of *independent*. The first meaning of the word (*Webster's Ninth New Collegiate Dictionary*, p. 612) is "not subject to the control of others: self governing."

Consider how this definition may play itself out within the agency/practice's professional treatment staff. The professional staff came to the agency/practice with certain sets of training and skills concerning their profession: psychotherapy, case management, social work, and so on. They may have come to the agency/practice with a set of professional beliefs about the uniqueness of their relationship to their client, patient, and consumer. They may believe that because of their unique relationship with "their consumer" (Note: Whose patient/client/consumer is it? It is their consumer. That is, the client who comes to the agency/practice is perceived as the clinician's consumer, not the agency/practice's consumer.), They are the only one that has the right to decide on a course of treatment for the consumer they are treating. It is possible that the clinician's training included a useful set of beliefs about the importance of supervision and taking treatment direction from a supervisor. This belief helps to mediate the other belief that they as clinicians with the unique relationship have the sole right to set the practice or treatment parameters for or with the consumers with whom they have a treatment relationship.

Consider then, if this set of beliefs exists in even half of the current therapists, the CEO and the management team and the board of directors make the announcement that evidence-based practice guidelines and protocols are going to be used. These practices will spell out clearly and directly possible courses of treatments for a variety of clinical conditions. What will be the reaction of this set of staff that is operating within the belief set that they are the only ones who can really make treatment decisions? Will their reaction not be, "They are trying to tell me how to do therapy?"

Or, take the potential proposal one step further. Consider that the agency/practice decides to participate as part of a replication study in which the agency/practice staff will replicate a treatment methodology for a specific clinical condition. A replication study requires that treatment protocols be followed specifically and exactly once a subject has met the criteria for inclusion in the study. Consider that in a university setting, you have graduate students or postgraduate students who are operating within the subtext of wanting to graduate. They are following the treatment protocols. It is highly likely, since graduating is one of their immediate goals, that they will follow the treatment protocols with great care and precision.

However, within the agency/practice, there are clinicians who have been providing treatment, that is, their own special brand of treatment, perhaps for years. They believe, probably in the absence of good outcome studies or any outcome studies, that they have been doing great work with this set of clinical conditions. They are part of the agency/practice culture belief set that says that because they are the ones with the special relationship with "their clients" (again, note where the ownership of the client lies, not with the study or the agency/practice, but with the clinician), they will consider that they are the only ones who can properly decide what the correct treatment course will be. This set of clinicians is chosen to participate in the replication study specifically because of their long-term work with this clinical condition. What is the likelihood or probability that they will follow the replication protocol with the precision required by the replication protocols?

This is not to say that the clinicians will maliciously sabotage this replication project. What might happen, however, is that these clinicians, acting out of their belief systems and within what they perceive to be the agency/practice culture of "clinician knows best," will filter the replication protocols through said culture of beliefs. They will follow the protocol but will apply their belief system and thus, perhaps, their preferred additions to the protocol since they know what will really help "their" client. The consequences of the imposition of the clinician's belief system on the replication project will be to invalidate the replication. The protocol will not have been followed with precision.

The economic impact for the agency/practice will be that the time, staff resources, and dollars spent on the project will have been wasted. The impact in terms of the efficacy of the treatment protocol will continue to be unknown since the protocol wasn't followed. Further, the outcome for the consumer who agreed to participate in the replication study will be statistically unknowable, although the consumer might report satisfaction with the results—all because of the belief system and culture of beliefs within the agency/practice that were played out in the clinician who was participating in the replication project.

A careful examination of the culture of beliefs existing within the agency/practice is, thus, very important. This should not be taken as an indication that it is impossible to do evidence-based work in agency/practice settings. It is warning, however, that all, or as many as possible, of the subtexts, belief systems, and so forth that are silently in operation within the agency/practice must be evaluated as to their possible effect on the decision to do evidence-based work.

How do you decide what might be all of the maladaptive belief systems at play in terms of this decision? One method of such discovery is to call together any clinical staff who might have an objection, tell them that leadership is considering this project, and elicit their criticisms of the project. Carefully take down all of their objections, without argument or attempts at persuasion, and then as a performance improvement team, analyze each and every objection and criticism for their underlying belief set. This will let the leader know what and where the resistances may be encountered as evidence-based practices are attempted.

EVALUATE THE READINESS AND ABILITY TO CHANGE/INFLUENCE STAFF PRACTICE

The following topics—Expect Resistance and Evidence-Based or Best Practice—are considerations to assist an agency/practice to evaluate its ability to influence staff practice.

Expect Resistance

I may have seemed a bit heavy handed, if not negative, up to this point in continuously listing various aspects and attitudes within agencies that might impede the implementation of evidence-based practice protocols. Nevertheless, it is both fair and appropriate to say that everyone in the agency/practice structure, from the board of directors through the chief executive officer to the janitor, has the potential to sidetrack, if not derail entirely, the use of evidence-based practice protocols or any other performance improvement initiative.

The list of concerns given so far is based partially on comments relayed to me by staff at a variety of levels within agencies following various lectures around the United States. The comments have varied but have been fairly consistent: "How can we establish meeting guidelines when the high-level executive is routinely 30 minutes late for our practice planning meetings?" "How can we ensure the use of our practice protocols, approved by our management team and supported by our board, when the high-level executive routinely makes pejorative remarks about their use?" Thus, this list of considerations has its beginnings in the remarks that were actually pleas for help as I discussed the implementation of evidence-based practices. I do not believe that they are isolated remarks, but suspect that these and similar events are the rule and not the exception in the administration of behavioral healthcare agencies and practices around the States.

The list is based additionally on growing best practices that are being established in thriving agencies around the country. The suggested practices (and/or areas to clean up in the organization) are those practices that are helping struggling and failing behavioral health agencies to move from what David Lloyd identifies in his workshops as "striving to thriving" (Lloyd, 2001). They are practices that help set the tone for following evidence-based protocols, for collecting evidence, for analyzing and evaluating data, and for making decisions based on this analysis.

Further, the laundry list is based on my study/reflection on resistance to change within the behavioral health field. When I began to work full time in the field, I was amazed to find that behavioral healthcare staff, experts with specific training in helping other people to make changes in their lives, had great difficulty making changes in their own professional lives. Far from finding it easy to make changes because of their training, behavioral healthcare professionals on the whole seemed to have as much difficulty as anyone else in making changes. Having the skills to help people change does not guarantee that behavioral healthcare staff will be readily or easily able to make changes themselves.

This experience led me to propose (Hayes & Nelson, 2000) that acceptance of new processes requiring changes within an agency/practice will follow a variation of the Pareto or 80/20 effect: 10% of a staff will willingly accept a new process, 10% will automatically reject a new process, while 80% of a staff will take a wait-and-see attitude toward the innovation. The overall result of this Pareto effect process is that the innovation within an agency/practice will probably stall unless specific steps are taken to ensure that the improvement will be followed. (See Richard Koch, 1998, for a further explanation of the Pareto effect.) This is part of the reasoning behind having an entire chapter devoted to evaluating the readiness of the agency/practice to implement the evidence-based practices described in this book.

The type of evidence-based practice an agency/practice decides to implement may be dependent on the extent that the agency/practice as a whole and the staff responsible for the implementation of the evidence-based practice specifically are ready and willing to accept the changes associated with the new practice. There is nothing more discouraging for a staff that has designed a protocol or selected an evidence-based protocol for implementation than to have the protocol languish in disuse.

The MISA best practice protocols devised at my agency, Sinnissippi Centers, Inc., and for which the agency/practice was awarded a JCAHO Ernest A. Codman award in 2002, were widely accepted and largely implemented because the management team members who were responsible for the initiation of the developmental idea for the protocol development took great and careful pains to invite the participation of staff members who were ready and willing to make the changes necessary to design and implement the best practice protocol. They elicited and received support from upper-level management and from the board of directors before the design of the program was begun. The design and implementation staff were sent to initial trainings by leading researchers in the field. Later, the same staff were included in doing all staff trainings within the agency/practice. Further, because they had based the treatment protocol they developed on the best evidence available, they were able to elicit buy-in from other staff to be involved in the implementation because the research they shared with other staff, the research they had built their protocol on, resonated with the actual experience of the staff to be brought into the project.

This is one instance where ownership of a protocol helped to spread the use of the protocol and was not counterproductive. It was not handed down from on high with orders to implement, but was instead developed, as it were, from the ground up by the key stakeholders who would be responsible for the implementation of the protocol they developed. The development team had a great deal of ownership and enthusiasm for the project and were able to convey that enthusiasm to other staff to increase buy-in to the process. Further, they had a commitment to a specific process design (the design, measure, analyze, and improve methodology), accurate note keeping, and knew the need to have a variety of data collection and measurement points built into their design.

The ability of this team to build their own research-based protocol came only after years of preparatory work within the agency/practice. For example, staff in the agency/practice were trained in the design methodology. Further, staff were trained in the basics of statistical analysis and databased decision making. This was not a one-time training, but a series of trainings over a number of years. This continuous training helped to mold the agency/practice culture into a design-oriented, databased decision-making culture.

Thus, the type of evidence-based practice an agency/practice decides to participate in depends on the agency/practice's culture and the extent that there is resistance or lack of resistance to the concept of evidence-based practice. The more an agency/practice staff is familiar with databased decision making, or following protocols, or responding to other types of accountability systems, the more structured a system of evidence-based practice the agency/practice will be able to easily accomplish. The less an agency/practice staff is familiar with (and/or accepting of) the preceding practices, the more difficult it will be, thus, the more costly it will be to establish the evidence-based practice because it will take more preparatory work before the evidence-based practice can be easily accomplished, that is, designed and integrated within the system.

Evidence-Based or Best Practice?

One important question to consider then, depending on the analysis of the agency/practice based on the preceding discussion, is whether leadership wants to establish and use true evidence-based practices or if someone will design best practice protocols for the treatment staff to use.

What is the difference between an evidence-based practice protocol and a best practice protocol? Evidence-based practices are practices that are based on the results of research. The preceding chapters have concentrated on six specific sets of evidence-based treatment protocols. All of these treatment designs have gone through numerous research implementations, and some of them, replication efforts. Their effectiveness has, thus, been well established. The ability of an agency/practice to replicate these practice protocols may have also been established.

There exist in the research literature and journals many similar types of evidence-based practices or protocols. Following chapters discuss how to find and evaluate these other practices. There is one important consideration in the use of evidence-based protocols. To produce the results achieved in the various research settings (i.e., in which the effectiveness was established), the protocols have to be followed very closely. Following the evidence-based practice protocol closely is, thus, a requirement if you want to be assured of having similar results. The question to ask is whether, or to what extent, the staff is ready to precisely follow treatment protocols—treatment protocols that may be rigid and demanding.

A best practice protocol, on the other hand, is a series of practice parameters that are based on the available research, or they may be "consensus protocols." Currently, there are a number of evidence-supported, as they are called, treatment books available in the marketplace (see Hofmann & Tompson, 2002, for example). These books follow the trends in practice that the research seems to be indicating yield good results.

Another approach to best practice protocols is to develop specific protocols for use in the agency/practice, either through some modification of or a combination of a variety of evidence-based practices concerning the diagnosis or functional deficit they were originally designed to ameliorate. However, these best practices will be either modifications of evidence-based practices or combinations of those practices. They, in their modification or combination, have not been specifically researched. Thus, they are not specifically guaranteed to render the results that were originally achieved in the research from which they were modified or drawn. Their effectiveness in their modified form is unknown. This necessitates, if this approach is going to be followed in the agency/practice design of the best practice protocols, that careful outcome or functional measures be taken to establish the effectiveness of the protocol within the own agency/practice. This important step may be overlooked if the design team is not sensitive to the differences between evidence-based and best practice protocols.

A second type of best practice protocol is not so much a combination of researched protocols as it is based on the best practice advice of the leading theorists within a specific field. Marsha Linehan's dialectic behavioral therapy (1993) might be considered an example of this type of best practice protocol. Another example of this type of best practice protocol might be found in the best practice protocols published by the American Psychiatric Association (2002). These best practices are the recommendations of the best minds and thinking currently available. These practices can be put in the format of a decision tree for staff to follow. The same caution is given as before: Functional measurements should be planned into the design of implementation of this type of practice.

One last approach to initiate the general concept of following protocols would be to standardize some of the current practices to specific diagnostic categories. A databased approach to this, which is described in detail in Chapter 13, is to examine the demographics of the practice and standardize the practices currently associated with the top (i.e., by number of recipients) several diagnostic categories. You are not necessarily adding any new elements of treatment in this approach. You are merely taking the current practices and, for example, arranging them in a decision tree format/process, so that the staff can get used to the idea of following treatment protocol. This is suggested as a possible path of least resistance for agencies starting at ground zero and is discussed further in Chapter 13.

Ultimately, however, the CEO, the clinical director, the management staff, or someone or ones with appropriate knowledge of both the clinical and administrative needs of the agency/practice will have to make a decision that is both clinically and financially sound for the needs of the agency/practice. This decision will revolve around the extent that the practices, whether they are evidence-based, or best practice, or a standardization of the agency/practice's current practices, are to be followed as suggested practice or as a strict requirement with accountability and fidelity measurement built in as part of the process of implementation.

The decision does not have to be an either/or proposition. It, in fact, may need to be a developmental designed decision. If the agency/practice is starting at ground zero and wants to develop slowly, the decision might entail starting with best practice suggestions for treatment that will be monitored. A developmental GANT chart could develop a time line for the current practice suggestions to evolve into a set of best practice (required) guidelines or protocols for which staff will be eventually held accountable. Once the staff has demonstrated the ability to follow the required guidelines, the leadership will know that they have moved the agency/practice from an independent practice approach with each consumer to an agency/practice or businesslike approach to each consumer. At this point, the decision to move toward the next developmental step, evidence-based practices, can be made with some ease and assurance that the staff will be both able and willing to follow the practice protocols.

EVALUATE THE STAFF

The following sections are considerations to assist an agency/practice evaluate its staff.

Critical Staff Involvement

Who are the critical staff that absolutely must be involved in this practice project? As indicated earlier, the CEO must carry the vision for this project to the board and to the administrative leadership. Once this process has occurred, the selection of the actual staff to carry out (i.e., to research and design the protocol and plan for its implementation) the project must take place.

The clinical leader, whatever this position may be called within the agency/practice, should be involved in the staff selection process of the design team. The clinical leader will have the knowledge of which professionals might have a passion for this new direction. Further, the clinical leader will know which staff have the knowledge of the selected diagnostic area for use of the evidence or best practice protocol.

If the selected area is a dual diagnosis or co-occurring area, for example, mentally ill, substance abuse (or mentally ill, chemical abuse), it is important that the design or planning team be composed of professionals with training and experience in both of these areas. One of the tragedies of treatment for the MISA consumer has been the lack of planning and conversation between these two sets of professionals (see Hayes et al., 2003). Since dual diagnosis consumers will need the expertise of at least two sets of treatment professionals, it is important that both sets be involved in the design and implementation of the evidence base or best practice protocols.

If the selected area for evidence-based or best practice protocol use will include the services of medical personnel, either doctor or/and nurses, it is important that representatives from these professionals are part of the design team. If the decision is made to design the agency/practice's own best practice protocols, the advice of the Joint Commission on the Accreditation of Healthcare Organizations (Poniatowski, 2000) is that the design team be composed of licensed independent practitioners (LIPs). These are the professionals in the organization who are licensed in their field to provide treatment services.

It is also critical to include in the design team some staff members who have sufficient direct, day-to-day contact with the consumers that the protocol is to be implemented with. They can add invaluable direction in terms of how the treatment protocol might be implemented with the specific population.

Last, but certainly not least in terms of inclusion in the design team, are staff that have the training and expertise to help the team design the outcome measures and/or functional measures that will be used to determine the effectiveness of the treatment protocols.

Support Staff Involvement

The next set of staff to consider for involvement in the design team is a representative of the support staff: secretarial, financial, and the information technology. Why include them, and what is the appropriate time to consider their introduction to the team? We examine this set of staff in reverse order.

Information Technology Staff Inclusion

It may seem a logical inclusion without need of explanation to include a member of the information technology (IT) system in the design team. This is especially and critically true if it is known from the outset that the design team wants to capture the functional and outcome data or any of the other process measurements using the information system. The IT professional can, thus, help the team decide how and when to input this data. The IT person might also have important suggestions as to what kinds of data can be the easiest to capture this way.

What if the design team did not consider data capture using the information system and do not believe that they would? First, evaluate this decision carefully. Electronic data capture is efficient when the alternatives are considered—capture on paper. A paper trail of measures, housed in consumer charts, is acceptable for tracking the process and progress of an individual consumer within the agency/practice. However, the integration of evidence-based or best practice paradigms into the system broadens the need for tracking.

Tracking outcomes of individual consumers plays a dual purpose in the integration of evidence-based protocols. On the one hand, the tracking allows the clinician and psychiatrist, if psychotropic medications are involved in the treatment paradigm, a better opportunity to measure the results of the effectiveness of the treatment paradigm for an individual. However, the paradigm is being introduced to a number of individuals through the agency/practice who are experiencing the same condition. It is a time-consuming process to manually collect data from individual client records. Further, once the information is collected from the records, it will have to be input into some electronic format for analysis anyway. Ultimately, it will save time and, thus, cost, to capture electronically as much of the data as possible that is associated with the project.

If the design team members have primarily all come from the "collaborative independent practitioners' model," they may not be aware of what data is already collected within the agency/practice, nor may they be familiar with what could be collected by the information system (IS). If an IS professional is not going to be included in the actual design team, it will be important to at least have an IS consultant appointed to the team. Acting in the role of a consultant, the IS professional can function as an adjunct member of the design team and give advice about data incorporation as the design is formalized.

Do not wait until the entire design has been completed, the program instituted, and data collection started before the IS professional is consulted. This delay could result in some backtracking on processes and could mean some redesign of the data collection. It could also mean increased costs.

Financial Staff Inclusion

Consider the extent that the clinical staff is aware of all of the requirements of the various funding sources. In the design of my agency/practice's MISA protocol, the financial department had to have a large presence because of financial considerations. In Illinois, the two treatment areas, mental illness and addictions, are funded by two different state agencies that have two completely different sets of documentation requirements for reimbursement. Unfortunately, this problem exists all over the United States—funding streams are separated for separate problems: developmental delays from addiction, addiction from mentally ill, mentally ill from family-related problems, and so on ad nausea. If a financial representative is not going to be part of the design team, then, as with the information systems professional, a financial consultant should be appointed. Further, this consultant should be regularly utilized to ensure that all of the elements included within the design are (1) reimbursable according to the funding source requirements and (2) financially sound.

What happens if the debate is initiated between the financial staff's position of "We can't afford this process" and the clinical staff's position of "We have to do this"? The first rule of inclusion of financial within the design team is this: The financial consultant is not a member of the team or a consultant to the team as a project veto plug puller. This must be clear to all members of the team, or they may view the financial representative/consultant with suspicion from the onset. However, the clinical members of the team do not have financial/business veto override either.

The purpose of having a multifunctional area design team is so that all functional area concerns can be worked out before the implementation of the project. If teams have been assessed as suggested earlier, there should be some awareness by this point whether the various staffs have the ability to work cooperatively. If they do not, initial training in consensus building, super majority voting, understanding and acceptance, or some similar process will be necessary so as to not waste valuable time and resources in design meetings that become divisive.

Secretarial Inclusion

How often are projects designed and brought to implementation without considering the effect the implementation will have on the secretaries and receptionists who are the ones that keep our agencies open and running? It should go without saying that almost every aspect of a project will in some way, if not many ways, affect the secretaries and receptionists. Again, it is suggested that if a support staff is not a member of the design team, a support staff consultant should have the opportunity to evaluate how the project design will affect the current support processes. What will the project's implementation mean in terms of increased support staff time? How much of the treatment protocol will the secretaries have to carry out? For example, will they have to distribute more forms or questionnaires or other items associated with the protocol that will take them from their current activities? The effect of the project on the support staff needs to be carefully evaluated and dealt with in the protocol.

"Dangerous" Staff Involvement (Including Possible Naysayers)

At some point, the design team may want to consider extending an invitation to the one or two staff who are seen as the agency/practice naysayers. The naysayer is the one who is most likely to be negative and/or reluctant about the proposed initiation of the evidence-based or best practice protocols.

As indicated earlier, I developed a theory based on the 80/20 or Pareto effect. While most (80%) of a staff take a wait-and-see attitude toward a proposed change, roughly 10% willingly adopt the protocol. They are the willing changers (Hayes & Nelson, 2000). The other half of the 20% from the 80/20 rule are the unwilling changers and tend to oppose, at least initially, whatever the change is, for whatever reason or sets of reasons. It doesn't make any difference that a proposed change may immediately benefit these staff. They are automatically opposed to any change.

It is one of these staff who should become part of the development team. This person is invited as a team member with a specific charge, however. This charge is to review all of the proposed changes with a mind to their possible negative effects on agency/practice processes. This person may not—and this point must be made clear from the onset—review the decision to move in the direction of best practice or evidence-based protocol use. That decision has already been made by the board and management and is a given. It must be clear in initial meetings with this staff member that the decision to use best practice/evidence-based protocols is not debatable.

The charge given to this naysayer staff member as part of the committee, a charge that becomes a role in the implementation of the protocols, is, thus, to assist in the implementation of the project by using his or her skill to see the negatives inherent in the new process. As this person discovers or realizes the various roadblocks to implementation, which is part of the implementation process and needs to be done in any change-related project, he or she is charged with keeping a list of these aspects and developing, with the help of a subgroup of the larger design committee, action plans to ameliorate the potential roadblocks.

This type of action could be considered a form of manipulation by some readers. It is, without a doubt, a form of co-opting of the staff person. It is also making use of a characteristic of the staff, that is, the ability to see the negative, and making it a usable skill in the initiation process. It is making use of the corollary of the saying, "Our strengths are also our weaknesses." In this case, a staff weakness, that is, the tendency to be negative and fault finding about proposed project changes, can become a strength that is put to good use in the agency/practice. As indicated earlier, it is important in the design process to look for the possible barriers, and who better to do the looking but one of the people most likely to be involved in using the barriers to avoid the change.

The Change Cheerleader or Champion

A second member of the 80/20 proposition for the design/implementation is a staff person from the 10% who are ready to adopt change: the change cheerleader. This person has also been called the "quality champion" in the quality improvement literature. Instead of naysaying, this is the staff person who willingly accepts any and all changes and will implement them without question. This is not the person to ask to critique a process, for he or she will see only the possibilities and not the pitfalls. This person is, however, the person to invite in the process to talk up the process, that is, to spread goodwill toward the innovation. (See Hayes and Nelson, 2000, for a further discussion of the role of this person in a quality improvement process.)

The Project Manager

The last person to mention in the overview of the development process is the project manager. If your agency/practice has a history of using project managers, you already know the importance of this team member for any project. Who among us has not watched a task force struggle for months, discussing and debating the same topics over and over with no end in sight, either in terms of delivering their product or ending their interminable session of meetings? Or who has not seen task forces meet and work on a product, only to have one team member miss several meetings and then return with questions and proposed changes to the product as developed in their absence?

The days have passed that the behavioral healthcare industry can afford ill-run task forces and design groups. The role of the project manager is to ensure that the project comes in on time, on budget, and delivers the product assigned. It is a strict business model that has broad applications within the behavioral health field, especially for agencies that are just starting to adapt themselves into a business model. The project manager needs to either be in a position to have sufficient authority or to be given sufficient authority so he or she can get the assigned task completed. The management or administrative team members must be aware of this assignment and the authority attached. Further, they must be willing, if not required, to follow up on any concerns expressed about the design team members, for example, the team member described earlier that misses meetings, fails to complete assignments, and so on. Again, it is remembered, or the administrative/management team needs be reminded, that both they and the project manager serve the needs of the agency/practice as a whole.

Training

Unless the agency/practice is very fortunate or is an agency/practice that is on the cutting edge of the industry, it is probable that there are not specific professionals with some of the skills described in this chapter as part of the agency/practice's workforce. Obtaining training for the staff selected to participate in the implementation design is of great importance. One consideration, rather than sending off one or two staff for training in, for example, project design or project management, is to bring in a trainer to educate not only the design team for this project but also the entire management team, administration, board members, and any appropriate supervisors. These are skills that will serve the agency/practice well in the years to come, for not only this project but also the behavioral healthcare business as a whole.

EVALUATE THE TECHNICAL READINESS

The following are considerations to assist an agency/practice evaluate its technical readiness to pursue evidence-based practices.

Evaluate the Information Technology Department

The question to evaluate here is simple in its formulation but broad and deep in its reality: How ready is the information technology department to accept the added demands inherent with evidence-based or best practice protocols, including both data gathering and protocol fidelity verification? If the IT department cannot readily add functional measures, for example, to the information already gathered daily on consumers via staff data gathering, what will be the time and costs associated with adding this component to the system? For example, my agency/practice found early in our quest to add routine outcome measures to our system that a "level of functioning" data input level was already part of the base system for reporting client contact. The initial functional level gathering was, thus, relatively simple to add to the system.

The system to add further functional measures, however, was not in place or part of a base system. These measures required a more complicated program upgrade that took months of clinical staff time as well as IT consultant/programming time to implement. However, the more aspects of these processes that can be automated via the IT department, the less time clinical staff will need to be gathering this information by hand. Thus, the evaluation of the IT department needs to include looking at the time and costs associated with not only what the system can currently do in terms of outcome collection but also the potential time and costs for any needed upgrades to the system for this collection.

The preceding is also true for the tracking of the fidelity of the staff in their use of the treatment protocols. It is highly probable that unless the IT system allows complete decision rules in terms of diagnoses and treatment codes, the IT system software will need some kind of upgrade. Again, this is not to say that the fidelity tracking cannot be done by hand. It can, but at the cost of clinical staff time to manually inspect client case records.

There is also a need, if the IT department is going to be used to track the outcome data, to evaluate the current equipment deployment. Do staff who will be inputting the outcome data into the IT system have computers, the appropriate software, and the necessary skills?

Evaluate the Statistical Readiness

To what extent is the agency/practice statistically ready to implement best practice or evidence-based practice protocols? Have the board, management, and staff been trained in statistical processes? Does the agency/practice have any staff on the design team with the required statistical skills necessary to analyze the outcome data that will be collected? As indicated earlier, this is a cost of time and potentially training dollars that should be made if the agency/practice is going to make full and correct use of the treatment protocols that will be added. Further, this is not a feature that can be added later or neglected entirely. Although not necessarily required with best practice protocols, aggregation and analysis of both the outcome data and fidelity to the process are part and parcel of any evidence-based treatment system.

Evaluate the Training Readiness

How ready is the agency/practice to undertake the degree of training necessary to use evidence-based protocols? The following questions are presented for consideration:

- Is there an ongoing training committee or is training one of many duties of one staff person in human resources? Depending on the scope of the best practice or evidence-based project, more training may be required than is usual for the agency/practice. Best practice protocol use will require less intense training than evidence-based protocol use, which will require more intense training and initial monitoring.

- Does the agency/practice have staff with sufficient training skills to ensure that the training will be presented in a manner that staff will learn the required skills? Adult learners have a variety of learning styles. Efficient and effective training needs to take these learning styles into consideration. Good use of computer-assisted learning is one method of reducing some training costs and further ensures consistency of presentation.

- Once the training has been presented, will trainers use both pre- and posttests to ensure that the staff have actually learned the processes and treatment protocols presented? This can be one important aspect of the fidelity process that could be built into the project design, that is, the degree that there is a correlation between staff posttraining test scores and process fidelity.

Evaluate the Current Clinical Record Review Process

The extent that an agency/practice has a thorough clinical record review process may be the quickest evaluation method for determining the current readiness to undertake a best practice or evidence-based treatment methodology. Chapter 13 thoroughly examines this process, but an overview and explanation is in order.

A clinical staff that knows that they are expected to thoroughly document their diagnostic decisions in terms of the *Diagnostic and Statistical Manual of Mental Disorders,* fourth edition (*DSM-IV;* American Psychiatric Association, 1994), for example, is a staff that has an understanding that there are basic clinical requirements expected of them. Further, the establishment of a correct diagnosis is paramount in the execution of an evidence-based practice. A practice or protocol that has been proven effective for generalized anxiety disorder (*DSM-IV* 300.92) may have little or no proven efficacy for adjustment disorder with anxiety (*DSM-IV* 309.24). A protocol that has proven effectiveness for a major depressive disorder, single episode (*DSM-IV* 296.2x) may have little or no proven effectiveness for adjustment disorder with depressed mood (*DSM-IV* 309.0).

The extent that staff have already been examined for their diagnostic accuracy via the documentation review process is critical and is an appropriate place to start if this practice is not currently being followed. If it has been, so much the better in terms of initiating evidence-based or best practice protocols. If it has not, it would be appropriate to begin to institute the thorough chart review that is discussed in Chapter 13 as part of the process of developing the practice implementation. If this is not feasible, the thorough clinical record review to determine diagnostic accuracy should be one of the first steps in the best practice or evidence-based practice implementation design.

HOW READY ARE YOU?

The question in one sense is: How ready is the agency/practice? In a larger sense, however, the question really is: How ready are you, the reader? If you are a CEO, to what extent have you committed or are you willing to commit your time and effort to this project? How ready are you to take this project to the board of directors and stand behind it with your vision and enthusiasm? How ready are you to take the idea of evidence-based or best practice project to your administrators and managers?

If you are an administrator or manager, how ready are you to take this idea to the CEO, to be prepared to pitch it, if necessary? If the CEO already is standing behind you, how prepared are you to carry your enthusiasm for evidence-based treatment to your staff?

If you are a front-line clinician, how ready are you to carry forth this project, perhaps as a member of the design committee, perhaps as the agency/practice cheerleader for the project?

At whatever staffing level within a behavioral health treatment agency/practice these words are reaching you, you need to ask the readiness question: How ready am I? Any performance improvement project requires the commitment of all those staff charged with its implementation. The change to evidence-based or protocol-driven treatment requires this question because it may be a significant change in procedures as usual and, thus, engender initial reluctance, if not occasional hostility. This is the way of change within organizations.

The advantages of evidence-based treatment for consumers, as outlined in the proceeding chapters, are tremendous in terms of the positive changes in quality of life. As staff can see the effects of the new treatment protocols, the results of their hard work to change their habits to be able to follow the new treatment methods, the initial reluctance fades into celebration for the lives that have changed because of the protocol use.

REFERENCES

American Psychiatric Association. (1994). *Diagnostic and statistical manual of mental disorders* (4th ed.). Washington, DC: Author.

American Psychiatric Association. (2002). *APA practice guidelines for the treatment of psychiatric disorders: Compendium.* Washington, DC: Author.

Hayes, R., Andrews, N., Baron-Jeffrey, M., Conley, C., Gridley, K., Norman, R., et al. (2003). Service enhancement to a dual-diagnosis population: Mental illness/substance abuse. *Quality Management in Health Care, 12*(3), 133–150.

Hayes, R., & Nelson, L. (2000). *Handbook of quality change and implementation for behavioral health care.* Revere, MA: C&R.

Hofmann, S., & Tompson, M. (2002). *Treating chronic and severe mental disorders: A handbook of empirically supported interventions.* New York: Guilford Press.

Jennings, J. (2002). *Less is more: How great companies use productivity as a competitive tool in business.* New York: Portfolio Penguin Putnam.

Koch, R. (1998). *The 80/20 Principle: The secret to success by achieving more with less.* New York: Doubleday.

Linehan, M. (1993). *Cognitive-behavioral treatment of borderline personality disorder.* New York: Guilford Press.

Lloyd, D. (1998). *How to maximize service capacity.* Rockville, MD: National Council for Community Behavioral Healthcare.

Lloyd, D. (2001, December). *Service capacity enhancement.* Paper presented at the meeting of the Community Behavioral Healthcare Association of Illinois, Chicago.

Lloyd, D. (2002). *How to deliver accountable care.* Rockville, MD: National Council for Community Behavioral Healthcare.

Merriam-Webster's collegiate dictionary (9th ed.) (1991). Springfield, MA: Merriam-Webster.

Morrison, D. (2001, October). *What's new in practice guidelines?* Paper presented at the meeting of the National Council of Community Behavioral Healthcare, Chicago.

Poniatowski, L. (2000). Clinical practice guidelines: Consider, adopt, or do your own [Electronic version]. *Nursing Management, 1331*(2), 13.

CHAPTER 13

How to Start with Your Agency, Practice, or Facility

Randy A. Hayes

The purpose of Chapter 12 was to help you determine the general readiness of your agency/practice to undertake evidence-based or best practice-based therapy. At this point, however, you may not have yet made the decision to undertake this task. There are several specific questions that are clinically related readiness questions that should be evaluated before undertaking the evidence-based or best practice route.

The purpose of this chapter is to overview one last set of readiness indicators and suggest action steps needed based on the analysis of those indicators. The bulk of the chapter then offers suggestions concerning possible courses of action, depending on the analysis of the state of readiness of the agency/practice and the needs of the consumers.

A GROUND ZERO START

The term *ground zero* is not meant to be a pejorative indicator of the state of readiness of an organization. It is used as an indication that the clinical prerequisites needed to initiate best practice or evidence-based practices are absent, in total or in part, from the processes of an agency/practice. While not absolutely necessary prior to the initiation of best or evidence-based practices, these prerequisite practices may ease the way for more formal evidence-based or best practice protocol use.

The Treatment Process Questions

The treatment process questions, listed in Table 13.1, are taken from the work of my agency, Sinnissippi Centers, Inc., Dixon, Illinois (Hayes, 2001). For the most part, these processes were not specifically engineered as evidence-based prerequisites. They were designed and instituted as part of the agency's overall commitment to providing and ensuring the provision of high-quality services. The impetus for the general initiation for the processes came out of the study and consideration of the requirements and the suggested guidelines of funding sources, accreditation (for my agency, the Joint Commission on the Accreditation of Healthcare Organizations [JCAHO]), and considerations garnered from the clinical record review process.

Table 13.1   Treatment Process Questions

1. Does your agency/practice assure that diagnosis is accurate per *DSM-IV* criteria and appropriate to the presenting problem?
2. Does your agency/practice use a standardized diagnostic specific measurement for principle diagnoses (e.g., Beck Depression for the depressive related disorders, CAP or Conners for ADHD)?
3. Does your agency/practice measure the functional level of consumers by some means (e.g., GAF, BSI) at admission? For each individual appointment or at regular intervals? At discharge? Do you aggregate, analyze, and use this data in any way to improve treatment processes?
4. Does your agency/practice assure that the treatment plan problem is clearly related to the presenting problem identified in the assessment?
5. Does your agency/practice assure that the treatment plan has measurable objectives that are clearly related to the presenting problem, and *DSM-IV* diagnosis?
6. Does your agency/practice assure that the treatment plan objectives are followed?
7. Does your agency/practice assure that treatment objective measures are being collected?
8. Does your agency/practice aggregate or chart the results of measures for use in the treatment of individual consumers?
9. Does your agency/practice aggregate and/or chart the results of measures for use in improving treatment processes in general?
10. Does your agency/practice benchmark the results of any of your data collection efforts?
11. Has your agency/practice developed standardized treatment protocols for any specific diagnostic categories?
12. Has your agency/practice trained staff to use the protocols with consumers?
13. Has your agency/practice trained in the statistical processes necessary to interpret the results of measurements?
14. Does your agency/practice assure that the treatment protocols, including measurement usage, are being followed?
15. Has your agency/practice aggregated data from your protocols to determine effectiveness of protocol?

Source: From "Evidence-Based Therapy: Is There a Practical Approach?" by R. Hayes, 2001, *Behavioral Health Management, 21*(6), pp. 20–24. Reprinted with permission.

Continuity of Care

One method of introducing the questions in Table 13.1 is to consider the phrase *continuity of care,* a phrase that has been in use in the behavioral health industry in the past decade. *Continuity,* in its most basic sense, means an "uninterrupted connection, succession, or union" (p. 284, *Webster's 9th).* Continuity of care has been used in terms of ensuring that care of an individual continues between two different agencies, both involved in the care of an individual. For example, continuity of care in Illinois refers to the treatment of an individual between a behavioral health provider and a state-operated psychiatric hospital. There are various continuity of care agreements between the various community behavioral health agencies and state-operated psychiatric hospitals across the state (Illinois). The processes these agreements establish ensure that care of the individual continues, for example, when the individual is released from a state-operated psychiatric hospital into the community. The processes establish the methodology for continued care by the community behavioral healthcare agency/practice. This is one highly specified meaning of the term continuity of care.

However, if this term is applied to behavioral health treatment in a larger sense, a concept that applies to all of the processes within a behavioral healthcare agency/practice can be seen. This concept can be stated simply as a business mission or goal: to provide an interrupted connection between the initial presenting problem when the consumer first comes to the agency/practice and the ultimate treatment outcome in which the consumer's problem is ameliorated or sufficiently modified for the consumer to report increased functioning and/or life satisfaction. All of the processes in an agency/practice's system should be designed to ensure this goal.

When applied to the treatment-specific processes within the agency/practice, the processes might be thought of as the golden thread that links every aspect of treatment efficiently (i.e., in terms of resource utilization) and effectively (i.e., in terms of producing the outcome or improvement desired by both the consumer of the treatment and the professional staff charged with ensuring such an outcome).

THE GOLDEN THREAD

The set of questions presented in Table 13.1 has a primary goal of linking all of the treatment elements that are or might be associated with improved outcomes for consumers. The first question was discussed initially in Chapter 12. The particulars in terms of the relationship to protocol use are discussed here.

Question 1: Accuracy of Diagnosis

Accuracy of diagnosis is especially important in a best practice or evidence-based protocol system if the best practice or evidence-based protocol system is going to be diagnoses based. (The alternative, a functional deficit-based protocol system or problem-based system, is discussed later.) The diagnostic taxonomy, for example, the *Diagnostic and Statistical Manual of Mental Disorders,* fourth edition (*DSM-IV;* American Psychiatric Association, 1994), makes frequent use of the same basic terminology in listing similar but discrete psychiatric problems. For example, the term *depression* or variants of *depression* (e.g., depressed mood) are used for a number of diagnoses that have similar symptoms, but nonetheless have been separated into distinct diagnoses. These distinct diagnoses may require similar, but different, treatment methodologies that do not lend themselves into one generic best practice or evidence-based protocol.

My agency, for example, selected depression as one of the three initial best practice protocols for development from the best practice treatment literature. The best practice protocol development task force had selected depression as the result of a databased decision process. The task force used a census count of the numbers of consumers in each distinct diagnostic category within the agency population of current consumers. The total population was typically around 3,800 individuals at any given time. The team aggregated the diagnostic counts in terms of use and ranked them from highest use to lowest use. Because several of the depressive diagnoses were on the top 10 list of most frequently occurring diagnoses within the agency population of consumers, depression was selected for a protocol development.

Because of this mix, and perhaps in the initial inexperience in developing treatment protocols, the team wondered if, in developing a protocol for depression, we would mix all of the depressive diagnoses together and arrive at one common protocol for the mixture of various depression-related diagnoses. This is where the multidisciplinary protocol development team, suggested in Chapter 12, was important. The chief psychiatrist, James Daly, MD, believed that to provide the best quality of service for consumers, separate treatment protocols for each of the diagnoses associated with depression would be required. There are differing treatment needs for each subset category within the general depression taxonomy. These treatment differences could possibly make a protocol developed as a one-size-fits-all methodology unyielding because it would require numerous decision trees, treatment paths, dosing paths, and so on. The one-size-fits-all model was given up for a single diagnosis treatment protocol.

However, the discussion of the differing treatment needs for the differing depressive diagnoses led to further considerations in terms of the ability of the treatment staff to clearly and consistently differentiate among the various depressive diagnoses. One of the processes in the clinical record review system was to determine the accuracy of diagnoses based on the information presented in the chart clinical assessment. Senior staff doing the clinical record review were asked to determine the extent that the stated diagnosis was supported by the material presented in the clinical assessment. Aggregated results from these chart reviews indicated that, frequently, diagnostic criteria were missing from the summary section of the clinical assessment. Diagnostic criteria and, thus, diagnostic appropriateness, had to be inferred from the text portion of the assessment. In fact, clinical record review instructions specifically allowed for a reading between the lines in terms of finding specific diagnostic indicators. While a system that allowed the inferring of symptoms within a clinical assessment may have been sufficient in the past, the design team believed that such a system did not sufficiently allow for accurately and efficiently reviewing the accuracy of a diagnosis for work with the proposed best practice protocols.

Thus, the treatment design team initiated a specific protocol/process for the clinical assessment. The protocol required the use of *DSM-IV* criteria in the summary of the clinical assessment to support the diagnosis. Further, any diagnostic criteria indicated in the summary had to have supporting documentation text clearly discernable within the text of the assessment. If these conditions were not met, the assessment was to be referred back to the therapist (with a notice to the appropriate supervisor) for inclusion of the appropriate and substantiating diagnostic criteria.

The use of treatment protocols for specific diagnoses required assurance that the diagnoses given by the staff are correct. The process within the clinical record review process already in place to check diagnostic accuracy was, thus, put to use in the development of the adjunct processes needed for the projected use of the treatment protocols. Before the agency began the actual implementation of the depression protocol, clinical leadership made sure of the accuracy of the diagnostic assessment associated with the consumers with whom the protocol would be used.

These discussions led to another improvement project for clinical staff to improve their differential assessment abilities. The chief psychiatrist provided specific training for clinicians to better differentiate and document the differences among the various depressive treatment categories. This process was taken as one further effort to ensure that the diagnoses would be correct so that the treatment protocols could be appropriate and successfully applied.

Question 2: Measurement

Following close behind or alongside the preceding improvements was another effort to both ensure accuracy of diagnosis and obtain a base measure of the degree of impairment so that the effectiveness of the treatment methodology could eventually be measured. A set of best practice measures was instituted agencywide for two of the three diagnostic categories chosen for protocol development. The specific diagnoses chosen were depression (Beck Depression Inventory) and attention deficit hyperactive disorder (the Children's Attention Problems scale [CAP] and the Connors' Rating Scale Revised). An additional screening tool (Michigan Alcoholism Screening Test [MAST]) was chosen for alcohol abuse and dependence. Although the MAST is not a measure in the sense that it can be used to track outcomes, it was instituted to help clinicians who were not hired and/or trained in the addictions field to better be able to screen for this condition.

Because of the number of consumers believed, based on a review of current research literature, to be potentially displaying co-occurring diagnoses, these measures were required of all consumers presenting at the agency for an assessment to better screen for alcohol abuse among the mentally ill population and depression or its variants among the addicted population. The measures were integrated into a larger best practice measurement process requirement for all consumers being assessed within the agency. The process was, thus, designed to enable clinicians to screen for and include as many as possible of consumers potentially displaying the symptoms of either diagnosis and to ensure that those screened into the specific treatment protocol use had a base line objective measure of their degree of impairment within that diagnostic category. The measure was also one other method of ensuring that the consumers were appropriate for the treatment protocols.

Suggested Best Practice or Required Best Practice?

A *suggested* best practice means that the treatment clinician has the choice to follow the practice protocol or set of measures, as described here, or not. The use of suggested best practices, especially in terms of initial assessments, is insufficient to establish full treatment team use. Busy clinicians, when given the choice, may choose nonimplementation of the measures as one method of reducing their overall documentation workload. This especially may be true with more experienced clinicians who believe, rightly or wrongly, that they have sufficient generalist diagnostic experience to discover whatever problem is covered by the assessment (measurement) tool. An agency/practice could establish a stringent competency assessment to document such a diagnostic ability for each clinician. This could prove to be a daunting task, however, even if a portion of all possible presenting problems were included in this competency assessment. The use of best practice assessment/measurement tools is probably an easier task for an agency/practice to undertake.

If an agency/practice's plan to implement evidence and/or best practice treatment protocols covers a substantial time period, the use of suggested best practice assessment/measurement tools will allow the treatment staff to begin to get used to the idea of these measures. If, however, the agency/practice is attempting to institute best or evidence-based practices in a rapid-fire sequence, the specific use of the terminology *required* is recommended. *Required* leaves no room for consideration as to the appropriateness of the use with consumers presenting at the agency/practice.

Question 3: Functional Assessment

Functional level assessment for consumers is encouraged in this methodology of establishing best practice or evidence-based protocol use. A functional level, such as the Global Assessment of Functioning (GAF; APA, 1994), allows a general overview of the state of the consumers receiving the treatment protocol. This general overview, that is, the change between beginning functional level and subsequent functional levels, can, thus, be used as a preliminary indicator for the effectiveness or lack of effectiveness of the protocol within the overall diagnostic category with which the agency/practice is working, for example, depression.

Use of the GAF is sometimes associated with complaints or concerns about inconsistency and inaccuracy of scoring among staff taking the measure. In research, these concerns are often expressed using the terminology, *interrater reliability,* which means that a variety of raters, given the same situation, rate the consumers' functional levels similarly. For a best practice or evidence-based practice initiation, steps are taken to ensure that staff would similarly rate consumers presenting with the same condition. Because of these concerns, GAF calibration training is strongly encouraged for all staff. Calibration training entails providing staff with clear guidelines and instructions on the meaning of the GAF scores, which can be done using vignettes in which the GAF scores are established, with explanations of each appropriate GAF score.

Treatment Plan Congruence

Ultimately, the purpose of a best practice or evidence-based protocol is to ensure that once an accurate diagnosis is confirmed, following the indicators on the protocol, a specific course of treatment is followed. A course of treatment is usually outlined or specified within a treatment plan. The next step of the golden thread—presenting problem followed by assessment of presenting problem, followed by accurate diagnosis of presenting problem—is the development of a treatment plan that adequately addresses that presenting problem.

Do not assume that the preceding process is occurring in your agency/practice without strong evidence based on a thorough clinical documentation review that it is occurring. The list of agencies being audited and fined for failure to provide adequate documentation grows daily, at least among those professional consultants who are called in to help these agencies correct their practices. Although the golden thread as a concept has been required by funding sources and recommended by accrediting bodies for the past decade, unless the agency/practice has taken specific steps to train staff how to achieve this process and has further taken steps to review that the golden thread process is taking place and correct instances where it is not occurring, there is no assurance that it is.

Questions 4 and 5 in Table 13.1 relate to treatment plan congruence with the presenting problem.

Question 4: Treatment Plan Problem Statement

Question 4 makes some assumptions about both the purpose and structure of a treatment plan. The first assumption is that the treatment plan is specifically designed to formally address the presenting problem that is documented in the formal clinical assessment. The second assumption, about the structure, is that the treatment plan is designed to formally highlight in some manner the presenting problem addressed. *Assurance,* the key word in this question and all of the following questions, relates to the processes the agency/practice takes to determine both the presence and the accuracy of the presenting problem as listed in the treatment plan.

A question for the team charged with designing a best practice treatment protocol relates, thus, to assurance in terms of accessibility of the presenting problem. How accessible is the presenting problem as the treatment plan is designed? Is there a place for the presenting problem that the treatment plan is addressing to be clearly spelled out? Is this place prominent in the beginning portion of the treatment plan?

Structure and Efficiency

Efficiency is a word that becomes prominent when the costs of processes must be considered. During the times of unlimited funding for social services, efficiency was not necessarily a value for consideration in the field. However, during any period in which funding is scarce or limited, efficiency should be a priority concern. This is especially true when considering documentation for evidence-based or best practice treatment protocols. A hallmark of the best practice or evidence-based protocol is required elements or processes. How will required elements be handled within the agency/practice processes? This is a critical question for consideration not only for clinical compliance, but also for clinical assurance. For example, the more prominent a required element of a treatment protocol is on a treatment plan, the greater is the likelihood that a treatment clinician will consider it for completion and the easier it will be for the team assigned to ensure the element's inclusion to do their job.

To this end, the design team must consider the extent that the current structure of the agency/practice's treatment plan allows ease of inclusion for required elements. Can a required element be placed in one specific area of a treatment plan, or can it be placed in one of several areas? How much time will a treatment clinician or other professional assigned to complete a treatment plan spend in trying to determine where a required element goes, for example, the score to a best practice measure? For the clinical record review team, how much time is required in reading between the lines to discover where the various elements that are to become required will be found? The more reading between the lines for required elements is found in the structure, the greater the time needed to provide assurance that the required elements are occurring. The more time needed to provide assurance, the greater the cost. Thus, accessibility is a key concept in terms of the assurance of any of the elements to be included in the protocol.

Prominence of the required elements can be one key to accessibility. Prominence can be achieved by highlighting, the use of an asterisk, the use of special instructions, and so on. In terms of the presenting problem, location early in the treatment plan is a key to accessibility. By early location, the busy treatment clinician is reminded as the treatment plan is started that treatment must be specifically linked to the presenting problem.

Assurance

The assurance process itself, only alluded to in the preceding questions, has to do with the practices in the agency/practice that may be called by many different names: chart review, clinical record review, utilization management per record review, and so on. What are the current structures for determining the completeness and adequacy of the clinical record? Which staff is involved in this process? How structured is the review process? These are a few considerations in determining the adequacy of the agency/practice's current process for redesign in terms of use for the evidence-based or best practice protocol use assurance.

The best practice or evidence-based practice assurance/fidelity process can be based on the clinical record review. A clinical record review is typically a process to determine the extent that the clinical record meets various requirements for completeness and adequacy. These requirements can be those of funding bodies, licensing bureaus, and/or accrediting agencies. In the process, the various requirements are listed in some fashion, and the clinical record is checked against the list. This type of review is only as good as the list; if the list is incomplete, it follows that the review will be incomplete. That is, the review will not cover all of the necessary or important items. While an incomplete review may suffice for many agency/practice processes, it would be inadequate in terms of a fidelity review for best practice or evidence-based practice.

Completeness of the review or assurance list is, however, only the first consideration. A second consideration is the quality of the list of elements for review. A simple listing of elements can yield only a simple assessment of the presence of required elements. It cannot yield an assessment of the quality of those elements. At best, it can yield the highly individualistic interpretation of the quality of the required elements. This interpretation will be based on the understanding of the person who is doing the evaluation and, thus, subject to individual interpretation as to what is required. That is, the simple list form of review is entirely subjective. A subjective review may be sufficient if the person doing the review is thoroughly based in the best practice treatment design protocol and has an exceptional memory for all of the details of the protocol. Lacking this proficiency, however, a simple listing of required elements is woefully inadequate.

While it may not be possible to make the assurance process entirely objective, the inclusion of specific instructions with each required element helps to eliminate some of the individualistic interpretation. The more thorough the instructions for each element of the protocol to be reviewed, the more objective that review can be. The more quality markers that are included in the review instructions, the higher the level of the quality of the record is ensured. Quality markers in this instance are highly specific instructions relating to the process or element that is being examined. Consider, for example, the following sets of instructions:

1. *Treatment plan:* "Presenting problem is present." This is an example of a simple listed element. It has no quality evaluative marker associated with it and, thus, will yield a subjective evaluation.

1A. *Treatment plan:* "Presenting problem present on the treatment plan is the same presenting problem listed in the clinical assessment." This example takes the preceding example one step in the right direction in that it ties the presenting problem in the treatment plan with the presenting problem in the clinical assessment. It is still a question that measures more presence and similarity than quality.

1B. *Treatment plan:* "The presenting problem listed on the treatment plan is the presenting problem listed in the clinical assessment and is specifically and clearly related to the final diagnostic formulation." This example ties the presenting problem to the final diagnosis and gives some quality markers—specifically and clearly. A good assurance process has specific questions related to the adequacy of the diagnosis before reaching the treatment plan question. The review question can be made more specific, however.

1C. *Treatment plan:* "The presenting problem listed on the treatment plan is the presenting problem listed in the clinical assessment and is specifically and clearly related to the final diagnostic formulation. *Specifically* means that there is a direct and logical link between the presenting problem and the final diagnosis such that you do not have to read between the lines or otherwise make an intuitive leap to reach the same diagnostic conclusion. *Clearly* means that any reasonable person reading the same presenting problem and diagnostic indicators could come to the same conclusion." In this review instruction, the quality markers, clearly and specifically, are defined and, thus, help to yield a more precise evaluation.

I do not advocate defining every word in a review instruction. This example is provided to illustrate the point that the more precise and complete the review instruction, the more precise and complete the review will be.

Question 5: Measurable Objectives

Question 5 relates specifically to the extent that the presenting problem is adequately addressed in the treatment plan. It again assumes a process and structure that is present within the treatment plan. The process is twofold: It assumes that the treatment plan will formulate a specific set of treatment goals and objectives that are related to the presenting problem and diagnosis; and it assumes that not only is there an expectation that these objectives be addressed in treatment but also that process toward meeting these goals and objectives will be measured as part of treatment. This question assumes that there is some process or place in the treatment plan where specific goals and objectives can be described. It also assumes that there is a structure for the indication of the measurement methodology.

Question 5 ties the treatment objectives squarely to the needs associated with the presenting problem. How does the presenting problem manifest itself in the thoughts, emotions, or behaviors of the consumer, and how specifically will therapy or counseling or other services address these needs? It is specifically the troublesome thoughts, emotions, or behaviors associated with the presenting problem that must be addressed in the objectives.

Assurance, as it relates to question 5, has to do with the extent that the agency/practice review process carefully examines the relationship of the presenting problem to these treatment goals and objectives. Specificity of objectives has to be carefully examined as objectives relate to the presenting problem. As described, a simple review listing of this element will yield a simple evaluation of the element. Following are examples of such a listing:

2. *Treatment objectives:* "The treatment plan has objectives that are related to the presenting problem." This type of listing is primarily a very loose question as to the general presence of such an element. It contains no quality markers.

2A. *Treatment objectives:* "The treatment plan contains objectives that are related to the presenting problem and, if applied, would lead to a reduction or amelioration of the presenting problem." The quality element is introduced in this version in that a direction or purpose of treatment is supplied—that of reduction or amelioration of the presenting problem. Further quality could be introduced via the use of the terms *specifically* and *clearly,* as discussed earlier.

Measurement

The inclusion of a method of measurement is critical in the adjudication of the effectiveness of a best practice or evidence-based treatment protocol. If an agency/practice is using a treatment protocol from one of the tool kits, the measurement method may be included in the tool kit. If the agency/practice has established best practice assessment or measurement protocols, these may be included in the objectives. If neither of these is available, a simple calibration scale can be included as part of the objective.

A calibration scale is simple for clinicians to formulate with a consumer. A calibration scale attempts to numerically quantify the extent of a problem or the degree or intensity of an emotion. The scale can be any set of numbers and is similar to a Likert scale. For example, "On a scale of 1 to 10, with 1 being no problem and 10 being the greatest problem, please rate your experience of this problem." Consumers can also be asked to indicate where on this scale they would like to be, thus giving a specific objective to work toward. For example, "Using the same scale, please indicate where you would like to be in relationship to this problem." As a further clinical tool, consumers can be asked how they will know they have reached this level; that is, what specific things will they be thinking, feeling, or doing differently to know that they have reached the desired level? This helps to make the treatment objective much more measurable and adds more quality measurement terms to the objective.

If such a calibration scale is used as part of the development of a best practices protocol, it is important to make the actual calibration scale consistent among treatment providers so that outcomes of the treatment protocol can be compared among consumers.

The inclusion of the measurement into the objective adds a further element of quality:

2B. "The treatment plan contains objectives that are related to the presenting problem and, if applied, would lead to a reduction or amelioration of the presenting problem as measured by the XXX scale for XXX problem."

The extent that a treatment staff is used to formulate specific treatment goals and objectives will relate to the ease in which they will be able to follow a specific best practice or evidence-based treatment protocol. The extent that a treatment staff is familiar with treating specific thoughts, emotions, and/or behaviors, the greater ease in which they will be able to follow a best practice or evidence-based treatment protocol. However, the following caveat is in order: The ease in following a best practice or evidence-based treatment protocol will relate specifically to the extent that treatment staff currently follow the goals and objectives set in the treatment plan.

Questions 6 and 7

Questions 6 and 7 relate to the congruence of the treatment plan to the actual treatment and the measurement of that treatment. Again, an admonition relating to *assure* is in order. A thorough clinical documentation review traces the golden thread as outlined earlier from the presenting problem all the way to a progress note that spells out specifically how the treatment proposed on the treatment plan was delivered and the extent the treatment was measured to determine how specifically the delivered treatment affected the presenting problem. The more an agency/practice has this type of procedure in effect, the greater ease there will potentially be in establishing a best practice or evidence-based treatment protocol because the staff will already be familiar with the processes required by such a protocol.

Question 6: Treatment Plan Objectives

Question 6 relates to the specific processes or procedures used by an agency/practice to determine if the treatment objectives are actually addressed as part of the treatment process. One method is through the review of the treatment progress notes. Again, both a process and a structure are assumed to be present in the agency/practice considering embarking on best practice or evidence-based practices. The process assumed is some type of required documentation concurrent with or following the provision of therapy, counseling, or other service. The structure relates to some method that is part of the progress note in which the service provider can link the service to the specific objective. Such a linkage requires that the treatment plan objectives be numbered or lettered or use some other process of identification and that the selected method of objective identification can be addressed on the progress note.

Once this linkage, as described earlier, has been established, the assurance questions can be applied to the progress notes. Specificity with quality markers is just as important a part to this process as to the previously described processes, as shown in the following examples:

3. *Progress notes:* "Progress notes are related to the treatment plan objectives." This measure of assurance is minimal subjective approximation of an attempt to determine possible linkage between treatment plan and actual treatment.

3A. *Progress notes:* "Progress notes indicate which treatment objective they are related to." This type of measure ties the objective identifier, described earlier, to the progress note. It is still a very rough measurement of linkage between treatment plan and progress note, but it is at least a specific indicator.

3B. *Progress notes:* "Progress notes indicate which treatment objective they are related to by treatment plan identifier and are appropriate in content to the intent of the treatment objective." Quality is beginning to be assessed in this measure in that appropriateness of content is introduced. Assurance of treatment plan linkage to actual treatment must be more than a simple placement of "A" in a box labeled "Treatment Objective." Content of the description of the service provided must be linked to whatever was indicated in the treatment plan as needing to occur with treatment objective A.

3C. *Progress notes:* "Progress notes indicate which treatment objective they are related to by treatment plan identifier and are clearly and specifically appropriate in content to the intent of the treatment objective." The markers *clearly* and *specifically* or other similarly defined markers could be added to give this review measure further quality and relevance.

Question 7: Measures Being Used

Question 7 relates specifically to the use of the assessment or measurement tool or process that is linked with each treatment plan objective. In the early days of designing objective and measurable treatment objectives, far more often than not, the measurement was included in the treatment objective but never carried through to session application.

There was, however, one notable exception—when the specific measure was required for another service, primarily a psychiatric service. When the psychiatrist required, for example, a Children's Attention Problem (CAP) score for a medication check, this measure, as indicated on a treatment plan, would be included in the progress note. It helped in the implication, perhaps, that the psychiatrist applied negative reinforcement when the measure was not included. This is an important lesson for those of us charged with designing and implementing best practice treatment protocols: That which is required and monitored by someone is more likely to be performed. A psychiatrist can be a powerful informal monitor of the use of best practice measures in service to the total implementation of a larger best practice treatment protocol. Thus, the inclusion of psychiatric services as part of the multidisciplinary design process can be crucial to successful implementation of the treatment protocol:

3D. *Progress notes:* "Progress notes indicate which treatment objective they are related to by treatment plan identifier and are clearly and specifically appropriate in content to the intent of the treatment objective and contain the required measurements/assessments listed in the treatment objective." This qualifier of the specific measurement or assessment tool brings the progress note to a utilitarian level in terms of assessing the effectiveness of a treatment protocol. When the measurement or assessment tool score is recorded in the clinical record, that clinical record can be data mined (see later discussion) in the process of determining effectiveness of the treatment protocol.

Question 7 also relates specifically to the concept and practice of fidelity measurement. Fidelity to process is an important consideration and was discussed earlier. If an agency/practice does not engage in a formal fidelity assessment, at least in terms of the use of measurement and assessment tools, all that agency/practice may have to rely on are the incidental reports of the psychiatric staff in response to clinicians who are not following the required processes and who may or may not be representative of the entire treatment staff. The results of a question such as 3D could be aggregated as an indication of fidelity to process. While this would and should not take the place of fidelity to the entire treatment protocol, it could be taken as one indicator of that larger process.

3E. *Progress notes:* "Progress notes indicate which treatment objective they are related to by treatment plan identifier and are clearly and specifically appropriate in content to the intent of the treatment objective and contain the required measurements/ assessments listed in the treatment objective. Further, there is evidence in the note that the clinician has used the results of the measurement to appropriately adjust the treatment of the consumer." The last qualifier, "used the results of the measurement to appropriately adjust the treatment," is ultimately the reason for including measures and for designing and implementing best practice and evidence-based treatment protocols.

First and foremost, the results of the measure must be applied to the treatment protocol to serve the needs of the consumer. The treatment protocol could, for example, call for either an increase or decrease in intensity of service based on the results of the measurement/assessment tool. The treatment protocol could also call for a specific type of service if the score was at or within a certain level. Part of the determination of the effectiveness of the protocol is the determination that the associated tools not only could be used but were used in getting the consumer to the correct level or correct type of service. A further question would be whether the measures were effective in differentiating that use, which is part of an analysis methodology that is discussed later.

Question 8: Aggregating Measurement Results

Question 8 relates specifically to the use of the measurement in the service to the needs of the consumer. My agency has found it particularly helpful to aggregate the best practice measures initially within the clinical record. With the chief psychiatrist, a set of graphing tools was developed for each best practice measurement tool. The results of the best practice-required measures were graphed on these charting tools and were located in the clinical record of each consumer who was being treated for that specific diagnosis. Thus, as appropriate treatment was being received and symptoms were, thus, reduced, the results of the measure appropriate for the diagnosis were clearly shown on the graph. This type of graphing allows primarily for data use in service to the needs of the consumer. Individual graphing in clinical records can be used in determining effectiveness of a treatment protocol but is time and labor intensive in that each consumer record must be individually examined.

Question 9: Use of Aggregated Results

Question 9 relates specifically to the aggregate use of the data collected in relationship to the treatment protocols. While it is possible to examine entire sets of clinical records, efficiency of determining clinical effectiveness of treatment protocols should be considered. It is important that these outcome measures be part of a clinical record so that the process can serve the needs of the consumer. It is also important to consider what an exceptionally laborious process it is to examine individual clinical records looking for said outcome measures. An electronic method of data capture should be considered as part of the protocol as designed. Electronic data capture allows for a more efficient use of time and further allows or could allow a more immediate aggregation of treatment data when there are a number of clinicians applying the best practice protocols with a number of consumers.

Both questions 8 and 9 relate to the processes an agency/practice has established to make use of the data that it is collecting. Some call these processes *data mining*. Although the term data mining is technically a subset mathematical process in the arena of knowledge management, in its common usage, it means using data to achieve some result. Agencies and practices that collect data simply and solely because some funding or accrediting body requires it are being called into question. For example, failure to show actual use of data to improve performance can result in a score of noncompliance during a JCAHO accrediting survey.

In terms of implementing evidence-based or best practice treatment protocols, the data collected must be used to determine the extent that the best practices being followed are achieving the results they were designed to achieve. That intent is the meaning of question 9. On the one hand, this question is an extension of the fidelity process discussion. But on the other hand, it has far wider reaching implications than mere fidelity. The results of looking at the data can be used to determine the effectiveness of the treatment process and, further, if the treatment process is shown to be ineffective, to improve the treatment processes.

In a research setting, the findings could lead to improvements that would perhaps be integrated in subsequent iterations of the treatment design. In an agency/practice process, the fidelity findings would probably be used to ensure that the treatment design was being followed more closely. The outcome findings would be used to determine the extent that a treatment process would be continued or developed further. This further development might not necessarily be part of a second iteration of a treatment design, but might more likely be part of a continuous improvement process.

Continuous improvement of a process would not be appropriate for researching the effectiveness of a treatment process in the research setting. If the effectiveness of a certain process is going to be established, that treatment process must remain constant throughout the trial. However, in the agency/practice setting, continuous improvement could be undertaken with certain provisos.

If a treatment protocol is to be improved or otherwise changed, the improvement should be based on an analysis of a statistically significant set of outcome data. It should not be modified just because the initial outcomes may not be as expected. Further, there should be some clear indications on or within the tracking mechanisms that the treatment protocol was modified. For example, if seven data points had been collected on the measurement/assessment tool and the treatment protocol was modified, every charting mechanism for that measurement/assessment tool should be clearly marked as to the change in protocol to allow for the specific tracking of the effect of the change in the treatment design on the outcomes.

The extent that an agency/practice has established the practice of using data to improve processes will be another determination of its ability to use or easily use best practice and/or evidence-based treatment protocols. The more an agency/practice has a practice history of using data to improve or correct procedures, the easier it will be to adapt the design/redesign portion of the best practice-based processes.

Question 10: Benchmarking Data

Question 10 concerns the practice of relating the results or outcomes of the agency/practice's processes with those of other agencies or with national standards. The problem, at least at this early stage for the behavioral healthcare industry in the process of designing and testing best practice protocols, is that there are no other agencies with outcome data with which to compare process outcomes. This is not true for those agencies that choose to follow the evidence-based practices as outlined in the preceding chapters. There are sufficient outcomes with which to compare data.

The outcome data as described in the preceding chapters can also be put to use for benchmarking if an agency/practice has decided to modify certain of the recommended best practices in the tool kit. Did the modified process produce as good as, better, or worse results than the original process? A similar parallel benchmarking process can be used if the agency/practice has developed its own treatment protocol for an area in which there are published outcome results of another treatment protocol for the same diagnosis or functional area. Did the agency/practice's protocol achieve the same results as the published protocol? If not, should the design team consider modifying the protocol to more closely match the protocol with the better results? You will have to decide the answer based on the needs of your agency/practice and the consumer base for which the protocol was developed.

But further, especially in tight financial times, an agency/practice should ask itself whether it can afford to test run its own particular treatment protocols. Is its situation so unique that it cannot apply those treatment processes that have already been shown to be effective in producing positive consumer outcomes?

GROUND ZERO ACTIVITIES

The following are presented as preliminary activities to assist an agency/practice prepare to institute evidence-based practices.

Cooperative or Business, Revisited

Table 13.2 is a reiteration of the suggestions that are based on the questions listed in Table 13.1. Based on the experience of my agency, the preceding activities will ease the process of instituting either best practice treatment protocols or evidence-based treatment protocols with an agency/practice. The need to have these practices or some approximations of these practices relates to the discussions in Chapter 12 as to the status of the agency/practice. Is the agency/practice a cooperative of loosely affiliated semi-independent practitioners, or is it a business with consistent practices, including and especially clinical practices? The more consistent the clinical practices are within the agency/practice, the less you will need to adopt these specific recommendations. Here, consistency must be based on an actual and formal review of the practices, including the current informal treatment protocols, and not on the collective consensus of management or supervisory staff.

Table 13.2   Ground Zero Activities

1. Assessment/diagnosis that meets *DSM-IV* criteria.
2. Presenting problem in assessment is consistent with *DSM-IV* diagnosis.
3. Treatment plan problem statement consistent with *DSM-IV* diagnosis.
4. Treatment plan objectives designed to reduce *DSM-IV* diagnostic problems.
5. Tx plan objective is measurable.
6. Tx plan objectives have a standardized measurement.
7. Progress notes consistent with problems per *DSM-IV* diagnosis.
8. Progress notes consistent with objective.
9. Progress notes measures, per Individual Treatment Plan measurement, the objective.

Source: From "Evidence-Based Therapy: Is There a Practical Approach?" by R. Hayes, 2001, *Behavioral Health Management, 21*(6), pp. 20–24. Reprinted with permission.

Informal Protocols and Practices

Informal treatment protocols are those processes that clinical staff are currently using for the treatment of the various disorders present in the agency/practice. Informal protocols are likely to be based either solely on a particular theoretical training model the professional staff learned, either in their initial professional training or in subsequent training experiences, or on an amalgamation of the various theoretical models to which they have been exposed. These theoretical models are coupled with the practices that are required, either formally or informally, in the agency/practice. Informal required practices are those practices that are not specifically disseminated by agency/practice policy or written practice but are the practices, nevertheless, that were developed by the staff who are responsible for the particular service or aspect of service and must be followed if staff want to access that service. For example, if you hear, "That's just the way Staff Name wants it done," you know you have informal practices.

Informal practices may be appropriate to the current needs of the clinical practice. They may lead to improved outcomes for the consumers. They may even be worth disseminating as best practices for the entire agency/practice. Informal practices and protocols, however, are bound to the person originating them and may or may not be continued after that person leaves the position or the agency/practice. Outcomes relating to the informal protocol or practice will be lost. If the practice is good, that would be unfortunate, both for the agency/practice and for the consumers. However, what usually happens is the opposite: "Staff Name is gone, so now we can do this the way it really should be done."

The behavioral health cooperative is fraught with informal practices and protocols based on years of clinical habits that may or may not bring positive results, either for the agency/practice or the consumer. Following the steps as listed in Table 13.2 will begin to move a staff from informal and personal practices ("I will do as I believe best") to formal, consistent agency/practicewide practices ("I will follow the agency/practice-required processes").

An agency/practice that is ready to begin the use of formal treatment (either best practice or evidence-based) protocols will have a formal assessment process that leads to a diagnosis that meets *DSM-IV* criteria. The presenting problem listed in the assessment will be consistent with *DSM-IV* diagnosis. The treatment plan problem statement (i.e., the statement in the treatment plan that indicates why the treatment plan is being drawn up) will be consistent with *DSM-IV* diagnosis and will have specific goals and objectives that are designed to reduce the *DSM-IV* diagnostic problems and, thus, relieve the presenting problem. Further, the treatment will have objectives that are measurable and, preferably, use standardized measurement processes. The progress notes written by the treatment service provider will be consistent with problems listed on the treatment plan and will clearly relate to the *DSM-IV* diagnosis. The notes will be consistent with the objectives of the treatment plan and will clearly indicate which objective is being addressed by the specific treatment for the specific day. Further, the progress notes will adequately and appropriately reflect the measurement tool results as listed in the treatment plan and will show evidence that the results of the measurement have been incorporated into the treatment process. The fact that these practices are occurring is documented minimally by a specific and thorough clinical records review process and by direct supervision, as needed.

NON-GROUND ZERO START—DECISIONS

The following decisions are presented to assist an agency/practice determine what its next steps will be in moving toward an evidence-based practice.

Evidence-Based or Evidence-Supported Practices

You may have determined that your agency/practice has met many or most of the preceding indicators. Perhaps leadership and the implementation team have decided that the agency/practice can incorporate these factors into the initial design of your evidence-based project. Perhaps they are unsure but are still considering whether the agency/practice can or will implement evidence-related practices and want more information before making the decision. Whatever the case, you are ready for the next step in the decision-making process.

Will your agency/practice use evidence-based or evidence-supported protocols? A number of questions follow from this question: What, exactly, is the primary difference between evidence-based and evidence-supported practices? How does this difference play itself out in any possible implementation in an agency/practice?

Chapters 2 through 9 have delineated the six tool kit practices supported by the Substance Abuse and Mental Health Administration and the Robert Wood Johnson Foundation, as well as the National Alliance for the Mentally Ill. These practices are examples of evidence-based practices. In essence, evidence-based practices have been thoroughly researched and have proven to be effective in producing and maintaining therapeutic changes within the areas they address. That is, when an agency/practice follows the treatment protocols for the given client population, that population consistently shows improved functioning and maintains that higher level of functioning. There is no guessing as to whether the treatment is effective. It has been proven to be effective in the research setting.

Further, many of these tool kit practices have been replicated in settings outside the initial research setting with similar consistent results, which means that outside the initial research setting, other populations of similar clients for which the treatment protocol was designed have also shown improved functioning when treatment protocol was followed. The latter is most important in terms of the decision of an agency/practice to use these or other evidence-based practices.

The proven ability, via research, to replicate an evidence-based practice has practical implications for the agency/practice. When the agency/practice follows the particular practice parameters of the evidence-based treatment with the population for which it was designed, the likelihood or probability is very high that similar treatment-related results will be produced for the clients in that agency/practice. All else being equal, the evidence-based, replicated treatment protocol is, thus, a cost-effective methodology for producing improved levels of care in the intended population for which it was designed; therefore, scarce treatment dollars will not be wasted on treatment methods that do not work or that produce inconsistent or insufficient results.

In contrast, evidence-supported treatment methodologies are treatment methods that are in the process of being researched (see Hofmann & Tompson, 2002). For the most part, they have passed initial stages of research that prove their basic effectiveness in the research setting. They may be in the early replication stage of a complete research design, or they may not have yet started the replication stage. In a complete research design, replication is considered a critical and important step to demonstrate that the results of the initial research are not contingent on other indiscriminate factors associated with the initial research.

For the agency/practice in the process of deciding where it will allocate treatment funds, the evidence-supported treatment protocol is somewhat less of a sure thing. For the past 3 years, I have received mass mailing from a variety of publishing concerns and workshop providers advertising the promise of "evidence-supported" treatments for a variety of possible treatment considerations in a behavioral health practice. These fliers may or may not be accompanied by references for obtaining the evidence that supports the proposed practice. Thus, from a practical and financial standpoint, there may be more upfront time involved in the use of evidence-*supported* as compared to evidence-*based* treatment protocols. The use of evidence-supported protocols may require more preliminary research as to applicability of the protocol to the agency/practice's setting. The important consideration is that, short of replication research, the applicability of the protocol to the agency/practice's specific setting may be entirely unknown. This could require more upfront preparation, in terms of carefully comparing the parameters of the *supported* protocol to the agency/practice parameters. This is not to say that an evidence-*supported* protocol would not produce desired results for an agency/practice's clientele; it is just that there may be more possibility or probability that it would not produce desired results than the fully evidence-*based* protocol.

The decision as to which protocol an agency/practice would participate in is dependent on the agency/practice's ability and/or design to manage the risks associated with the less sure, evidence-supported practice. However, the agency making this decision must also compare the risks associated with its current practices, which may have no evidence to support their use. Part of the impetus to switch to evidence-based or evidence-supported practices could be the desire to lessen the risk associated with using treatment methodologies based entirely on the theoretical understandings of one treatment guru. There may be far less risk associated with some evidence for efficacy than for no evidence of efficacy at all.

Diagnosis or Functional Problem

It seems highly probable that an agency/practice will not switch all of its practices to evidence-based or evidence-supported treatment protocols in one time period or in one single process but, instead, phase in the use of treatment protocols over a period of time and over a number of processes. Thus, the next set of decisions has to do with the population the agency/practice will choose for implementation of its best practice treatment beginnings. The experience of my agency may offer some guidance. Because a strategic plan element specifically called for "databased decision making" within all agency processes, it was decided to use demographic data as a guide for the selection of best practices to implement. This agency primarily provides outpatient therapy services, so it was decided to use the top three diagnostic categories seen in the agency. Data as to diagnostic categories were aggregated for the preceding 1 year, 5 years, and 10 years. The same three diagnostic categories were consistently in the top although their actual position varied. Therefore, these three diagnostic categories were selected for best practice treatment protocols use.

In other types of settings where diagnostic category may not be appropriate, functional concerns may be a more appropriate and effective consideration. Dual diagnosis, co-occurring mentally ill with substance or chemical abuse problems (MISA or MICA), is one such functional area that could be appropriate for best practice methodologies. Sexually aggressive youth in a residential setting could be another functional area that would be suited to best practice or evidence-based protocol use. Multi Systemic Family Therapy ® is one such evidence-based treatment model that is based on a variety of functional problems of the identified clients and not on any one specific diagnostic category. The setting of the agency/practice or program determines the appropriate emphasis.

A second guiding principle in determining areas for use in an evidence-based protocol is the one used by the Joint Commission for the Accreditation of Healthcare Organizations in its suggestions for determining performance improvement strategies The JCAHO recommends performance improvement efforts be made in areas that are "high risk, high volume, or problem prone" (Joint Commission on the Accreditation of Healthcare Organizations, 2002). In the preceding example, my agency chose high volume as a guiding principle with the initial three practice guidelines. However, in the development of the fourth practice guideline, my agency leadership chose the MISA population, a functional area, because of both the high risk and problem-prone nature of this population.

COLLECT EVIDENCE ON THE AGENCY/PRACTICE'S OWN PROCESSES

A third alternative, rather than using established evidence-based or evidence-supported treatment protocol, is an agency/practice collecting evidence on its own treatment processes to build an evidentiary case for effectiveness of its treatment. This process, described next, allows (permits) an agency/practice to research its own processes either as they are currently provided or as they are specifically designed or modified from evidence-based or evidence-supported practices. My agency, Sinnissippi Centers, Inc., has consistently taken this approach in the use of best practice protocols. It has also been recognized for one of its best practice program designs for the MISA population by both the Joint Commission, having been awarded the Ernst A. Codman Award in 2002, and the American Psychiatric Association, having received the APA Bronze Psychiatric Services Award in 2003. It is possible outside a university setting to design and research the effectiveness of treatment protocols.

Table 13.3 lists some questions for initial consideration in the task of designing and researching the effectiveness of a treatment protocol in an agency/practice or university setting. At this point, it is assumed that the conditions described in Tables 13.1 and 13.2 have been met, in whole or in part, by the agency/practice. The questions in Table 13.3 take the earlier questions to the next level of the evidence collection process.

Question 1: Standardized Treatment Protocols

Question 1 has an underlying assumption, namely, that many agencies already have delineated some standardized treatment protocols for either specific diagnostic categories or areas of functional deficits. These treatment protocols may be written, formal, and have some identification that labels them clearly as a treatment methodology. However, there may exist within the agency/practice any number of treatment methodologies that may be called by other names, but could nevertheless be considered a rudimentary form of treatment protocol. Therefore, question 1 should be considered carefully and by a multifunctional treatment team that is aware of all of the forms of treatment that occur in the agency/practice. For example, there may be rudimentary protocols that could be known as program plans, treatment suggestions, or treatment planning modules. These modules or plans or suggestions could form the basis of a more formal treatment protocol. Further, rudimentary protocols may exist as outlines for group content, as discussion guidelines for homework assignments, or within training outlines for the care of specific groups of consumers. Again, these outlines or discussion guides or training outlines

Table 13.3   Questions to Ask When Designing and Researching a Treatment Protocol

1. Has your agency/practice developed standardized treatment protocols for any specific diagnostic categories or specific areas of functional deficits?
2. Has your agency/practice trained staff to use the protocols with consumers?
3. Has your agency/practice trained in the statistical processes necessary to interpret the results of measurements?
4. Does your agency/practice assure that the treatment protocols, including measurement usage, are being followed?
5. Has your agency/practice aggregated data from your protocols to determine effectiveness of protocol?

Source: From "Evidence-Based Therapy: Is There a Practical Approach?" by R. Hayes, 2001, *Behavioral Health Management, 21*(6), pp. 20–24. Reprinted with permission.

could serve as the basis for the development of a more formalized treatment process for which outcomes could be gathered.

There are advantages of using methodologies such as described previously that already exist in some semiformal manner within the agency/practice. There should be fewer formal training needs associated with this approach, formalizing and structuring a current methodology, since the treatment staff will already have some degree of familiarity with it, which could mean a quicker and easier start-up of the project with less initial resistance from staff. It could also mean a less cost-intensive start-up, as compared to training a staff on an entirely new process. Further, the cost of development for the treatment protocol is reduced when an agency/practice chooses to formalize a current practice. Time in researching and structuring is significantly lessened, although it may not be entirely eliminated.

Researching the agency/practice's current practice for formalization into a treatment protocol is needed. It is important to ensure that there is no research indicating that the methodologies currently being used are counterindicated for the population to be served with the formalized approach.

However, it could be helpful in treatment protocol development to discover if there is available a researched treatment protocol similar to the practices that the agency/practice is attempting to formalize. If there is, a hybrid approach to formalizing the current treatment methods could be developed. In this hybridization approach, the current practices could be mapped to the researched practices. Areas of similarity could be carefully noted. Areas of difference could also be noted, either for possible inclusion into the practice or as a point of comparison in terms of outcomes. If there is a great deal of similarity of approaches, the researched model could become the agency/practice's formalized treatment protocol. It would be important to use the same outcome measures as the researched model, if available, so that the agency/practice could benchmark its treatment results with that of the researched model.

If no similar treatment models are found or, as is the likelihood, absolutely no researched treatment protocols are discovered for the diagnosis or functional problem that is to be addressed, it is important for the development of the treatment protocol to follow carefully the steps outlined in Chapter 12 to do adequate research in the effectiveness of the treatment protocol.

There is one further consideration as to question 1 of Table 13.3. As indicated earlier, there may be a number of informal methodologies in the agency/practice that could prove useful in the development of a formalized treatment protocol. The team charged with the development of the treatment protocol could call together a special development group of clinicians experienced in the proposed area of development. Before this group meeting, members of the protocol development team should meet with each clinician individually to determine this staff's treatment approach to the specific area or problem. Do a thorough and exhaustive examination of how the clinician provides treatment. Ask multiple "What if" questions: "What if the consumer doesn't respond to this? What do you do next?" Also ask multiple "How" questions: "How do you know the consumer is doing better? How do you know if the consumer is doing worse?" The development team could next aggregate all of the responses in terms of points of similarity and dissimilarity of approaches. Put the approaches in the form of a decision tree or flow chart, the initial best practice treatment protocol. Next, call together the senior clinicians to discuss the initial treatment protocol the design team has developed from their input. Do any necessary refinement or make changes as suggested by the clinicians. Get their input as to the usefulness of this structured approach in the current system to help ensure early buy-in to the designed, formalized process. Remember the admonition to research the completed protocol.

Question 2: Staff Training

Question 2 deals once again with the need to train staff in the use of the best practice treatment protocols. The length and intensity of the training will vary depending on the level of prior formal protocol use within the agency/practice. If the agency/practice has had no experience in the use of a formal treatment protocol, staff will need some general training on treatment protocols as well as specific training on the use of the diagnosis or functional deficit area protocol.

General training on the use of treatment protocols should be provided for several specific reasons. One reason concerns optimum learning for the staff involved. Research in the field of adult learning indicates that adult learners have a variety of learning styles (Hayes & Nelson, 2000). Each learning style has a somewhat different method of learning that requires a specific type of training for optimal learning. The staff that need to be trained will have these various learning styles, although they may not be aware of their own specific learning style or need. Understanding the learning styles of the staff and training to those learning styles will help the training to be more effective and help the staff to more quickly apply the protocol and apply it correctly.

If the agency/practice has made the decision based on the preceding questions that it can do a non-ground zero start, the agency/practice may already have a formal training committee in place that can work with the best practice protocol committee in designing the specific training for the treatment protocol. The training committee should seriously consider learning styles in developing the training plan for this project.

Training and Learning Styles

There are several models of learning style representation. Felder and Silverman (1988) represent adult learning styles as pairs of opposites. The opposite pairs are: active or reflective, sensing or intuitive, visual or verbal, and sequential or global. Each extreme of the pair of learning characteristics has a specific training methodology attached to it.

Active learners learn by doing. They do best in group activities and do not fare well in lecture situations, especially if taking notes is required. If a lecture situation is chosen for the best practice protocol training, these learners will need copies of the materials presented and, minimally, an outline of the lecture. Group discussion about how to specifically apply the treatment protocol to a case study will help this group of learners more quickly.

Reflective learners have to think through a process to understand it and need to have time alone to work on understanding new material. These learners will find the lecture situation just as difficult as the active learners. They can, however, be given the information about the history of treatment protocol use and the newly developed protocol and how it is to be used in the agency/practice to read and study on their own. A pretest/posttest can be used with reflective learners to ensure that they have completed the training. Having reflective learners attend mandatory group lecture trainings is a waste of their time and a waste of agency/practice resources.

Sensing learners like established training methods. They do not like surprises. They deal well with memorization, details, and lab-type work, but not necessarily a lecture situation. These learners need lots of concrete examples of how the treatment protocol will be applied in a variety of situations.

Intuitive learners like to discover and understand relationships. If the agency/practice has adopted a research-based treatment protocol that was similar to a formal or informal process already being used within the agency/practice setting, intuitive learners should be given copies of the mapping as suggested previously so they can see the relationship between what they were doing and what they are supposed to be doing in the new methodology. If such a map was not developed, this would be a good project for intuitive learners to help them learn the new methodology. That is, have them map out what they are currently doing for the treatment group and relate that process to what they are going to be required to do in the new treatment protocol. Intuitive learners prefer the innovative, new concepts and abstractions. They need the history of treatment protocol development and the theoretical and philosophical reasons the agency/practice is switching to the use. They will also be allies in the dissemination of this innovation.

Visual learners remember what they see. The current computer-based slide projection training techniques (e.g., PowerPoint™) are made for these types of learners. They need diagrams, sketches, maps, and so on. They also respond well to color coding of concepts. Most people are visual learners, which is one reason the use of computer-based slide presentations is very popular. For these learners, the lecture that accompanies the projected slide is less important than the slide. It is important, therefore, to be sure to get the important information about the protocol use on the slides.

Verbal learners are made for the straightforward lecture situation. Most people, however, do not learn this way. This is an important consideration for the training committee that is using valuable agency/practice resources in doing training. A strict and straightforward lecture will be ineffective in training most staff and, therefore, is a waste of agency/practice resources.

Sequential learners understand material when it is defined in clear, linear logical steps. The material has to be presented to them sequentially—first, second, third, and so on. They are invaluable to have both on the training committee and in the treatment protocol development team because they will be the first members to see the holes in the protocol. They will be the first to know the steps that have been left out because they will not be able to continue either in the training or the discussion or the development of the protocol until the next logical step has been provided or discovered. Identify the agency/practice's sequential learners and use them for this project.

Global learners tend to need the big picture to adequately understand the material they are being presented. They understand in large jumps and random steps. They can get from point A to point R without going through all the in-between steps. They may or may not even consider the need for the intermediate steps. Global learners need the history of best practice and evidence-based treatment protocols to get the big picture before they can or will adequately learn the protocol. Because they are not necessarily good at detail work, they also need close monitoring after the implementation of the treatment protocol to ensure that they are following it.

Although they are essential in designing the global aspects of the treatment protocol, global learners are ill prepared for developing the intermediate steps. When paired with sequential learners, they can help the team keep the project focused on the big picture while sequential learners deal with the details of the protocol.

Efficiency and effectiveness in training require consideration of all of these learning styles so as to not waste precious agency/practice resources. This can be accomplished using computer-based slide presentations, one of the current best practice training technology methods available. Copies of the slides can be handed out in advance of any presentation, with any other supporting documentation. Intuitive learners can be offered the option of reading the material on their own and taking a posttest to opt out of the training, thus, not wasting their time in a lecture. For those staff who might attend a presentation on the treatment protocol, learners can be divided into similar learning styles for appropriate learning-related activities. It is possible to let the learners self-select into their appropriate learning style by designing the postpresentation learning opportunities to match each style's learning needs. For example, the training team could devise a set of vignettes of presenting cases. One activity could be group discussion (active learners); another activity could be relating the new protocol to the former treatment method (any intuitive learners present and the sequential learners). Global learners and verbal learners could take the posttest to determine what further training they might need. Linking the training to the learning style in this manner or in some other method increases the effectiveness of the training and, thus, increases the probability that the treatment protocol will be carried out appropriately. It also adds to the cost-effectiveness of the training.

Question 3: Statistical Process Training

Have staff been trained in statistical processes? Is this absolutely necessary? While staff do not need to be capable of postgraduate-level statistical analysis, they do need to be aware of the basic meaning of what they read in the evidence-based literature, as well as the training material they will be given on the treatment protocols the agency/practice has developed.

If the agency/practice is going to be data driven in making decisions, the basic data analysis tools for doing this are absolutely essential. Supervisors and management personnel will need to know the basic processes for making appropriate decisions based on the analysis of the data they and the staff are collecting. They need to know the basics of statistical process control, a process developed specifically for use in industry, but with practical application for the behavioral healthcare industry.

For example, raising the staff's awareness level of the term and concept of statistical significance can help to prevent errors in interpreting data. In my experience in working with agencies, decisions have been made based on a single data point that was common cause or random variation and, thus, not statistically significant. Because the datum was from common cause variation and because changes were made to the system based on that random variation, the system subsequently produced worse results than if the agency/practice had appropriately chosen to wait for further data. Valuable resources had been wasted in making changes to the system, changes that were based on the wrong interpretation of the available data. If someone in a meeting discussing these changes had asked, "Is this result statistically significant or is it just random variation?" the resources this agency/practice wasted could have been saved and better used.

Most staff at a master's degree level will have had some statistical training. Staff with bachelor- or associate-level degrees and nondegreed staff will not have had such training. Even for those staff with college training, there is little probability of their remembering the training. More importantly, however, there is little probability that even if they do remember the statistical training, they will have had no specific training in how to interpret statistical results and use them to make treatment or management decisions. The training committee of the agency/practice starting on the journey toward the use of best practice and evidence-based treatment protocols should include at least elementary training on statistical processes for the general staff and some type of advanced training for management and supervisory staff.

Staff should be familiar with these basic statistical terms and processes: mean or average, random variation, normal curve, special cause and common cause variations, standard deviation, control charts, correlation, standard score, standard difference, trending, statistical significance. In my agency, all supervisors and management staff are required to pass competency tests on elements of program design and on statistical processes.

Questions 4 and 5: Making Use of the Data

Questions 4 and 5 relate to the extent the agency/practice is making use of the data that is being collected. Question 4 relates to the concept of fidelity to process referred to earlier in the text. Do leaders know the extent the treatment clinicians are following the processes prescribed in the treatment protocols currently in use? Question 5 asks if leaders are using the data to make decisions about the effectiveness of the treatment protocol in use. Both questions emphasize the need to make the collection of data more than an exercise. Data, to produce meaningful results, must be both analyzed as to statistical significance and, when statistically significant, used to address the process they were collected from. If the process is producing statistically significant results, that process can be and should be continued and perhaps expanded. If a treatment system or protocol is not producing statistically significant results, that system must be examined to discover why and what can be modified within the system or added to the system so that positive statistically significant results do occur. This examination process needs to occur for two reasons: (1) so that consumers can get better through the treatment staff provides and (2) so that the agency/practice does not continue to waste resources on treatment methods that in effect do not produce positive results.

FINANCE, FUND, OR INTEGRATE CURRENT PRACTICES

A further consideration in the decision to use evidence-based or supported treatment protocol has to do with financing such a new venture. In the previously described MISA best practice protocol development in my agency, no specific funding for the project was received. The best protocol in its development looked at both specific barriers to treatment and improvements in treatment for the population. The design also carefully examined barriers to the agency's receiving payment for services that the agency was already providing this consumer base. In designing the complete best practice protocol, both treatment and administrative (e.g., documentation) protocols were developed. In implementing the best practice, both the treatment guidelines—to increase consumer functioning—and administrative guidelines—to increase probability of correct processes so that payment was received—were used. This permitted processes to be instituted that allowed consumers to have statistically significant functional improvement, and the agency was able to capture funding that it previously had not been able to capture because of errors in meeting documentation requirements.

The development of a best practice treatment protocol in an agency/practice allows for all of the ancillary aspects of the treatment, that is, financial, support requirements, and so on, being considered in addition to the actual treatment aspects. The ability for an agency/practice to successfully accomplish this process is believed to be contingent on many of the ideas discussed in this chapter. While it may be possible for an agency/practice to accomplish such a development and successful implementation without the practices in place, there is a greater ease and higher likelihood of success when they are in place.

REFERENCES

American Psychiatric Association. (1994). *Diagnostic and statistical manual of mental disorders* (4th ed.). Washington, DC: Author.

Felder, R., & Silverman, L. (1988). Learning and teaching styles in engineering education [Electronic version]. *Engineering Education, 78*(8), 674–681.

Hayes, R. (2001). Evidence-based therapy: Is there a practical approach? *Behavioral Health Management, 21*(6), 20–24.

Hayes, R., & Nelson, L. (2000). *Handbook of quality change and implementation for behavioral health care.* Revere, MA: C&R.

Hofmann, S., & Tompson, M. (2002). *Treating chronic and severe mental disorders: A handbook of empirically supported interventions.* New York: Guilford Press.

Joint Commission on the Accreditation of Healthcare Organizations. (2002). *2003 comprehensive accreditation manual for behavioral health care.* Oakbrook Terrace, IL: Author.

CHAPTER 14

Build Your Own Best Practice Protocols

Randy A. Hayes

As discussed in Chapter 13, it is possible to design a best practice protocol for use within your agency/practice. The extent that this best practice protocol is or will become evidence-based is dependent on the extent that its efficacy is researched by the agency/practice. That research could be considered a major undertaking in many settings. Another possibility for the agency/practice wanting to initiate evidence-based therapy is to design a best practice protocol that is based on existing *evidence-supported* treatment protocols. In this option, the basic efficacy research has already been done. By designing a treatment protocol based on the original research, you are attempting to replicate the initial work and, as such, could add, if various fidelity requirements are met, to the available knowledge base on the protocol in question.

EVIDENCE-BASED/EVIDENCE-SUPPORTED AND THE BEST PRACTICE PROTOCOL: A REITERATION OF THE DIFFERENCES

At this point, the difference between a best practice and evidence-based or evidence-supported protocol needs to be clarified. The following definition is taken from my agency's staff training on the use of their best practice guidelines/protocols:

> A best practice treatment protocol is a suggested course of treatment and/or treatment services for a specific diagnosis, functional deficit or problem area. The protocol highlights the major therapeutic intervention points. It can identify choices of different courses or paths of treatment. It also suggests a logical order of flow of interventions. It suggests possible (or potential) comorbid diagnoses which should be taken into consideration as assessment and as treatment continues. Points to consider psychiatric consultation, as well as suggested follow-up guidelines/time lines are given. The guideline or protocol is not meant to replace or supercede clinical judgment. It is to provide a structured format for consistent consideration of treatment possibilities for a specific diagnosis or problem area. (Sinnissippi Centers, Inc., 1999)

A best practice guideline or protocol may be evidence-based; that is, it may be based on available research. However, it may also be based on best practice consensus. A consensus guideline is based on the combined recommendations of the experts of the field in general or of the experts within an area of specialty. The latter may be based on the available research, though not necessarily.

When researching the design of a best practice protocol for use in a practice, care must be maintained as to the extent available research has gone into the formulation of consensus guidelines. Presumably, the experts within a specialty field are more knowledgeable about a specific problem area or diagnostic category than the staff working at a local behavioral healthcare agency. This does not automatically mean, however, that their knowledge, however great, is based on the most current research in the specific field.

This consideration should not delay your decision to institute the use of a best practice protocol. The more a treatment staff is accustomed to following a treatment protocol, whatever its source or the extent it is based on the research, the easier it will be ultimately to move that staff from a less research- or evidence-based protocol to a more evidence-based protocol. This is the first concern for an agency/practice that is beginning its journey in evidence-based practices: accustoming the treatment staff to following a treatment protocol. The presumption is that as the research progresses over the years and decades, current treatment protocols that are based on the very best evidence possible will be replaced by other treatment protocols that are based on better or more complete research and evidence. Evidence-based treatment protocol should and undoubtedly will evolve and develop. Protocols can and will be replaced within agencies and practices.

The initial job for an agency/practice that is not used to following treatment protocols is to provide staff with at least one protocol to follow so that the staff becomes attuned to the concept of the treatment protocol (as compared to their own individualized treatment methodology) as an acceptable method of providing therapy.

A SCIENTIFIC APPROACH TO BUILDING A BEST PRACTICE PROTOCOL

Table 14.1 presents one method of developing a best practice protocol that follows a scientific methodology. Each step is discussed following an introduction to the scientific methodology, a methodology or process recommended for the development of the treatment protocol.

Table 14.1   One Method of Developing a Best Practice Protocol

1. A formal plan must be developed.
2. The plan contains hypotheses about treatment.
3. Treatment protocols that follow the plan must be developed.
4. Data collecting methods must be developed and used.
5. Training in procedures for following the protocol and the measures must take place for all staff.
6. Standardized methods for collecting, analyzing, comparing data must be developed and maintained.
7. Methodology to determine if staff are following the treatment procedures is developed.
8. Analysis methodology is used in interpreting your results to improve your system.

Source: From "Evidence-Based Therapy: Is There a Practical Approach?" by R. Hayes, 2001, *Behavioral Health Management, 21*(6), pp. 20–24. Reprinted with permission.

The Scientific Method and Protocol Development

A scientific method of developing clinical protocols is recommended over other types of protocol development. A scientific type of methodology seeks to establish the effectiveness of the protocol to determine if that protocol should be used to treat consumers with the same or similar presenting problems. That is, a scientific methodology seeks some verification of the truth of the protocol: Does it really work to help people achieve a higher functional level? Specifically, a scientific methodology might seek to determine whether the treatment protocol works better than doing nothing at all and might use a control or comparison group, or it might seek to determine whether this treatment protocol works better than another treatment methodology.

Other protocol developmental methodologies do not focus on effectiveness as much as they may focus on mere replication of the developer's technique. This replication focus was in fact what typified the behavioral healthcare field for many decades. Treatment methodologies were developed and disseminated by big names in the field, not so much to aggregate data as to the effectiveness of their methodology, but more to spread the use of that methodology. The overall effectiveness of the treatment methods or protocols was assumed from the experience of the practitioner disseminating the treatment methodology.

This method of developing a clinical protocol other than through the scientific method could be called a protocol development based on clinical experience. A protocol developed from clinical experience makes use of the experience that a seasoned professional has had in treating a diagnosis or a functional area. Developing practitioners believe that the protocol they have used has led to good outcomes. Further, they believe that because they have had good outcomes, anyone else following their protocol will achieve good outcomes. Such a protocol, thus, lists the steps that the seasoned practitioner has followed in treating the diagnosis. This protocol might look similar to a best practice or evidence-based protocol. This protocol might, for example, make use of functional measurement tools to determine if the consumer was showing improvement from the treatment. Perhaps the protocol would even have alternate treatment methodologies if the consumer was not showing sufficient improvement from the primary mode of treatment. However, the primary difference between this method (replication of a seasoned clinician's treatment method) and a scientific method is in how the measurement results were used in terms of proving or disproving the effectiveness of the actual treatment methodology. In a scientific methodology, the measurement results serve not only the needs of the individual consumer but also the overall effectiveness of the treatment for all consumers.

For example, staff could aggregate the results of the preceding treatment protocol based on clinical experience to attempt to determine the overall effectiveness of the protocol. It might be possible to find that in 75% of the individual cases, the treatment was ineffective in increasing the functional level of the consumer using the measurement tool called for in the treatment protocol. Is a 25% effectiveness rate good? Without some method of comparing data usually found in a scientific process, this answer could not be known. Without some sort of statistical analysis of the data found in a scientific process, staff and leadership would not know whether the effectiveness rate is satisfactory.

Thus, the true scientific nature of the protocol is found in step 8 of Table 14.1: The measurement serves the truth of the protocol. If it is determined to be ineffective, the treatment must be abandoned so that a new treatment may be discovered that does bring results, not only to the originator of the treatment but to anyone else appropriately applying the treatment.

A Formal Plan

A standardized, formal planning methodology is recommended for the development of the protocol. A formalized planning methodology encourages a design team to consider many aspects of a total process design that they might not otherwise consider. There are numerous design tools available, for example, the PDCA (plan, do, check, act; Deming, 1982) or the DMAI (design, measure, analyze, improve; Joint Commission, 2001). These tools are brief form representations of the whole design process. I use a modification of the DMAI methodology that includes a risk analysis as part of the initial design (DRMAI; design, risk assessment, measure, analysis, improve) and discuss its use later.

A Hypothesis

One of the hallmarks of the scientific method is the testing of a hypothesis. A hypothesis is the question about what is being tested by the design. In fact, the hypothesis is what drives the design. For example, a hypothesis about the treatment of depression might be that cognitive therapy, or some specific aspect of cognitive therapy, decreases the symptoms of depression. This hypothesis would lead to the construction of a treatment protocol that applies some aspects of cognitive therapy to consumers with this presenting diagnosis. The hypothesis for my agency's treatment protocol for its mentally ill substance abuse (MISA) consumers was the presumption that consumers wanted to access services for help with their problem; however, our services were constructed such that it was difficult to easily access the needed services. This hypothesis led the design team to create a different system for accessing available services. Hypothesis testing might include the use of the treatment protocol on a pilot group of consumers to test its effectiveness. Any treatment protocol that is truly novel should undergo the formal process of research approval, however, and follow all guidelines established for research of human subjects.

Research and the Treatment Hypothesis

It would be unfair to suggest that the hypothesis under which my agency designed its MISA treatment protocol was generated from thin air. My agency considers it a responsibility of all its program directors to be conversant with current research and best practice within the director's area of responsibility. Initial hypotheses, thus, for the treatment protocol design were established from the day-to-day reading that is part of the director's basic job.

However, day-to-day reading is insufficient for the design of a best practice treatment protocol. The very terminology—best practice—implies that there is some consistency of recommendation about a particular treatment modality from experts within the specific or particular field. Reading articles in one or two or several journals, while sufficient to catch the current flavor or direction of treatment research and best practice, seems insufficient when considering specific practices that could affect the functioning of a consumer's life.

Part of the initial design of the best practice treatment protocol should include a thorough and exhaustive inventory of available literature relating to the treatment area. There are a number of methodologies for accomplishing this exhaustive review.

The first methodology for literature review is the historic research methodology—the university library. Some larger metropolitan areas may have city libraries that contain sufficient research facilities for this project. However, the vast majority of behavioral healthcare facilities are located in nonmetropolitan areas that have local libraries that are not suited to advanced research.

Some states have junior colleges that may have libraries adequate to begin treatment protocol research. While these libraries may not have the needed journals that contain the research articles, they may have reference materials that would allow staff to begin a research project. For example, *PsycInfo,* a reference compiled by the American Psychological Association, would probably be available in the library of a junior college. This reference contains indexes, journal articles, chapters in books, as well as books on psychology and other related fields. This reference covers some 1,300 journals and, thus, is an example of one method of doing an initial, yet thorough, review of available research. Relevant articles can be determined through a review of this reference guide and then requested through an interlibrary loan service at many libraries. Failing the interlibrary loan service, an agency staff could do the preliminary research as indicated earlier and go armed with the article list to the university library to make the required copies of the articles.

A more time-efficient research mechanism is the online research methodology. Many, if not most, university libraries and state university library systems have online research capacities. My local university library, an hour's driving time for me and, thus, not exceptionally convenient for quick research, has such an online system that allows a considerable amount of preparatory research. This library lists two core databases under the psychology heading (*PsycInfo,* already mentioned, as well as *Mental Measurements Yearbook*) but further lists five related databases (Contemporary Women's Issues, ERIC, Family Studies Database, Social Sciences Abstracts, and Sociological Abstracts). Some of these databases contain the full text of articles. The online research facility also lists 9 general databases, 11 psychology-related web resources, 36 professional psychological organization web sites, 9 specific psychological research centers, and 2 electronic psychology journals. Online university library systems such as this can allow the agency/practice protocol design staff to do sufficient research on the available literature surrounding the treatment area or diagnosis.

There are other similar systems that local libraries may make available to their subscribers. One such system is the OCLC First Search (http://newfirstsearch.oclc.org). This online service allows access to more than 70 research databases and includes access to more than 10 million online full-text articles. This online service is particularly helpful in researching evidence-based methodologies.

An additional and helpful service is available to online researchers through the publishers of various psychological and psychiatric journals. Some journals and/or publishers make their journal articles available for search via their Internet web sites, usually for a fee. For example, the publisher of *Psychiatric Services* makes such a search available. Annual subscriptions or, for a small fee, 24-hour subscriptions are available that allow unlimited access to the full articles. There are also several sites, primarily in the United Kingdom, dedicated specifically to evidence-based practices. Although these practice sites are primarily concerned with medical treatment, they nevertheless allow an agency/practice staff the opportunity to gather general information, including training information, about the larger view of evidence-based practices. Two such sites are the Cochran web site (http://www.cochrane.de) and the Clinical Evidence web site (http://www.clinicalevidence.com), both located in the United Kingdom.

Another U.K. site is the United Kingdom Department of Health site, which has a listing of evidence-based and evidence-supported behavioral health treatments that have been selected for use in the U.K. system of healthcare. This site (http://www.doh.gov .mentalhealth/treatmentguideline) allows reproduction without formal permission or charge for personal or in-house use. The treatment guideline is an excellent introduction to evidence-based treatments and contains a reasonable bibliography for various behavioral health treatment categories.

One very helpful web site based in the United States is the National Guideline Clearing House (http://guideline.gov). This site is sponsored by the U.S. government and contains 1,094 guidelines at time of writing this chapter. The site lists treatment guidelines that are approved by appropriate groups of medical professionals. For example, the American Psychiatric Association has the following guidelines listed and may be found by doing a search for "APA" at the main web site http://guideline.gov:

Practice guideline for the treatment of patients with bipolar disorder (revision)

Practice guideline for the treatment of patients with borderline personality disorder

Practice guideline for the treatment of patients with HIV/AIDS

Practice guideline for the treatment of patients with major depressive disorder

Practice guideline for the treatment of patients with delirium

Practice guideline for eating disorders

Practice guideline for psychiatric evaluation of adults

Practice guideline for the treatment of patients with panic disorder

The American Academy of Child and Adolescent Psychiatry has the following guidelines that can be found doing a search for AACAP:

Practice parameter for the assessment and treatment of children and adolescents with schizophrenia

Practice parameter for the assessment and treatment of children and adolescents with suicidal behavior

Practice parameter for the prevention and management of aggressive behavior in child and adolescent psychiatric institutions with special reference to seclusion and restraint

Practice parameter for the use of stimulant medications in the treatment of children, adolescents, and adults

Practice parameters for the assessment and treatment of children, adolescents, and adults with mental retardation and comorbid mental disorders

Practice parameters for the assessment and treatment of children, adolescents, and adults with autism and other pervasive developmental disorders

Practice parameters for the assessment and treatment of children and adolescents who are sexually abusive of others

Practice parameters for the assessment and treatment of children and adolescents with obsessive-compulsive disorder

Practice parameters for the assessment and treatment of children and adolescents with language and learning disorders

Practice parameters for the assessment and treatment of children and adolescents with depressive disorders

Practice parameters for the assessment and treatment of children and adolescents with posttraumatic stress disorder

Each of the preceding guidelines is hyperlinked to both a summary of the guideline and to the complete text of the guideline. While these guidelines may be highly medical in orientation, they contain a wealth of practice information on the covered topics besides issues related to psychotropic medications. These are consensus best guidelines as opposed to research- or evidence-based guidelines. In addition, there are behavioral health-related treatment issues addressed in other specialization areas. This site offers a free e-mail subscription and provides weekly updates of new guidelines that are added to the site.

A word of warning: Not everything posing as research on the Internet is research. Not everything appearing in a published journal is adequate research. This warning is not intended to insult your intelligence, but included because of my experience with staff at a variety of agencies throughout the United States who have genuinely believed that any research is acceptable and appropriate research. A number of distinct methods and processes are available to help a novice researcher determine if legitimate research meets sufficiently high standards to be considered adequate for acceptance as having statistically significant results. There are a number of available resources on this process, called *critical appraisal*.

Critical Appraisal Skills

Critical appraisal is the process of examining a researched process to determine its adequacy and the degree that you can use the research results within a specific setting. The questions cover, for example, not only the researched population, but also the research design, the types of randomization of various treatment types, the extent that all subjects entering into the research protocol were accounted for when the research was concluded, and so forth. One web site containing several lists of critical appraisal questions is the site of Oxford University, Center for Evidence Based Medicine: http://cebmh.warne

.ox.ac.uk/cebmh. The critical appraisal skills can be found under the Resources tab. Another United Kingdom site contains definitions and examples of critical appraisal questionnaires. This site is hosted by the Aggressive Research Intelligence Facility, a specialist unit based at the University of Birmingham. Of special interest to the design team is a computer-based slide presentation on critical appraisal skills: http://www.bham.ac.uk/arif/casp/index.htm. This slide presentation can be downloaded free of charge and used in training. I recommend its use with the protocol design team as they begin to review research for the chosen topic of protocol development.

Treatment Protocols

The treatment protocol is the actual course of treatment (see the preceding definition). One aspect of the design of the treatment protocol is the research of possible treatment protocols as discussed previously. Another aspect could be how the design team would select the protocol, while a third is either the selection of the protocol to use within the practice or the design of modified treatment protocol based on several available treatment methodologies. A fourth aspect of the design is the form the treatment protocol will take: a flowchart, a decision tree, a set of verbal instructions, and so on. One important point in the design of the treatment protocol is to construct it so it is clear and simple for the treatment staff to use. A difficult protocol with too many decision points or an unclear or confusing protocol with not enough decision points will be met with frustration and may be quickly abandoned.

Data Collecting Methods

A second hallmark of the scientific method is the collection of data concerning the hypothesis. A scientific approach to a hypothesis is never to prove or disprove the hypothesis. It is merely to find out the truth concerning the hypothesis. In the case of a treatment protocol, does it work or not? Does the use of an aspect of cognitive therapy help someone who is depressed feel better? The only way to know is to collect data about the process. Thus, the design must include the methods that will be used to determine if indeed someone who has been depressed is actually feeling better. For depression, the method of proof could be a simple Likert scale, or it could be a formal and readily available measurement system such as the Beck Depression Inventory or similar inventories. The point is that some measure or measures must be part of a scientific process of developing treatment protocols.

Further, part of the design must include how the data will be collected, how often it will be collected, and who will be responsible for the collection of the data. Failure to include these steps as part of the process design will lead to their not being done. This aspect is discussed at length later.

Training Staff

Once the protocol has been designed and the data collection methodology worked out, the staff who will be responsible for implementing the treatment protocol must be trained first in how to follow the protocol. A treatment protocol may seem self-evident to the team that has designed it; however, it may look like a map of Mars to someone not intimately connected with its development. This is especially true if a number of decision trees are involved in the protocol. If a decision tree or flowchart is used, it is probably a good practice to develop specific instructions as to each point of the tree or flowchart. Numbering the elements of the flowchart or decision tree and linking them to the specific instruction for that element is also an aid to finding the instruction. If the decision was made to use a verbal flow of instructions for the treatment protocol, constructing a simple flowchart could assist in learning the process of the treatment. Both methods, that is, verbal instructions and some form of visual representation of the instructions, will help the staff learn the treatment process more quickly than just one or the other form.

Second, the staff has to be trained in how to use or implement the treatment protocol once they understand how to follow the treatment outline. This is the litmus test for staff. Case vignettes could be invaluable for this aspect of the training. These vignettes would describe a consumer with the appropriate presenting problem and then describe how the treatment protocol was applied to this consumer. A training vignette for several variations of the treatment protocol (assuming that the protocol will have a number of treatment decisions associated with it) could be developed so that staff can see how the decision choices can affect the course of treatment. Training before the treatment process is initiated and at some point a retraining after the process has been in use can be helpful to staff. At the retraining, staff will have more informed questions based on their actual experience, and they may also have important suggestions as to how to make the treatment protocol more useful or comprehensible.

Third, it will be necessary to train the staff on how to use the measurements associated with the protocol. Training occurs so that consistency in application of both the protocol and the measurements will take place. If the measurement is a process that the consumer completes, the training will center on the instructions the staff give to the consumer for the completion. If the measure is a process that the staff member completes, a more thorough training is needed to ensure that the staff completes the measure in a consistent manner. In a formal research process, this measure is called *interrater reliability*. This is one more way of ensuring that it was the actual treatment process that affected the consumer's functional level.

Standardized Methods for Collecting, Analyzing, Comparing Data

Standardization of methodology is also important in terms of making use of the data. Collection of functional measures at consistent points in the implementation of the treatment protocol will allow for examination of the effectiveness of the protocol at the various stages of the protocol. Effectiveness of the protocol is obtained by the use of standard analysis methods including statistical analysis. It is important to have on staff or available someone who is familiar with statistical methodology to do this analysis. Apparent "improvement" that has not been determined to be statistically significant improvement is not, in effect, improvement at all but merely random variation that has no relationship to the treatment protocol. Thus, statistical analysis is a critical aspect of this approach.

Comparison methodology is also a potentially important aspect of determining the effectiveness of the treatment protocol. Whether you can compare the results of a treatment protocol with the results of another treatment protocol will depend on a number of elements. Perhaps the most important aspect is whether any other agency/practice is testing the treatment protocol the agency/practice is using. If the design team has chosen to replicate a treatment protocol exactly as it was designed in the original research, the results of the original research can be compared to the agency/practice results. If the team has modified a treatment protocol or combined several different protocols, such a comparison would not be statistically valid. It could be possible to compare the results of the treatment protocol with a comparison group (matched as to demographics and diagnosis or functional problem) composed of individuals who did not receive the treatment protocol. This type of comparison would need to be part of the initial design so that the comparison group could receive the same set of measurements that the treatment protocol group received.

Analysis Methodology Is Used in Interpreting Results to Improve

The purpose of collecting data concerning the treatment protocol, besides ensuring that consumers are improving because of the treatment protocol, is to improve the treatment system or process. If during the treatment protocol initial or subsequent stages, based on an analysis of the measures, no consumer is showing improvement, the process needs to be examined.

A fidelity measure is one method of examining the process. Fidelity examines whether the staff who are supposed to be delivering the protocol are following the protocol. A fidelity process can require that staff regularly report in supervision how they are following the process. Some evidence-based models have very strict requirements for such processes, for example, multisystemic therapy (Center for the Study and Prevention of Violence), which is a concurrent monitoring process designed to ensure that staff do closely follow the prescribed processes.

A retrospective fidelity process can be examination of the clinical documentation of those consumers who have reportedly received the treatment guidelines to determine the extent that the treatment processes were followed. If examination of clinical documentation shows that the treatment protocols were not followed, training or other staffing considerations might be necessary. If the treatment protocols were followed and no improvement was seen, the design team needs to do a careful analysis of the processes developed, perhaps using both statistical and nonstatistical methodologies such as Pareto and/or Ishikawa charting to determine subsequent steps. Once again, this likelihood and methodology should be built into the treatment design so that the necessary tools are readily available.

If, on the other hand, analysis finds that the treatment processes are working, there is cause for celebration and reason to expand the use of the treatment protocols outside any initial pilot projects.

Can an Agency/Practice Really Pick and Choose?

Even a quick and cursory review of the research literature on the topic of behavioral healthcare evidence-based treatments will yield a wealth of various treatment protocols with various degrees of efficacy. It is unlikely that an agency/practice would be unable to find a protocol that could be used, modified, or adapted to its setting. If nothing else, an agency/practice could even adapt the processes it currently uses for any specific area, systematize the process, and determine the effectiveness of those processes using the methods described earlier and following.

Suggestions for the actual design of a treatment protocol are discussed next. These are not hard and fast rules—only suggestions to help an agency/practice to get started in the process.

The Design Model

The design portion of the DRMAI consists of four separate but interrelated elements. The following sections will explain each element in detail.

Objectives

In the initial element of the design process, the objectives of the project are set forth. These objectives could include the goals of the project as well as any philosophic or strategic plan elements relevant to the project and the hypothesis that the design is going to test.

Processes

In the second element of the design portion are the actual processes that will be followed in the production of the project design. This element might include the makeup of the design team (see later section), the meeting schedule, and design tools to be used (e.g., a Gantt chart, flowcharts, prioritization chart or process).

Risk Assessment

The third suggested element of the design portion is the risk assessment. A design team should be charged, as part of the design, to determine what risk factors might be associated with aspects of the proposed treatment process. Examples of the risk factors are financial risk (if the proposed best practice treatment protocol is an expensive protocol to follow), time management risk (if the proposed protocol requires extensive preparation or analysis time), methodological risk (risk of confusion of the protocol directions if fine differentiation is required), and productivity loss risk (i.e., not meeting production goals, if any). This last risk can occur if the proposed treatment area has a high initial no show associated with it (e.g., court-ordered addiction services) such that there is a great deal of downtime when consumers do not present for assessment. Clinical staff assigned exclusively to such a program could run the risk of considerable downtime and, thus, fall below productivity requirements—risk to the consumer. (This is the most serious risk of any treatment design. Any proposed treatment proposal that includes a significant risk to a consumer must follow established procedures for research with human subjects and should be entered into only after all these requirements are fulfilled. Any design that might have a consumer-related risk factor should have a high level of authorization within the agency/practice structure and should not be undertaken without such authorization.)

A formal risk assessment process should be completed if any risks are discovered in this process of the design formulation. One such approach is called *failure mode effects analysis* (FMEA; Lewis, 2000). This approach follows a process that estimates the aspects of a system that might fail, how it might fail, the likelihood of the failure, the effects or severity of the failure, the ability or likelihood of detecting the failure, and the ways to mitigate or reduce the failure. The FMEA is not only a useful process for behavioral healthcare agencies but also a process that began to be required by the Joint Commission on the Accreditation of Healthcare Organizations of its accredited organizations in 2003.

Measurement

The fourth element, the measurement process, can be divided into two parts, internal and external or comparison measures. It is possible to look at a number of different areas for internal measurements.

Administrative measures are first and foremost an indication of how well the agency/practice is following its mission, vision, and values. Presumably, the mission and vision have something to do with service to people in need. Necessarily, given this mission and vision, the values relate to how the mission and vision are to be designed and carried out. Vision and mission drive the values. The values are played out in the processes and practices that staff carry out in day-to-day activities. Thus, the degree that any process, procedure, or practice, even an evidence-based treatment or clinical practice, is meeting that mission is ultimately the only reason that any process, procedure, or activity should be measured. Leadership is ethically beholden to discover how well the mission of the agency/practice is being met. We are morally compelled to determine the extent that our values, as they are lived out in the day-to-day activities of the agency/practice, are meeting the demands of our vision and mission. If the mission of the agency/practice, the vision of the board, and the values of the treatment culture are not being measured via some process or preferably multiple processes, the degree to which the vision and mission are being met and the values are supporting the treatment culture is unknown except as opinion and well-meaning assumption.

Second, and perhaps more practically, administrative measures examine the extent that processes meet various administrative requirements. Productivity, mentioned earlier, is one such measure that looks at the rate staff are producing that is sufficient to fund their salaries and ancillary administrative costs. Another administrative measure could be as simple as whether the required planning meetings occurred, and its direct measure could be design meeting minutes. A further elaboration of meetings as an administrative measure could be the extent that the design meeting had an agenda, that each agenda item had a time limit associated with it, and so on. A third and important administrative measure is whether the design team met its required delivery date, that is, was the proposed treatment protocol produced within the required time lines? A time frame is a very important element of any process design. Failure to include a time frame or completion date tends to ensure that the design process will go on ad infinitum with a resultant high cost of the design process. The cost of the design process is, thus, one further measure to consider. Since the staff participating in the design will likely be higher salaried senior supervisors and administrative personnel, the actual cost of the design in terms of staff hours should be kept in mind and could be a measure of the efficiency of the design team.

Process measures relate to the ability of a system to function in either an effective or efficient manner. Access is one such process measure. Can a consumer access a program? This could be as simple as a yes/no response measure. If a consumer needs a program and cannot access it as part of the treatment protocol, the success of that treatment protocol is in danger. The ability of consumers to access the needed elements of the treatment protocol should be part of the initial risk assessment of the program design, described earlier. A no response to this measure could mean an analysis of the program design.

If the consumer can access the desired program or service, what is the average length of time to access the program or service? Is this time reasonable? Having to wait to access services can affect the decision of a consumer to participate in the treatment program. Does the consumer have to be on a waiting list to access the service? Being on a waiting list to access a service that is part of a treatment protocol could also seriously affect the outcome of the treatment protocol for the consumer base. These are measures that can and should be part of the evaluation of the treatment protocol.

What is the access goal of the program? A third consideration is, thus, the actual access goal for the various treatment elements of the protocol. An important consideration for all of the treatment elements in the protocol could be including access goals for each treatment element, and the meeting of these goals should be monitored closely.

Another process measure, related to the previous discussion, is whether there is any difficulty obtaining needed service across service or program area divisions. This measure is especially important if the treatment process includes access across various treatment or service areas within the agency/practice. Because of the common practice of organizing practices into service areas and because these service areas tend to have their own unique processes, access between such service areas can lead to a potential failure or slowdown of service. A potential process measure in this area could be a speed of access in terms of hours or days needed to access the service.

A further consideration as a process measure is actual consumer satisfaction with the service provided. Consumer satisfaction with service is part of the wider consumer empowerment movement in behavioral health services and could be an important consideration in evaluating any new program.

Functional measures focus on the extent that the treatment protocol produces desired results. One of the more simple methods of producing a functional measure is to design a Likert scale that is consistent with the goals of the treatment protocol. The steps for constructing a Likert scale are relatively simple:

1. List the various functional elements that are important in the person's life. Senior supervisors and staff with experience with the population can help ensure that the measure will have meaning.

2. Decide on a rating scale that makes sense to the project. The greater the number of points included in the scale, the finer the sensitivity potential for the scale. For example, "0 to 10" is an 11-point scale that would allow a greater sensitivity to potential changes than a "0 to 3" scale, which is a four-point scale.

3. Adding descriptors to the rating will help staff know how to score the person in terms of the element described. The larger the scale, the more descriptors are necessary if a finer sensitivity is desired. For example, if the element to be

measured is compassion, the descriptive elements could be 0 = Not present, 5 = Some present, and 10 = Totally present. A more sensitive scale could divide the same 11 points by adding a descriptor to every other point such that there were six descriptions starting at 0, with a descriptor at 2, 4, 6, 8, and 10. The design team should consider very carefully the desired sensitivity of the functional scale.

Once the Likert scale is devised, staff must then be trained in its use. If more formal research is being conducted, interrater reliability can be conducted once the scale is implemented. The use of this type of scale when implemented with the treatment protocol allows a comparison between pretreatment protocol functionality and post-treatment protocol functionality.

If a researched protocol is chosen for implementation, a standardized measurement process may be included as part of that protocol. In addition, there are numerous measures for a variety of diagnostic and functional conditions that are available for purchase and could be used as functional measures as part of the treatment protocol.

Fidelity measures were discussed earlier. Fidelity to internal process is an important consideration if a practice or agency/practice wants to make the claim that any improvements in a consumer or a group of consumers are related to the treatment they have provided. To be able to say that treatment makes a difference in people's lives, clinical leadership needs to be able to establish that staff provided consistent treatment. Otherwise, the best that leadership can claim is that, on occasion, Jane Therapist and Joe Counselor provide treatment that seems to help Sally Consumer feel better.

Comparison measures, briefly discussed earlier, allow a further verification of the effectiveness of the treatment protocol. For example, if the treatment protocol produced an average increase in functional level of five Likert points on an 11-point scale in the research population and the use of the same treatment protocol produces an average increase in functional level of six Likert points on the same 11-point scale, leadership could conclude that the rendition of the treatment protocol was just as effective as the one in the research population, everything else being equal.

If, however, a sister agency paired with us to use the same treatment protocol with the same population in their agency, but their consumers showed only two Likert points on average improvement, the reason for the difference would need to be discovered. Replicability of a process means that it should produce similar results in similar circumstances. The failure of the treatment protocol to produce the anticipated results means that the design team at a sister agency would need to drill down to discover the reason or reasons they did not produce results at the research level.

If, on the other hand, an agency/practice and a sister agency/practice were using a treatment protocol that they had designed together (rather than attempting to replicate a previously researched protocol) and there was no outside outcome comparison, as in the research, and differing results were produced, it would have to be concluded that the difference in outcome between the two agencies was more likely related to factors other than actual treatment protocol. Such a drill down would call for a point-for-point comparison of the two sets of methodologies to discover what the other factors could be. In this drill down, fidelity to process could play an important factor in the difference between outcomes and should be an initial consideration.

A well-designed protocol methodology includes possible points of comparison. As indicated earlier, it is possible, if no outside source of comparison is available, to establish a comparison group that is matched demographically (i.e., age, education, and sex) as well as by diagnosis or functional problem, but does not participate in the treatment protocol. This could be a formal control group if the agency/practice is using a formal research protocol. However, it could also be a comparison group of consumers who self-selected out of the treatment protocol or who had already been through a treatment process.

In designing the dual diagnosis treatment protocol, my agency determined to use a matched comparison group gleaned from the consumer database of current and past consumers. Because it is a relatively large database in excess of 65,000 consumers, it was possible to match each member of the pilot treatment group to a similar consumer (i.e., of the same age, sex, and dual presenting problems). It was, therefore, possible to examine the number of times the comparison group had been admitted to services, had used psychiatric hospital services, had used emergency telephonic support services, had dropped out of services, and so on. While this was not a formal research control type of group, it did give the agency a method of comparing the effectiveness of the treatment protocol versus not having the treatment protocol applied.

Statistical Process and Measurements

The design team should determine what statistical processes it would prefer to use with the measures that it is establishing. This step will help to determine in advance if those statistical processes will be possible given the design of the treatment protocol project. For example, the design team might want to have a statistical correlation between various elements of treatment. The team might decide to correlate the use or nonuse of a specific psychotropic medication in conjunction with a specific treatment pathway, for example, dialectic behavioral therapy (Linehan, 1993). Specific recording protocols will need to be established and implemented with training as to use so that this information can be easily retrieved.

If treatment staff will be expected as part of the treatment design to do some statistical calculations concerning treatment progress to determine the next treatment pathway, the staff will need to be carefully trained in this process and tested in the process to ensure competency to carry out the process. This training will also need to be designed into the overall implementation process. An alternate to this requirement could be to design the measurement recording format (e.g., plotting the score on a graph) so that the statistical relevance is readily apparent from the graph. A number of measurement tools that are available for purchase are designed this way. The design team needs to be aware of these possibilities and design this aspect of recording into the treatment protocol.

If the design team is planning to compare results with a sister agency/practice and has designed the measurement protocols to use the same measurement tools, the team will also need to ensure that the sister agency/practice is using the same statistical techniques to aggregate its data so that comparisons are possible. Further, the team will need to ensure that the same formulas are being used to determine specific functions. For example, if an electronic spreadsheet is being used to produce averages and standard deviations, the protocol needs to specify if the agency/practice is to use the simple standard deviation formulas found in the spreadsheet or the standard deviations for populations, a formula also available in most spreadsheets. Or, if statistical correlations are to be figured using the electronic spreadsheet, will the simple correlation formulas be used or will the Pearson formulas be used? Failure to plan this ahead could lead to confused data comparisons.

The Multidisciplinary Team

A key in designing a treatment protocol is that the design team be multidisciplinary. *Multidisciplinary* means different things in different settings. Multidisciplinary for a hospital setting could include far more potential disciplines than in an outpatient behavioral healthcare setting. For the purposes of designing a treatment methodology, the meaning of multidisciplinary is clearly related to the setting and the population. A multidisciplinary treatment protocol design team in any setting should include a representative from all of the potential service area providers to ensure that all needed processes are included in the design and to ensure that design team members properly understand how current processes are carried out. There is always a danger that design team members who are not part of a nonrepresented process will design or include a process that will require special training, equipment, and so on, unaware that it could affect the outcome of the treatment protocol. Therefore, as new or additional processes are added to the treatment protocol, it will be important to include representatives from those areas in the design team.

Further, a design team should include representatives from the support staff. It is important that the team not make treatment changes that affect the support operations without including a representative from the support operations. Including a support operations supervisor or other representative will give the design team a clear understanding of how the proposed process change will impact support operations. Support operation consideration is critical to the success of any treatment design. Designing processes that will heavily impact the use of support personnel without consideration for the support operation could affect the success of the treatment protocol.

For example, if the initial design treatment protocol calls for an attending receptionist to distribute by hand the presenting consumer a required measurement tool, this task would presumably have little impact on the other required tasks of that support staff. However, suppose the treatment protocol also called for the attending receptionist to score that protocol and log the results into the clinical record before the consumer sees the treatment professional. These additional tasks could seriously impact the completion of the receptionist's other duties. The required measurement tool might or might not get done if other and equally important duties were required of the reception staff at the same time the consumer is presenting for treatment within the newly designed protocol. This kind of unnecessary complication could be avoided by the inclusion of a support supervisor as part of the design team.

These types of complications could perhaps also be avoided by asking for a support supervisor review of any processes designed. The disadvantage of a retrospective review for job impact is that valuable staff design time could be wasted if the support review turns up processes that, as designed, are unacceptable.

My agency's best practices design team illustrates one multifunctional involvement approach. The design team for the 2002 JCAHO Codman Award for Behavioral Healthcare consisted of a wide variety of staff from within the agency. The staff involved in the planning and implementation of the initiative included management, supervisors, and frontline clinicians. They represented licensed clinical social workers, licensed clinical professional counselors, certified addiction and drug abuse counselors, registered nursing/certified psychiatric, and nonlicensed, noncertified staff. These staff came with master's in social work, master's in psychology, master's in nursing, bachelor's degrees, and nondegreed. The group members all had numerous years of experience in working with both populations and were specifically selected because of this knowledge base. Although the chief psychiatrist did not specifically sit on the design team, he reviewed the clinical processes to ensure that they met with appropriate psychiatric interfaces.

Although support staff were not used in the design of this best practice protocol, they played an important part in the design of best practices for the reduction of failure rates within the agency because it was believed that support staff would play a large and critical role in this process.

A second learning point from this team is that part of their research concerning the available evidence-based treatment models for the functional area chosen for treatment protocol development (mentally ill substance/chemical abuse) included attending, as a group, various regional trainings on the topic. Attending training together deepened their cohesiveness as a group and allowed them to do group work and discussion while it was fresh in their experience. They were, thus, able to examine, discuss, and suggest connect and disconnect possible points of the material presented while still at the conferences. They were, as an added benefit, able to discuss points of concern with the researchers who were presenting the information.

A SUGGESTED STRUCTURE FOR THE TREATMENT PROTOCOL

The structure of the protocol may vary with the needs of the organization. We have found at my agency that a flowchart with decision trees is one helpful way for staff to understand the treatment process. The decision tree is especially helpful when there are multiple courses of treatment possible. It is important to remember in designing a treatment protocol that follows a flowchart/decision tree model that the flowchart is an abbreviated form of the entire model. Explicit directions and guidelines are needed for many of the elements that are abbreviated on the flowchart. A procedural manual should also be developed in the overall treatment protocol design.

Suggested components of the protocol, either in the decision tree/flowchart form and/or in a more elaborate treatment process manual form, are discussed next.

Target Recipients

Who is the protocol designed for? The recipients could be either a diagnostic category or a functional problem area. It is important to clearly and carefully delineate the target recipients. What are the age ranges for which the protocol is designed? Is the protocol for men, or women, or both sexes? Is the treatment protocol for a specific and narrow diagnostic category or subcategory, or is it for a broad range of categories? For example, if the protocol is for depression, will the protocol be applied to every consumer who presents with any variation of the diagnosis or only for those with one specific diagnosis? If the protocol applies to only one specific diagnosis or subdiagnosis, will there be instructions or treatment protocols for other consumers with similar diagnosis but not this specific diagnosis?

Assessment Elements

Will the consumers be required to complete a specific type of assessment for inclusion in the treatment protocol? Will the regular assessment process be sufficient? Are supplemental assessments to be part of the inclusion process? If there are to be special supplemental assessments, which staff will be required to do these assessments? What will be the process for the primary assessment staff to request the supplemental assessment? What will be an acceptable time frame for the completion of the supplemental assessment, if it is required? Who will be responsible for ensuring that the supplemental assessment occurred? Do not leave any aspect of this process unclear or nonspecific.

Associated Assessment Measures

Which specific measurement tools are to be used as part of initial assessment in the treatment protocol? Will there be inclusion or exclusion thresholds associated with these tools? Will there be any other specific psychometric tests used? Who will be responsible for ensuring that the consumer completes the measure? Who will be responsible for scoring and notating the score of the measure in the clinical record?

Target Screening-In Elements

Are there specific elements that should screen consumers into the treatment protocol? These elements could be used to narrow the treatment field. However, if a variety of consumers are desired for the treatment protocol, a wide selection protocol could be used. The more variation in terms of multiple diagnoses or multiple problems, the more difficult it may be to determine effectiveness of the protocol for any specific problem.

What are the target or threshold screening-in scores for the associated assessment measures listed in the Associated Assessment Measures section described earlier? What is the treating professional supposed to do in terms of treatment when a consumer falls below the screening-in score? Will the treatment be as usual? Will the non-screened-in consumer receive other types of services?

Risk Management Screening Measures/Procedures

If one of the initial measures reaches a critical need for immediate action threshold, what is the procedure to be followed? This procedural element should specifically and clearly delineate the steps that must be followed. If not, a flow element indicating something to the effect of "refer to crises services immediately" should be considered. The inclusion of this risk management element is to ensure that it is clear to the treating clinician that the treatment protocol does not override the need to secure immediate action in cases of the likelihood for harm to self or others.

Target Screening-Out Elements

Are there specific diagnostic elements, associated presenting problems, demographic features, life conditions, and so on that the design team will want screened out of use for this protocol? If the agency/practice wants a narrow and specific population, this would be a second opportunity to cut inappropriate consumers out of the treatment protocol. Will there be a need to screen out any consumers with comorbid conditions? For example, will agency/practice treatment or assessment staff be expected to screen out children presenting with a conduct disorder diagnosis as well as attention deficit hyperactive disorder? Every additional disorder screened into the treatment protocol requires a specific methodology of treating or otherwise dealing with that element. If it is not dealt with, it will be a variable that will somehow have to be taken into consideration when the treatment protocol is evaluated.

Treatment Protocol

The actual treatment protocol could have a number of treatment columns in the flowchart/decision tree—comorbid considerations (if they have been included), psychotherapy or counseling methodologies, or psychiatric and medication paradigms.

How specific will these protocols need to be for the agency/practice's staff? This is a point that the design team will need to consider carefully. It is the actual implementation of the treatment protocol that can give staff the most concern. Treatment staff will wonder the extent that the treatment processes (which they, up to the initiation of the protocol, have been in charge of) will delineate the steps they will now have to follow. This could be a potential point of resistance and, therefore, is a point that needs to be managed carefully, especially if the protocol is going to be very specific.

If the design team indicates, for example, that "six sessions of cognitive therapy for depression will precede psychiatric consultation" as part of the treatment protocol, will the treatment protocol then need to spell out specifically the elements to be included in the cognitive therapy? Will the design protocol need to delineate what each session must cover? Will the design protocol need to list the order that the elements need to be covered? If the design team wants to ensure that every consumer will receive the very same process, they should list every topic, in the desired order, if they have reason to believe that the order of topics can have an influence on the functional outcome. If the design team chooses to use a flowchart methodology to display the treatment protocol, this specific type of listing would not be possible on the flowchart itself.

Thus, if the treatment protocol indicates a process such as "six sessions of cognitive therapy," it is advisable to spell out the elements of the "six sessions" that would be included in a procedural manual to accompany the flowchart. These session elements could be as simple as a list of topics to cover in each of the six sessions. The list could include a set of homework assignments to be done by the consumer and so on. Unless the agency/practice already specifically trains therapists in a methodology and/or already has a detailed guideline for the treatment method referred to in this protocol, it will be necessary to detail this guideline for the clinicians who will be providing the service. This issue will also be a point of training in the program design. To fail to do so assumes that every clinician carrying out the treatment protocol will know exactly what the design team had in mind when they said "cognitive therapy."

If the design team decides that the content label *cognitive therapy* is sufficient for whatever reason, specifics do not need to be listed. This decision, however, leaves the protocol open to numerous interpretations and variables in the actual treatment of the consumer. For example, will the treatment professional use the cognitive therapy of Albert Ellis or Aaron Beck? Or will the treatment professional use the cognitive therapy aspects of some other theoretician? It will be difficult to determine what actually produces an effect if a variety of cognitive therapies apply as part of the treatment protocol.

If, however, this is the agency/practice's first attempt to introduce a staff to the use of a treatment protocol, listing "cognitive" therapy and leaving the staff free to continue to use their own methodologies will help ease that staff into the process of using a treatment protocol. If the use of best practice is going to be gradually enhanced into a use of evidence-based practices, this more loose structure could help to improve initial acceptance of the process.

Measurement Points

Measurement points should be included as part of the flowchart diagram. In the preceding example, what is to happen after the six sessions of cognitive therapy? A second Beck Depression Inventory score could be indicated at this point in the flowchart with specific thresholds included for processing to the next step of the protocol. If the score is at or above threshold A, will consumers be referred for psychiatric consultation and possible medication? Will they be assigned an additional three sessions of cognitive therapy and so on? Include the specific flow of treatment that is to be associated with each measurement score or grouping of scores.

Psychiatric Protocol

The details of the psychiatric protocol should be discussed with the psychiatric staff, if they have not been part of the design. It is important to have these discussions early in the process and protocol design, that is, long before the protocol development is completed. What additional information will the psychiatrist need or require? How will these elements be worked into the general protocol? What specific markers or thresholds will the psychiatrist look for in terms of establishing that the consumer is stable or is at risk? These markers (thresholds) need to be included in this portion of the protocol. Again, an abbreviated version can be included as part of the flowchart/decision tree, with the expanded guidelines explained in the procedural manual.

The team will need to decide that it will adopt or suggest the adoption of any specific best practice or evidence-based medication algorithms. This issue should be discussed with the psychiatric staff.

Intermediate Measurement Time Lines

The times that the required measurements are to be taken should be indicated on the flowchart and include the specific measure and all follow-up time lines. The flowchart should also indicate what steps are to be taken if the benchmark scores are achieved or not achieved. There should be specific procedures to follow if the measurement shows a decline in functioning, as well as if there is an improvement. These should be linked back to the appropriate element in the flowchart/decision tree. It should also refer to the appropriate emergency procedures should any of the scores indicate an emergency.

Termination of Treatment Elements

This section includes the markers and thresholds for when the consumer has reached the desired level of care. This section could also include the markers as to when the consumer would be referred to a lower level for maintenance processes. If the treatment protocol is open ended, it is especially important to include any specific termination reporting procedures in this section.

Reporting Procedures

While not an actual part of the treatment protocol, the reporting requirements as to use of the protocol, measurement results, and so on should be included, both on the flowsheet and in the manual. If they are not included, the unfortunate reality in a busy practice could be that there will be very little actual reporting, and it will then be very difficult to evaluate the effectiveness of the program. Part of the reason for undertaking such a program is to determine its effectiveness, and timely and consistent reporting is an invaluable part of that process.

THE TREATMENT PROTOCOL: PILOTING THE DESIGN

One of the methods to ensure that a design will work within the agency/practice setting is to institute the treatment design initially as a pilot project. The pilot, as such, is more to test the mechanics of the process and not necessarily the effectiveness of the treatment protocol with the intended population. The pilot project, when it is so designed, allows an agency/practice to determine the fit and operational effectiveness of the treatment mechanisms and processes on a small scale before integrating the protocol within the total processes of the agency/practice. It also allows the design team to work out any details or unconsidered elements as soon as they arise, which is usually easier within the smaller setting of a pilot project than it is after the process has been disseminated throughout an agency/practice. For example, changes to an assessment process or treatment plan can be "tested" by senior clinicians to determine if the changes are workable within the organizational structure. If the senior clinicians find that the changes are not workable, the design team will either need to redesign the changes or consider redesigning the structure within which the changes were to occur.

Pilot Design: Length of Pilot

The structure of the pilot project may determine in part the results of the project. The length of the pilot is one initial important consideration. Will the pilot project be a number of weeks or a number of months? This time line should be developed by the design team in terms of (1) the problem area or diagnostic category the pilot is designed to address and (2) the portion of the larger project that the agency/practice is piloting and the general readiness of the organization to attempt this type of change.

If the agency/practice as part of its initial assessment system or process has never used an assessment measure, for example, the Beck Depression Inventory, and the design team has included its use as part of the treatment protocol, it could be important to pilot the training and implementation of this instrument before piloting the entire protocol.

Staff who are not accustomed to a systematic use of this type of instrument will need some time to understand and adjust to its use. If the system is not yet organized around the formal use and reporting of this type of instrument, a process for this use and reporting will need to be developed and instituted as part of the pilot; thus, the time needed for this aspect of the pilot will vary. The pilot needs to be long enough to get the process and system glitches worked out before it is instituted throughout the entire system.

As suggested earlier, one way to help decrease the number of bugs (glitches) in the process before it is piloted is the multidisciplinary team. The more diverse the membership of the team is, the more likely the team will realize the potential implementation problems and design methods of countering these problems.

System-related glitches will be manifested very soon on implementation of this type of new process, perhaps within the first week or even the first attempt of a few senior clinicians to implement the process, in this case, the measure. The time needed to correct the problem will vary according to the magnitude of the discovered problem. The design team will need to carefully differentiate true system-related glitches from potential initial resistance to change on the part of the implementing clinicians.

The length to run the actual complete treatment protocol will depend on the manner in which the design team decides to establish it. Suppose the protocol, for example, treatment of major depression, will be applied to every consumer who presents with this diagnosis. The design team has determined that the agency/practice has annually a sufficient population of consumers manifesting this problem. The design team calculates the average number of consumers presenting with this diagnosis per quarter. If that number is 30 (a number that is usually considered a minimum for providing statistical sufficiency) or higher, the length of time needed to ensure that a sufficient number of individuals have been processed using the treatment protocol would be one quarter. One quarter would not be long enough to determine if the treatment protocol was effective with the individual consumers. It would only be long enough for an initial determination as to whether the actual process was being carried out properly by the staff.

Pilot Design: Intermediate Measures?

The first intermediate measure should be a *fidelity to process* measure, as discussed earlier. Is the treatment (protocol implementation) staff following the protocol? The sooner this measure can be taken, the better for the accuracy of implementation of the protocol. A design team might want to include as part of the design of the protocol implementation a process for checking every specific case record that relates to the treatment protocol to allow immediate feedback to the implementation staff. If the design does not include this immediate fidelity measure, it should be completed by the end of the first quarter of implementation. Any discrepancies in the protocol implementation should be corrected.

The second consideration is the more important consideration: Are people getting better from the use of the protocol? The design team will have included some type of functional measures as part of the treatment protocol. The design team will have devised the process of collecting, reporting, and aggregating these measures. This process should have included a time frame for collecting the data. How long will it take to ensure that a treatment protocol is effective? My agency in designing its award-winning MISA treatment protocol believed that, because of the multiple difficulties inherent with the population, 18 months into the project was sufficient to do the initial functional measure. Interestingly enough, treatment staff began to talk about how well certain individuals were responding to the protocol long before this time period ended. Retrospectively, the design team believed that it should have scheduled the initial functional measurement to occur sooner, possibly as early as 6 months into the implementation.

The design team will need to give the functional measurement time frame careful consideration. Some measures, again the Beck Depression Inventory, could be taken at every psychiatric appointment for a medication check. Other measures, for example, the Global Assessment of Functioning (GAF), could be taken at every individual session. Some Likert scale functional measures could be taken quarterly, especially if they are designed to address more global functional areas. What is important, ultimately, besides how often the consumer measurements are taken, is how often the measurement results will be aggregated and analyzed in determining the effectiveness or continued effectiveness of the treatment protocol in general. The design team will have to balance the costs of the aggregate data collection and analysis and the cost of letting a project continue if it is not producing effective results for consumers.

PROJECT MANAGEMENT

Project management, alluded to earlier, is a process borrowed from the manufacturing industry that can be used in behavioral health. Project management refers to a variety of techniques that are used to ensure that a project is completed along expected guidelines and within an acceptable and expected budget. It is, in brief, doing the right things in the right way to get the project accomplished (paraphrased from Burlton, 2001).

The importance of a project manager was explained in Chapter 12. The project manager's responsibilities are to ensure the completion of the project along the guidelines indicated. The project manager needs to have the authority to get these tasks accomplished along these same guidelines. The project manager also needs to have the skills as well as personal characteristics to get the tasks accomplished by the members of his or her team. Further, the project manager needs to have the confidence that he or she can get the task accomplished.

One of the tasks of the project manager is to resolve any political or cross-organizational conflicts that might occur and that might hamper the completion of the project. Within the behavioral healthcare organization, this role is especially important given the grant-based organization features that remain in many agencies. One of the tasks of this role, therefore, is to gain acceptance for the plan once it is developed.

The project manager can be assisted in this process by the project champion. The role of project champion specifically is to assist in the clearing of roadblocks for the project and the smoothing of political frictions. The project champion must continually in the tribal or silo-based behavioral healthcare agency or large practice defer to the good of the agency/practice as a whole and must work to refocus any tribal or silo alliances to the greater good of the larger agency/practice.

According to Burlton (2001), there are four primary stages to any project to be managed: defining the work, planning the work, working the plan, and accepting the work.

Initially, the work is defined by the board and administration of an agency/practice through its mission and vision. An administrative or management team may make the initial definition of the work that the actual project team is supposed to complete, although it is up to the project team to further refine and define its understanding of the required task.

Planning the work has been discussed in various aspects in this and the preceding chapters. The project team designs not only the treatment protocol (or assigns its design to a subgroup) but also the method by which the completed treatment protocol will be carried out. One of the common techniques of this planning stage of project management is the Gantt chart (Lewis, 2000). In the Gantt chart, each activity is listed in one column to the far left, while a time line of due date columns spreads out to the right of the activity column. This chart is one of the methods the committee uses to measure the degree that it is on target with its deliverables.

Other planning activities are researching the treatment protocol, writing the specific protocol, designing the training plan for the protocol's use, planning the implementation of both the training and the subsequent use of the protocol, planning the collection of the protocol data, planning for the aggregation of the data, and determining the acceptable values for assessing the success of the treatment protocol (i.e., what rate of improvement will be considered acceptable). The planning activities also include the delineation of what will constitute acceptable benchmarking and other comparison activities.

Working the plan follows only after the careful planning has taken place. How often has leadership in behavioral healthcare only partially or inadequately planned what we were going to do in terms of providing treatment or adding services? Project management requires not only careful planning as described but also careful implementation. The training on the protocols and measurements and reporting must be initiated before the actual implementation of the treatment protocol. Close supervision could be a valuable part of the early implementation steps. Frequent reporting of measures could also be a part of the initial workings of the plan. Fidelity to process is unquestioned in business but is a very new concept in behavioral healthcare that must be carefully planned and meticulously monitored. An agency/practice must determine not only if its proscribed processes are being followed but also the extent that those processes are being monitored.

Accepting the work in a manufacturing sense means that the administration decides at some appropriate level that the work to be accomplished by the plan was not only accomplished, but was accomplished within the acceptable level of quality, within the time frames, and within the budget. Did the project come in on time, on budget, and of a quality staff can be proud of? In behavioral healthcare, these questions apply, but they apply in terms of the results of the services designed. That is, did the treatment protocol adopted, developed, or used as part of a published evidence-based research protocol that had been planned and executed produce the requisite results: statistically improved functioning levels for the aggregate group of consumers for which it had been selected or developed? Are the consumers for whom the treatment protocol was devised also pleased with the treatment process and their treatment progress? It is also important to consider whether the treatment providers are pleased with the treatment processes as designed and implemented. Are they able to effectively follow the processes and access the ancillary prescribed services? Acceptance of the product includes acceptance by all of the stakeholders.

PROCESS MANAGEMENT ESSENTIALS

Project management is one aspect of the larger structure of process management. Process management represents a number of systems of activities that enable an agency/practice to better ensure its final product. Process management is also a system of activities that enables an agency/practice to better manage change within that agency/practice. Besides project management, process management consists of the following subcategories: risk management, knowledge management, and human change management.

Risk management was referred to in the design process described earlier. The design team of the project needs to consider what potential risks might be associated with the adoption and use of the treatment design. In a larger sense, however, the agency/practice administrative and management staff need to consider the risks associated with not advancing toward the use of evidence-based practices. The potential financial risks associated with establishing new practices must be balanced against the long-term risks of continuing to provide treatment services that have not been established as being effective.

Knowledge management in a specific sense is part and parcel of the use of best practice and eventually evidence- or research-based practices. The process of using best practice and evidence-based practices has to do with discriminating knowledge about these practices, both to the professional staff who are charged with the implementation of the knowledge and to the consumers who will be the recipients of that knowledge. But in a larger sense, knowledge management has to do with the extent that staff involved in the evidence-based projects, staff who work to support their efforts, and other staff within the agency/practice as a whole are given the basic knowledge about the project. This includes the importance of the practices to the agency/practice, both in the immediate time frame and for the future. This knowledge also includes the reasons the practices are being implemented, the practical reasons in terms of providing better treatment, which will result in improved outcome reasons for the good of the consumers. It also should include the methods being used to implement the practices, as well as the role each staff member in the agency/practice plays in that implementation.

REFERENCES

Burlton, R. (2001). *Business process management.* Indianapolis, IN: Sam's Publishing.

Deming, W. (1982). *Out of the crisis.* Cambridge, MA: MIT Press.

Hayes, R. (2001). Evidence-based therapy—is there a practical approach? *Behavioral Health Management, 21*(6), 20–24.

Joint Commission on Accreditation of Healthcare Organizations. (2001). *Comprehensive accreditation manual for hospitals.* Oakbrook Terrace, IL: Author.

Lewis, J. (2000). *The project manager's desk reference* (2nd ed.). Boston: McGraw-Hill.

Linehan, M. (1993). *Cognitive-behavioral treatment of borderline personality disorder.* New York: Guilford Press.

Sinnissippi Centers, Inc. (1999). *Best practice guideline training* (Unpublished training paper). Dixon, IL: Sinnissippi Centers, Inc.

APPENDIX

Resources and Sample Treatment Plans

The following forms, flow charts, and so on represent a small portion of the work involved in the MISA Consumer Process Improvement Initiative referenced in Chapters 10 through 12 at the Sinnissippi Centers, Inc. This project was awarded the Joint Commission on the Accreditation of Healthcare Organization (JCAHO) 2002 Ernst A. Codman Award for Behavioral Healthcare, and the 2003 American Psychiatric Association's Bronze Psychiatric Services Award. Both awards were for the use of outcome data in improving the functional levels of the MISA (Mentally Ill Substance Abusing) consumer.

CLINICAL SCREENING TOOLS BEST PRACTICE CHECKLIST
R = Absolute Requirement   *** = Required for All Medication Checks**
 # = Administer if Appropriate

Check the column or enter the date each item is completed.

REQUIRED FOR ADULTS: The following screening/assessment tools/information are required for all adult clinical assessments. Items with * are required for each medication check.

R-01 * _____ 21 Question Beck Depression Inventory
R-02 * _____ 21 Question Beck Anxiety
R-03   _____ Mood Disorder Questionnaire
R-04   _____ 24 Question MAST (*Clinical & Family Division Assessments*)
R-05 * _____ Check consumer weight and log on SCI Medication Record (*for consumer's receiving medications from SCI*)

WHEN APPROPRIATE FOR ADULTS: The following screening/assessment tools are required for all adult clinical assessments, if appropriate. Items with * are required for each medication check.

#-06 * _____ PANSS (*for Schizophrenia/Psychosis—every 6 months*)
#-07 * _____ Mini Mental Status Exam (when cognitive impairment suspected)
#-08 * _____ Yale Brown for OCD if OCD suspected—*Do both sides initially then Quantitative side only for additional appointments*
#-09 * _____ Young Mania Scale if Diagnosis is bipolar
#-10   _____ Multnomah (CILA, PAS evaluation, PSR (*Vocational only*))
#-11   _____ pre CASIG (*PSR services*)
#-12   _____ Hawthorn for Adult ADHD if presenting problem
#-13   _____ List numbers of any screening tools consumer refused:_____

REQUIRED FOR CHILD/ADOLESCENTS: The following assessment/screening tools/information are required for all child/adolescent clinical assessments. Items with * are required for each medication check.

R-01 * _____ CDI (Age 17+ use Beck) If positive, repeat as indicated
R-02 * _____ CAP (Every medication check)
R-04   _____ EKG (for all children who are to be seen for physician consultations)
R-05 * _____ Check height and weight and enter in CSR
R-06   _____ SA Screening Tool (Age 10–17: any positive findings requires further evaluation)

WHEN APPROPRIATE FOR CHILD/ADOLESCENTS: The following screening/assessment tools required for all child/adolescents clinical assessments, if appropriate. Items with * required for each medication check.

#-07   _____ CAFAS: if SASS, complete every 90 days
#-08 * _____ Child Y/BOC if OCD
#-09 * _____ Young Mania if Diagnosis is Bipolar
#-10   _____ List numbers of screening tools client/guardian refused: _____

Consumer Name: _____

Case Manager:_____
    This is an example of a set of best practice measures that are required for initial assessment. Each measurement has an associated tracking mechanism. See the following CAP tracking tool for an example.

Children's Attention Problem Scale Plotting Sheet
Child: ───────────────────────────

Clinician: ─────────────────────────

Instructions: Plot total score in columns below:

Date	
Scores	
24	
23	
22	
21	
20	
19	
18	
17	
16	
15	
14	
13	
12	
11	
10	
9	
8	
7	
6	
5	
4	
3	
2	
1	
Notes:	

This is an example of how an agency can track the results of a best-practice measurement tool. Use only one column per date. For multiple scores, put a slash mark for each score in a range box. Use notes for comments about changes in medications.

Menu of Services Grid

This Menu of Services was developed to assist clinicians in selecting services for dually diagnosed consumers. It is not intended to be a rigid prescription of services. Best practice recommends consultation between clinicians and/or supervisors while developing treatment strategies and plans. Be encouraged to consult. Services within each cell of this grid are arranged from least to most restrictive.

Low Addictions
Low Psychiatric

LL (ASAM Level .5) Mentally Ill and Substance Abuse

Case Management	MEGA (MISA education group)
Psychosocial Rehabilitation (PSR)	ATOD education

Low Addictions	**High Addictions**
High Psychiatric	**Low Psychiatric**
LH Serious Mentally Ill and Substance Abuse	**HL Mentally Ill and Substance Dependence**
Case Management	Case Management
Psychiatric Services	Psychiatric Services
Medication Monitoring	Medication Monitoring
Linkage Case Management	Psychosocial Rehab (PSR)
Psychosocial Rehabilitation (PSR)	Bridge (MISA group)
ATOD education (Level .5)	MEGA (MISA education group)
MEGA (MISA education group)	Intensive Outpatient (IOP) (Level 2)
Community Integrated Living Arrangement (CILA)	
Intensive Day Treatment (IDT)	
Crisis Services (Crisis Bed)	
Linkage to Psychiatric Inpatient	

High Addictions
High Psychiatric

HH (ASAM Level 2) Serious Mentally Ill and Substance Dependence

Case Management	Intensive Outpatient (IOP)
Psychiatric Services	Intensive Day Treatment (IDT)
Medication Monitoring	Linkage to Addictions Inpatient (Level 3)
Linkage Case Management	Crisis Services (Crisis Bed)
Psychosocial Rehabilitation (PSR)	Linkage to Psychiatric Inpatient
CILA Intermediate	
Community Integrated Living Arrangements (CILA)	

High Psych High Addictions (ASAM Level 2) = **BDI 21 + and/or BAI 16 + and/or PANSS X and MAST 5 +**
High Psych Low Addictions (ASAM Level 1 = **BDI 21 + and/or BAI 16 + and MAST 2 to 4**
Low Psych High Addictions (ASAM Level 1) = **BDI 11 to 20 and/or BAI 8 to 15 + and MAST 5 +**
Low Psych Low Addictions (ASAM Level .5) = **BDI 11 to 20 and/or BAI 8 to 15 and MAST 2 to 4**
© Sinnissippi Centers, Inc.

Sample of a Likert Scale, Developed for the MISA Consumer

MISA Consumers' Functional Measurement Tool

Name of Consumer: _____

Case Manager: _____

Id #: _____

Diagnoses: Psychiatric: _____

              Addiction: _____

              Psychiatric: _____

              Addiction: _____

              Psychiatric: _____

              Addiction: _____

Date of SCI admission: _____

Date began MISA services: _____

1. Is this consumer receiving CILA services? _____ Yes _____ No

2. Is this consumer receiving PSR services? _____ Yes _____ No

3. Is the consumer currently using alcohol? _____ Yes _____ No

4. Is the consumer currently using drugs? _____ Yes _____ No

ANSWER EITHER 5A OR 5B

5A. Approximate length of CURRENT sobriety/non-use: _____ months **or**

5B. Approximate of LAST sobriety/non-use: _____ months.

Please rate as best you can this consumer on the following **before** he/she started MISA Services. Use a 0 to 10 scale, with 10 being the highest evidence of the attitude or skill and 0 being the lowest. The actual descriptors follow each attitude or skill.

	10 9 8 7 6	**5 4 3 2**	**1 0**
_____ 1. Medication compliance	Compliant	Occasional	Not Compliant
_____ 2. Treatment compliance	Compliant	Occasional	Not Compliant
_____ 3. Control of psychiatric symptoms	Controlled	Occasional	Not Controlled
_____ 4. Ability to keep home	Able	Some Ability	Not Able
_____ 5. Living (i.e., self care) skills	All Necessary	Some Skills	No Skills
_____ 6. Relationship problems	No Problems	Some Problems	Many Problems
_____ 7. Legal Problems	No Problems	Some Problems	Many Problems
_____ 8. Commitment to sobriety	Total Commitment	Some Commitment	No Commitment
_____ 9. Active support system	Sufficient Support	Some Support	No Support
_____ 10. Maintenance of sobriety	Maintained	Some Lapses	Not Maintained
_____ 11. Attendance in AA/NA, etc.	Attended	Some Attendance	No Attendance

MISA Best Practices
Fidelity to Guidelines

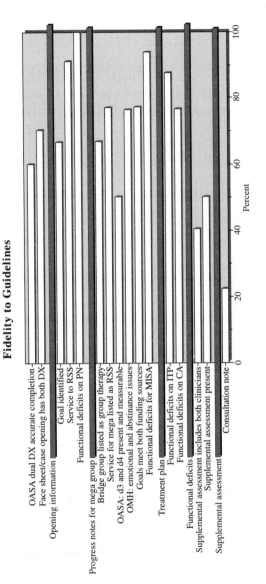

Sample of a fidelity to guidelines graph indicating percents of adherence to the specific element of the best-practice guideline.

MISA Service Flow Chart

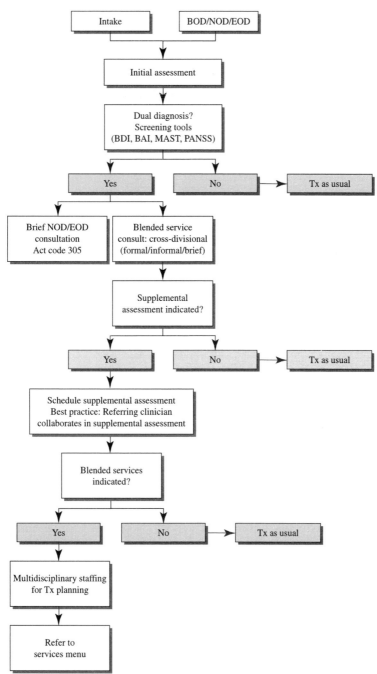

Author Index

Subject Index